OXFORD READINGS IN SOCIO-LEG

A Reader in Environmental Law

A Reader in Environmental Law

EDITED BY

Bridget M. Hutter (LSE)

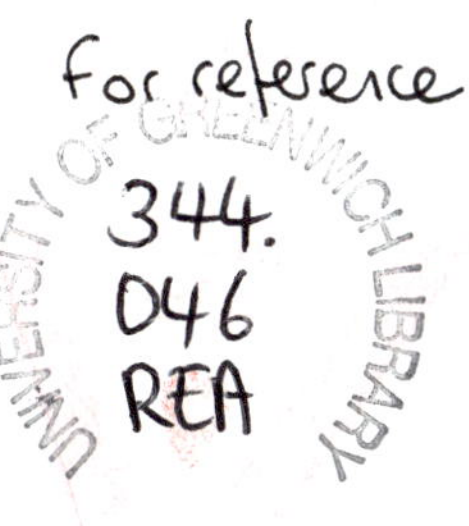

OXFORD
UNIVERSITY PRESS

Oxford University Press, Great Clarendon Street, Oxford OX2 6DP

Oxford New York
Athens Auckland Bangkok Bogota Bombay Buenos Aires
Calcutta Cape Town Dar es Salaam Delhi Florence Hong Kong Istanbul
Karachi Kuala Lumpur Madras Madrid Melbourne Mexico City
Nairobi Paris Singapore Taipei Tokyo Toronto Warsaw
and associated companies in Berlin Ibadan

Oxford is a registered trade mark of Oxford University Press

Published in the United States
by Oxford University Press Inc., New York

First published 1999

British Library Cataloguing in Publication Data

Socio-legal reader in environmental law / edited by Bridget M. Hutter.
p. cm. – (Oxford readings in socio-legal studies)
Includies bibliographical references.
1. Environmental law. 2. Environmental policy. 3. Environmental protection. I. Hutter, Bridget. II. Series.
K3585.4.S63 1999 344′.046–dc21 98–51480

ISBN 0–19–876550–9
ISBN 0–19–876549–5 (pbk.)

1 3 5 7 9 10 8 6 4 2

Typeset in Dante by Pure Tech India Ltd., Pondicherry
Printed in Great Britain on acid-free paper by
Biddles Ltd., Guildford and King's Lynn

To
Richard, Corin & Esther

Preface

There are several people who should be thanked for their help in the preparation of this Reader. The Socio-Legal Editorial Board and Richard Hart recognized the significance of this area of academic study and persuaded me to spend time going through this important literature again and looking afresh at its development. Searching through the massive literature on the environment for specifically socio-legal work was an enormous task. I am indebted to a number of people for giving me direction and help in that task. Keith Hawkins and Peter Grabosky helped direct my searches of some areas, especially those where I could find little material. I am also very grateful to John Braithwaite for sending me a draft chapter from his forthcoming book with Peter Drahos and to Peter Bartrip and Christine Garwood for helping with the historical section. Several colleagues at the LSE also helped with references on specific topics. Keith Hawkins should also be thanked for going through a draft of my introduction and for allowing me to use him as a sounding board. Michaela Coulthard from OUP took over the production of the Reader part of the way through its gestation and she and Yvonne Brown, of the LSE, should be thanked for their various contributions to the production of this book.

Finally, as always, I would like to thank Clive Briault for patiently reading through draft after draft of the introduction. His advice on clarity was invaluable and I am grateful for his comments. I dedicate this book to our children who will hopefully benefit from improved regulation of environmental pollution and from the insights offered by work such as that included in this Reader.

BMH

Note on Readings

The readings included in this book represent a cross-section of socio-legal work on environmental law over the past twenty years. While there are few works that can regarded as 'classics' in this area, there is much excellent research from which to choose.

I have used a number of criteria to select readings. First and foremost, I have only considered work which has a distinctively socio-legal focus. The pieces by Ogus and Richardson, Yeager, and Aalders explicitly explain this approach. Some prominent writers on environmental law and the environment have not been included because so many of them cannot be regarded as *socio*-legal. Second, I have tried to include work from a variety of disciplines and perspectives. So, for example, the disciplines of economics, law, management, policy studies, and sociology are represented; interactionist and structuralist approaches are included; and the readings draw their data from a variety of different sources. Third, I have included work from different parts of the world, although there is a European, North American, and Australian bias. Socio-legal research is most developed in these regions and much of the work that has been undertaken to date—including that on environmental law—has been highly ethnocentric. Fourth, I have aimed to cover different stages and aspects of the socio-legal interest in environmental law. Where possible I have tried to select material which fulfils more than one of these criteria.

This cross-section should give readers some idea of the breadth and development of socio-legal approaches to environmental law. One consequence of this approach is that a few lesser known (but nevertheless excellent) authors are included and some significant writers in the area are not included. Where this is so I have tended to include a fuller discussion of these omitted works in the Introductory Chapter. Conversely I have not dwelt too much in this chapter on works included in the Reader.

The Reader is organized around the major themes of the introductory chapter. It should be borne in mind that many of these papers contain material that falls into more than one section. Indeed this is partly why they have been selected.

Contents

PART IV: ALTERNATIVE METHODS OF ENVIRONMENTAL REGULATION

PART V: INTERNATIONAL ENVIRONMENTAL LAW

Acknowledgements

Grateful acknowledgement is made to all the authors and publishers of extract material which appears in this book, and in particular to the following for permission to reprint material from the sources indicated:

American Economic Association: M. Porter and C. van der Linde, 'Toward a New Conception of the Environment—Competitiveness Relationship'. Reprinted by permission of the publisher from the *Journal of Economic Perspectives*, 9 (1995), 97–118, © 1995 by the American Economic Association.

Blackwell Publishers Ltd: M. Alders, 'Regulation and In-Company Environmental Management in the Netherlands'. Reprinted by permission of the publisher from *Law and Policy*, 15 (1993), 75–94, © 1993 by Blackwell Publishers Ltd. J. DiMento, 'Can Social Science Explain Organizational Noncompliance with Environmental Law?' Reprinted by permission of the publisher from *Journal of Social Issues*, 45 (1989), 109–32, © 1989 by Blackwell Publishers Ltd. P. Grabosky, 'Green Markets: Environmental Regulation by the Private Sector'. Reprinted by permission of the publisher from *Law and Policy*, 16 (1994), 419–48, © 1994 by Blackwell Publishers Ltd. R. W. Hahn, 'The Political Economy of Environmental Regulation: Towards a Unifying Framework'. Reprinted by permission of the publisher from *Public Choice*, 65 (1990), 21–47, © 1990 by Blackwell Publishers Ltd.

Cambridge Law Journal: A. Ogus and G. Richardson, 'Economics and the Environment: A Study of Private Nuisance'. Reprinted by permission of the copyright holders from the *Cambridge Law Journal*, 36 (1977), 284–325, © 1977 jointly by the Cambridge Law Journal, A. Ogus and G. Richardson.

Cambridge University Press: G. Hoberg, 'Sleeping with an Elephant: The American Influence on Canadian Environmental Policy'. Reprinted by permission of the publisher from the *Journal of Public Policy*, 11 (1991), 107–32, © 1991 by Cambridge University Press.

Oxford University Press: N. Gunningham and D. Sinclair, 'Designing Smart Regulation'. Reprinted (in abridged form) by permission of the publisher from N. Gunningham and P. Grabosky, *Smart Regulation* (Oxford: Oxford University Press, 1998) ch. 6, © 1998 by Oxford University Press. K. Hawkins, 'Compliance Strategy'. Reprinted by the permission of the publisher from K. Hawkins, *Environment and Enforcement: Regulation and the Social Definition of Pollution* (Oxford: Oxford University Press, 1984) ch. 6, © 1984 by Oxford University Press.

Sage Publications, Inc.: M. S. Brown and K. Lyon, 'Holes in the Ozone Layer: A Global Environmental Controversy'. Reprinted by permission of the publisher from D. Nelkin (ed.), *Controversy: Politics of Technical Decisions* 3rd edn., (London: Sage Publications Inc., 1992) ch. 4, © 1992 by Sage Publications, Inc. S. Jasanoff, 'Cross-National Differences in Policy Implementation'. Reprinted by permission of the publisher from *Evaluation Review*, 15 (1991), 103–119, © 1991 by Sage Publications, Inc.

University of California Press: P. Yeager, 'Structural Bias in Regulatory Law Enforcement: The Case of the U. S. Environmental Protection Agency'. Reprinted by permission of the copyright holder from *Social Problems*, Vol. 34, 4 (October 1987), 330–44, © 1987 by The Society for the Study of Social Problems.

Introduction

Socio-Legal Perspectives on Environmental Law: An Overview

BRIDGET M. HUTTER

Introduction

Environmental law was amongst the earliest subjects of socio-legal research.[1] This introduction will outline the main socio-legal approaches to environmental law over the past twenty years highlighting common themes and new developments. There are imbalances in the work that has been done and this will be reflected in the themes addressed by this chapter. For example, the great weight of socio-legal literature and indeed legal activity has been in the area of public rather than private law. Early socio-legal research took environmental law as an exemplar of social regulation. This has remained a central theme, but the focus of socio-legal interest in environmental law has changed over time. This chapter will trace the way in which the focus has moved from social regulation at a local level, particularly from an enforcement perspective, to consideration of alternative methods of protecting the environment in broader arenas and from different perspectives. These developments have taken place partly in response to a growing interest in the environment, to increasing environmental legislation, and also to changing academic trends.

Socio-Legal Approaches to Environmental Law

Although the shelves of academic and legal bookshops are bending under the weight of the increasing volume of books on the subject of the environment and environmental law, only a small proportion of these can be regarded as distinctively socio-legal. There are many dimensions to socio-legal interest in environmental law. The socio-legal focus is upon the law in context, most especially the law in social context. The perspective draws upon a range of theoretical perspectives within and across disciplinary boundaries.[2] Moreover, it is characterized by the interplay and interdependence of theory and empirical data. Often the very nature of the subject matter means that the work is of policy relevance, but this is not a requirement, nor necessarily an aim, of socio-legal research (Hutter and Lloyd-Bostock, 1997).

Socio-legal studies are motivated by the belief that it is necessary to consider the law in its social context rather than for its own intrinsic value as legal text. For this reason it is commonplace to draw a distinction between the 'law in books' and the 'law in action', since the consideration of just the law in books tells us very little about what difference the law makes (Cotterrell, 1992, p. vii). The socio-legal approach considers the practical expression of legislative mandates. This is not to argue, however, that socio-legal studies ignore the law in books; indeed, legal texts and the provisions and procedures encoded in law are problematized within their social contexts (McBarnet, 1981; Nelken, 1981). Thus socio-legal scholars are as concerned to understand the social, economic, and political processes that bring law about and shape its form and content as they are to examine its enforcement and impact at the micro everyday level. More than this, they are keen to understand the relationship between the two—for example, how the broader structures incorporated in law influence the everyday actions of legal actors (Hutter, 1997; McBarnet, 1981). An important strand of socio-legal studies has been the empirical treatment of much that has been taken for granted—for example, the importance of the law in out-of-court contexts and the meaning of legal concepts such as discretion, compliance, and enforcement (Hutter and Lloyd-Bostock, 1997).

Socio-legal studies thus considers environmental law from a variety of multi-disciplinary and theoretical perspectives, each of which has its own distinctive methodology. The central characteristic running through all of these is a focus and emphasis upon the role of the law, in particular its socially situated role.

Environmental Law as a Form of Social Regulation

Environmental law represents a major, and perhaps one of the most important, regulatory regimes in western industrialized societies (Ogus, 1994, p. 204). This perspective upon environmental law has been an early and enduring focus of socio-legal research into environmental law. There are many definitions of regulation (Mitnick, 1980). Traditionally it refers to the use of the law to constrain and organize economic activity (Kagan, 1978). It therefore directs attention to state intervention through law and typically it involves regulation through public agencies charged with the implementation of the law. This is often referred to as the 'command and control' approach to regulation. It involves the 'command' of the law and the legal authority of the state. Typically it involves regulatory law backed by criminal sanctions. But this definition has been broadened to encompass both non-legal forms of regulation and supranational regulation (Baldwin, 1997). Indeed, the development of environmental law has led to new ways of conceptualizing regulation and new directions for socio-legal research into environmental law.[3]

This focus immediately raises a number of important themes concerning the general effects and implications of regulation. The first relates to *government attempts to intervene and control the operations of the market* and other aspects of economic life. This is a subject fraught with contention as advocates of the so-called 'free market' or 'laissez-faire' approach contend with those who believe that governments can and should intervene to regulate the undesirable aspects of economic activities. This subject has had particular resonance in America and Britain since the 1980s when deregulation was prominent on the political agenda. The meaning of deregulation is open to much speculation and controversy (Majone, 1989). What is much clearer is the fact that right-wing rhetoric took as central the notion that governments should reduce the extent to which they attempted to regulate economic activities. Generally this seemed to involve reducing the number of regulatory laws and cutting the resources of regulatory agencies.[4] Environmental regulation represents an interesting challenge to this rhetoric. However much governments engaged in political rhetoric about reducing regulatory burdens, the area of environmental control was one where they had to be especially careful due to an increasingly active environmental movement. Indeed, environmental law is one area of social regulation that has undoubtedly expanded over the past twenty years (Ogus, 1994, p. 10), and where deregulation is clearly seen to have limits (Yeager, 1991). This is in part a result of an increasingly important and vocal environmental movement (Ayres and Braithwaite, 1992, p. 12) and part of a backlash against deregulatory rhetoric (Sigler and Murphy, 1988).

A second general theme emerging from the regulatory literature is the *criminalization of regulatory offences*. New categories of criminal law and criminal behaviour have been created, as much environmental law is directed to the regulation of corporate activities. Thus transgression of environmental legislation is typically a criminal offence punishable by criminal sanctions in a criminal court. The use of the criminal law and criminal sanctions to control regulatory behaviour has proved controversial. Divisions have emerged, for example, over the criminality of corporate offending. Regulatory offences, including environmental pollution offences, have been referred to as 'quasi-criminal' or 'technical' offences, and it has been argued that such offences are administratively and morally distinct from traditional crimes (Baucus and Dworkin, 1991; Shover, 1980).

Environmental regulation exemplifies some of the reasons why regulatory offences may be regarded differently from more traditional crimes. For instance, the extension of the criminal law has created 'criminals' who are not readily identifiable with those who are the subjects of, for example, orthodox criminology (Taylor, Walton, and Young, 1975). This is partly a matter of class and status as directors and managers of business and industry do not fit the conventional stereotypes of working class criminality. It also raises the subject of corporate offending, which may be regarded differently from individual wrong-doing (Wells, 1992). Another reason for the differential handling and perceptions of much regulatory and environmental law is that it seeks to control activities proactively.[5] It typically regulates situations and activities which are potentially harmful. In other words actual harm need not have been caused for an offence to have been committed. Even when harm has been caused the source of an offence may be difficult to detect because of the complex technical nature of the activities subject to control (Hawkins, 1984). Another factor which may affect perceptions of environmental legislation is that much of it (in Britain for instance) has abandoned the concept of *mens rea* and accepted the principle of strict liability. Notions of individual guilt and moral culpability are firmly embedded in the criminal legislation so their abandonment may be seen as a dramatic change which may have diluted the moral force of the law (Hutter, 1988; Justice, 1980; Paulus, 1974; Richardson et al., 1983).

The third general theme raised by the focus upon regulatory legislation is the *limits of the law*, or of its effectiveness. Socio-legal research into environmental law raises questions not only about the efficacy of the criminal law as a regulatory tool but also the status of the law itself. For example, as the second theme reveals, questions are raised about the relationship between the law and morality and the law and class—how useful is the law as a regulatory tool, particularly when it is attempting to control activities which may be regarded as central to the economy? Studies of environmental regulation raise important issues on these subjects. They help us to understand, for instance, the social, political, economic, legal and organizational parameters of regulation and more specifically, the circumstances which encourage and foster regulation and those that do not (Kagan, 1994; Yeager, 1991). The case of environmental regulation also highlights the problems surrounding evaluation of regulatory law. As Ogus (1994, p. 251) explains, evaluating environmental harm (and thus benefit) is extremely difficult because of geographical and temporal factors plus the complex interaction of varying sources of pollution and variations in such factors as the weather.

These are all themes which run through the socio-legal literature on environmental law. They will emerge and re-emerge throughout this reader. Another organizing theme of environmental law is the relationship between science and law. It is to this subject, which pervades the regulatory process, that I now turn.

The Interface between Law and Science

Socio-legal interest in environmental law highlights a variety of issues relating to the interface between law and science. For example, it underlines the difficulties in legislating in situations of scientific uncertainty. Moreover it raises the issue of risk and its relationship with the law and the status of scientific 'evidence'. While there is an established and growing literature on the subject of science and technology and society,[6] and part of this literature focuses on the relationship between the environment and science,[7] there is very little serious socio-legal work which examines the relationship between environmental law and regulation and science and technology. The authors of the *Handbook of Science and Technological Studies* note in their introduction the absence of work on law and science (Jasanoff et al., 1995, p. xiv). Yet the subject is clearly an important one, which demands reference in much socio-legal work on the environment.

Sociological studies of science regard science as a social process, so scientific knowledge and technology are regarded as social products in much the same way that socio-legal studies regard the law a social product. This has a number of implications for the examination of the interface between law and science. First, it draws attention to the fact that science and technological issues are related to political values (Nelkin, 1992). Thus these issues become subject to struggles over meaning and morality, the distribution of resources and the loci of power and control (Lewenstein, 1995, p. 344). Second, it assumes that there is no simple division between facts, values, and opinions (Wynne, 1989, pp. 28–9). And third, it relates science and technology to broader societal changes. This is most starkly illustrated with reference to the German sociologist Beck (1992), who argues that the risks generated by science and technology have fundamentally transformed modern society. Indeed, they have ironically created risks which have led to a growing scepticism of science and technology, due in particular to the environmental problems created by science and technology and the fear of the risks involved (Nelkin, 1992). All of this relates to law in a number of ways, but centrally through the notion of science as a subject of political contestation. So Smith and Wynne observe: 'Science and law now interact in very complex ways as part of a broadly political process' (1989, p. 2). The environment is of course but one area in which science, technology, and the law interact, but it is a particularly important and interesting one.

Environmental law and science may come into contact for a variety of reasons.The law may provide the public with access to information about science, this being especially the case in the United States (Nelkin, 1995, p. 455). The law may be called upon for the resolution of uncertainty, so it may mediate between competing scientific evidence (Smith and Wynne, 1989, p. 8). Alternatively the law may be used in pursuit of interests, for example, the interests of environmental groups, industry or government, in which case science and technology become policy resources (Yearley, 1995, p. 465).[8] But most notably science becomes part of the regulatory policy-making process, which as we have seen, is concerned with reconciling competing aims.

Once in legal settings, scientific and technological knowledge becomes 'expert knowledge' which is framed and negotiated in a legal context. Scientific expertise is questioned from in legal settings outside the scientific community according to legal procedure and often it is subject to public deconstruction (Wynne, 1989, 34 ff.). The legislative process thus lays bare competing conceptions of science (Bimber and Guston, 1995, p. 559). Technical problems about environmental protection become subject to political and legal framing. So, for example, the siting of nuclear power stations has to reconcile environmental values and political priorities (Jasper, 1992); the choice of environmental technology is influenced by political and economic decisions (Clarke, 1992); and individual rights have to be reconciled with social goods (Nelkin, 1992). Brown and Lyon (1992, p. 60, reprinted in this volume), for instance, explain how policy-makers involved in the decision to ban CFCs were embroiled in decisions with complex scientific, technical, environmental, and economic dimensions.

Policy-makers are also forced into marking the boundaries around science, policy, and the ways in which the two should interact (Yearley, 1995, p. 467). Jasanoff has been especially important in developing our understanding of the interactions between regulatory policy and science

(1989; 1990). She documents, for instance, divergent conceptions of the role of science in regulatory decision-making in the U.S.A. She takes the example of the regulation of chemical carcinogens during the period 1974–1986 by the Environmental Protection Agency (EPA) and Occupational Health and Safety Administration (OSHA). Both agencies had to accommodate competing notions of science and rationality in setting policy within the same adversarial legal setting. Essentially EPA opted for flexible risk assessment guidelines which acknowledged that carcinogen regulation might need case by case negotiation between scientists and policy-makers. OSHA, however, took a less flexible approach. It took the advice of the scientific experts and then drew up explicit legalistic rules to cover all cases. So in these two cases the role of the scientific advisors was very different.

National political and cultural forces also shape environmental controversies (Jasper, 1992). It is therefore perhaps not surprising that environmental policies have developed differently in different countries (Brickman et al., 1985; Vogel, 1986; Yearly, 1995). Jasanoff (1991, reprinted in this volume) provides an account of differences in national regulatory policies for controlling chemicals in Europe and North America. She discerns varying approaches to policy formation and implementation and differences in the use made of scientific information. She fears that this diversity could prove an obstacle to global agreements. Rayner (1991), however, takes a different view in his consideration of the cultural influences on scientific issues; cultural preferences for different policy instruments; and the ways in which these affect policy formation and implementation. He sees potential in diversity: 'Cultural diversity seems to be a source of potential strength in humanity's attempts to come to grips with global environmental challenges' (1991, p. 99). In essence he regards a greater understanding of these issues as a basis for developing future effective policies.

Environmental Law: The Regulatory Process

Socio-legal research on environmental law which adopts a regulation perspective can usefully be considered from the 'natural history' approach to regulation. This approach regards regulation as a process which involves the enactment of legislation; its drafting and the legal form selected; its implementation by the administrative bureaucracy charged with enforcement; and the impact of the regulations upon those they seek to control and protect. It is also a reflexive process in which the relationship between the regulators and regulated is one of constant examination, re-examination, and adjustment to new information (Dodd and Hutter, forthcoming).

Emergence

Discussion of the enactment of environmental legislation has taken place in two main areas of socio-legal studies. The first area comprises historical and sociological accounts of the emergence of environmental legislation. The second concerns an economics literature which considers the reasons for regulatory legislation.

Whilst the rise of environmentalism has been the subject of lively historical attention (Clapp, 1994; Thomas, 1983; Wall, 1994),[9] historical work on environmental law is relatively limited. It is not surprising that much of the work that has been done has concentrated on the past 150 years. Although pollution is not a new phenomenon it is undoubtedly the case that levels of environmental pollution increased dramatically at the time of the industrial revolution. Indeed, mid-nineteenth century Britain witnessed increasing state intervention to control environmental pollution through the use of the law.[10]

The most prevalent historical studies of this process focus on the enactment of particular laws and their enforcement, most particularly the Clean Air Acts in England and Wales.[11] The message of these works is very much one of a struggle for protective legislation and an adequate administrative machinery. Early air pollution legislation was very restricted in its scope. The English and Welsh Alkali Act, 1863, referred to just one pollutant, namely hydrogen chloride gas, from one process—the reaction between sodium chloride and sulphuric acid.[12] Further air pollution legislation was passed in 1874 and 1881 but neither Act widened the scope or powers of the Inspectorate substantially. Arguably such shortcomings with the legislation (Ashby and Anderson, 1981) and limited technology (Bowler and Brimblecombe, 1990) led to a cooperative, persuasive enforcement approach. Certainly difficulties in enforcement were encountered at both the local and national level (Flick, 1980; Hawes, 1995). Moreover all of this took place in an era of changing attitudes to pollution and the environment (Ashby and Anderson, 1981; Beck, 1959) and in the context of the conflicting demands of protectionism and the economic demands of industry.

The socio-legal literature is divided on the issue of why governments intervene to protect the environment. In the sociologically oriented discussions there is a division between two main views. Accommodative or consensual theories regard environmental laws as protective of 'public goods'. The activities of relatively powerful groups are thus regulated in favour of a less powerful majority. Conflict theorists, however, believe that regulatory laws and policies do nothing to curb significantly the activities of business and industry, who they believe to be major players in the shaping of regulatory policies and favoured in the implementation process.

Whilst all socio-legal theories recognize the tension between regulation of the environment and business interests, and recognise the presence of conflicting interest groups, they regard the resolution of these tensions in different ways. Accommodative theorists portray regulatory legislation as the result of an accommodation between interest groups. They adhere to a consensual, pluralist model of society and argue that the legislation is neither as interventionist as the reformers would want it to be nor as lax as business would prefer (Carson, 1974; Paulus, 1974).

Conflict theorists, who tend to adopt a dominant power group model of society, regard economic interests as paramount. They argue that the dominant class has ensured that their interests are not seriously affected by regulation. For example, they argue that business and industry are well represented in government and are therefore significant in shaping the legislation (Gunningham, 1974). Yeager (1987, reprinted in this volume; 1991) adopts a conflict perspective in his examination of the US government's attempts to regulate industrial water pollution in the twentieth century. He argues that there is a dynamic tension pervading the legislation and implementation process between the limits on economic activity and the constraints on regulation. Ultimately, argues Yeager, these structural contradictions weaken the impact of environmental legislation.

Sociological theories of regulation are mirrored in other social science approaches to regulation. Ogus (1994), in the most comprehensive and detailed discussion of law and economic theory to date, draws a distinction between two broad economic theories which in many respects mirror the sociological theories outlined above. Ogus (1994, 1 ff.). identifies a tension between two systems of economic organization, namely the market system and the collectivist system. In the market system individuals and groups are largely free to pursue their own goals, whereas in the collectivist system the state seeks to correct deficiencies in the market system for the collective good. The market system gives rise to a private interest theory of regulation which regards private interest groups as securing regulatory benefits for themselves through their use of the political and legal systems. The work of Stigler (1971) and Pellzman (1976), for example, examines how powerful interest groups may influence regulation. Becker

(1989) argues further that more efficient regulation may be promoted through political competition between different interest groups. Such competition, it is argued, is an efficient mechanism for correcting market failures. A collectivist view of regulation gives rise to public interest theory, which regards regulation as a corrective to the operation of the market and as operating in pursuit of collective goals. In this model, regulation is designed for the good of all. Moreover, it aims to correct biases introduced by powerful private interests (Olsen, 1982; Hahn, 1989).

These economic accounts of regulation underline the political context of regulation. Different interest groups may coordinate and coalesce around different issues (Yandle, 1989), and political forces may shape the regulatory strategies adopted (see, generally, Shogren, 1989). All of this is arguably unavoidable given the inherently political nature of the regulatory task and environment, namely balancing the competing concerns of the environment and economic interests.

Legal Form

The different perspectives upon the reasons for the emergence of environmental law colour historical accounts of how and why this legislation came into being. They also influence the interpretations placed on the content and framing of environmental legislation. For example, much environmental legislation in Britain is characterized by unspecific, broadly framed standards such as 'best practicable environmental option' (BPEO), 'best available technology not entailing excessive costs' (BATNEEC), or even a provision about 'preventing or minimizing pollution of the environment' (Ogus, 1994, p. 207). One interpretation of such broad standards is that they are necessary in order to take account of technological change and varying circumstances. In other words, they are necessary to encourage flexibility. Indeed, there is not always the scientific knowledge upon which to base standards (Yeager, 1991), and this may be yet another reason for broad standards. A rather different perspective upon such standards is that they lead to inconsistency and that they favour business, particularly as they involve consideration of the costs and benefits of pollution control and arguably the costs are always much clearer and easier to calculate than to the benefits.[13] Rule-making is a political as much as a technical process.

Some authors regard environmental legislation as intentionally vague and ambiguous and some even regard it as symbolic legislation, which appears to promote the protection of the environment but which fails to specify to the regulatory agency and the courts how to 'transform symbolic guarantees into enforceable standards' (Dwyer, 1990, p. 233). Dwyer takes the example of the Clean Air Act enacted in the United States in 1982. Particular attention is focused on section 112, which required the Environmental Protection Agency (EPA) to set 'health-based' emission standards for hazardous air pollutants. But this Act did not allow the Agency to consider implementation costs and technological feasibility when setting standards—something that the Agency considered unrealistic. Thus, argued Dwyer, the legislature minimized the political costs and maximized the political credit of protecting health. It appealed to interest groups and growing public concern for environmental controls whilst transferring the conflicts and resolution of the tensions of balancing the different competing interest groups to the regulatory agency and the courts. The effect of this was to render the legislation ineffective as the EPA responded by delaying standard-setting and misconstruing the statutes. This regulatory delay in turn increased the risks to health and undermined the integrity of the regulatory agency. Again this case raises the intensely political nature of the regulatory process, summed up by Dwyer as 'symbolic legislation is a political gesture' (1990, p. 316).

Discussions such as these of course touch on broader legal debates about discretion and legalism (Davis, 1969; Galligan, 1986; Hawkins, 1992). They also lead directly to consideration of the decision-makers in the legal process; that is, to regulatory bureaucracies and inspectors who are allocated, or may appropriate, wide discretion in their interpretation of the law.

Implementation

The enactment of environmental legislation has typically been accompanied by the establishment of a bureaucracy charged with the implementation of environmental legislation. These bureaucracies may be under the jurisdiction of either central government or local government, or both. It is the work of these agencies which has received the earliest and most extensive socio-legal attention. This is in large part explained by the relative newness not only of socio-legal research but also research into social regulation. The early focus was upon the most accessible and visible aspects of regulation (Hawkins and Hutter, 1993, p. 213 n. 3). Moreover, this early focus on 'command and control' regulation was a reflection of the fact that this was at the time the traditional, the most prevalent, and the most visible method of regulation.

Implementation embraces two main aspects, namely policy-making and enforcement. Policy-making is typically undertaken at the centre of a regulatory bureaucracy and involves standard setting and organizational interpretations of the law. Environmental policy-making is little understood by socio-legal researchers. In particular, there is a dearth of empirical studies of the policy-making process. The work of Hahn (1990, reprinted in this volume) is an interesting contribution from an economist working in an advisory capacity to government. His paper considers economic explanations of instrument choice. It rejects the economic efficiency perspective in favour of interest group theory, which regards environmental policy as the result of a struggle between key interest groups. Lawyers have concentrated more on the type of standards and rules that may be selected by policy-makers. However, much of this work does not specifically consider environmental law, but is part of a more general discussion of discretion or choice of rule type (Baldwin, 1995) or of regulatory techniques (Baldwin, 1997). Gunningham and Sinclair (1998, reprinted in this volume), however, do specifically discuss the design of effective strategies to combat environmental degradation. Drawing upon existing empirical studies they seek to identify core regulatory design principles for policy-making and in so doing embrace much of the work discussed in this reader.

The second aspect of implementation is enforcement. This refers to implementation of the law and of agency policies by lower grade field-level officials. It is this aspect that has received most socio-legal interest. This is partly because the work of lower level officials is more tangible and observable. Also, those at the centre of regulatory bureaucracies have been rather more willing to grant researchers access to the work of their staff than they have to be researched themselves.

The work of field-level inspectors has been seen as especially important, as these are front-line inspectors who serve as the gatekeepers to the enforcement process. These inspectors have the discretion to decide what constitutes an offence or problem and whether to refer a case to their supervisors for further attention, so their interpretation of the law and of agency policies is of particular significance: they constitute the bridge between the government's decision to intervene and protect the environment and the impact of this intervention upon both the environment and the regulated.[14]

Research into the enforcement of environmental law has, along with similar research into other forms of regulatory control such as occupational health and safety and environmental health, made important contributions to our understanding of the law in social context. For example, the focus on enforcement has challenged our understanding of the meaning and definition of enforcement. Studies of regulation, many of which were studies of environmental law enforcement, identified the adoption of frequently used law enforcement practices by regulatory officials. These practices directly challenged the view that enforcement refers simply to legal action. Rather, law enforcement was seen also to encompass a wide array of informal techniques such as persuasion, education, advice, and negotiation. These studies thus emphasized the negotiated and processual nature of much law.

The varying styles of enforcement have been conceptualized as distinctive enforcement models. Hawkins (1984, ch. 6 reprinted in this volume), like Reiss (1984), adopted a binary model of enforcement in his research into the work of staff in two Regional Water Authorities in England in the 1980s. He termed the style approximating that often adopted by regulatory officials the compliance model.[15] This refers to a style of enforcement which is cooperative and conciliatory, its aim being to secure compliance through the remedy of existing problems and, most importantly, the prevention of others. The use of formal legal methods of enforcement, notably prosecution, is regarded as a last resort, something to be avoided unless all else fails to secure compliance. This style of enforcement allows for compliance over a period of time: instant remedy is not necessarily sought or considered feasible. This model contrasts with the deterrence (Reiss, 1984) or sanctioning (Hawkins, 1984) model, in which a penal style of enforcement accords prosecution an important role. Its objective is to prohibit certain activities. It is also accusatory and geared to catching out those who break the law.[16]

The compliance and sanctioning models of enforcement have been developed to increase our understanding of variations in the enforcement of environmental legislation. Variations have been identified as follows: intra-agency (Hutter, 1988); inter-agency (Braithwaite, Walker, and Grabosky, 1987); and cultural (Vogel, 1986). Explanations of the variations range from an emphasis upon the regulated activity through to the motives of the regulated or more broadly upon the social, political, economic, and organizational contexts of enforcement.[17] Hawkins, for example, considers how the nature of the activities regulated by environmental law may be significant (1984, ch. 6, reprinted in this volume).

Vogel (1986) concentrated on another aspect of variation, namely that between different countries. His comparison of the British and American pollution control systems in the 1980s led him to identify the British system as approximating a compliance approach and the American system as being more akin to a sanctioning approach. These differences were largely explained in cultural terms; for instance the American system was identified as more adversarial and litigious than the British one (see also Hawkins, 1992; Kagan, 1995).

Different theories give varying interpretations of enforcement activity. Accommodative theorists regard low levels of prosecution as a rational response to limited agency resources, ambiguous legislation, and weak sanctions (Cranston, 1979; Hutter, 1988; Richardson et al., 1983). Conflict theorists, however, cite a reluctance to prosecute as evidence of ineffective legislation—the 'capture' of the regulatory agency by business and the power of business (Bernstein, 1955; Box, 1983; Clinard and Yeager, 1980; Gunningham, 1974; Yeager, 1991). Both groups agree that tactical manoeuvres at the time of legislating weakened regulatory law but, whereas conflict theorists believe the law has been weakened to the point of ineffectiveness, consensual theorists believe that improvements have been effected, albeit not on a scale the reformers would have wished.

Impact

There are two main dimensions to the issue of the impact of environmental law: its impact upon the environment; and its impact upon the regulated. The first of these has attracted virtually no socio-legal interest and the second, the impact of regulatory laws and bureaucracies upon industry, is a topic which attracted relatively little socio-legal research interest until recently when the impact of regulation upon nation states in a global context has been discussed (see below).

The neglect of these topics is clearly not related to their importance, since the impact of environmental law must be one of the central socio-legal questions. The dearth of material relates more to the complexity of the issues involved. As noted earlier, evaluating environmental harms and benefits is extremely difficult. There is no clear-cut method for measuring the improvements to the environment which may have been effected by the law. In particular, it is difficult to isolate this from the complex of other factors which may be involved in environmental improvements. In his consideration of the effect of environmental regulation on mercury and sulphur dioxide pollution in Canada in 1970s, Dewees (1990) concluded that it is necessary to consider a combination of factors:

> These differences in the character of the problem, the scientific information, the tort environment, and the nature and distribution of the harm all work together to lead to different outcomes. These outcomes are developed through the regulatory system, through tort litigation, through public pressure, and through the firm's own self-interested actions. This suggests that in cases where regulatory action

seemed to have been particularly successful the regulation does not exist in a vacuum. Rather the factors that make regulation successful also yield other pressures, such as tort liability and public opinion, leading toward the same outcome (1990, p. 347).

The work which has been done has therefore tended to focus upon the regulated, most especially at the level of the individual company and also upon the activities of the regulatory agency. This aspect of regulation draws attention to a number of important issues relating to such matters as how much those subject to regulatory laws and policies know and understand about their provisions and about the regulatory apparatus in place for their implementation; the extent to which the law might cause individuals and institutions to change their behaviour and practices; whether or not environmental regulation influences commercial decisions about the location of industry and sites; and how these matters relate to industries, perceptions of the national and transnational environmental risks posed by their activities.

All of these themes relate to important theoretical concerns in the socio-legal area. These include deterrence theory in its investigation of the extent to which those subject to regulatory law know about its provisions and the sanctions for noncompliance with the law; and compliance theory in its consideration of the trade-offs between compliance and other factors such as risk. At a wider level, research into corporate responses to regulation will contribute to theories of corporate criminality as environmental violations are often the outcome of collectivities rather than individuals (DiMento, 1989, reprinted in this volume).

The impact of environmental law and its enforcement is hotly debated. Some authors maintain that the law has little impact. Some attribute this to weak enforcement (Cable and Benson, 1993, p. 465). Indeed, some (almost polemically) assert and assume a causal relationship between noncompliance and weak enforcement. Another explanation is that environmental regulation may, on occasions, be counterproductive because it may, for instance, create black markets or lead to displacement or relocation (Grabosky, 1995[a]). Others claim that businesses adapt to legal regulation and, moreover, that regulation may lead to innovation (Porter, 1990; Porter and van der Linde, 1995, reprinted in this volume).

The international debates about the impact of national, transnational, and international environmental laws will be discussed later. Here I want to concentrate on what is known about the impact of the regulatory regime at the level of the individual company. How much do companies actually know about environmental law? And what explains their compliance and noncompliance with these laws? In short, we know surprisingly little about either of these issues.

One of the early—and most detailed—empirical studies of the impact of pollution control on industry is Brittan's 1984 study of water pollution control in England and Wales. She found that water pollution control had become a significant part of everyday life for the regulated. She found high levels of knowledge about consent limits and the allocation of responsibility within companies for the day-to-day control of water pollution. But she discerned little detailed knowledge or comprehension of the law and the penalties which could be incurred for noncompliance. Brittan also found that smaller businesses tended to be affected disproportionately by the regulations. This is corroborated by Genn's 1993 paper on the impact of health and safety at work legislation, which found that those working on the most hazardous and largest sites were the most knowledgeable and the most motivated to comply.

The reasons for compliance or non-compliance with environmental law are much talked about but little researched. As Olsen (1992, p. 16) remarks, different theoretical traditions offer different theories. Also the whole issue depends very much upon how compliance is defined (DiMento, 1986; Hutter, 1997). Bardach and Kagan (1982), writing about their fears of overregulation and unreasonableness in 1980s USA, argued that a complex of reasons explained compliance with regulatory legal regimes such as those designed to protect the environment. The threat of inspection and punishment alone, they argued, were insufficient to secure compliance. Other additional factors were necessary and these included economic pressures; the threat of private legal action; self-interest; worry about compensation; high accident rates; reputational reasons; and intra-organizational pressures for compliance. Brittan (1984, p. 69) found moral obligation to be the overwhelming explanation for compliance amongst her sample. This included a moral obligation to be socially responsible; to fulfil legal obligations; to maintain corporate reputation; internal pressure; and recognition that the effluent may be dangerous. Genn (1993) suggests that motivation varies and is in part explained by self-interest, notably the nature of the risk posed. DiMento (1989, reprinted in this volume) meanwhile points to reputational factors, such as a concern to avoid adverse publicity and maintain goodwill. In turn, of course, these may be fed into perceptions of the cost and benefits of compliance.

A variety of reasons for non-compliance are suggested by Bardach and Kagan (1982), including deliberate evasion; ignorance; incompetence; inadequate supervision; poorly trained operators; and indifference.

DiMento (1989) argues that non-compliance is immensely complex and requires a multivariable approach. He focuses specifically on just a few of the relevant factors such as enforcement, communication, and the characteristics of the actors involved. But, as he explains, the evidence on any of these is often partial and contradictory.

Methods of Protecting the Environment Through Law

As the environment has become a subject of increasing political and public interest there has been a growth in both the volume and variety of methods used to protect it. This has been accompanied by broader socio-legal interest in the limits of public law approaches to regulation. The command and control strategies which had been the focus of so much early socio-legal research in the 1970s and 1980s came under increasing scrutiny and attack. In particular much criticism was levelled at the regulatory agencies responsible. At one extreme these agencies were criticised for being in danger of being captured by the regulated population; that is, identifying too closely with their interests and thus becoming too lax in their enforcement of the law.[18] At the other extreme there were criticisms that regulatory officials were unreasonable, legalistic, and increasing the burdens on industry (Bardach and Kagan, 1982).

The complexities of regulatory enforcement raised a number of concerns. The first centred on the resource capacity of regulatory agencies. This included, for example, the staffing of these agencies in terms of both the levels of staffing and the quality of the staff employed. These factors, it was charged, could lead to an inability to see through the regulatory mandate.[19] These arguments are related to the second major set of criticisms which concerned the relative regulatory capacities of regulatory agencies and business. Some authors identified an imbalance between the regulatory capacities of the regulatory agencies and big business. Business, it was argued, has many advantages over the public agencies. For instance it has more money, more specialized staff, a greater capacity to fight the agency on both technical and legal grounds, and more information about the regulatory problem and its extent and possible technological remedy.[20]

The other main area of criticism was the efficiency and, most important, the effectiveness of command and control regulation and of regulatory agencies. Of particular concern here was the negotiated style of enforcement which some regarded as a sign of weakness or even capture. This, together with persistent environmental problems, led to disillusionment with regulatory officials (Boyer and Meidinger, 1985, p. 837; Dwyer, 1993, p. 105). Some regarded command and control regulation as oversimplified (Grabosky, 1995, p. 529), others regarded it as a failure of environmental regulation (Cable and Benson, 1993, p. 465). Consequently governments and socio-legal scholars turned their attention to alternative methods of regulation and the term regulation became construed broadly to include a wide range of policy instruments (Grabosky, 1995[a], p. 347).

Methods of Regulating Environmental Pollution

Business and industry may be regulated in a variety of ways. Apart from command and control regulation through public law backed by criminal sanctions, governments may enact civil law remedies. Alternatively they may opt for economic incentives such as effluent charges or taxation policies; administrative measures, such as licensing; or self-regulation or self-audit, where government seeks to establish the principle that businesses and industries regulate themselves.[21] In addition there may be non-governmental influences upon environmental regulation.

The different methods of regulating environmental pollution fall into a number of broad analytical categories. Before continuing to outline socio-legal discussions of a few of these it should be borne in mind that these are analytical categories, which in reality often overlap. Moreover, most of the methods discussed are used in some form or another in advanced industrial societies, although very few have been adequately evaluated.

Private Enforcement and Civil Law

For centuries private law was the main instrument of pollution control, its main objective being the pursuit of private interests rather than the public good. While the rise of the modern state led to new forms of regulation through public law, the civil remedies remained in place as an alternative means of control. However, these remedies have attracted very little socio-legal interest and the place of the civil law and private enforcement is one of the under-researched areas of environmental law.

One of the earliest socio-legal papers on the subject of environmental law took the law of private nuisance in England and Wales as its main focus. The paper by Ogus and Richardson (1977, reprinted in this volume) took an explicitly socio-legal approach in applying an economic analysis to private rights legislation, in particular its role in the enforcement of the law. The findings of this paper perhaps help to explain why subsequent researchers were not encouraged to examine the subject further, as Ogus and Richardson concluded that there is only a limited role for private law in pollution control (1977, p. 324). Yet they ascribed this method an important subsidiary enforcement rôle and a more important and central role in compensating the victims of pollution. The role of common law has recently been tested in the Cambridge Water Case (Cambridge Water Company *v.* Eastern Counties Leather plc House of Lords, 9 December 1993) where the House of Lords provided an authoritative set of common law principles governing civil liability for damage caused by pollution. The judgement again implied that the common law has a limited role in dealing with many types of environmental pollution and led to calls for the government to develop more effective statutory mechanisms (*ENDS Report* 227, 1993: 43). This said, it remains the case that parts of this judgement are thought to leave open a large potential for liability.

It is, of course, not surprising that individual citizens have not made great use of the civil law. The cost of private law is beyond the pocket of most members of the population. For perhaps similar reasons there have been few private actions under public and criminal law concerned with environmental protection. Indeed, in England and Wales some of the early environmental legislation prohibited members of the public from bringing a prosecution. This apart, it would be extremely difficult for them to acquire data to support their case because of restrictions on their access to company and government information (Austin, 1989; Frankel, 1974). In the United States, however, recent work has pointed to different and sometimes novel ways in which civil law and private enforcement may play a role in pollution control and environmental protection. First, there is evidence that federal regulators have been using civil injunctions against corporate violators. Ostensibly this is because of difficulties they encounter in controlling corporate offenders, the argument being that civil injunctions are more efficient and effective than the available criminal remedies. For example, civil sanctions require a lower burden of proof than criminal law. But, as Cable and Benson argue, there are potential negative consequences of this for society: 'Unlike criminal penalties, civil injunctions do not stigmatize offenders. They lack the punitive and deterrent effects of criminal sanctions, making corporate environmental crimes less costly for corporations and hence more likely to occur' (1993, p. 467).

The second development in the United States concerning the use of law by private citizens is the rise of large-scale citizen-suit litigation by private environmental organizations. This follows the enactment of environmental legislation which gave the public a right to be heard in enforcement decisions and also provided for the reimbursement of expenses they incurred. This form of private action is discussed at length by Boyer and Meidinger (1985), who explain that this action represents an attempt by private organizations to take over the administration of regulation. So it does not represent private enforcement in pursuit of private wrongs, but private action about the content of policy and the routine enforcement of cases. The purpose of the action is to change the behaviour of polluters by changing the incentives to comply. Boyer and Meidinger (1985, p. 957) are cautiously optimistic that private enforcement modelled on the citizen-suit provisions is a useful method of environmental control. But again they regard it as a supplement to the command and control approach. These developments, together with the uncertainties of English case law, point to this being an important area for future research.

The problems with private enforcement centre on their costs and the fact that the cases which tend to be pursued are ad hoc and selective rather than part of any well thought out environmental strategy and policy. The advantages are that they represent yet another source of environmental pressure on the regulatory agencies, the government and business. Indeed, Grabosky (1995) argues that private litigation may result in substantial damages and deterrent effects.[22]

Economic Incentives

The most discussed forms of economic incentive to reduce pollution are *emissions charges* and *marketable permits*. Both adhere to the 'polluter pays' principle. Emissions charges charge dischargers either a fixed price per unit of pollution or a variable rate according to the level of compliance (Meidinger, 1985). Charges may be used to fund environmental improvements or alternatively they will be directed to unspecified government funds in the form of a tax. Emissions charges have been used, particularly in relation to water pollution, in France, Italy, Germany, the Netherlands, and Japan (Tietenberg, 1990). Marketable permits are a form of emissions charge. Essentially they are a permit to pollute which may be traded (thus the term emissions trading). Thus over-compliance in one area may be traded for under-compliance in another area—either within one site; one company; or between companies. The transferrable pollution permit permitted by the EPA in the United States is a prime example of this method of pollution control (see Meidinger, 1985).[23]

The advantages of economic-based regulations are seen to centre on the choice they offer polluters either to opt out of burdensome regulation or to develop pollution control technology. Indeed, economic-based incentives may be regarded as a very real incentive to innovate, if not by individual companies then through the revenue generated by emissions charges. The fact that the costs are borne by industry is regarded as a major advantage of these methods (Hahn, 1990, p. 33). According to some authors these methods are cheaper than command and control regulation (Tietenberg, 1990, p. 23). Moreover, some regard them as an important 'pressure valve' for regulators charged with implementing strong environmental controls (Dwyer, 1993, p. 117).

There is, however, some debate over the administrative costs and efficiencies of economic incentives and some studies point to administrative considerations as significant disadvantages of economic-based regulation. For example, the administrative costs may be very high. Opschoor and Vos (1989) found that half of the revenue generated from German water effluent charges went to pay for the administration of the system. There may also be bureaucratic obstacles to the successful use of economic-based methods, including the difficulties of the economic calculations involved. For example, there may be no precise measures of the emissions involved because there may be no reliable technology available to undertake the measurement. Thus the change in emissions effected by pollution control may be difficult, even impossible, to estimate, let alone calculate (Dwyer, 1993). It may be difficult to obtain data about the costs of pollution damage so an appropriate price cannot be either calculated or charged (Ogus, 1996). Even if all of this can be estimated it is often the case that the transaction costs of emissions trading are such that only large companies can absorb the costs involved (Tietenberg, 1990). The efficiency gains may be diffuse and this may be accompanied by controversy in deciding how the funds generated will be distributed—that is, if they are available for environmental improvements at all (Hahn, 1990). Over and above all of these problems, it is typically very difficult to assess the impact of economic-based incentives as there is typically a regulatory mix and this means that it is nigh on impossible to isolate the effects of one method as distinct from the others employed (see Hahn, 1989).

Commercial Environmentalism

Commercial environmentalism is an interesting variant on the role of the market in the furtherance of environmentalism. The focus here is not upon government intervention to promote environmentalism, but upon the commercial incentives that may already exist in the market. This topic is most fully discussed by Grabosky (1994, reproduced in this volume). The main points to draw out are the variety of pressures to commercial environmentalism that exist in the market. There may, for example, be a very direct appeal to commercial profits and gains. Environmental concerns may create new markets such as the demand for recycling and waste-management industries. Alternatively, green markets may be fostered by means of consumer pressure such as the preferential purchasing of so-called green products, the boycotting of environmentally unfriendly products, or selective institutional investment according to environmental criteria. There are clear links here with interest groups who may lead campaigns on such matters (see below). Government may also be involved, for instance, as major purchasers and by building environmental considerations into their domestic and international policies (see Grabosky, 1994).

Symbolic Incentives

Symbolic incentives such as environmental rewards and praise may also be used to improve environmental quality. Grabosky (1995; 1995[b]) discusses a range of alternatives from the regulatory authorities, praise to the formal recognition of successful pollution control. While 'public affirmation of good citizenship' may be important in its own right (see Makkai and Braithwaite, 1993), symbolic incentives may also be accompanied by economic rewards. These may take the form, for example, of reputational capital or lower insurance premiums.

The advantages of symbolic rewards are perhaps self-evident. They are less coercive and invasive than many other forms of control. Moreover, they are cheap, educational, and regarded positively. Indeed, they may increase support for the regulatory agency and regulatory objectives. The disadvantages centre on the lack of agency accountability and fears that these methods are manipulative or are accompanied by the danger that compliance will appear optional rather than mandatory (see Grabosky, 1995[b]). What is clear is that symbolic rewards do have a place in environmental control but their effectiveness is likely to be increased if they are used sparingly, otherwise there is a danger of their being devalued.

Third Party Enforcement

Third party enforcement is an increasingly popular method of regulatory control (Gilboy, 1998). The range of methods falling into this category is wide, ranging from state conscription of third party enforcement through to the pressure exercised by interest groups. The first of these embraces a variety of techniques such as legal requirements to undertake environmental audits; or take out liability insurance; or keep full and accurate records of environmental emissions. Alternatively governments may, for example, contract out standard-setting to professional associations or enforcement tasks, such as motor vehicle emission testing, to garages.[24]

An important source of third-party enforcement may be the activities of *interest groups*, in particular the activities of non-governmental organizations (NGOs). There has been a dramatic increase in the number and profile of environmental organizations such as Greenpeace and Friends of the Earth at a national and international level. There are many community-based campaigns focusing on local environmental issues. Lobby organizations such as the Sierra Club have also emerged. These groups aim to bring environmental problems to public and, most particularly, political attention. Environmental groups often campaign for the enactment of new laws or the negotiation of international agreements. Local groups tend to be more concerned with the enforcement of existing laws and pressurizing companies to comply.

Environmental interest groups form for a number of reasons but central among these is a belief that the state is failing to protect its environment and population from pollution. Democratic pressure is therefore brought to bear through letters, press conferences, marches, and less conventional publicity stunts. Environmental organizations have come to be viewed as a form of social control (Cable and Benson, 1993). Indeed, they may be co-opted by governments and given some legitimacy in turn for legitimizing government actions and policies which they have been asked to comment on or help form. Grabosky (1995) explains that interest groups may provide data, interpretations, and perspectives not normally considered by the decision-makers.

Third-party enforcement has a number of attractions. From a governmental perspective it is a cheap form of control. For example, the delegation of standard-setting to a third party could reduce government expenditure on regulatory agencies. Interest groups may also be a potent source of regulation as publicity may be one of the more successful sanctions against business (Braithwaite and Fisse, 1985). Indeed the pressure that can be exercised by interest groups may be mobilized by regulatory authorities.[25] Some interest group activities have undoubtedly helped shape environmental agendas. There are, however, drawbacks to these methods, notably the loss of accountability as third parties are not democratically accountable for their activities. Likewise their activities are by definition not part of any coherent environmental strategy. They may even be regarded as an erosion of civic commitment. Interest groups, of course, aim to change or capture the policy process. This is not necessarily always in the public interest, for attention may be diverted away from more serious, less visible, problems.

Self-Regulation

Many of the alternative methods discussed in the literature fall within the broader category of self-regulation. Generally, self-regulation is taken to refer to the regulation of activities by members of the occupations or businesses engaged in the regulated activities. It is a broad concept which covers a wide range of arrangements. It may, for example, refer to self-regulation mandated by law (Ayres and Braithwaite, 1992) while, at the other end of the spectrum, it can refer to the decision of an individual firm or industry to set its own standards and enforce them.[26]

Self-regulation in some form or another is an important part of many environmental policies in many advanced industrial societies. Self-regulation may be an attractive option for a variety of reasons. It may be seen as an important recognition that compliance is the responsibility of the regulated company rather than the enforcement agency. It may also be regarded as an efficient way of coping with a lack of agency resources, which means that monitoring compliance across the full range and quantity of regulated forms may be sporadic and infrequent. There may also be reasons for industries to want to self-regulate. For example, high risk industries may have a self-interest in self-regulating because the risks of non-compliance may be catastrophic, either to themselves or the surrounding environment and population (Genn, 1993). Companies also have an interest in promoting a good image for their industry or in being seen to exercise industry control as a means of reducing demands for stricter government control (Gunningham, 1995, p. 60).

Gunningham (1995) discusses Responsible Care, a chemical industry initiative adopted in Australia. The aim was to reduce chemical accidents, increase industry credibility, and involve the community in decision-making through the establishment of codes of practice and a commitment to community participation and consultation. Gunningham argues that the scheme favours the interests of large industry players to the extent that they are better able to cope with the weaknesses of the scheme. The two main weaknesses are identified as short termism—which may place demands for short-term profits above long-term environmental improvements—and the divergence of the interests of transnational corporations' and small- and medium-sized companies, divergent regulatory capacities, for example.

In Gunningham's view Responsible Care programmes need a number of ingredients to be effective: first, good methods of monitoring compliance;

second, the institution of performance indicators to demonstrate that pollution is being controlled; and finally, third-party oversight concerning, for example, audits or a community right to know. Once these have been achieved, there remains the problem of collective action: namely, ensuring that all companies participate and the elimination of the 'free rider' problem. In achieving such an effect a variety of the methods discussed above may be employed. For instance self-policing could be important.[27] Corporate shaming or praise may also be useful as may product stewardship, which involves a company exercising concern over the product when buying in raw materials and through the production process to the selling and ultimate use of the product. So, for example, companies could require information, or even an audit, to establish the environmentally friendly production of raw materials before placing a contract for their supply. What Gunningham is proposing here is 'regulatory mix' and ultimately he suggests that co-regulation between government and industry, or tripartism between industry, government, and the community, will be most effective. This is an important topic to which we will return shortly. But let us first consider the advantages and limitation of self-regulation.

The advantages of self-regulation centre upon cost savings that may be achieved on behalf of the public when the costs of standard-setting and enforcement are internalized by the trade. Also important are the high levels of expertise and technical know-how which may reside within the industry, possibly making enforcement and monitoring both easier to achieve and less costly. Since self-regulation is less formalized than public enforcement it can theoretically at least be more flexible and more sensitive to the market and technical innovations. The disadvantages centre on the degree to which we are prepared or able to trust industry to regulate itself. Self-regulation is open to abuse and is marked by a lack of accountability. There are also anti-competitive pressures which may be exerted by established and stronger members of an industry to the detriment of smaller and medium-sized companies.

Trends in Environmental Regulation

There has been an increasing tendency for both public and private forms of regulation to co-exist and it is partly because of this that it is difficult to evaluate. Despite its limitations and 'bad press', command and control regulation is still regarded by many authors as an important and necessary underpinning of other regulatory methods (Boyer and Meidinger, 1985). Several commentators argue for a mixture of positive and negative sanctions which may reinforce each other in promoting the environment (Grabosky, 1995[b]). In such cases the government may be central to the provision of the necessary 'carrots' and 'sticks'. The government is also one of the main players in tripartism (Aalders, 1993; Gunningham, 1995). In his discussion of the Dutch government's adoption of a new regulatory strategy, Aalders (1993, reprinted in this volume) observes that governmental attempts to encourage the voluntary adoption of environmental management as an integral part of corporate management was regarded as additional to government monitoring. He wrote 'The "big stick" is still there, but the speech is smoother than ever' (1993, p. 88). A key ingredient of the 'regulatory mix' is flexibility; namely, the flexibility to adapt different methods to individual circumstances (Ayres and Braithwaite, 1992; Bardach and Kagan, 1982; Grabosky, 1995[a] 363; 1995[b], p. 272). Indeed, the importance of a regulatory mix—or 'instrumental combinations'—is central to the design of smart environmental regulation discussed by Gunningham and Sinclair (1998, reprinted in this volume). They argue for a policy mix and recommend core design principles but are also careful to emphasize that instruments need to be matched to particular circumstances such as the particular environmental problem subject to control.

A second strong trend in environmental regulation has been the move to a broader holistic conception of the environment and its protection. Early definitions of the environment were typically limited to local environmental problems and their regulation was often through the enforcement of national regulatory legislation at a local level. Pollution was often dealt with using a sector-by-sector approach so that, for example, water pollution and air pollution were seen as separate and were dealt with through different legislation and even different enforcement agencies. Increasingly, however, it was recognized that environmental problems are interrelated, and more far-reaching and long-term than previously understood. This led to a wider view of how to regulate and protect the environment which is reflected in the emergence of integrated pollution control in the British Environmental Protection Act 1990.

There has thus been a recognition that pollution control in one area could lead to displacement effects to other mediums and localities. Accordingly the legislation and the regulatory agencies have become more generic. In the Netherlands, for example, there has been a movement from a sectoral character to environmental protection to an integrated approach. This has involved shifting responsibility from local to central government, so larger and more specialized agencies were created. Also a standard procedure was introduced for controlling the various sectors of pollution. In essence this was a form of integrated pollution control covering, for example, air pollution, water pollution, chemical waste and noise nuisance (Bennett and von Molke, 1990). In England and Wales there have been two main steps to create a generic pollution inspectorate. In 1987 the H.M. Inspectorate of Pollution was created[28] and in 1995 a new Environment Agency came into legal existence and began work in April 1996.[29] One of the main objectives of these moves was the development of a more integrated approach to protecting the environment from pollution and other hazards.

The trends towards a broader conception of the environment and increasingly integrated approaches to regulation have characterized Sweden, Switzerland, the U.S., and Germany (Haigh and Irwin, 1990). Sometimes this has taken place with the encouragement of international bodies such as the European Union and the OECD which has had an important informational role. The move from local to national environmental concerns and a more integrated approach to environmental protection within the national state has developed into broader international concern about the environment. More recently, this has broadened into a global view.

International Environmental Law

Conceptualizations of the environment have changed dramatically in the past 20 to 30 years and there is now a broader understanding that environmental issues extend beyond geopolitical borders (Braithwaite and Drahos, forthcoming). Transnational and global environmental initiatives have been prompted by an increasing recognition that some types of environmental deterioration are contributed to by all countries. There has been an increasing understanding that decisions taken in one country may have a detrimental environmental effect elsewhere.[30] Moreover, there has arguably been greater internationalization of the environment, of politics and of economies (Vogel, 1995). Socio-legal work in this area is still relatively limited and it is only in the past five years or so that serious attention has been paid to international attempts to control transnational pollution by use of the law.[31] This socio-legal interest has mirrored changes in conceptions of the environment and regulation. It has also accompanied wider academic interest in globalization.[32]

International attempts to protect the environment have involved national and international attempts to regulate transnational environmental problems. It has also introduced new participants to the regulatory arena and changed the role of some existing players. The role of the *nation state* has become the subject of intense debate. Some argue that the nation state has a more restricted role because it has been superseded by supranational organizations. Others argue that it has expanded its role and influence more directly and forcefully in the international context, by becoming not only the exporter of goods but also the exporter of regulatory standards and knowledge. It certainly appears difficult to accept that the role of the nation state is diminishing (Braithwaite and Drahos, forthcoming; Dodd and Hutter, forthcoming). What is important is to differentiate among nation states, as some are more powerful than others; for example, the U.S.A., Germany, and Japan figure prominently in the debate about environmental control. What is also certain is that there is a tension between demands for internationally-effective regulations and even-handedness on the one hand, and for national economic advantage on the other.

Transnational organizations, such as the European Union (EU) and OECD, have assumed greater importance in discussions of environmental regulation (Vogel, 1995, ch. 8). The OECD, for example, has taken a leading role in regulating environmental issues relating to the chemicals industry. It has worked with both states and business to assemble information and set standards (Braithwaite and Drahos, forthcoming). *Multinational companies* have also appeared as significant participants and here the emphasis is very much upon big business which operates on a global, international level, rather than small, localized businesses. These large companies are important because they may be major polluters. They may also represent a significant economic force in their own right and be able to exert political pressure at the level of the nation state. Braithwaite and Drahos (forthcoming) associate the lead role of Du Pont in the development and manufacture of CFC substitutes with the willingness of the U.S. Government in international discussions to promote the control of CFCs. This is contrasted with European opposition to such controls, which may be seen as related to pressure from Du Pont's rival ICI.

Non-governmental organizations (NGOs) can also play an important role in international environmental regulation. In particular they form part of a *community of environmental actors* which has emerged, comprising networks of states, NGOs, businesses, and international organizations (Braithwaite and Drahos, forthcoming). Peter Haas (1989), in his discussion of epistemic communities, has highlighted the importance of these communities and how they extend into the arenas of knowledge and science.

International efforts to regulate pollution may involve any number and variety of actors. Transnational environmental regulation may, for example, be bilateral or extend further across the international community.

Bilateral Environmental Regulation

The most prominent example of bilateral environmental regulation is that between Canada and the U.S. These nations share an extended land and water border which has located within its proximity many major industrial cities (Bruning, 1991). The external influence of the U.S. on Canadian domestic public policy reveals the dependency of a relatively small nation on a large one. Generally the impact of the U.S. on Canada is much greater than vice versa. Bruning, for example, estimates that the U.S. is responsible for nearly two to four times as much acid rain falling on Canada than vice versa. The two countries have very different economic and political priorities and differing attitudes to environmental regulation (Bruning, 1991; Hoberg, 1991, reprinted in this volume). Whereas Canada has an interest and commitment to transboundary environmental issues, the U.S. government has proven itself rather more interested in domestic issues, especially during the early 1980s when the Reagan Government was not concerned with environmental issues.

There is some dispute about the extent of regulatory expertise. Bruning (1991, p. 149) argues that Canadian technical expertise about regulating transboundary environmental issues is much greater than that of the U.S. federal and state agencies. Hoberg (1991, p. 109), however, believes that Canada is dependant on the U.S. for knowledge and policy leadership. The net effect of both arguments is much the same, namely that there is little effective resolution of the transboundary environmental problems experienced, especially by Canada. Bruning (1991, p. 144) argues that the problems are *managed* not *resolved* and the resolution is primarily diplomatic. The Canada–U.S. example is important because it highlights the significance of the power dimension in international negotiations (or lack of them) about environmental regulation. And this is a theme that runs through the international literature.

Global Environmental Regulation

Much of the socio-legal literature on this subject considers what efforts towards global regulation have emerged in the past 20 to 30 years. In contrast to the work undertaken at the local and national levels, there is more discussion of the policy issues involved in international environmental regulation and their effects than there is of enforcement.

Discussions of *policy-making* present a general picture of considerable activity but variable substance. There are many treaties and conventions relating to environmental regulation and protection—so many that Braithwaite and Drahos refer to 'convention fatigue'.[33] But these developments have been piecemeal, with little coherence, limited mandates, and typically small budgets. The longevity and maturation time for many environmental problems is in many respects at odds with political democracy which does not tend to favour long-term planning, especially if it is costly in the short-term.

One issue which is the matter of much debate is the type of rules and standards which may be implemented. Harmonization of laws and standards may be an attractive political option, but conditions vary widely and different standards may be more desirable. Braithwaite and Drahos suggest that continuous improvement should be the principle underlying and guiding international standard setting. This is an approach which favours a ratcheting up of standards rather than compliance with strict rules. Indeed, as Vogel (1995, p. 7) reminds us, stricter standards do not necessarily mean more effective standards. Another policy related problem is the need to embrace different legal cultures and traditions, a subject which is hardly researched and an area which warrants serious attention.

Internationally there is a lack of *enforcement* mechanisms for the implementation of internationally agreed regulations. Supra-national enforcement of environmental agreements is virtually non-existent. Typically there is national enforcement of internationally agreed standards and not surprisingly there is a great variety of arrangements for such enforcement between nations, sometimes even within nations. Formally these different enforcement arrangements and approaches are mutually recognized (Braithwaite and Drahos, forthcoming) for, as Esty (1994, p. 148) comments, enforcement goes to the heart of national sovereignty. National command and control approaches have limited success in the enforcement of international standards (Esty, 1994, p. 148). This has led to consideration of other measures to influence environmental behaviour (see, generally, Braithwaite and Drahos, forthcoming), including third-party enforcement; the use of rewards such as funds to promote environmental regulation and compliance in developing countries and Eastern Europe; and different types of self-regulation. In addition alternative verification techniques need to be used to check compliance. The three main means here are NGOs; the media; and incidents of noncompliance which can be readily traced back to source. The sanctions which may then be utilized are few—for instance, shaming, but more typically trade sanctions. Indeed, it is on the subject of the nature and the implications of the relationship between trade and environment that the most substantial literature exists in the area of international environmental regulation.

The debate about the relationship between trade and environmental protection goes directly to the heart of the tension between economic goals and environmental protection and the limits of political attempts to intervene to control the operations of the market.

Environmental Protection and Economic Growth/Competition

One method of promoting global environmental protection is the incorporation of environmental concerns into trade agreements. Examples of this include the Montreal Protocol, which aims to phase out CFCs and ban trade in certain goods with countries that do not comply with the agreement; the North American Free Trade Agreement (NAFTE) between the U.S., Canada, and Mexico; the European Union (EU); and GATT. The linking of these two issues has led to increasing conflicts and disputes, in part because they lead to allegations of discriminatory and protectionist practices.

There are two fundamental and opposing views caricatured by Esty (1994) as an opposition between environmentalists and free traders, one with the main objective of protecting the environment and the other with the main objective of free trade. Esty (1994, p. 37) refers to this as a clash of paradigms where judgements are opposed and criteria of 'success' and 'failure' differ, as do the means of assessment. The extent to which the environment and free trade are opposed to each other is a matter of some controversy. Vogel (1995) accepts that while environmental regulation is to some extent an obstacle to trade its incompatibility with free trade is exaggerated. He maintains that trade liberalization does not necessarily weaken domestic standards, indeed it could do the reverse and strengthen them. The debate thus turns on the effects of environmental protection on economic competition, this is a subject about which there are strong and very different views. This debate is sometimes characterized as the debate between the 'race to the top' and the 'race to the bottom'.[34] The 'race to the bottom' idea is that stricter standards are the source of competitive disadvantage and will lead companies to move to the lowest cost location. The state response in such a scenario is deregulatory both nationally and internationally.[35] According to this point of view corporations resist compliance and may relocate to avoid the costs of regulation. One strong advocate of this point of view is Stewart (1993), who argues that stringent environmental regulation harms the international competitiveness of nations promulgating such regulation. Meanwhile, the 'race to the top' argument maintains that those at the cutting edge of environmental regulation are at a competitive advantage because (in global terms) domestic producers can comply most easily. The state response is a strategic trade policy where the state acts to encourage international regulatory efforts. The argument is basically that a ratcheting up of standards is effected and strict regulation is an opportunity for companies to upgrade (Porter, 1990; Porter and van der Linde, 1998, reprinted in this volume).

Each side regards the same 'evidence' rather differently. Indeed, the whole notion of 'evidence' is problematic as very little rigorous research has been undertaken into this subject. This is a difficult area to research given the difficulties in obtaining comparable data. Most of the work so far has been undertaken by economists and with reference to the U.S., where it seems to be generally accepted that there is a particularly stringent regulatory regime.[36]

It is generally accepted that most of the empirical studies to date have found that strict regulation has had little effect upon the competitive standing of the U.S. (Esty, 1994, p. 21; Stewart, 1993, p. 2041). On the subject of cost, for instance, Esty (1994, p. 159) quotes research that claims that spending on pollution control is less than 2 per cent of the value added for 86 per cent of U.S. industries. Likewise there is little evidence of relocation because of strict regulation. Gunther (1991) notes that very few U.S. industries have relocated because of strict environmental regulation in the U.S. However, there is some evidence that at the margin, in a few high polluting industries, strict regulation does cause pollution costs to be factored in when deciding where to locate (Esty, 1994, p. 160) and it may even cause relocation to developing countries (Stewart, 1993, 2084).

Those who believe that strict regulation is incompatible with economic growth or competitiveness argue that empirical research to date ignores two important points. The first is the existence of large invisible costs which depress innovation and the development of new products. These include the opportunity costs of compliance; the costs incurred by delays to production; the uncertainties involved; and the risks of liability and the need to comply with liability rules (Stewart, 1993, 2063). The second criticism is that existing work is outdated. It considers the costs of regulation during a period of de-regulation and does not take into account increasing pollution controls and their associated costs (Esty, 1994, p. 160; Stewart, 1993, 2084).

These are essentially cost–benefit arguments, and like all such arguments the costs and the benefits can look very different according to your standpoint and allegiances. So different evidence is considered and the same evidence is differently interpreted. One of the benefits of strict regulation should be the environment, but to date there has been little research on this topic, largely because of the difficulties of estimating the benefits of regulation. Those adhering to the 'race to the top' point of view believe that far from stifling competition regulation promotes it by prompting innovation. This embraces the development of new control technologies, more energy saving processes and new products.

What is noticeable in this debate is that the costs are short-term and the benefits are long-term. Indeed, the social benefits may be ignored altogether (Palmer et al., 1995). This is one fundamental difficulty with the debate, another being the need to differentiate between large and small companies. Clearly more research is needed and the complexities of differing situations and variables need elaborating.[37] In particular, there is a need for more studies which consider regulatory effects across a range of different countries.

Developing countries are an important consideration in debates about the impact of global environmental agreements. They may be the location of so-called 'dirty manufacturers'. Moreover, the costs of dealing with global environmental issues may be levied disproportionately on them (Saunders, 1991, p. 167). Developing countries may be reluctant to divert their limited resources to environmental issues. They may, for instance, have more pressing social needs and may regard 'northern' intrusions into their sovereignty as offensive, as an imposition of values and priorities. They may also be suspicious of the developed world's motives in trying to impose strict environmental standards. The environmental challenges posed by the industrialization of such major nations as India and China surely pose among the most serious regulatory issues of the next century. Of particular concern is how supranational institutions will cope with these changes and what sort of environmental policies can be agreed upon (see, generally, Hewitt et al., 1992; Redclift and Benton, 1994).

Another problem for developing countries is that environmental regulation may be counter-productive. Esty (1994, p. 188) explains, for example, how restrictions placed upon the import of tropical timber may lead to a limited market which lowers the price and may result in more trees being felled to maintain income. The problem is very much one of global co-operation between advanced industrialized nations and developing countries.

Even within advanced industrialized countries some nations are clearly more powerful than others. This is exemplified by the work of Vogel (1995), who examines six trade agreements and treaties and their relationship to national environmental and consumer regulations. He highlights the importance of powerful nations in promoting stricter environmental standards, in particular the role of the U.S. in NAFTA and Germany in the EU where, he argues, Germany's pressure for stricter standards has contributed to a strengthening of standards amongst its trading partners (1995, 260 ff.).

The global dimension to environmental protection highlights the complexity of factors and dynamics involved in making environmental law effective. On the one hand globalization may have increased the pressure to find the lowest-cost location. But on the other hand it can introduce dynamics pushing in the opposite direction. For example, NGOs can push for increasing standards and global acceptance of higher standards (Braithwaite and Drahos, forthcoming). The role of political and business considerations are brought to the fore and 'solutions' seem hard to agree upon. As Esty (1994, p. 172) remarks, there is a fear of loss of national sovereignty involved in these debates and the more international and global the effort becomes, the further removed the process may become from public participation and possibly the closer it may become to business interests.

Conclusion

Socio-legal interest in environmental law has developed over the past 20 years in response to, and as a reflection of, broader environmental concerns, changing regulatory trends, and shifting academic interests. It has also been shaped by pragmatic concerns such as the accessibility of data and restricted by technical and normative considerations, notably in evaluating the impact of law. Despite these developments there has been a constancy in the underlying themes and problems. A central and enduring focus of research is the ambiguity surrounding environmental law in its quest to regulate economic activities at the core of advanced modern societies. This is reflected in the different theoretical approaches taken in research, which reflect the ideologies of their authors and the complexity of the subject matter.

Despite the growth of environmental law and the 'greening' of academic interest, there are still noticeable and large gaps in the socio-legal literature on environmental law. There is surprisingly little historical work which adopts an expressly socio-legal perspective on environmental law. While a lot of effort has been concentrated on environmental law as a form of 'command and control' regulation, we know remarkably little about the use of environmental law in civil cases. Policy-making at both the national and international levels is ill-understood, and in particular we lack the rich ethnographic accounts and analysis that have taught us so much about the enforcement of environmental law. Studies of the impact of environmental law upon business and the environment are still a major gap in our knowledge, particularly studies which look beyond the U.S. Meanwhile, consideration of international attempts to use law to protect the global environment is both rudimentary and at the cutting edge of socio-legal interest in environmental law.

We can only hope for further socio-legal research into these areas, since environmental law is a rich field of socio-legal analysis. It is one where the interactions between law and broader social relations are starkly revealed and contested. And while much of the literature is critical of environmental law as a protective mechanism, very few authors are willing to abandon law. It is seen as an important underpinning to other attempts and methods to protect the environment. The vital task is to establish the circumstances under which law can be effective and this is the important socio-legal task ahead of us. But it is important that this is pursued as part of a broader effort to develop a theoretical understanding of the place of law in society and in particular to develop the conceptual tools which will enable research of a high quality to be undertaken.

Notes

1. Institutionalized socio-legal research is some 25 years old. For example, the Centre for Socio-Legal Studies at Oxford University celebrated its first 21 years of existence in 1995. Members of the United States-based Law & Society Association critically reflected on their 25th Anniversary in 1989/90 (see, for example, Trubek and Esser, 1989).
2. These include, for example, anthropology, economics, history, law, political science, psychology, social policy, and sociology.
3. A distinction is often drawn between social and financial regulation. Environmental law clearly falls into the first of these categories, and refers to laws protecting the environment, consumers, and employees. It concerns the regulation of industrial processes that may cause harm to workforces, the public, and

the environment. The distinction between economic and social regulation is largely a heuristic division and is not always so clearcut as these definitions would suggest. See Dodd and Hutter, forthcoming; Yeager, 1991, p. 24.

4. This does not on its own mean less regulation, since while many specific laws have been repealed they have often been replaced by less but more inclusive legislation. In other words, the change has been one of reregulation rather than deregulation.
5. Proactive enforcement is law enforcement through agency initiative so it involves officials seeking out offences. This is in contrast to reactive enforcement where the agency response is prompted by an outside person or event, typically a complaint or accident. See Reiss, 1971.
6. See, generally, the work of Sheila Jasanoff; Dorothy Nelkin; Brian Wynne; and Steven Woolgar.
7. See, in particular, Yearley, 1992. It is interesting to note that in 1995 Yearley comments that even science studies have not yet properly considered environmental issues.
8. The marshalling of scientific expertise by competing environmental groups may of course contribute to a conception of science as untrustworthy.
9. I am indebted to Christine Garwood for an excellent bibliography and summary of historical work on environmental protectionism in Britain. Peter Bartrip has also given me very helpful advice on this section.
10. This was a period of increasing governmental regulation. See, generally, Taylor, 1972. For discussion of the emergence of other protective social regulation see Alderman, 1973; Bartrip and Fenn, 1980; 1983; Carson, 1974; Martin, 1983; Parris, 1965.
11. See, for example, Ashby and Anderson, 1981; Beck, 1959; Brimblecombe; 1987; Flick, 1980. On the subject of river pollution see Breeze, 1993; Luckin, 1986; Smith, 1982.
12. Within its first year the Inspectorate managed to reduce this pollutant from 1000 tons a week to 43, but this did not apparently improve the atmosphere greatly. This was because the scope of the Act was so limited and did not allow for the regulation of the many other substances polluting the atmosphere (Ashby and Anderson, 1981; Frankel, 1974).
13. These standards are the subject of much controversy. See Bugler, 1972; Gunningham, 1974; Owens, 1990; Ponsford, 1988; Yeager, 1991.
14. Another reason for this emphasis upon field-level officials may be found in the intellectual traditions from which many of socio-legal researchers working in this area, especially in its formative years, emanated, namely the interactionist tradition. This perspective had done much to increase our understanding of the police as street-level bureaucrats. See Rock, 1995.
15. This is sometimes referred to as the accommodative strategy. See Richardson et al., 1983; Hutter, 1988; 1997. These models of enforcement are extrapolations of the most distinctive enforcement characteristics identified amongst

regulatory officials and the police. No one claims that they will be found in these precise forms in the real world. Neither is it claimed that one style is the exclusive province of one type of enforcement agency. Rather it is acknowledged that all enforcement officials will use both styles but with differing levels of commitment.

16. Reiss uses the term deterrence model and Hawkins refers to the sanctioning model, the latter being deliberately less specific. Reiss argues that the object of prosecution is simply to prevent the occurrence of violations although Hawkins argues that the objective is broader and includes an element of retribution for wrongdoing.
17. See Kagan (1994) for an excellent summary.
18. The classic text on regulatory capture was written much earlier. See Bernstein, 1955.
19. In the U.S.A., for instance, the EPA struggled to achieve the standard-setting goals required by environmental legislation (Dwyer, 1990). Mashaw and Harfst (1990) discuss similar difficulties in the area of motor vehicle safety in the US where there was also a move to regulate through agency rule-making. Standards which took some three months to prepare in the 1960s took several years in the 1970s, partly because of the agency's ability to undertake to work involved in preparing specific standards and because of industry resistance and technological uncertainty.
20. See Yeager (1991). Much of this criticism stems from the United States where many of these problems were probably more exaggerated than in the United Kingdom.
21. See Grabosky and Braithwaite, 1986, Chapter 14; DiMento, 1986, Chapter 3; and Ogus, 1994, Parts III and IV for a more detailed discussion of the various forms of regulation available to governments. See Cheit, 1990, for a discussion of private standard setting by such bodies as trade associations and professional societies.
22. This includes civil cases, which may be taken by third parties, such as the violation of standards set by professional bodies.
23. A variety of other policies fall within this category. For example, the *offset policies* discussed by Dwyer (1993) are a form of economic incentive, these allow firms to build new facilities or modify existing ones so long as they employ strict pollution controls on the new source and offset all residual emissions by reductions at other existing sources. Other policies falling into this category include the 'bubble policy', netting and emissions banking. See Tietenberg (1990), pp. 18–19.
24. Grabosky (1995) provides an excellent overview of third-party enforcement. See also Cheit (1990); Gilboy (1998).
25. Regulatory agencies may have an ambivalent relationship with interest groups which may both be critics of the regulatory agency and also powerful allies against business. See Hutter (1997).

26. See Ogus (1995) for an excellent summary of the various definitions of self-regulation.
27. This is not part of the Australian Responsible Care programme but it was an integral part of the U.S. Nuclear Power Industry self-regulation, see Rees (1994).
28. This agency was charged with undertaking the work of the former Industrial Air Pollution Inspectorate, the Hazardous Waste Inspectorate, H.M. Radio-chemical Inspectorate, and a Water Pollution Inspectorate.
29. It merged the responsibilities of the H.M. Inspectorate of Pollution, the National Rivers Authority, and the local authority waste authorities and is responsible for integrated pollution control for most industrial processes, the regulation of waste disposal, and the control of the main river watercourses (Hutter, 1997).
30. For example, the build-up of greenhouse gases in the atmosphere, caused by carbon-dioxide emissions through the burning of fossil fuels, has led to unprecedented global warming. The destruction of the ozone layer has been caused by internationally used chlorofluorocarbons. The atomic power industry presents global environmental problems. Deforestation, oil spills, and countless other examples are now understood to have detrimental environmental effects beyond geopolitical borders.
31. See Hurrell and Kingsbury (1992) and Birnie and Boyle (1992) for a more general discussion of the international political and legal dimensions of environmental protection.
32. It should be noted that there is little agreement about what the concept of globalization means and what it entails. See Featherstone (1990); Giddens (1990).
33. Braithwaite and Drahos estimate that there are now over 500 framework conventions relating to the environment.
34. In the U.S. the race to the top is sometimes known as 'the California effect' as California is considered to have higher standards which have pushed standards up and benefitted businesses based in California. The race to the bottom is known as 'the Delaware effect' as it is maintained that lower standards in Delaware have attracted business to the area and led to a general lowering of standards.
35. Braithwaite and Drahos (forthcoming) cite a useful summary by Robyn Eckersley of the two points of view.
36. Kagan (1995) refers to adversarial legalism. Kagan et al. (1996) further contests that this strict regulation leads to greater social or environmental benefits.
37. Esty (1994, p. 159), for example, notes that strict regulation may spur innovation and create a competitive advantage, but only when there is flexible enforcement and enlightened corporate management.

Bibliography

Aalders, M. (1993) 'Regulation and In-Company Environmental Management in the Netherlands', *Law and Policy*, Vol. 15, No. 2, 75–94.

Alderman, G. (1973) *The Railway Interest*, Leicester: Leicester University Press.

Ashby, E. and Anderson, M. (1981) *The Politics of Clean Air*, Oxford: Clarendon Press.

Austin, R. (1989) 'Freedom of Information: The Constitutional Impact' in Jowell, J. and Oliver, D. *The Changing Constitution*, 2nd edn. Oxford: Clarendon Press.

Ayres, I. and Braithwaite, J. (1992) *Responsive Regulation*, New York: Oxford University Press.

Baldwin, R. (1995) *Rules and Government*, Oxford: Clarendon Press.

——(1997) 'Regulation: After "Command and Control"' in Hawkins (ed).

Bardach, E. and Kagan, R. (1982) *Going by the Book: The Problem of Regulatory Unreasonableness*, Philadelphia: Temple University Press.

Bartrip, P. W. J. and Fenn, P. T. (1980) 'The Administration of Safety: The Enforcement Policy of the Early Factory Inspectorate, 1844–1864', *Public Administration*, 58, 87–102.

——and——(1983) 'The Evolution of Regulatory Style in the Nineteenth Century British Factory Inspectorate', *Journal of Law and Society*, Vol. 10.2.

Baucus, M. and Dworkin, T. M. (1991) 'What is Corporate Crime? It Is Not Illegal Corporate Behaviour', *Law and Policy*, Vol. 13, No. 3, 231–244.

Beck, A. (1959) 'Some Aspects of the History of Anti-Pollution Legislation in England, 1819–1954', *Journal of the History of Medicine and Allied Sciences*, 14.

Beck, U. (1992) *Risk Society: Towards a New Modernity*, London: Sage.

Becker, G. S. (1989) 'Political Competition Among Interest Groups' in Shogren (ed.).

Bennett, G. and von Molke, K. (1990) 'Integrated Permitting in the Netherlands and the Federal Republic of Germany' in Haigh and Irwin (eds.).

Bernstein, M. H. (1955) *Regulating Business by Independent Commission*, Princeton: Princeton University Press.

Bimber, B. and Guston, D. H. (1995) 'Politics by the Same Means: Government and Science in the United States' in Jasanoff et al. (eds.).

Birnie, P. W. and Boyle, A. E. (eds.) (1992) *International Law and Environment*, Oxford: Clarendon Press.

Box, S. (1983) *Power, Crime and Mystification*, London: Routledge.

Boyer, B. and Meidinger, E. (1985) 'Privatizing Regulatory Enforcement: A Preliminary Assessment of Citizen Suits Under Federal Environmental Laws', *Buffalo Law Review* 34, 833–964.

Braithwaite, J. and Drahos, P. (forthcoming) *Global Business Regulation*, mimeo.

Braithwaite, J. and Fisse, B. (1985) 'Varieties of Responsibility and Organizational Crime', *Law and Policy*, Vol. 7, No. 3, 315–343.

Braithwaite, J., Grabosky, P. and Walker, J. (1987) 'An Enforcement Taxonomy of Regulatory Agencies', *Law and Policy*, Vol. 9, 9, 323–351.

Breeze, L. E. (1993) *The British Experience with River Pollution 1865–1876*, New York: Peter Lang.

Brickman, R., Jasanoff, S. and Iilgen, T. (1985) *Controlling Chemicals: The Politics of Regulation in Europe and the United States*, Ithaca, NY: Cornell University Press.

Brimblecombe, P. (1987) *The Big Smoke: A History of Air Pollution in London*, London: Routledge.

Brittan, Y. (1984) *The Impact of Water Pollution Control on Industry*, Oxford: Centre for Socio-Legal Studies.

Brown, M. S. and Lyon, K. A. (1992) 'Holes in the Ozone Layer: A Global Environmental Controversy' in Nelkin (ed.).

Bruning, E. R. (1991) 'Canadian–US Transboundary Environmental Issues: An Institutional Assessment' in McKee (ed.).

Bugler, J. (1972) *Polluting Britain*, Harmondsworth, Penguin.

Cable, S. and Benson, M. (1993) 'Acting Locally: Environmental Injustice and the Emergence of Grass-Roots Environmental Organizations', *Social Problems* 40, 4, 464–477.

Carson, W. G. (1974) 'Symbolic and Instrumental Dimensions of Early Factory Legislation: A Case Study in the Social Origins of Criminal Law', in Hood, R. (ed.) *Crime, Criminology and Public Policy*, London: Heineman.

Cheit, R. E. (1990) *Setting Safety Standards: Regulation in the Public and Private Sectors*, Berkeley: University of California Press.

Clapp, B. W. (1994) *An Environmental History of Britain Since the Industrial Revolution*, London: Longman.

Clarke, L. (1992) 'The Wreck of the Exxon Valdez' in Nelkin (ed.).

Clinard, M. B. and Yeager, P. C. (1980) *Corporate Crime*, New York: Free Press.

Cotterrell, R. (1992) *The Sociology of Law*, 2nd edn. London: Butterworths.

Cranston, R. (1979) *Regulatory Business: Law and Consumer Agencies*, London: Macmillan.

Davis, K. C. (1969) *Discretionary Justice*, Baton Rouge: Louisiana State University Press.

Dewees, D. (1990) 'The Effect of Environmental Regulation: Mercury and Sulphur Dioxide' in Friedman (ed.).

DiMento, J. F. (1986) *Environmental Law and American Business: Dilemmas of Compliance*, New York: Plenum Press.

——(1989) 'Can Social Science Explain Organizational Non-Compliance with Environmental Law?', *Journal of Social Issues*, 45, 1, 109–132.

Dodd, N. and Hutter, B. M. (forthcoming) 'Geopolitics and the Regulation of Economic Life', mimeo.

Dwyer, J. P. (1990) 'The Pathology of Symbolic Legislation', *Ecology Law Quarterly* 17, 233–316.

——(1993) 'The Use of Market Incentives in Controlling Air Pollution: California's Marketable Permits Program', *Ecology Law Quarterly* 20, 103–117.

ENDS Report 227 (1993) London: Environmental Data Services.

Esty, D. C. (1994) *Greening the GAAT: Trade, Environment and the Future*, Washington: Institute for International Economics.

Featherstone, M. (ed) (1990) *Global Culture: Nationalism, Globalization and Modernity*, London: Sage.

Flick, C. (1980) 'The Movement for Smoke Abatement in Nineteenth Century Britain', *Technology and Culture*, 21: 1: 29–50.

Frankel, M. (1974) *The Alkali Inspectorate: The Control of Industrial Air Pollution*, London: Social Audit.

Friedman, M. L. (ed) (1990) *Securing Compliance: Seven Case Studies*, Toronto: University of Toronto Press.

Galligan, D. J. (1986) *Discretionary Powers*, Oxford: Clarendon Press.

Geis, G. and Stotland, E. (eds.) (1980) *White-Collar Crime: Theory and Research*, Beverly Hills, CA: Sage.

Genn, H. (1993) 'Business Responses to the Regulation of Health and Safety in England', *Law and Policy*, Vol. 3, 15, 219.

Giddens, A. (1990) *The Consequences of Modernity*, Cambridge: Polity Press.

Gilboy, J. (1998) 'Compelled Third-Party Participation in the Regulatory Process: Legal Duties, Culture and Non-Compliance', *Law and Policy*, Vol. 20, No. 2, 135–155.

Grabosky, P. (1994) 'Green Markets: Environmental Regulation by the Private Sector', *Law and Policy*, Vol. 16, No. 4, 419–448.

——(1995) 'Using Non-Governmental Resources to Foster Regulatory Compliance', *Governance*, 8, 4, 527–550.

——(1995a) 'Counterproductive Regulation', *International Journal of the Sociology of Law*, 23, 347–369.

——(1995b) 'Regulation by Reward: On the Use of Incentives as Regulatory Instruments', *Law and Policy*, Vol. 17, No. 3, 257–282.

——and Braithwaite, J. (1986) *Of Manners Gentle*, Melbourne: OUP.

Gunningham, N. (1974) *Pollution, Social Interest and the Law*, London: Martin Robertson.

——(1995) 'Enforcement, Self-Regulation, and the Chemical Industry: Assessing Responsible Care', *Law and Policy*, Vol. 17, No. 1, 57–109.

——and Grabosky, P. (1998) *Designing Environmental Policy*, Oxford: Oxford University Press.

——and Sinclair, D. (1998) 'Designing Smart Regulation' in this volume, abridged from Gunningham and Grabosky (1998).

Gunther, W. D. (1991) 'Plant Locations and Environmental Regulation' in McKee (ed).

Hahn, R. W. (1989) 'Economic Prescriptions for Environmental Problems: Not Exactly What the Doctor Ordered' in Shogren (ed.).

——(1990) 'The Political Economy of Environmental Regulation: Towards a Unifying Framework', *Public Choice*, 65, 21–47.

Haas, P. M. (1989) 'Do Regimes Matter? Epistemic Communities and Mediterranean Pollution Control', *International Organization*, 43, 377–403.

Haigh, N. and Irwin, E. (1990) *Integrated Pollution Policy Control in Europe and North America*, Washington: The Conservation Foundation.

Hawes, R. (1995) 'The Control of Alkali Pollution in St. Helens, 1862–1890', *Environment and History*, 1.

Hawkins, K. (1984) *Environment and Enforcement: Regulation and Social Definition of Pollution*, Oxford: Clarendon Press.

——(1992a) *The Regulation of Occupational Health and Safety: A Socio-Legal Perspective*, Report to the Health and Safety Executive.

——(ed) (1997) *The Human Face of the Law*, Oxford: Clarendon Press.

Hawkins, K. H. and Hutter, B. M. (1993) 'The Response of Business to Social Regulation in England and Wales: An Enforcement Perspective', *Law and Policy*, Vol. 15, No. 3, 199–218.

Hewitt, T., Johnson, H. and Wield, D. (eds.) (1992) *Industrialization and Development*, Oxford: Oxford University Press.

Hoberg, G. (1991) 'Sleeping with an Elephant: The American Influence on Canadian Environmental Regulation', *Journal Public Policy*, 11, 1, 107–132.

Hurrell, A. and Kingsbury, B. (eds.) (1992) *The International Politics of the Environment*, Oxford: Clarendon Press.

Hutter, B. M. (1988) *The Reasonable Arm of the Law?: The Law Enforcement Procedures of Environmental Health Officers*, Oxford: Clarendon Press.

——(1997) *Compliance: Regulation and Environment*, Oxford: Clarendon Press.

——and Lloyd-Bostock, S. (1997) 'Law's Relationship with Social Science: The Interdependence of Theory, Empirical Work, and Social Relevance in Socio-Legal Studies' in Hawkins (ed.).

Jasanoff, S. (1989) 'The Problem of Rationality in American Health and Safety Regulation' in Smith and Wynne (eds.).

——(1991) 'Cross-National Differences in Policy Implementation', *Evaluation Review*, 15, 1, 103–119.

——(1990) *The Fifth Branch: Science Advisors as Policymakers*, Cambridge, MA: Harvard University Press.

——Markle, G. E., Peterson, J. C. and Pinch, T. (eds.) (1995) *Handbook of Science and Technology Studies*, London: Sage.

Jasper, J. M. (1992) 'Three Nuclear Energy Controversies' in Nelkin (ed.).

Justice (1980) *Breaking the Rules*, London: Justice.

Kagan, R. A. (1978) *Regulatory Justice*, New York: Russell Sage Foundation.

——(1994) 'Regulatory Enforcement' in Rosenbloom, D. H. and Schwartz, R. D. (eds.) *Handbook of Regulation and Administrative Law*, New York: Marcel Dekker.

——(1995) 'Adversarial Legalism and American Government' in Landy and Levin (eds.).

——Axelrad, L. and Ruhlin, C. (1996) 'Convergence or Divergence in National Modes of Regulation: Multinational Corporations and American Adversarial Legalism', paper presented at the Annual Meeting of the Law and Society Association, Glasgow, 1996.

Landy, M. and Levin, M. (eds.) (1995) *The New Politics of Public Policy*, Baltimore: Johns Hopkins Press.

Lewenstein, B. V. (1995) 'Science and the Media' in Jasanoff et al. (eds.).

Luckin, B. (1986) *Pollution and Control: A Social History of the Thames in the Nineteenth Century*, Bristol: Adam Higler.

Majone, G. (ed) (1989) *Deregulation or Reregulation?*, London: Pinter.

Makkai, T. and Braithwaite, J. (1993) 'Praise, Pride and Compliance', *International Journal of the Sociology of Law*, 21, 73–91.

Martin, B. (1983) 'The Development of the Factory Office up to 1878: Administrative Evolution and the Establishment of a Regulatory Style in the Early Factory Inspectorate', paper presented to 'Regulation in Britain: A Conference', Trinity College, Oxford University, September 1983.

Mashaw, J. L. and Harfst, D. L. (1990) *The Struggle for Auto Safety*, Cambridge, MA: Harvard University Press.

McBarnet, D. J. (1981) *Conviction: Law, the State and the Construction of Justice*, London: Macmillan.

McKee, D. (ed.) (1991) *Energy, the Environment and Public Policy*, New York: Praeger.

Meidinger, E. (1985) 'On Explaining the Development of "Emissions Trading" in U.S. Air Pollution Regulation', *Law and Policy*, Vol. 7, No. 4, 447–479.

Mitnick, B. (1980) *The Political Economy of Regulation*, New York: Columbia University Press.

Nelken, D. (1981) 'The "Gap Problem" in the Sociology of Law: A Theoretical Review', *Windsor Yearbook of Access to Justice*, 1, 35–61.

Nelkin, D. (ed.) (1992) *Controversy: Politics of Technical Decisions*, 3rd edn. London: Sage.

——(1995) 'Science Controversies: The Dynamic of Public Disputes in the United States' in Jasanoff et al. (eds.).

Ogus, A. (1994) *Regulation: Legal Form and Economic Theory*, Oxford: Clarendon Press.

Ogus, A. I. and Richardson, G. (1977) 'Economics and the Environment: A Study of Private Nuisance', *Cambridge Law Journal*, 36, 2, 284–325.

Olsen, M. (1982) *The Rise and Decline of Nations: Economic Growth, Stagflation and Social Rigidities*, New Haven, CT: Yale University Press.

Opschoor, J. and Vos, H. (1989) *Economic Instruments for Environmental Protection*, Paris: OECD.

Owens, S. (1990) 'The Unified Pollution Inspectorate and Best Practicable Environmental Option in the United Kingdom', in Haigh and Irwin.

Palmer, K., Oates, W. E. and Portney, P. R. (1995) 'Tightening Environmental Standards: The Benefit–Cost or the No-Cost Paradigm?', *Journal of Economic Perspectives*, 9, 4, 119–132.

Parris, H. (1965) *Government and the Railways in the Nineteenth Century*, London: Routledge and Kegan Paul.

Paulus, I. (1974), *The Search for Pure Food*, London: Martin Robertson.

Pellzman, S. (1976) 'Towards a More General Theory of Regulation', *Journal of Law and Economics*, 19, 211–240.

Ponsford, B. (1988) 'Logic and Practice in Environmental Pollution Control', *Annual Occupational Hygiene*, 32, 3, 261–270.

Porter, M. E. (1990) *The Competitive Advantage of Nations*, London: Collier Macmillan.

Porter, M. B. and van der Linde, C. (1995) 'Towards a New Conception of the Environmental Competitiveness Relationship', *Journal of Economic Perspectives*, 9, 97–118.

Rayner, S. (1991) 'A Cultural Perspective on the Structure and Implementation of Global Environmental Agreements', *Evaluation Review*, 15, 1, 75–102.

Redclift, M. and Benton, T. (eds.) (1994) *Social Theory and the Global Environment*, London: Routledge.

Rees, J. V. (1994) *Hostages of Each Other: The Transformation of Nuclear Safety Since Three Mile Island*, Chicago: Chicago University Press.

Reiss, A. (1971) *The Police and the Public*, New Haven, CT: Yale University Press.

——(1984) 'Selecting Strategies of Social Control Over Organisational Life' in K. Hawkins, and J. Thomas (eds.) (1984) *Enforcing Regulation*, Boston: Kluwer-Nijhoff.

Richardson, G. M. with Ogus, A. I., Burrows, P. (1983) *Policing Pollution: a Study of Regulation and Enforcement*, Oxford: Clarendon Press.

Rock, P. (1995) 'Sociology and the Stereotype of the Police', *Journal of Law and Society*, 22, 1, 17–25.

Saunders, R. J. (1991) 'Developing Countries and the Potential for Global Warming' in McKee (ed.).

Shogren, J. F. (ed.) (1989) *The Political Economy of Government Regulation*, Boston: Kluwer.

Shover, N. (1980) 'The Criminalization of Corporate Behavior: Federal Surface Coal Mining' in Geis and Stotland (eds.).

Sigler, J. A. and Murphy, J. E. (1988) *Interactive Corporate Compliance: An Alternative to Regulatory Compulsion*, New York: Quorum Books.

Smith, P. J. (1982) 'The Legislated Control of River Pollution in Victorian Scotland', *Scottish Geographical Magazine*, 98: 2: 66–76.

Smith, R. and Wynne, B. (eds.) (1989) *Expert Evidence: Interpreting Science in the Law*, London: Routledge.

Stewart, R. B. (1993) 'Environmental Regulation and International Competitiveness', *Yale Law Journal*, 2039–2106.

Stigler, G. J. (1971) 'The Theory of Economic Regulation', *Bell Journal of Economics*, 2, 3–21.

Taylor, A. J. (1972) *Laissez-faire and State Intervention in Nineteenth-Century Britain*, London: Macmillan.

Taylor, I., Walton, P. and Young, J. (1975) *Critical Criminology*, London: Routledge and Kegan Paul.

Thomas, K. (1983) *Man and the Natural World: Changing Attitudes in England 1500–1800*, London: Allen Lane.

Tietenberg, T. H. (1990) 'Economic Instruments for Environmental Regulation', *Oxford Review of Economic Policy* 6, 1, 17–31.

Trubek, D. M. and Esser, J. (1989) 'Critical Empiricism in American Legal Studies: Paradox, Program or Pandora's Box?', *Law and Social Enquiry*, 3–59.

Vogel, D. (1986) *National Styles of Regulation: Environmental Policy in Great Britain and the United States*, Ithaca, NY: Cornell University Press.

——(1995) *Trading Up: Consumer and Environmental Regulation in a Global Economy*, Cambridge, MA: Harvard University Press.

Wall, D. (ed.) (1994) *Green History: A Reader in Environmental Literature, Philosophy and Politics*, London: Routledge.

Wells, C. (1992) *Corporations and Criminal Responsibility*, Oxford: Clarendon Press.

Wynne, B. (1989) 'Establishing the Rules of Laws: Constructing Expert Authority' in Smith and Wynne.

Yandle, B. (1989) 'Bootleggers and Baptists in the Market for Regulation' in Shogren (ed.).

Yeager, P. C. (1987) 'Structural Bias in Regulatory Law Enforcement: The Case of the U.S. Environmental Protection Agency', *Social Problems*, Vol. 34, No. 4, 330–344.

——(1991) *The Limits of the Law: The Public Regulation of Private Pollution*, Cambridge: Cambridge University Press.

Yearley, S. (1992) *The Green Case*, London: Routledge and Kegan Paul.

——(1995) 'The Environmental Challenge to Science Studies' in Jasanoff et al. (eds.).

PART I
Theoretical Approaches

Economics and the Environment: A Study of Private Nuisance

A. I. OGUS* AND G. M. RICHARDSON†

The English lawyer has been notoriously unwilling to admit the relevance of social sciences to his discipline. In part, this may be attributed to his lack of formal training in economics or sociology. As regards the latter, there are some signs of the handicap being overcome: much current research effort is now being directed to the interpretation of law and the legal system as social phenomena.[1] But the application of economic reasoning to legal instruments and institutions has been limited and tentative. Although it has long been recognised that a marriage of the two disciplines is necessary for the procreation of effective norms in areas where the law clearly governs economic activities, for example, the regulation of trade[2] and income redistribution,[3] so far, in this country at least, creative thinking about central legal institutions such as tort, contract, property and crime has remained relatively untouched by such a mode of analysis.[4] Yet, as Americans have demonstrated, there is nothing inappropriate in such an exercise. At first sight the subject areas of economics and law will appear to diverge significantly: the former is 'concerned with the manner in which a society produces, distributes and consumes wealth when it is constrained by scarcity, either of tangible resources or of intangible resources,'[5] while the latter is often viewed as a system of norms governing the conduct of individuals and institutions. Yet such conduct will generally involve the transfer and acquisition of resources. With this congruence of interest, therefore, the opportunity exists to compare economic analysis with prevailing legal rules on particular issues to see whether the 'right' solution is reached.

But what is meant by 'right'? In the most positivist legal sense, it is that which is prescribed by the proper interpretation of the applicable sources, common law or statute. On a broader view, 'right' indicates that which is dictated by policy considerations in the light of society's needs. One important such policy consideration is that provided by a form of economic analysis which attempts to achieve optimal social welfare by ascertaining the 'efficient' means of influencing, through policy, the use of resources by society. At the general level 'efficient' outcomes are those in which given increases in individuals' welfare are obtained at the *least cost* to society, or alternatively a given quantity of resources is utilized in such a way as to maximize the welfare which society derives from it.[6] Much of the analysis of efficiency in economics is concerned with the ways in which institutions (markets, government units, legal rules, etc.) influence the allocation of resources between competing uses, and the ways in which this influence could be improved.

This form of analysis may be illustrated with a typical problem of resource allocation: should the costs incurred as a result of the manufacture of defective products be reflected in the price of those products, or should they be borne by the injured consumer himself?[7] The efficiency criterion, where general welfare is associated with the least cost, will seek to encourage avoidance of the harm by the cheapest means. It must therefore be ascertained whether the manufacturer or the consumer is the least cost-abater. On that party will be imposed the cost of the harm inflicted in the expectation that he will thus be encouraged to take appropriate precautions. In the case of defective products the manufacturer is generally the cheapest cost-abater: he has the required technical expertise and facilities. The efficient solution may be reached therefore by imposing liability in damages for the loss inflicted on the consumer. Whether the increase in the price of goods reflects the compensation itself or higher insurance premiums the anticipated deterrent effect will be the same.[8] There are, on the other hand, instances where the consumer might reasonably be regarded as the least cost-abater: *e.g.*, where injury might be avoided by use of seat belts or crash helmets. Efficiency then demands that he bears a significant proportion of the costs incurred.

The legal solution will often coincide with the economically efficient solution. For the cases mentioned there is tort liability for injuries caused by defective products[9] and a reduction in damages for the non-use of safety belts.[10] But, as was mentioned above, efficiency is only one possible component, albeit an important one, of the 'right' solution: it pays no heed to the ethical and distributional implications of the solution it favours. It may be that the efficient solution conflicts with society's concept of justice or fairness. A tenant may be able more cheaply to repair his premises and yet society sees fit to impose the obligation on the landlord.[11] Here distributional and broader policy issues are plainly allowed to prevail over those of efficiency.

Linked to this is another general principle. The private law is formulated in terms of individual rights,[12] and one traditional judicial maxim is that, subject to precise legislative intervention, they are not to be sacrificed to general efficiency.[13] The law of tort, for example, is concerned with individual claims and it would be rash to impute to it an overall strategy in terms of accident prevention.[14] It is through compensation that the individual claim is to be satisfied. The restoration of the *status quo ante* is seen as the prime objective: it will prevail over the efficient solution in the event of conflict. The danger is that at this point our stereotype lawyer, always suspicious of the social scientist's interference, will blithely declare the economist's model to be irrelevant. But it is not. The predominant criticism of the tort action is that it is not even an efficient means of achieving compensation.[15] An ideal policy solution must take account of both the efficiency and the justice objectives.[16]

The central purpose of this study is to apply economic analysis to a specific legal instrument in an attempt both to determine the extent to which that instrument fulfils the efficiency criteria and to speculate on the identity of such other policy dictates as may be involved. Environmental pollution, a field where the economic implications of legal rules are direct and visible, is the subject area chosen. The policy maker who is required to construct a legal framework for such control is confronted with an array of alternative though not necessarily mutually exclusive instruments: regulatory standards, ambient or emission; charges, pricing or taxation; subsidies; and private rights.[17] It is proposed to take the last and examine it in some depth. The discussion concentrates on the law of private nuisance since it is the primary instrument for the protection of private rights in this area.[18] It must, however, be recognised that certain 'inefficiencies' in the application of private nuisance might be remedied by recourse to alternative actions, such as those in negligence, *Rylands v. Fletcher* or public nuisance,[19] and reference will be made to the possibility at relevant points in the discussion.

In section II the economic model is described and then applied to the private nuisance action. Section III is concerned with the relevance of the model to an evaluation of the role of private nuisance in the control of pollution. To see the study in its proper context, however, it is first necessary to describe what is meant by the 'pollution' problem.

The Pollution Problem

An analysis of the efficacy of the nuisance action as an instrument of pollution control presupposes an agreed definition of 'pollution.' In every organized society certain activities will be proscribed by reason of the intensity of harm they inflict on the environment, the degree of tolerance being relative to the economic and social conditions then prevailing. Typically the initial concern is with health. In Britain, since the thirteenth century, controls have been imposed on activities which are seen to present an immediate threat to health.[20] In the nineteenth and early twentieth centuries, the threats became more acute with increasing industrialisation, and the controls multiplied.[21] The legislature decided that such activities as sewage disposal, discharges of industrial waste, and chemical industrial processes created serious health hazards, and minimum standards of hygiene had to be imposed.[22]

The attainment of any higher standard of environmental quality was not, at that time regarded as society's concern. But for centuries individuals had had the capacity through the private law to pursue for themselves a greater freedom from polluting activities.[23] In an agricultural community the full use and enjoyment of land necessarily involved some control over the neighbour's use of his property. Initially this would have been achieved through individual transactions, but such a contract technique would prove to be inefficient when land changed hands. Restrictive covenants were therefore devised to ensure that the original contract would run with the land and be enforceable by and against successors in title.[24] In time, some of the controls might be and were joined automatically with the ownership of land, so that the relative rights of adjacent landowners were to that extent both enlarged and limited, notably by the private nuisance action:[25] a man must not so unreasonably conduct affairs on his land so as to cause 'harm' to his neighbour.[26] In terms of private property rights, actionable 'pollution' may thus be defined as any adverse change in the environment which the purchaser might not reasonably anticipate when he buys his interest in land.[27]

There emerged, in effect, a two-tiered system: the general goal was determined by the legislature while the achievement of any superior environmental quality was left to the individual through the assertion of private rights. Society's concept of the appropriate goal does not, however, remain static. On the one hand, there has been a greater readiness to recognise environmentally-related illness and hence to lower the levels of tolerance especially in particularly sensitive areas, *e.g.*, working conditions.[28] On the other hand, at least in industrialised societies, there has been a growing concern with the protection of the environment *per se*.[29] The stated aim is to preserve the ecological cycle intact; to have regard to the interests of future generations; to maintain what is loosely, and generally rhetorically, referred to as 'the quality of life.'[30] The question is thus raised whether the establishment and enforcement of these elevated environmental standards may best be achieved, as previously, within a framework of private rights or rather by other legal instruments, notably legislative regulation. In reaching a decision the 'society manager' must determine which method or combination of methods is the most 'efficient,' 'just' and 'fair' in the light of society's distributional preference. One such distributional preference may be the financial compensation of pollution victims. The traditional private action is designed to fulfil the dual function of compensation and the enforcement of standards—the nuisance action provides a method both of obtaining damages in tort and of protecting, by an injunction, a property interest in the environment. But confusion will ensue if these two functions are not considered independently. If on distributional grounds compensation is desirable, the means of securing it may be totally divorced from the appropriate apparatus for the enforcement of standards. The main concern of this paper is with the latter.

The Efficiency Issue

The Economic Model

In recent years economists have differed over the appropriate framework for controlling the quality of the environment.[31] Traditionally, a polluting activity has been as one which imposes uncompensated harm (costs) on third parties.[32] On this view the result is an inefficient allocation of society's resources, for the price a consumer pays for such a good will not reflect its true production costs.[33] Suppose that the smoke from a factory chimney is causing damage to the crop grown by a neighbouring market gardener. Unless, by some means, the factory owner is made to pay for the costs thereby imposed, the price he charges for his goods will not reflect the true cost of their production. Such a result will be inefficient because it will lead to over-production of the factory owner's goods and under-production of the crop, for the consumer will be encouraged to buy more of the former and less of the latter.[34] The legal solution might appear to be simple: efficiency will be attained if the polluter is made liable for the harm he caused.[35] But for Coase, writing in 1960,[36] it was not a sufficient argument for a broadly based system of polluter liability. For him pollution was not a unilateral imposition of harm but rather the result of a conflict in land use.[37] In such a situation the conflict may be resolved by the operation of market forces. It is for each land user, whether 'polluter' or not, to assess what price he is prepared to pay for the unimpeded continuance of that activity. In our example, therefore, the question is whether the factory owner, through the price his consumers are prepared to pay, values his land use more highly than does the market gardener through the prices he can secure for his products. Whichever land is valued the higher, the owner in question will be prepared to enter into transactions to restrict any competing land use. The market equilibrium necessary for efficiency will thus be achieved since the price paid by the consumer will reflect the costs incurred in securing its production. Coase goes on to demonstrate that, provided the impact of transaction costs are ignored,[38] the introduction of legal rights, in whosever favour they are drawn, will not affect efficiency. Thus if the market gardener's activity is more highly valued, an imposition of an injunction on the factory owner will result in an efficient resolution of the land use conflict. Conversely, if the market gardener's activity is the less highly valued of the two, efficiency will be achieved by the absence of liability on the factory owner. Should either legal solution conflict with the respective evaluations of land use, efficiency will nevertheless be achieved through market transactions.[39] The legally liable factory owner may buy off the gardener; the 'rightless' gardener may buy off the factory owner. Of course one land use need not prevail wholly over the other: a compromise solution may be reached whereby one land use will abate to a degree compatible with the use of the other.

The seminal article by Coase, with its reliance on the operation of free market forces, has had enormous influence on the development of a certain form of economic analysis of law, concentrated in Chicago, and epitomized by Posner's monograph on the subject,[40] but hitherto has been neglected by English legal literature.[41] The application of the Coasian theorem to the private regulation of the environment has been much elaborated by other American writers.[42] For the purposes of this study it is proposed to adopt as a model that advanced by Calabresi and Melamod in 1971.[43] This has been chosen because of its application to specific legal rules and its orientation towards a legal audience. We are aware that the model has been subjected to substantial criticism by economists.[44] As lawyers we do not consider that it is our task to analyse it from such a perspective. Our reservations are of a different nature: the model is based on assumptions as to the attitudes and conduct of individuals and the availability of information which many would consider unjustified. The issues will be pursued at a later stage in the discussion.[45] Whatever doubts may emerge, however, this scrutiny of legal rules will force account to be taken of their economic implications.

The chief import of the Coasian theorem was that the efficient solution *might* be reached whatever the location of legal rights. Calabresi and Melamed have found in the choice of different legal rules a means of reaching the efficient solution when regard is had to other important factors, such as transaction costs,[46] the number of parties involved,[47] and their relative abilities to abate damage.[48] These will have implications both for the location of liability and its form, *i.e.*, injunction or damages. Taking the question of location first, it will be evident from what has already been said that if one party is clearly the cheapest cost-abater efficiency criteria dictate that liability should be imposed on him. In our crude example, supposing that the factory owner could cheaply and easily install a filter, he is to be made liable. In many cases the identity of the least cost- abater will not be obvious and it then becomes necessary to determine which party is in the best position to negotiate.[49] Liability is then placed on him on the assumption that as 'best briber' he will, by initiating transactions, persuade the other party to abate, should the latter be able to do so more cheaply. Assume that the relative costs of a factory filter and a protective greenhouse are unknown, but the factory owner with his extensive legal and scientific staff is in a better position to initiate negotiations. If in practice a greenhouse is cheaper than a filter the factory owner will be able to 'bribe' the gardener to erect one.

The nature of the liability (injunction or damages) becomes relevant to the economic model if the initial location of rights does not of itself achieve the efficient solution and recourse must be had to market transactions. As regards the injunction, it is assumed that the party on whom it is imposed may negotiate privately to modify his obligations thereunder at a mutually acceptable price.[50] As in the last example, the gardener's greenhouse is cheaper than the filter, and yet the gardener obtains an injunction. In these circumstances an efficient result will be achieved if the gardener agrees to release the factory owner on payment by the latter of the price of a greenhouse. In practice this type of negotiation might be extremely expensive and prolonged especially if there are two or more parties who will benefit from the injunction. There is always the risk that one of the parties may refuse to accede at less than an extortionate price.[51] The alternative is an award of damages. As will be appreciated, the net result of this remedy will not be dissimilar from that arrived at after negotiating a release from the injunction. The only, but significant, difference is that the price of the bargain is in this instance stipulated by the court in accordance with its evaluation of the harm inflicted, and the obstinate landowner will not be able to hold out for more than the judicial award.

To meet the efficiency criteria contained in the above analysis, tort law may choose between three solutions.[52]

(i) Liability on discharger—specific enforcement. The pollution resulting from the discharge may be abated by an injunction.
(ii) Liability on discharger—monetary payment. Discharger liable in damages but on payment he may continue discharging. He effectively compulsorily purchases the right to pollute.
(iii) No liability on discharger—the discharger has a right to pollute. He is subject to no legal remedy and must be 'bought off' at an agreed price.

But, as Calabresi and Melamed have revealed, there exists a theoretical fourth solution to complete the symmetry.[53]

(iv) The discharger's right to pollute may be bought at a judicially determined price.

This form of 'compulsory purchase' is the converse of that in rule ii where the plaintiff's right to quiet enjoyment is 'purchased' by an award of damages. Here the discharger is forced to sell his right to pollute by means of an injunction for which the plaintiff must pay. The initial justifications for this solution are similar to those for rule ii, namely the uncertainty as to the cheapest cost-abater or best briber, and high transaction costs, rendering a court determination desirable. The existence of rule iv gives the court the choice of evaluating the abatement costs rather than, as in rule ii, the harm inflicted.[54] In addition rule iv may be more compatible with distributional and justice considerations.[55] For example, the smoking factory, in this instance, is in an urban setting surrounded by a recently constructed high-income housing development. The factory burns cheap but dirty fuel, employs an otherwise redundant work force, and produces essential low cost goods. The householders obtain an order forcing the factory to abate, *i.e.*, by using more expensive fuel, for which the householders must pay the balance.

Private Nuisance

It seems gratuitous to observe that the form of analysis propounded above is far removed from that encountered in legal text books or court judgments, but it is nevertheless valuable to discover the extent, if any, to which prevailing legal solutions to given factual problems diverge from those dictated by efficiency criteria. Efficiency is, of course, not the only guideline to the 'right' principles and at some points must yield before, and at other points compromise with, other guidelines, notably those of justice and fairness. In a world of limited resources, however, a solution which is compatible with efficiency demands is not to be dismissed lightly.[56] The next task then is to ascertain whether the rules governing liability for private nuisance (the primary instrument for enforcing private rights in the environmental field) accord with the economic model.[57] In legal terms the four rules in this model deploy two different variables: actionability (location of liability) and remedy (nature of liability). The analysis of private nuisance will proceed accordingly.

Actionability

If the English courts decide that a nuisance is actionable they are in effect preferring the solution in rules i, ii, or iv to that in rule iii. To satisfy economic efficiency criteria they should, in broad terms, only refuse the plaintiff a remedy when they are certain that he is either the cheaper cost-abater or the better briber.[58] It remains to be seen whether the law of nuisance is consistent with these precepts. Broadly defined, the tort embraces any condition or activity which unduly interferes with the use or enjoyment of land.[59] To succeed the plaintiff must overcome eight hurdles.

(i) He must have a legal interest in the occupation or enjoyment of land.[60] Although failure to comply with this condition will be fatal to a nuisance claim, a plaintiff without such an interest may nevertheless succeed in other causes of action, notably negligence. However, the tort of negligence, essentially covering unintended events causing physical harm, does not extend to forms of intangible environmental harm remediable in nuisance.[61] The requirement of an interest in land may thus be crucial. Yet it is difficult to rationalise the limitation in efficiency terms, except perhaps in so far as it increases the certainty of legal decision-making. The law is rendered more certain and thus more predictable, in turn reducing transaction costs, by 'labelling' interests in a cause of action[62]: 'duty of care' for negligence,[63] 'non-natural uses' for *Rylands* v. *Fletcher*,[64] interest in realty for nuisance.[65] Deriving more from historical associations than from modern social conditions, these 'labels' may often produce artificial results. The well-known case of *Malone* v. *Laskey*,[66] where a wife failed to recover in nuisance because only her husband had a legal interest in the premises, provides sufficient illustration.

(ii) The interest must be of a kind which the law of nuisance will protect.[67] It is true that the nuisance action has extended its protection beyond tangible physical harm to cover such loss of amenities as that resulting from noise and smell. But, in contrast to other legal systems,[68] English law has persistently refused to condemn aesthetic nuisances.[69] Wray C. J.'s dictum of 1587 that ruining a view would create no cause of action, 'for prospect . . . is a matter only of delight and not of necessity'[70] still holds sway and its influence can be seen in a more recent decision that recreational facilities, for example the use of a television set, will not sound in nuisance.[71] For the purposes of economic efficiency these distinctions seem to be of dubious validity—the deprivation of such facilities, as much as other forms of interference, result in the diminution of land value and there are certainly no grounds for assuming that the plaintiff here will be the cheaper cost-abater.[72] No doubt the disregard of aesthetic nuisances can be traced historically to pre-industrial revolution conditions where such problems would not frequently arise,[73] and in modern times pragmatically to the feeling that such matters are the province of planning rather than tort law[74] and to a basic dislike of the unquantifiable nature of aesthetic judgments.[75] As regards the decision on the reception of television one can only suspect that the judge is here being led by his own blinkered view of its social utility.

(iii) The plaintiff must prove interference with the enjoyment of his interest and the extent of the interference required will depend on the nature of that interest.[76] Some rights are drawn in almost absolute terms and damage will be presumed (*e.g.*, a riparian owner need only show a 'sensible' alteration in water quality or quantity).[77] Others require proof of actual damage, *e.g.*, fumes, smell or noise.[78] There appears to be no historical justification behind the attribution of absolute status to certain interests, and equally in economic efficiency terms the elevated status of certain interests appears to be somewhat arbitrary. No doubt in a fair proportion of water pollution cases it may be proper to assume that the discharger will be the cheapest cost-abater or, failing this, the best briber, but the same may be equally the case for other less favoured land users. It is, of course, true that an absolute standard may reduce dispute costs.[79]

(iv) In cases of interference with amenity rather than physical damage the plaintiff must show that the defendant's activities constituted an unreasonable use of his land.[80] It is at this point that the court is given the opportunity to consider topographical, economic and social factors.[81] In theory, to achieve an efficient allocation of land use, the court might indulge in balancing between the costs of pollution, individual and social, and those of abatement, individual and social.[82] These will include the nature of the area in terms of amenities, employment and general welfare, balance of payments, relative social utility of the parties and community morale. In cases of physical damage, following the decision in *St. Helens Smelting Co.* v. *Tipping*,[83] such balancing is excluded: liability follows automatically on proof of injury. As regards amenity damage, in practice the courts have limited themselves to the so-called 'neighbourhood test': analogously to a zoning process, they attribute land use characteristics to specific areas.[84] The plaintiff may expect only standards considered appropriate for his particular neighbourhood. 'That may be a nuisance in Grosvenor Square which would be none in Smithfield Market.'[85] A contravention of the standards appropriate to the locality then becomes decisive in the choice between rules i, ii or iv on the one hand and iii on the other, and not without reason. Should the defendant's activities be consistent with the environmental standard of the locality, there has been no adverse change in quality unforeseeable by the plaintiff. In addition the legitimate assumption is that the complainant is the least cost-abater. In *Adams* v. *Ursell*[86] the plaintiff, a veterinary surgeon, obtained an injunction to restrain the defendant from carrying on his fish and chip shop which, though situated 'in the lowest district' adjoined property belonging to the plaintiff and others 'of a much better character.'[87] The defendant could 'carry on his business in another more suitable place somewhere in the neighbourhood'[88]—he was the cheapest cost-abater.

But the neighbourhood test can at best provide a crude guide to cost-abatement. Were the court to have regard to *all* factors relevant to determine the actual costs of abatement in some cases it might reach a different conclusion. For example in *Rushmer* v. *Polsue and Alfieri*[89] a milkman who had lived and managed his dairy for eighteen years in a neighbourhood devoted to printing and allied trades brought an action against a neighbouring printing firm which had installed a new machine. When normally operated at night it interfered with his sleep. The court upheld an injunction imposed on the night activities on the basis that the inconvenience was unreasonable even within such an area. Here the court can be seen to be focusing solely on its conception of the neighbourhood, to the exclusion of such relevant factors as the unique nature of the plaintiff's land use (he was the only resident in the area), the changing techniques and needs of the printing trade and the importance to the trade of night work. The decision may accord with the justice notion that the plaintiff should be protected against adverse changes in the environment but on pure efficiency criteria it probably resulted in the printer subsidizing the milkman's use of his land.[90]

In cases where interference is of limited duration the courts have shown a readiness to advert to factors external to the neighbourhood test. In *Andreae* v. *Selfridge & Co. Ltd.*[91] a hotel owner was not allowed to recover the full amount of loss of custom alleged to have been caused by the defendant's noisy and dusty demolition and construction work. The operations were only temporary: 'it would be unreasonable to expect people to conduct their work so slowly or so expensively, for the purpose of preventing a transient inconvenience, that the cost and trouble would be prohibitive.'[92] Cognisance was also taken of 'new inventions and new methods' which 'enable land to be more profitably used.'[93] Such damages as were awarded were those resulting from harm which the defendants in all the circumstances might reasonably have abated.

Quite apart from the limited nature of the neighbourhood test, the distinction between physical and amenity damage derived from the *St. Helens* case is itself extremely suspect. Why should zoning techniques be relevant to the latter but not the former? One possible justification which is evident on the face of the opinions in the *St. Helens* case is that property damage rather than amenity damage leads to a diminution in land value[94]—a fallacious argument since land values clearly reflect environmental amenities.[95] A second possible rationalization may be based on cost-abatement considerations. It might be argued that an inflicter of physical harm is invariably the cheapest cost-abater. Such an assumption is demonstrably false: if cost abatement may be considered when smoke gets in your eyes, it is equally relevant when smoke gets at your cabbages. Thirdly, it may be seen as an attempt to exclude from the arena of litigation trivial claims. From a nineteenth-century viewpoint amenity loss was trivial in comparison to physical damage and was remediable only if seen to be acute in terms of the locality.[96] Since then attitudes have changed and medical science is more convinced as to the implications of environmental hazards.[97] Fourthly, the distinction may reflect judicial concern to maintain minimum standards for the protection of property enjoyment. Just as in the nineteenth century public law was concerned to protect minimum standards of health leaving refinements to the private sphere,[98] analogously it can be argued that public policy considerations exerted their influence on the court's enforcement of private rights. Certain conditions were not to be tolerated at any price. Today we would regard such an objective as falling more properly within the province of legislative regulation. The final, and perhaps most persuasive justification derives its force from the certainty principle already referred to. A tort of strict liability (to which the infliction of property damage in effect gives rise) provides for stability and predictability creating a basis of known legal rights from which bargaining may spring.[99]

(v) The plaintiff must establish that the interference resulted from the defendant's activity.[100] This may give rise to serious problems in cases involving multiple-polluters.[101] Once able to establish the causal link with one polluter, a plaintiff who suffers indivisible harm, as is likely with most forms of industrial discharge, may recover from that polluter damages for the whole.[102] The principle of contribution enables the defendant to recover a proportionate indemnity from the other tortfeasors.[103] The combination of these two rules constitutes an efficient method of achieving the allocation of resources chosen on grounds of, for example, cost-abatement or justice.

However, the causal link with the individual polluter is not easily established. In principle, the plaintiff must satisfy the so-called *sine qua non* test: he must show that but for the defendant's activity he would not have sustained the harm in question.[104] In many cases, a single defendant might persuasively argue that the same damage would have accrued irrespective of his activity, an excuse which may operate for each polluter in turn. The courts have not been impressed by this argument. It has been held that the existence of another tort feasor whose activities were themselves sufficient to produce the harm inflicted would not relieve the defendant.[105] In other circumstances, where it is only the cumulative effect of a number of discharges that creates the actionable wrong, the courts have gone even further. Notwithstanding the fact that the plaintiff would be unable successfully to sue any one discharger individually, he may apparently bring an action against them all.[106]

It is evident that in these two situations the courts have been inclined to assist the plaintiff by overcoming technical legal difficulties. In the second situation it is likely that by so doing they will reach the efficient solution. The judgment against all the dischargers should force them to negotiate between themselves to take the cheapest steps to reduce the pollution load to within the appropriate standard. The assumption is that their joint effort to abate will be cheaper than any steps which might foreseeably be taken by the victim. In the first situation (alternative causes) each discharger must abate since his own load is itself unlawful, and the cost thereby incurred may well exceed that of the plaintiff. The existence of multiple-polluters will often indicate that the neighbourhood is industrial. If so, the cost-abatement objectives described above must accord also with the neighbourhood test, though, as has been seen, the English courts exclude cases of physical damage from its ambit.

(vi) The defendant must not have acquired the right to pollute by prescription.[107] It is necessary that for a period of at least twenty years the nuisance has existed, it has been exercised as of right, the owner of the servient tenement knew of its existence and the nature of the nuisance has been certain and uniform throughout that period.[108] This last criterion has led to the suggestion[109] that it cannot be possible to obtain a right by prescription to annoy your neighbour by noise, vibration, smells or smoke since the nature or intensity of the annoyance must vary. There do not seem to have been reported cases in which a prescriptive right to commit such nuisances has been upheld in this country, although there is a dictum suggesting that it is possible.[110]

Quite apart from the justice argument that calls for protection only where there has been an adverse change in the environment,[111] the prescription rule may be explained in terms of efficiency.[112] Where the discharger has acquired a prescriptive right the assumption is that the victim has consciously been prepared to bear the cost. The discharger has presumably relied on this fact and has organized his business accordingly. If the victim were suddenly to prevent the polluter from discharging it might involve the latter in considerable expenditure or could result in the closure of his plant. The law will not contemplate such a result and will uphold the prescriptive right to discharge in the absence of statutory regulation. Where a change of mind on the part of the plaintiff is involved this will probably be the efficient solution: it should be cheaper for him to adapt than for the polluter to abate. On the other hand, where a change of use is involved the situation may be different. No doubt in many cases it will still be cheaper for the new use to be located elsewhere and the prescriptive rule should apply. But account should be taken of the social costs resulting from the freezing of land use. If these exceed the cost of abating the first use, the rule will be inappropriate.

The critical decision is *Sturges v. Bridgman*.[113] In 1865 the plaintiff, a physician, came to occupy premises the garden of which adjoined a property occupied by the defendant confectioner who had operated noisy machinery there for over twenty years. In 1873 the plaintiff erected at the end of his garden a consulting room the use of which was impaired by the activity of the defendant. The court held the nuisance to be actionable and granted an injunction. Once the surgery had been built, it was not at all clear which of the two parties was the cheaper cost-abater, but the court paid some heed to social costs by considering the zoning implications of its decision. Had the surgery been erected in an industrial neighbourhood the plaintiff would not have succeeded, but in areas of land not so developed the court regarded it as 'inexpedient that the use and value of the adjoining land should, for all time and under all circumstances, be restricted and diminished by reason of the continuance of acts incapable of physical interruption, and which the law gives no power to prevent.'[114] It therefore saw no reason to withhold the injunction. The case illustrates the possible conflict between a solution efficient between the parties and one taking heed of social costs. If the prescription rule, or a variant thereof, had applied, the doctor would not have chosen to build his surgery in the noisiest corner of his property and the dispute would never have arisen. The confectioner's abatement costs (x) would have been avoided at the price of some inconvenience (y) to the doctor. This would have been an efficient result on the reasonable assumption that x was greater than y. In *Sturges* v. *Bridgman* the court with its welcome acknowledgment of social costs (z) disliked such a result and imposed an injunction. For the ruling to have been efficient z plus y should have been greater than x—a conclusion which, on the facts as reported, is highly unlikely since it is difficult to attribute a high value to z.

Coase in the original exposition of his theorem uses this decision to demonstrate, at least to his own satisfaction, that even if the court had misplaced the liability in terms of cost-abatement, the error would have been redressed by means of negotiation between the doctor and the confectioner,[115] a prognosis that will be challenged in the second half of this paper. Where the social costs issue does not intrude, the defence of prescription achieves efficiency. There is, however, no magic in the twenty years and a general defence of 'coming to the nuisance'[116] would not tie the court to any such arbitrary period.[117]

(vii) The discharger may plead in defence that the plaintiff's activity was unduly sensitive.[118] The law will not allow an individual by virtue of his special land use to make unusual demands on his neighbours. It lays down environmental standards which, though to some extent relate to general neighbourhood conditions, do not cater for individual needs. If individuals require greater protection they must procure it through private transactions governed by the law of contract. Although for these reasons a legal solution imposing liability on the discharger can only be regarded as hypothetical, nevertheless the question remains whether the present legal solution is efficient.[119] In cases where the sensitive user is outnumbered by many dischargers, it is reasonable to assume, as in the neighbourhood test, that the former is the cheapest cost-abater. So also where the sensitive use is subsequent in time to the more normal use. On the arguments developed in the last section it is contended that the present solution will usually be efficient. In cases not falling within these two categories, and despite an instinctive reaction to the contrary, there are no obvious inferences as to the identity of the cheapest cost-abater. This is the paradigm case which Coase and his followers use to reinforce their concept of reciprocity in their description of pollution.[120] As between a not particularly smoky chimney and an orchid grower who is to say who is 'polluting' whom? Of course Coase would argue that the market will discover and allow to prevail the most highly valued land use. If on this view a choice between liability and no liability is a matter of indifference, nevertheless the prevailing legal solution of no liability (rule iii) can be justified on the 'best briber' principle. The argument can be made that a party with greater knowledge of the special character of his land use is in a better position to evaluate the likely costs created and to appreciate the degree of abatement required thereby rendering him the more appropriate initiator of transactions.[121] Finally, for the sake of completeness, the same conclusion would seem to be favoured by justice and distributional considerations: why should the 'normal' user and his consumers be penalised by the presence of an abnormal neighbour?

(viii) The existence of a nuisance act on may, of course, be barred by statute.[122] Many enterprises, particularly public utilities, act under legislative authority. Some of the relevant Acts do not explicitly consider the availability of the private nuisance action, some are ambiguous. It therefore becomes a question of statutory interpretation whether an action will lie and what degree of liability will be imposed. In theory the answer is provided by the legislature, presumably after having made the appropriate efficiency and distributional evaluations. But this is, of course, in most cases a fiction: no clear guidance is given to the court which consequently must apply its own judgment. It does so in accordance with a vintage rule of statutory interpretation that common law rights prevail in the absence of clear contrary intention.[123] As a result, decisions as to the actionability of nuisances committed by authorised enterprises have no greater regard to costs of abatement than those affecting other enterprises. But arguably the abatement of the operation of public utilities will usually generate greater social costs than that of private enterprises. There has been some judicial recognition of the distinction. On the one hand, a few decisions have diverged from the principle of statutory interpretation demanding priority for common law rights.[124] On the other hand, as will be seen, there is some evidence that courts do take cognisance of social costs of abatement in selecting the appropriate remedy.[125]

Remedies

(i) Available Remedies

In terms of the Calabresi and Melamed analysis, the effect of the decision on actionability is to exclude from further consideration rule iii: if the defendant is held not liable, there is no remedy, and the plaintiff's only recourse will be to buy the discharger's right to pollute. If the nuisance has been held actionable the court must then select the appropriate remedy. The economic model postulates at this stage three possibilities: injunction (rule i), damages (rule ii), injunction at a price (rule iv). The law is in fact more complex than the model would suggest. Five different solutions must be distinguished.

(a) *Common law damages for past losses.* Damages can be awarded either at common law or in equity. Because nuisance is a continuing tort, common law damages can only be awarded for past losses.[126] Consequently it does not prejudice the plaintiff's ability to return to court and claim afresh for further infringements. Equitable damages, on the other hand, may be awarded for future losses and will exhaust the plaintiff's right to further remedy for that particular nuisance.[127] In cases where the nuisance is not a continuing one, or unlikely to be serious, or intended to be repeated only at long intervals, the court is likely to restrict the remedy to compensation for past losses, hence common law damages.[128]

The economic model attempts by the choice of the appropriate legal rule to induce the parties to reach an efficient resolution of their land use conflict. Its primary concern is therefore with the future behaviour of the parties rather than with the compensation of losses already inflicted. It follows that cases of non-continuing pollution, and the award of common law damages, have no direct application to the model, though they may be of indirect relevance in so far as the apprehension of a damages award may act as a general deterrent to *other* discharges,[129] and the pattern of damages awards may be used as a guideline either for future equitable damages, or for bargains struck where judicial evaluation is sought but proceedings do not reach judgment.

(b) *The immediate granting of an injuction.* The court may impose an injunction compelling the discharger to abate the nuisance as from the date of the judgment.[130] The solution is exactly that envisaged in rule i. It will often be accompanied by an award of common law damages for losses already incurred, but, as indicated in the last paragraph, that will not affect the efficiency considerations involved in the solution.

(c) *The award of equitable damages.* Since 1858 the court has had the power to award damages in lieu of an injunction,[131] thus effectively enabling the defendant compulsorily to purchase the right to perpetuate the nuisance. This is the clear equivalent of rule ii.

(d) *Suspension of injunction with damages.* The injunction, being a discretionary remedy, can be imposed in such circumstances and on such conditions as the court thinks appropriate.[132] A frequent exercise of this power has been the suspension of the injunction. If this is combined with an undertaking by the defendant to pay for damage inflicted pending the implementation of the injunction, the court has in effect opted for a compromise solution midway between rules i and ii.

(e) *Suspension of injunction without damages.* Alternatively the injunction may be suspended but no undertaking as to damages secured. In this case the costs of the pollution incurred during the suspension will fall on the plaintiff. In terms of the model the immediate effect of this solution is similar to that of rule iii (right to pollute without compensation) but after the expiration of the specified period it will revert to rule i. For reasons that will emerge in the next paragraph, English law, at least on the evidence available, appears not to have at its disposal rule iv, and suspension without damages is the closest analogy to it: effectively the plaintiff is paying a price for the injunction as eventually implemented.

(f) *Injunction on condition of payment.* The breadth of the equitable discretion is technically unfettered, and there is thus in theory no impediment to imposing a monetary payment as a condition for the implementation of the injunction as required by rule iv. English Chancery judges, however, have tended to condition the use of their broad powers by their great—some would say excessive—reliance on precedent and practice.[133] No decision has been found in which the judge rendered an injunction conditional on payment by the person in whose favour it was granted. In present circumstances, therefore, there seems little prospect of any direct application of this particular solution. One American state has been more adventurous. In *Spur Industries* v. *Del E. Webb Development*,[134] the defendants had been producing cattle foodstuffs for three years when the plaintiff property developers purchased adjacent property. Before completion of development but after several residents had entered into possession, the plaintiffs sought to compel the defendants to abate the nuisance of flies and smells emanating from their property. The court decided to impose an injunction but only on condition that the plaintiffs would indemnify the defendants for the reasonable costs of relocating their business.

(ii) Judicial Practice

(a) *Quantification of damages.* Whether damages are at common law or in equity the aim is to evaluate the plaintiff's loss resulting from the defendant's nuisance and award him such a sum as will put him in the position he would have been in if the wrong had not been committed.[135] The equitable award, of course, requires the judge to predict the future extent of the loss and is therefore highly speculative. This factor makes precise evaluation impossible but, in general, the court will follow the common law method of quantification. Traditionally, this bases the award on the diminution in the market value of the plaintiff's property,[136] a concept which has rightly been criticised in the pollution field for underestimating the subjective value of the property to the resident occupier.[137] The diminution method assumes that the property is worth no more to the plaintiff than its market value.[138] Economists refer to this difference between the subjective and objective market evaluation as 'consumer surplus.' Some commentators have argued that for a satisfactory judicial determination under rule ii the damages award should include a bonus payment reflecting the consumer surplus.[139] In fact, the law of damages may already be sufficiently flexible to account for this important element. In cases of physical damage to property, as an alternative to the diminution method, the court may base the award on the reinstatement measure: the cost of restoring the property to its pre-injury condition.[140] The method has not been universally popular primarily because the doctrine of mitigation prescribes that the plaintiff must accept the least costly method of redeeming his loss. Where a motor vehicle is damaged to such an extent that the cost of repairing it would exceed the cost of replacing it in its pre-accident condition, the reinstatement method is understandably excluded.[141] But in special circumstances the judiciary have recognized that if the property has some particular subjective value to the plaintiff the doctrine of mitigation might legitimately be overreached.[142] So in pollution cases the problem of consumer surplus may also be solved by the reinstatement method: a man's special interest in his choice of residence is more important than his attachment to a particular motor vehicle. Where amenity (as opposed to physical) damage is inflicted the method may be less appropriate—there is little you can do about a smell—but here the court may allow for the consumer surplus in its award for non-pecuniary loss.[143] Such damages are at large and clearly give the court great freedom in the choice of an appropriate figure.

(b) *Availability of Injunctions.* On satisfying the criteria of actionability, the plaintiff is entitled to common law damages as of right. Both the equitable remedies, damages and injunction, are at the discretion of the court and the question now to be considered is how it is exercised, in particular whether regard is had to efficiency objectives. There are two fundamental principles. The first, expressing the primacy of injunctive relief, was enunciated by Sir Raymond Evershed M.R. in the leading pollution nuisance case of *Pride of Derby* v. *British Celanese*[144] 'if A proves that his proprietary rights are being wrongfully interfered with by B, and that B intends to continue his wrong, then A is prima facie entitled to an injunction, and he will be deprived of that remedy only if special circumstances exist.' The second, complementary, principle specifies the situations in which the damages alternative is to be preferred:

(1) If the injury to the plaintiff's legal right is small,
(2) and is one which is capable of being estimated in money,
(3) and is one which can be adequately compensated by a small money payment,
(4) and the case is one in which it would be oppressive to the defendant to grant an injunction—
then damages in substitution for an injunction may be given[145]

The principles reveal the clear English judicial preference for rule i over rule ii. Only where it is certain that the defendant is either the cheapest cost-abater or the best briber should the injunction be preferred if the result is to accord with the economic analysis. But the case law manifestly demonstrates that in their initial preference for the injunction, the judiciary have little regard for economic considerations. They have not in general been prepared to 'balance the equities,' to weigh up the detrimental consequences to the defendant of granting an injunction against those to the plaintiff of refusing one. In the *Pride of Derby* case the Court of Appeal specifically rejected the plea that it would be very expensive and perhaps impossible for the defendant local authority to abate the nuisance, given the inadequacies of the sewerage system.[146] The injunction was granted, though its operation was suspended to give the defendants time to carry out the necessary extensions to the system.[147] The same view was expressed more recently by Lord Upjohn in the House of Lords: 'an argument on behalf of the tortfeasor... that this will be very costly to him... receives scant, if any, respect.'[148]

It follows *a fortiori* that if economic consequences to the defendant are regarded as irrelevant, so also the social and economic effects on third parties of the granting or non-granting of an injunction are to be ignored. In *Att.Gen.* v. *Birmingham*,[149] Page-Wood V.-C., while granting injunctive relief, commented: 'it is a matter of almost absolute indifference whether the decision will affect a population of 250,000 or a single individual carrying on a manufactury for his own benefit.' English law has traditionally been wedded to the protection of individual property rights. Subject to legislative intervention, they are to prevail over the public interest. In *Shelfer* v. *City of London Electric Lighting Co.*,[150] the fact that the tortfeasor was a public benefactor was not considered to be a sufficient reason for refusing an injunction. The nineteenth-century social philosophy was perfectly expressed by Lindley L. J.: 'Courts of Justice are not like Parliament, which considers whether proposed works will be so beneficial to the public as to justify exceptional legislation, and the deprivation of people of their rights with or without compensation.'[151]

Some easing in the judicial attitude is perhaps evident in the very recent decision of *Miller* v. *Jackson and Another.*[152] An injunction was claimed to prevent a village cricket club playing on the ground they had used for seventy years and from which occasional 'sixes' had landed in neighbouring property developed for residential use some three years previously. The majority refused an injunction on the grounds that the cricket club had been there first, had spent 'money, labour and love' in preparing the field, and there was no alternative site in the locality. Moreover, the public interest 'in preserving our playing fields in the face of mounting development, and enabling our youth to enjoy all the benefits of outdoor games' out-weighed the private interest in 'securing the privacy of a home and garden...'[153] Damages for the physical damage caused and for the past and future interference with enjoyment were, however, granted. The case is significant in that it takes account of social costs, allowing them to outweigh private property interests. The decision itself is consistent with the second complementary, principle quoted above, and it remains to be seen whether it heralds a new judicial attitude to land use conflicts.

The traditional English approach was followed for a time in the North American jurisdictions but the majority soon established an independent position.[154] Property rights were no longer seen as absolute—they were relative. In a case of conflicting land uses they may sometimes have to cede where the court considers that the claims of the neighbour to use his land for his particular purpose are superior, notwithstanding that the latter amounts to an unlawful use. Where economic consequences of an injunction would cause much greater hardship to the defendant's enterprise than would its absence to the plaintiff, relief is limited to damages.[155] The crucial question then arises as to the criteria to be adopted in determining the equities: is it simply a matter of balancing the value of the defendant's investments against the loss in the resale value of the plaintiff's property? or, if the plaintiff's use is residential, should special account be taken of this? Should the court have resort to locational considerations (*e.g.*, whether the area is primarily industrial or residential)? Should it matter which of the two users was first in time? Most important of all, should the court consider the interests of any third party and of society in general (*e.g.*, the interest of the neighbourhood in the quality of the environment, or its interest in full employment in the defendant's enterprise)? There has been no uniformity in the answers to these questions.[156] But in the recent case of *Boomer* v. *Atlantic Cement*[157] the New York Court of Appeals adopted an unambiguous stance. It dismissed an application for an injunction (awarding instead damages based on diminution of land value) on the ground that the economic hardship on the defendants would be disproportionate to the (economic) benefit to the plaintiff, a neighbouring residential landowner. In so doing it categorically refused to take into account the interests of any but the parties to the action. The difficulty the New York court experienced in attempting to assess social costs reveals the serious obstacles encountered in using the private action as a general solution to the environmental problem. These same difficulties are consciously or unconsciously avoided by the English judiciary's straightforward preference (at least until the *Miller* case)[158] for the injunction over damages. They see the choice of remedies as determined by the protection of the individual's property right rather than by general environmental considerations.

(c) *Suspension of injunction.* While economic factors are generally regarded as irrelevant in the choice of remedy, they re-emerge as significant factors in deciding how the remedy is to be implemented. In particular, great flexibility is achieved through the ability to suspend the injunction. This device has been used by the court to achieve the efficient result in three different situations.

(i) In the first, efficiency demands the eventual abatement of the nuisance but also that time is necessary to achieve that goal. The costs, both individual and collective, resulting from the immediate disruption of the defendant's activities would be much greater than those incurred by the plaintiff, pending more gradual abatement. So, in the well-known case of *Halsey* v. *Esso Petroleum Ltd.*,[159] the neighbourhood test dictated that the smell and night-time noise emanating from the defendants' oil depot was unreasonable, and hence in terms of the efficiency analysis they were the cheapest cost-abaters. But the burden of an immediate injunction would have been excessive: apart from internal costs, consumers would have suffered. Veale J. suspended the order for six weeks. In cases where an injunction is imposed on a public utility the court has no alternative to suspension since essential services must be maintained.[160]

(ii) The second category involves situations where there is real uncertainty as to the identity of both the cheapest cost- abater, and the best briber and for which a rule ii damages award would provide the efficient solution. As has been seen,[161] however, the judges feel compelled by their distrust of 'compulsory purchase' to avoid this solution. They choose instead to suspend the injunction, thus mitigating the defendant's burden. In *Shelfer* v. *City of London Electric Lighting Co.*,[162] the working of powerful engines in the defendant company's premises created vibrations and noise in a neighbouring inn of which the plaintiff was the tenant. At first instance, Kekewich J. held that though the defendant's acts constituted a nuisance the plaintiff should be awarded damages rather than an injunction 'having regard to the fact that the profits of his business had not been interfered with, and to the character of the nuisance, and to the great inconvenience that would be caused by stopping the business of the defendants.'[163] The Court of Appeal was less convinced by the defendant's allegations—'the evidence as it stands does not satisfy me that this is really true,'[164] (indicating uncertainty as to cost-abatement). It reversed the judgment and imposed an injunction, on the grounds that equitable damages should be awarded in lieu only in exceptional cases, (*e.g.*, where the injury is a small one) and that 'expropriation, even for a money consideration, is only justifiable when Parliament has sanctioned it.'[165] A suspension was subsequently granted.

(iii) In some circumstances there is no uncertainty: it is clear on the evidence available that the plaintiff is the least cost-abater. Here efficiency would dictate the adoption of rule iii and confer no remedy on the plaintiff, but as has been seen there are several areas where the law will hold a nuisance actionable despite efficiency criteria. This is particularly evident in cases where physical damage is inflicted or in which the property right is absolute. Of course, in the eyes of the proponents of the economic model, this selection of the rule is not fatal to an efficient outcome: it is assumed that market transactions will achieve the appropriate relocation. The court, having imposed liability, is faced with a choice between rules i, ii and iv. If forced to consider this problem the model would favour that rule which would encourage a satisfactory bargain at least cost. Rule i would be appropriate where transaction costs are low and the parties might easily reach a bargain. Otherwise rule ii, judicial evaluation of abatement cost, should apply. The typical response of the English court does not proceed along such lines. Unlike economists, judges seldom contemplate that parties to an action will immediately resort to the market place and reverse the effect of their ruling. Accordingly, in their eyes, there can be no justification for rule i. For reasons already given rule ii is generally not favoured,[166] and they have no conception of rule iv as such. They are left then with their dependable compromise solution, the suspended injunction. A good illustration is *Stollmeyer* v. *Petroleum Development Co. Ltd.*[167] The plaintiff owned but did not use a small plot of land downstream from the defendant's oil field. On the basis of his riparian right he claimed an injunction to prevent the pollution of the stream by the defendant's discharges. The Supreme Court of Trinidad and Tobago refused an injunction, a decision reversed by the Privy Council. 'The grant of an injunction is the proper remedy for the violation of right according to a current of authority, which is of many years' standing and is practically unbroken.... Their Lordships see no reason to depart from so uniform a practice, and although they fully appreciate the reluctance expressed by the Courts of Trinidad, in view of the special circumstances of the petroleum industry, they do not think they differentiate the present from other cases. There must be an injunction, therefore.... Their Lordships are, however, of the opinion that it would not be right to enforce the injunction at once. The loss to the respondents would be out of all proportion to the appellant's gain....'[168]

(d) *Suspension with or without damages.* The suspension of an injunction leaves open the question of who is to bear the cost before the order takes effect. If the defendant is to bear the cost the court will award damages for the interim period, thereby selecting rule ii for the short term and rule i for the long term. In the language of property law this is tantamount to a compulsory leasehold of the plaintiff's right to quiet enjoyment. It also conforms with the standard practice of the courts. If the plaintiff so requests it seems that damages will usually be granted, but generally in the form of an undertaking by the defendant to pay either at the time the injunction takes effect[169] or from 'time to time' throughout the suspension,[170] for damage actually inflicted. The decision to impose the interim costs on the plaintiff by not awarding damages is a short-term rule iii, forcing the plaintiff to pay the market price if he wants to secure abatement for the earlier period. The combination of this solution with an eventual injunction (rule i) could be the closest analogy in English law to rule iv: the plaintiff gets his injunction but the price he pays for it is the period of delay. There have certainly been cases where the injunction has been suspended and no provision for damages made,[171] but it is difficult to draw precise conclusions from them. The refusal may have resulted from a failure to claim damages[172] or alternatively the court may have been unable to predict sufficient material injury on which an award could be grounded.

Assumptions of Model

The analytical model devised by Calabresi and Melamed rests on certain key and traditional economic notions, particularly those of the free market in which rational individuals seeking to maximise their self interest will achieve efficient resource allocation.[173] The successful operation of such a market assumes ability and desire to bargain and access to full information.[174] These assumptions give rise to acute problems in the pollution field, owing to the wide dispersal of its effects and its inevitable impact on sections of the community, uncoordinated, inarticulate and financially disadvantaged. We have attempted to examine these problems elsewhere[175] and it will be sufficient here to summarize our arguments.

Transaction Costs

Selection of rules under the model is made dependent on transaction costs in two sets of circumstances. It will be recalled that where the identity of the least cost-abater is uncertain, liability should fall against the best briber. A party may be regarded as the best briber if it is cheaper for him to initiate appropriate transactions.[176] Secondly, resort is to be had to judicial determination (rules ii and iv) where the costs of reaching agreement in the market are high on both sides.[177] While going some way towards coping with the problem of transaction costs, the model seems to ignore certain key issues which are of particular significance in a typical industrial pollution case. The chief failing is the insufficient regard for litigation costs. If rule i is chosen on the grounds that the discharger can more cheaply initiate transactions and is therefore the best briber, is there not an inherent inconsistency in expecting the other party to enforce, or credibly to threaten to enforce, his property right? The inconsistency is exacerbated by the fact that the entitled party in this case would typically be a passive recipient of the discharge, whose only effective method of enforcement is by means of the prohibitively expensive litigation process.[178] Rule iii is more satisfactory since the entitled party will be the active discharger who may successfully enforce his right by merely continuing the discharge. But wherever the law of nuisance adopts this solution any adjustment necessary can only take place in the market, thus presupposing the 'victim's' ability to bargain. It is true that the American contingency fee system goes some way to alleviate the problem,[179] but in this country the problem is solved neither by the existing legal aid scheme,[180] nor by the rules as to costs.[181]

One method of reducing litigation costs is to formulate the law in more certain terms; in this context, by the adoption of strict liability. This could lead the law to favour an apparently inefficient solution, for example, giving riparian owners the benefit of rule i. The advantage of strict liability is that in the great majority of cases it obviates the need for litigation and enables the parties to proceed with Coasian bargaining, which will be cheaper than forcing the court to indulge in expensive cost-abatement inquiries.[182]

Attitudes

The second difficulty with the efficiency approach is less easy to define or quantify, but is nevertheless of great significance. According to the model, the world is peopled by inveterate bargainers and litigators. The serious problem of individual initiative towards the assertion of rights is one worthy of profound and detailed study. It is sufficient here to enumerate three fundamental doubts.[183] First, it cannot be assumed that individuals have sufficient time, energy or inclination successfully to pursue their own self interest. Secondly, they are seldom in a position, either financially or psychologically to bargain with large corporations. Finally, the suspicion is that the average English householder is unlikely to perceive environmental protection as a problem involving individual rights and therefore requiring the assistance of the legal profession.

Information

The efficiency model envisages two types of conduct: prosecuting a legal right and negotiating in the market. Both impose heavy information requirements and, though precise empirical confirmation is lacking, few would dispute the proposition that there is likely to be a very marked asymmetry between polluters and householders regarding their access to information in certain key areas.[184] These will include the evaluation of the costs to themselves of maintaining the status quo or of any proposed charges, abatement or avoidance; sufficient technological knowledge to recognise the nature of the harm caused and its connection with the discharge; the awareness of legal rights.

Justice

It has already been suggested that the choice of the most efficient solution will not necessarily be 'good' law. Society may prefer an inefficient solution on the ground that it is more just or equitable. It is true that a utilitarian theory of justice[185] does not conflict with efficiency. If a rule results in an aggregate of social benefits which exceed social costs it is both efficient and, on this theory, just. The theory is now discredited.[186] The subordination of individual rights to general welfare with compensation being payable only where the actions of others do not promote general welfare is regarded as 'unfair.' In a case of pollution, the point may be simply illustrated. The noise from X's machinery unduly disturbs the sleep of Y living in a nearby house. In terms of cost-abatement, it may be cheaper for Y to install double glazing. If so, the efficiency model would indicate rule iii, no liability on X. Y would therefore have to pay for the double glazing, a solution which many would regard as unjust. What then are the criteria of justice which are or may be given priority over efficiency? The problem is an immense one which has attracted the attention of many moral and political philosophers.[187] Rather than attempt any comprehensive or critical survey of their views, we propose to enumerate some of the principles which, in the context of an environmental conflict, *may* explain the application by the courts of an inefficient rule.

Distributional Justice

The efficiency analysis disregards distributional issues.[188] Economics regards the maximization of output as a primary goal since it will make available the greatest amount of resources for distribution but it does not concern itself with the political preferences for such distribution. If parties start from an unequal position, it may be regarded as unjust to promote a solution which maintains or reinforces that position. The analysis of the distributional effects of alternative solutions may thus indicate a preference for a just, though inefficient, rule. On the other hand, the analysis may reveal such a complex web of variables that a comprehensive regulatory scheme is required to achieve society's distributional aims. In such circumstances, the private action might have to be abolished to avoid a clash of competing objectives. Whether or not the private action should be used as a direct instrument for redistributional policies is highly questionable.[189] Whatever view be taken on this, it is important to analyse the distributional effects of particular rules to see if they accord with common ideas of justice or fairness. For example, the second of Rawls's two principles of justice, the so- called 'difference principle,' prescribes that 'the higher expectations of those better situated are just if and only if they work as part of a scheme which improves the expectations of the least advantaged members of society.'[190] Thus, if it could be shown that the adoption of say rule iii, while contributing to a cleaner environment which is beneficial to a broad cross-section of society, at the same time is detrimental to a group which is already economically disadvantaged, this particular formulation of justice would be infringed. On such an issue there are grave dangers of over-simplification. It is not unusual for commentators to see pollution as the product of a capitalist economy the cost of which is borne by the underprivileged classes.[191] An analysis of the costs and benefits of pollution control in fact reveals a more complicated position.[192] As regards benefits, an improvement in water standards will profit those who consume the water, whether for drinking or for recreational purposes. On the face of it, the reduction of atmospheric pollution, noise and smell will directly raise the amenities of those living nearest to industrial areas, typically the poorer sections of the community. But, in the long term, it may be more in the interest of the landlord whose property will be increased in value, and who can thus command higher rents. The poor may then have to move to a less desirable area. Such considerations suggest that redistributional policies might be served better by uniform standards imposed by legislation, rather than by the random improvements resulting from private actions. The 'polluter-pay-principle' has generally been regarded as a just (if not necessarily efficient) criterion for allocating the costs of implementation.[193] If the discharger is a public utility, the burden will be borne by the taxpayer or ratepayer, and should therefore accord with distributional dictates. If, however, it is an industrial enterprise, the effects of control will depend on whether, in the light of prevailing market conditions, the industry is able to pass on the cost in the form of prices. If this is possible, it is the consumer who will suffer and, according to traditional analysis,[194] this is likely to involve regressive redistribution because lower income groups pay a higher proportion of their income on goods and services. If the enterprise is unable to pass on the cost, it will have to reduce its output and thus its profitability. In such a case, the effect will be felt not only by shareholders and consumers but also by the region generally through reduced employment prospects. It may also have an adverse impact on the gross national product and the balance of payments. The very complexity of such issues should indicate that they more properly come within the province of the policymaker who has to decide the overall strategy for pollution control rather than within that of the judge who is concerned to find a solution to an individual land use conflict. The nuisance action is not, it is submitted, an appropriate instrument for redistribution except in the limited sense of corrective justice: compensation is payable to restore the parties to their distributional status prior to the commission of the unlawful act. This is far removed from the objective of altering the distributional structure, a task more suited to the public law.

While the nuisance action, therefore, exists to protect existing distribution, there is some evidence that the judiciary are allowing their own distributional preferences to infiltrate the description of the *status quo ante* for which protection is sought.[195] They sometimes allow their own view of what is worth protecting to colour what should be an objective judgement. So in *Bridlington Relay* v. *Yorkshire Electricity Board*[196] Buckley J. was not prepared to protect television reception from electrical interference: 'I do not think that it can at present be said that the ability to receive television free from occasional, even if recurrent and severe, electrical interference is so important a part of an ordinary householder's enjoyment of his property that such interference should be regarded as a legal nuisance . . .'[197] Contrast this with *Vanderpant* v. *Mayfair Hotel Co.*[198] in which Luxmoore J., while reaffirming that for a nuisance to be actionable it must materially interfere 'with the ordinary physical comfort of human existence, not merely according to elegant or dainty modes and habits of living . . .'[199] nevertheless accepted as an important evidence of nuisance, that 'so far as lunch and dinner times are concerned . . . it is frequently necessary to shut the windows of the dining room at No. 62a Curzon Street to prevent the noise interfering with the conversation . . .'[200]

The Concept of Change

Akin to the notion of preservation of the *status quo ante*, is the judicial perception of the type of situation which will justify intervention. The law of nuisance is not concerned with environmental conditions; it is rather directed to prevent or compensate for damage.[201] Implicit in the notion of 'damage' is that of 'change.' It may be fair to complain of adverse changes in the environment which are the result of your neighbour's activities. It will certainly be unfair to complain about them if you knew of their existence at the time you bought the interest in your property: for it should be the case that the detrimental effect of the activities will have been reflected in the price you paid.[202] As will have been apparent in the analysis of nuisance decisions this dimension of justice has been used to justify solutions on such key issues as neighbourhood,[203] prescription[204] and sensitivity.[205] If the principle is adhered to, and there seems to be no reason to question its appropriateness, it must follow that there are limits to the role of the nuisance action as an instrument for planning land uses generally.[206] Its own limited perception of 'pollution' prompts recognition that as an instrument of control its role can never be more than a subsidiary one.

Just Protection

There has been an interesting recent attempt to analyse the principles of fairness underlying the law of tort.[207] The theory postulates that in any given society there exist certain risks to which all members would rationally submit themselves. There are others which they would not accept at any price. Midway between the two are risks which are to be tolerated only if accompanied by commitments to compensation should the evil materialise. Corresponding to these three categories of risks are three appropriate legal solutions: for the first, no remedy; for the second, an injunction; and for the third, damages. It will be recalled from the analysis of nuisance decisions that one important respect in which the court may fail to achieve efficiency is in its jealous preference for an injunction (rule i) over damages (rule ii). Now in accordance with the 'fairness' theory of tort liability there would appear to be two possible rationalisations of the practice. The first would advert to the nature of the apprehended hazard for which the discharger is responsible—it is so great that it must be avoided at any price—and the second to the interest of its potential victim—it is of such paramount importance to him that he will not countenance its destruction. In both cases, the court would prefer to impose an injunction rather than force the victim into the market. This rationalisation reflects a view to which reference has already been made,[208] that the law should intervene positively to protect minimum environmental standards and tolerate market solutions only for conflicts in amenities above those standards. But it is not the only explanation. There is at play another principle which is regularly invoked by the judges: unless sanctioned by the legislature, common law property rights are not to be compulsorily purchased.[209] It is possible to see in this excerpt from the judicial catechism direct overtones of Rawls's principle, that 'each person is to have an equal right to the most extensive basic liberty compatible with a similar liberty for others.'[210] In his scheme this principle of liberty takes priority over the distributional objective[211] (difference principle) and *a fortiori* must always prevail over efficiency.

Judicial Role

Another rationalization for the non-application of efficient solutions might be expressed in terms of formal or procedural justice.[212] Judicial decisions should be made in accordance with the 'inner morality of the law': judgments should be based on the prevailing law, not on external policy criteria; the law applied must have an element of generality; like cases must be treated alike. 'The law must deal with classes of cases, based on typically recurring situations. The classes of persons, whom the rule concerns, and the type of conduct, whose legal effect it lays down are identified by isolating particular elements in the situation. These elements are then regarded as the material facts, the only ones which are legally relevant, and everything else is ignored, as being irrelevant to the application of the rule.'[213]

All these postulates are in fact question-begging. They do not provide criteria for distinguishing between what is 'law' and what is 'policy,' for determining what is the 'likeness' in like cases, for identifying the 'material facts.' Yet there is an underlying theme which, at least in the context of a dispute between private rights, seeks to distinguish between the roles of the legislature and judge by limiting the creativity of the latter. The idea has been most fully developed in Dworkin's study of 'Hard Cases.'[214] As a tenet of political philosophy, he argues that while the legislature may properly be concerned with 'policies,' by which he means the collective goals of society as a whole, the judge must make decisions according to 'principles,' which reflect and protect existing rights of individuals or groups. These rights are enmeshed in the traditions of the common law, and reflect standards considered fundamental in a democratic society. Economic efficiency is explicitly categorized as a 'collective goal' and thus a question of 'policy' rather than of 'principle.' The efforts of Posner and the Chicago school to superimpose efficiency analysis on judicial decisions is not regarded as subverting the thesis.[215] There is little evidence that judges when reaching decisions which are in fact efficient do so on the basis of economic reasoning. Such decisions are in fact reached only when they may be seen to accord with the rights of the parties in the individual case. As such, the fact that a decision might make economic sense does not alter its character from one of principle to one of policy.

It is difficult to accept the principle/policy distinction as a universally applicable description of judicial practice. It seems to pay insufficient heed to the importance judges ascribe to transaction and litigation costs. Occasionally, it would appear, they are prepared to solve a hard case by reference not to principle but to the policy objective of a more efficient legal system. In the *Pride of Derby*[216] case, for example, Harman J., with scant respect for the distinction between joint and independent tortfeasors, held that the plaintiffs could recover the whole of the damage sustained from any one of the defendants, thus obviating the need for a multiplicity of actions at great expense. Yet subject to this single qualification, the thesis does provide an illuminating account of the relationship between justice and efficiency as it operates within judicial practice. It also helps to explain limits on the common law's willingness to adapt to social change.

Three conclusions may be derived from our analysis of the English nuisance decisions:

(i) The judges are to a limited extent aware of efficiency considerations. The latter are well to the fore, for example, in the use of suspended injunctions to mitigate the inefficiency which would otherwise result from a strict application of legal principles.

(ii) Even where the judiciary do not appear to have regard to the economic implications of their decisions, nevertheless an application of the rules of nuisance themselves will often lead to an efficient solution. The use of the neighbourhood test for amenity damage and the defence of sensitivity provide perhaps the best examples. The consistency with economic analysis might be purely fortuitous, but it is certainly arguable that judicial decisions reflect intuitively the fundamental utilitarian tradition, which has had such a pervasive influence on our social institutions and policy.

(iii) Conversely, there are many important rules which clearly conflict with efficiency dictates, and which can be justified only by principles, some of which we have outlined in this section. The pre-eminence of property rights over compulsory purchase is the leading example.

Conclusion

The focus of this paper has been an internal study of the law of private nuisance. We have attempted to reveal the extent to which the rules applied by the judges achieve an efficient resolution to the land use conflict, and the extent to which other objectives take priority over this essentially economic dictate. It remains now to take an external stance and consider the role of the nuisance action as an instrument of pollution control in the light of these findings.

Such conclusions must be prefaced by a warning that in certain significant respects the study has not been a comprehensive one. In the first place, no attempt has been made to provide an economic critique of the model adopted.[217] Secondly, as was stated in the introduction, the thrust of the article has been towards the nuisance action as an instrument of control. Its efficacy as a method for providing compensation for injuries already inflicted, though ripe for careful scrutiny, has not been brought into question here. Thirdly, we have not attempted to compare the nuisance action with other instruments for environmental protection, though before any policy decisions as to its viability can be taken such a comparison will be necessary.

The primary conclusion is that the nuisance action can play at best a subsidiary role in any system of pollution control having as its objective general social welfare. There are three main reasons for this. The first is the principle of justice which postulates that existing property rights must be protected even where the result will impose greater costs on society at large. The second is the private law's limited ability to deal with generally inferior environmental conditions, both because it can intervene only where there has been a perceptible change (damage) and because the system of control presupposes an interest in neighbouring land. Finally, enforcement of standards created by the private law is likely to be only selective. The system assumes that the holders of property rights will be aware of their entitlement and will be willing and able to assert them, and that those without such rights will be willing and able to enter into appropriate market transactions to secure the necessary protection.

While the conclusion is not a surprising one—the broad areas of statutory regulation constitute sufficient evidence of the policy maker's recognition of the private law's limited role[218]—it does not follow that the nuisance action is redundant. On the one hand, it may continue to prosper as a means of providing compensation for pollution victims. We have not attempted here to judge its efficiency in this respect, but in the absence of a publicly controlled fund for indemnifying environmental harm,[219] it is the only instrument available for this purpose. On the other hand, there is a growing awareness of the function of the tort action as an 'Ombudsman,' the ability to use the court as a forum to vindicate an individual's legitimate grievance against wrongdoers and publicly to condemn unlawful conduct.[220] The effectiveness of governmental enforcement agencies is not beyond question and so long as public participation in the prosecution process continues to be circumscribed[221] there may still be a need to recognise what Linden referred to as the 'appeasement function of tort law... Our imperfect world still contains people who will utilize antisocial means to wreak vengeance on those that injure them. The tort remedy is one vehicle whereby this urge may be assuaged.'[222]

Notes

* M.A., B.C.L., Senior Research Fellow, Centre for Socio-Legal Studies, Oxford; Research Fellow, Wolfson College, Oxford.

† LL.B., LL.M., Research Officer, Centre for Socio-Legal Studies, Oxford. We wish to express our gratitude to Paul Burrows, Keith Hawkins, John Kay, Jim Krier, Jenny Phillips, and William Twining who read the paper in its various drafts and made many helpful comments.

1. For a recent survey see Campbell and Wiles, 'The Study of Law in Society in Britain' (1976) 10 Law & Soc. Rev. 547.
2. *e.g.*, Hughes-Parry, 'Economic Theories in English Case Law' (1931) 47 L.Q.R. 183; Swann *et al.*, *Legislation Regulating Industry* (1975).
3. *e.g.*, Peacock (ed.), *Income Redistribution and Social Policy* (1954); Titmuss, *Income Redistribution and Social Change* (1962); Culyer, *The Economics of Social Policy* (1971).
4. The one important area where the influence has been felt is that of accident and personal injury law: see, *e.g.*, Atiyah, *Accidents, Compensation and the Law* (2nd edn.), ch. 24; Phillips, 'Economic Deterrence and the Prevention of Industrial Accidents' (1976) 5 I.L.J. 148; Phillips and Hawkins, 'Some Economic Aspects of the Settlement Process: A Study of Personal Injury Claims' (1976) 39 M.L.R. 497.
5. Williams, 'Collaboration between Economists and Lawyers in Policy Research,' Paper delivered at the Ford Foundation Workshop on Law and the Social Sciences 1973. The whole paper illuminates the relationship between the two disciplines.
6. The theory of efficiency is described in the standard economics texts. For a modern critical survey see, especially, Rowley and Peacock, *Welfare Economics* (1975), Part I.

7. *Cf.* Symposium on 'Products Liability: Economic Analysis and the Law' (1971) 38 U.Chi.L.R. 8. See also *Goldberg* v. *Kollsman Instruments Corp.*, 191 N.E. 2d 81 (1963), for a judicial discussion of the problem.
8. Calabresi, *The Costs of Accidents* (1970).
9. For an account of the law in this area see Jolowicz, 'The Protection of the Consumer and Purchaser of Goods under English Law' (1969) 32 M.L.R. 1 and the Final Report of the Committee on Consumer Protection, Cmnd. 1781, (1962), para. 417. In the U.S.A., there have been considerable developments, a clear account of which is provided in Pasley, 'The Protection of the Purchaser and Consumer under the Law of the U.S.A.' (1969) 32 M.L.R. 241.
10. *Froom* v. *Butcher* [1976] Q.B. 286.
11. Housing Act 1961, ss. 32–33 and Defective Premises Act 1972, s. 4.
12. For historical accounts see Cohen, 'Property and Sovereignty' (1972) 13 Cornell L. R. 8, and Philbrick, 'Changing Concepts of Property in Law' (1938) 86 U.Pa.L.R. 691.
13. The principle and its theoretical foundations are analysed in depth in Michelman, 'Property, Utility and Fairness: Limits on the Ethical Foundations of "Just Compensation" Law' (1967) 80 Harv. L.R. 1165.
14. *Cf.* Atiyah, *op. cit., supra* note 4, ch. 24, criticising Calabresi, *op. cit., supra* note 8. See also Tunc, *International Encyclopedia of Comparative Law*, Vol. XI, ch. 1 and Horn, 'Zur ëkonomischen Rationalität des Privatrechts' (1976) 176 *Archiv fur die civilistische Praxis* 307.
15. Atiyah, *op. cit., supra*, note 4, pp. 456–64.
16. Horn, *supra*, note 14, pp. 332–3; Michelman, *supra*, note 13; Fletcher, 'Fairness and Utility in Tort Theory' (1972) 85 Harv. L.R. 537; Polinsky, 'Economic Analysis as a Potentially Defective Product: A Buyer's Guide to Posner's Economic Analysis of the Law' (1974) 87 Harv. L.R. 1655; Rawls, *A Theory of Justice* (1971), esp. pp. 66–75 and 157–75.
17. For discussion of the implications of the alternative instruments see Kneese and Bower, *Managing Water Quality: Economics, Technology, Institutions* (1968), Part III; Krier, *Environmental Law and Policy* (1971), ch. 3; Freeman, Haveman and Kneese, *The Economics of Environmental Policy* (1973), chs. 4–5; Thompson, *The Economics of Environmental Protection* (1973), chs. 5–6; Pearce, *Environmental Economics* (1976), ch. 5; Hagevik, 'Legislating for Air Quality Management: Reducing Theory to Practice' (1968) 33 Law & Contemp. Prob. 369; Wälde, 'Umweltschutz und Recht' (1974) 99 *Archiv für öffentlichen Rechts* 585; Lutz, 'Environmental Management Laws' (1976) 24 Am.J. Comp. L. 447.
18. For a comparative survey of the private law actions for environmental harm in England, France and Germany see Lang 'Grundfragen des privatrechtlichen Immissionschutzes in rechtvergleichender Sicht' (1974) 174 *Archiv für die civilistische Praxis* 381.
19. The application of these torts to a pollution problem was briefly described in our article 'The Role of the Private Law in the Protection of the Pollution

Victim' (1976) 40 *Rabels Zeitschrift für ausländisches und internationales Privatrecht* 449. See also Juergensmeyer 'Common Law Remedies and Protection of the Environment' (1971) 6 U.B.C. Law R. 215 and Elder, 'Environmental Protection through the Common Law' (1973) 12 W.Ont.I.R. 107.

20. In 1273 an Act was passed by Edward I to prohibit the use of coal as being detrimental to human health. See Chas & Feldman, 'Tears for John Doe' (1954) 27 S. Calif. L.R. 349.
21. For an account of the emergence of legislation designed to safeguard health from the increasing pollution in the mid-nineteenth century see Brenner, 'Nuisance Law and the Industrial Revolution' (1974) 3 J. Legal Studies 403, 424–431. He cites Nuisances Removal Act 1846 as the first statute with national scope.
22. *Cf.* Alkali Act 1863; Public Health Act 1875; Rivers Pollution Prevention Act 1876.
23. *Cf.* Philbrick, *supra*, note 12. For an account of the modern use of consensual instruments see Ellickson, 'Alternatives to Zoning: Covenants, Nuisance Rules and Fines as Land Use Control' (1972) 40 U. Chi. L.R. 681, 711–718.
24. Ellickson, ibid., and more generally, Simpson, *An Introduction to the History of Land Law* (1961), pp. 109–11, 238–43.
25. Newark, 'The Boundaries of the Law of Nuisance' (1949) 65 L.Q.R. 480. For the medieval development of the action see Fifoot, *History and Sources of the Common Law* (1949), Chaps. 1, 5 and for the nineteenth century, Brenner, *supra*, note 21.
26. *Cf.* Salmond, *Law of Torts* 16th ed., pp. 51–2.
27. Ellickson, *supra*, note 23, pp. 725–8.
28. *Cf.* Report of the Committee on Safety and Health at Work ('Robens Report') Cmnd. 5034 (1972), and the resulting Health and Safety at Work Act 1974.
29. In 1970 a standing Royal Commission was appointed to 'advise on matters, both national and international, concerning the pollution of the environment.' *Cf.* its First Report, Cmnd. 4585 (1971). On an international level see Report of the U.N. Conference on the Human Environment (1972) Internat. Legal Mat. 1416, and for European developments, Booth and Green, 'The European Community Environmental Programme and United Kingdom Law' (1976) 1 Eur. L.R. 444. For a general account of the emergence of concern for the environment see Gunningham, *Pollution, Social Interest and the Law* (1974).
30. First Report of the Royal Commission on Environmental Pollution, *supra*, note 29, para. 12.
31. For texts on the economics of pollution control see: Dales, *Pollution, Property and Prices* (1968); Kneese and Bower, *op. cit., supra*, note 17; Bohm and Kneese (eds.), *The Economics of the Environment* (1971); Dorfman and Dorfman (eds.), *Economics of the Environment* (1971); Victor, *Economics of Pollution* (1972); Freeman, Haveman and Kneese, *op. cit, supra*, note 17; Thompson, *op. cit., supra*, note 17; Kohn, *Air Pollution Control* (1975); Walters, *Noise and Prices* (1975); Pearce, *op. cit., supra*, note 17.

32. Kneese and Bower, *op. cit., supra*, note 17, ch. 5; Victor, *op. cit., supra*, note 31, pp. 17–23; Freeman, Haveman and Kneese, *op. cit., supra*, note 17, ch. 4; Culyer, *op. cit., supra*, note 3, pp. 25–41.
33. For an extended analysis of the 'polluter-pay principle' see Rehbinder, *Politische und Rechtliche Probleme des Verursacherprinzips* (1973), and for its general political acceptance, Lutz, *supra*, note 17, pp. 473–7.
34. Pigou, *The Economics of Welfare*, 4th edn.
35. 'The power of the courts to issue an injunction for nuisance has proved itself to be the best method so far devised of securing the cleanliness of our rivers,' *per* Denning L. J., *Pride of Derby and Derbyshire Angling Assoc.* v. *British Celanese Ltd.* [1953] 1 Ch. 149, 192. For other advocates see Katz, 'The Function of Tort Liability in Technology Development' (1969) 38 U.Cin.L.R. 587; McLaren, 'The Common Law Nuisance Action and the Environmental Battle' (1972) 10 Osg. Hall L. J. 505; Juergensmeyer, *supra*, note 19; Elder, *supra*, note 19.
36. 'The Problem of Social Cost' (1960) 3 J. Law & Econ. 1.
37. Ibid., p. 2.
38. 'Transaction costs' are the total costs incurred in the processes of bargaining, negotiating and litigating. Coase does not ignore them. At pp. 15–19 he recognizes that they may be sufficient to outweight the anticipated benefits of the transaction. In such circumstances, therefore, the initial location is important.
39. 'The Problem of Social Cost' (1960) 3 J. Law & Econ. 1., p. 8.
40. *An Economic Analysis of the Law* (1972). Two periodicals, both based in Chicago, contain many expositions of this form of analysis: *Journal of Law and Economics, Journal of Legal Studies*. In a recent article, Posner has described the history of the movement, reformulated its objectives, and defended it against its critics: 'The Economic Approach to Law' (1975) 53 Tex. L.R. 757.
41. 'The Economics of Water Pollution Control: An Application of Posner's Law?' (1976) 3 B.Jo. Law & Soc. 76 was contributed by an economist, D. J. Storey. The Germans appear to have been more receptive: see Horn, *supra*, note 14 and Wälde, *supra*, note 17. For a more recent British appraisal see now Cranston, 'Creeping Economism' (1977) B. Jo. Law & Soc. 103.
42. See particularly: Symposium on Coase Theorem in (1973) 13 Nat. Res. J. 507 and (1974) 14 Nat. Res. J. 1; Demnetz, 'When does the Rule of Liability Matter?' (1972) 1 J. Leg. Studies 13; Ellickson, *supra*, note 23; Michelman, 'Pollution as a Tort: A Non-Accidental Perspective on Calabresi's Costs' (1971) 80 Yale L. J. 647; Regan, 'The Problem of Social Costs Revisited' (1972) 15 J. Law & Econ. 427; Johnson, 'Meade, Bees and Externalities' (1973) 16 J. Law & Econ. 35; Freeman, 'Give and Take: Distributing Local Environmental Control Through Land-Use Regulation' (1976) 60 Minn. L.P. 883.
43. 'Property Rules, Liability Rules and Inalienability—One View of the Cathedral' (1972) 85 Harv. L. R. 1089. The model is based in part on the analysis of Michelman, *supra*, note 42.

44. A useful review of the criticisms is to be found in Dick, 'The Voluntary Approach to Externality Problems: A Survey of the Critics' (1976) 2 J. Environ. Economics and Management 185.
45. *Infra*, pp. 75–7.
46. Michelman, *supra*, note 42, pp. 673–4; Wälde, *supra*, note 17, pp. 610–12; Ellickson, *supra*, note 23, pp. 743–8; Note 'The Cost-Internalization Case for Class Actions' (1969) 21 Stan. L. R. 383.
47. Michelman, *supra*, note 42, pp. 673–4; Wälde, *supra*, note 17, pp. 606–8; Note *supra*, note 46; Ellickson, *supra*, note 23, pp. 725–42.
48. Ellickson, *supra*, note 23, p. 725.
49. Michelman, *supra*, note 42, pp. 649–58; Ellickson, *supra*, note 23, p. 725.
50. See, generally, Thompson, 'Injunction Negotiations—an Economic, Moral and Legal Analysis' (1975) 27 Stan. L.R. 1563.
51. The situation which Michelman, *supra*, note 42, p. 671, describes as a 'holdout.' This is the reverse of a 'free-loader' which may occur when a number of parties are affected but one benefits from the transaction without having contributed. Calabresi and Melamed discuss the impact of both hold-outs and free-loaders, *supra*, note 43, pp. 1107 and 1119. See also Thompson, *supra*, note 50, p. 1568.
52. Michelman, *supra*, note 42, p. 670; Calabresi and Melamed, *supra*, note 43, pp. 1115–16.
53. Calabresi and Melamed, *supra*, note 43, p. 1116.
54. Ibid., p. 1120.
55. Ibid., p. 1121.
56. Ibid., pp. 1093–1094; Posner, *op. cit.*, *supra*, note 40, pp. 4–8.
57. *Cf.* Ellickson, *supra*, note 23, pp. 719–61, and Freeman, *supra*, note 42.
58. *Supra*, pp. 292–3.
59. Clerk and Lindsell, *Torts*, 14th edn. (1975), para, 1391.
60. *Ibid.*, paras. 1393 and 1403. See also Newark, *supra*, note 25.
61. *Cf.* Salmond, *op. cit., supra*, note 26, p. 53; Friedmann 'Incidence of Liability in Nuisance' (1947) 63 L.Q.R. 59; Juergensmeyer, *supra*, note 19.
62. The point is made by implication, in Jolowicz 'Law of Tort and Non-Physical Loss' (1972) 12 J.S.P.T.L. 91. See also Ehrlich and Posner, 'An Economic Analysis of Legal Rulemaking' (1974) 3 J. Leg. Studies 257.
63. Green, *Judge and Jury* (1930), chs. 3–4; Atiyah, *op. cit., supra*, note 4, pp. 64–8.
64. Newark, 'Non-Natural User and *Rylands* v. *Fletcher*' (1961) 24 M.L.R. 557.
65. West, 'Nuisance or *Rylands* v. *Fletcher*' (1966) 30 Conv. 95.
66. (1907) 2 K.B. 141.
67. Clerk and Lindsell, *op. cit., supra*, note 59, para. 1455; Fleming, *Law of Torts*, 4th edn. (1971), pp. 344–5.
68. Note, 'Aesthetic Nuisances: An Emerging Cause of Action' (1970) 45 N.Y.U.L.R. 1075; Silverstone, 'Visual Pollution: unaesthetic use of land as a nuisance' (1974) 12 Alberta L.R. 542.

69. A recent example is *Coventry C.C.* v. *Cartwright* [1975] 1 W.L.R. 845, where Lord Widgery C. J. summarily dismissed the Coventry Justices' implication that visual impact could constitute a nuisance. See also *Dalton* v. *Angus* (1881) 6 App. Cas. 740.
70. *Aldred's* case (1610) 9 Co.Rep. 57b, at 58b.
71. *Bridlington Relay Ltd.* v. *Yorkshire Electricity Board* [1965] Ch. 436.
72. Ellickson, *supra*, note 23, pp. 733–5.
73. Silverstone, *supra*, note 68, p. 544; Noel, 'Unattractive Sights as Nuisance' (1939) 25 Cornell L. Q. 1, 2.
74. *Cf.* Bigham, *Law and Administration Relating to Protection of the Environment* (1973), ch. 12.
75. Ellickson, *supra*, note 23, pp. 734–5; and see *Morris* v. *Dominion Foundries and Steel* [1947] 2 D.L.R. 840, 844.
76. Clerk and Lindsell, *op. cit.*, note 59, paras. 1404–1405; Ellickson, *supra*, note 23, p. 737.
77. 'Every riparian proprietor is entitled to the water of his stream, in its natural flow, without sensible diminution or increase and without sensible alteration in its character or quality,' *per* Lord MacNaghten, *Young* v. *Bankier Distillery* [1893] A.C. 691, 698. See, generally, Elder, *supra*, note 19, pp. 127–42, and Storey, *supra*, note 41.
78. See *Halsey* v. *Esso Petroleum* [1961] 2 All E.R. 145 for an example of 'damage' resulting from fumes, smell and noise. The distinction between material and amenity damage is discussed under (iv) *infra*. See also Ellickson, *supra*, note 23, pp. 737–8.
79. See *infra*, pp. 315–16.
80. Clerk and Lindsell, *op. cit., supra*, note 59, para. 1395. For judicial discussion see *e.g., Rushmer* v. *Polsue Alfieri* [1906] 1 ch. 234 and *Sturges* v. *Bridgman* (1879) 11 Ch.D. 852. See also Ellickson, *supra*, note 23, pp. 728–33.
81. For discussion of these issues see Friedmann, *supra*, note 61; Eekelaar, 'Nuisance and Strict Liability' (1973) 8 Ir. Jur. (N.S.) 191; Juergensmeyer, *supra*, note 19.
82. On problems of assessing the costs of pollution see Burrows, 'Nuisance: the Law and Economics' (1970) *Lloyds Bank Review* 36. See also Michelman, *supra*, note 42, pp. 1193–6.
83. (1865) 11 H.L.C. 642.
84. Clerk and Lindsell, *op. cit., supra*, note 59, para. 1397. See also McAuslan, *Land, Law and Planning* (1975), esp. pp. 48–51; Comment 'The Role of Private Nuisance Law in the Control of Air Pollution' (1968) 10 Ariz. L.R. 107; McLaren, *supra*, note 35, pp. 533–6; Freeman, *supra*, note 42, pp. 923–4.
85. *Per* Pollock C. B., *Bamford* v. *Turnley* (1862) 3 B. & S. 66, 79.
86. [1913] 1 Ch. 269. This case is quoted by Coase, *supra*, note 36, pp. 21–2 as an illustration of the court's understanding (albeit inexplicit) of the reciprocal nature of the problem.

87. See statement of facts [1913] 1 Ch. 269, 270.
88. *Per* Swinfen Eady J., ibid., p. 271.
89. [1906] 1 Ch. 234.
90. Freeman, *supra*, note 42, pp. 893–9, however argues that residential amenities should generally outreign efficiency considerations.
91. [1938] ch. 1. This case is quoted extensively by Coase, *supra*, note 36, pp. 22–3. He draws attention to the economic factors considered by the court in their determination of what was 'reasonable.'
92. [1938] ch. 1, 10, *per* Sir Wilfrid Greene M. R.
93. *Ibid.*, p. 6.
94. (1865) 11 H.L.C. 642, 651. For a full discussion of the *St. Helens* case see Brenner, *supra*, note 21. See also McAuslan, *op. cit., supra*, note 84, pp. 71–3; *cf. Hammersmith Railway* v. *Brand* (1869) L.R. 4 H.L. 171 where it was held that vibration, noise and smoke did depreciate the selling value of land.
95. *Cf.* Michelman, *supra*, note 13, p. 1202.
96. The point made by Lord Wensleydale in *St. Helens* case, *supra*, note 94, p. 653. As Brenner has discovered (*supra*, note 21, pp. 415–20) the judicial view is hardly compatible with that of the House of Lords Select Committee on Noxious Vapours (Parl. Papers 1862, 14) which two years previously had investigated the town of St. Helens.
97. *Cf. supra*, pp. 53–4.
98. *Supra*, pp. 53–4.
99. *Infra*, pp. 76–7.
100. Clerk and Lindsell, *op. cit., supra*, note 59, paras. 1411, 1418. See also Dias, 'Trouble on Oiled Waters' [1967] C.L. J. 62 and Friedmann, *supra*, note 61.
101. Brenner, *supra*, note 21, gives this as one of the reasons for legislative intervention in the mid-nineteenth century. See also *infra*, note 78, p. 315.
102. *Clark* v. *Newman* (1847) 1 Ex. 131.
103. Clerk and Lindsell, *op. cit., supra*, note 59, paras. 203–208.
104. Hart and Honoré, *Causation in the Law* (1959) ch. 5.
105. Clerk and Lindsell, *op. cit., supra*, note 59, para. 317 and the cases there cited.
106. *Pride of Derby and Derbyshire Angling Assoc.* v. *British Celanese* [1952] 1 All E.R. 1326, affirmed on other grounds [1953] Ch. 149.
107. Clerk and Lindsell, *op. cit., supra*, note 59, para. 1469. See also *Jones* v. *Prichard* [1908] 1 Ch. 630.
108. Clerk and Lindsell, *loc. cit.* See *Hulley* v. *Silversprings Bleaching Co.* [1922] 2 Ch. 268.
109. Clerk and Lindsell, *loc. cit.*
110. *Halsey* v. *Esso Petroleum Ltd.* [1961] 2 All E.R. 145, 154–155.
111. *Infra*, pp. 79–80.
112. *Cf.* Attwood, 'An Economic Analysis of Land Use Conflicts' (1968) 21 Stan. L.R. 293; Freeman, *supra*, note 41, pp. 899–903.
113. (1879) 11 Ch. D. 852.

114. *Per* Thesiger L. J., ibid., p. 865.
115. *Supra*, note 36, pp. 8–13.
116. In the very recent decision of *Miller* v. *Jackson and Another* [1977] 3 W.L.R. 20, the Court of Appeal has resurrected the possibility of 'coming to a nuisance' as a defence, at least to a claim for an injunction. The majority appears not to have approved of the decision in *Sturges* v. *Bridgman*, Lord Denning M. R. explicitly referring to the 'different approach' of nineteenth-century judges. Damages for past and future losses were however granted and so the importance of the case is in relation to the question of remedy rather than liability, on which see *infra*, pp. 67–75.
117. Though a fixed period does have the advantage of certainty: *cf. infra*, pp. 76–7.
118. Clerk and Lindsell, *op. cit., supra*, note 59, para. 1396. See also *Robinson* v. *Kilvert* (1889) 41 Ch.D. 88 and *Heath* v. *Brighton (Mayor of)* (1908) 98 L.T. 718.
119. *Cf.* Ellickson, *supra*, note 23, pp. 751–7.
120. Coase, *supra*, note 36, pp. 2–6; Calabresi and Melamed, *supra*, note 43, p. 1102; Posner, *op. cit., supra*, n. 40, pp. 16–17.
121. Ellickson, *supra*, note 23, p. 725.
122. Clerk and Lindsell, *op. cit, supra*, note 59, para. 1471. See also *Geddis* v. *Proprietors of Bann Reservoir* (1878) 3 App. Cas. 430. Even in the absence of express statutory authority to create a nuisance such authority may be inferred if nuisance must inevitably result from the performance of the statutory duty: *London & Brighton Ry. Co.* v. *Truman* (1885) 11 App. Cas. 45.
123. Cross, *Statutory Interpretation* (1976), pp. 26, 28, 31, 145.
124. See, *e.g.*, *Smeaton* v. *Ilford Corp.* [1954] Ch. 450 where Upjohn J. refused to hold the local authority liable for the overflow of sewage on to the plaintiff's property.
125. *Infra*, p. 72–3.
126. McGregor, *Damages*, 13th edn. (1972), paras. 276–277.
127. *Tunnicliffe* v. *West Leigh Colliery* [1906] 2 Ch. 22.
128. *Hole* v. *Chard Union* [1894] 1 Ch. 293; *Chapman, Morsons & Co.* v. *Guardians of Auckland Union* (1889) 23 Q.B.D. 294.
129. For a discussion of the deterrent effect of damages awards see Calabresi, *op. cit., supra*, note 8, Michelman. *supra*, note 43, pp. 652–8, and Atiyah, *op. cit., supra*, note 4, Chap. 24.
130. See Kerr, *Treatise on the Law and Practice of Injunctions*, 6th edn. (1927), Lawson, *Remedies of English Law* (1972), pp. 211–26 and the standard textbooks on equity. For a comparative survey of the common and civil law systems see Kötz, 'Vorbeugender Rechtsschutz im Zivilrecht' (1974) 174 *Archiv für die civilistische Praxis* 145. For comments on the use of the injunction within the pollution field see: Comment, 'Equity and the ECO-System: Can Injunctions Clean the Air?' (1970) 68 Mich. L.R. 1254; McLaren, *supra*, note 35; and Juergensmeyer, *supra*, note 19.

131. Jolowicz, 'Damages in Equity—A Study of Lord Cairns' Act' [1975] C.L.J. 224.
132. Kerr, *op. cit., supra*, note 31, ch. 2 and Lawson, *op. cit., supra*, note 31, at pp. 222–7.
133. Allen, *Law in the Making*, 7th edn. (1964), pp. 415–21.
134. 494 P. 2d 700 (1972), noted in (1973) 26 Vand L.R. 193.
135. *Armstrong* v. *Sheppard and Short* [1959] 2 Q.B. 384.
136. *Moss* v. *Christchurch R. D. C.* [1925] 2 K.B. 750.
137. *e.g.* Ellickson, *supra*, note 23, at pp. 735–7.
138. Pearce, *op. cit.*, note 17, at pp. 2–6; Freeman, Haveman and Kneese, *op. cit., supra*, note 17, at pp. 73–6; Culyer, *op. cit., supra*, note 3, at pp. 28–30.
139. *e.g.*, Ellickson, *supra*, note 23.
140. Ogus, *Law of Damages* (1973), pp. 122–35 and on damage to land, pp. 162–5.
141. *Darbishire* v. *Warren* [1963] 1 W.L.R. 1067.
142. *O'Grady* v. *Westminster Scaffolding* [1962] 2 Lloyd's Rep. 238.
143. *Cf. Bone* v. *Seal* [1975] 1 W.L.R. 797.
144. [1953] Ch. 149, 181. See also Cozens-Hardy M. R. in *Price's Patent Candle Co.* v. *L.C.C.* [1908] 2 Ch. 526, 544, quoted *infra*, note 159.
145. *Per* A. L. Smith, L. J., *Shelfer* v. *City of London Electric Lighting Co.* [1895] 1 Ch. 287, 322.
146. *Supra*, note 45, at pp. 180 (Evershed M. R.), 192 (Denning L. J.), 194 (Romer L.J.).
147. Ibid., p. 182.
148. *Morris* v. *Redland Bricks* [1970] A.C. 652, 664.
149. (1858) 4 K. & J. 528, 539–540.
150. *Supra*, note 145.
151. Ibid., p. 316.
152. [1977] 3 W.L.R. 20.
153. *Per* Lord Denning M. R. at p. 30.
154. McLaren, *supra*, note 35, at pp. 552–6 and Comment, *supra*, note 130.
155. See, *e.g., Gilpin* v. *Jacob Ellis Realty*, 135 A. 2d 204 (1957).
156. In *Madison* v. *Ducktown Sulphur, Cooper & Iron Co.*, 83 S. W. 658 (1904), an injunction was refused on the ground that the resulting loss to the community in terms of unemployment would have been unreasonable. See also the Canadian case *Black* v. *Canadian Copper* [1917] O.W.N. 243, *per* Middleton J., p. 244.
157. 257 N.E. 2d 870 (1970). The case has met with severe criticism, *e.g.* (1970) 16 N.Y.L. Forum 666, (1970) 45 N.Y.U.L.R. 919, (1971) 43 U. Col. L.R. 225.
158. *Supra*, p. 71.
159. [1961] 2 All E.R. 145.
160. See *Price's Patent Candle Co.* v. *L.C.C.* [1908] 2 Ch. 526 and *Pride of Derby and Derbyshire Angling Assoc*, v. *British Celanese* [1953] Ch. 149, where suspended injunctions were granted against sewage authorities. 'Considerations of pub-

lic welfare may justify the suspension of an injunction upon terms, but they do not justify the denial of relief to the private person whose rights have been affected,' *per* Cozens-Hardy M. R., the *Price* case, p. 544. See also *Manchester Corp.* v. *Farnworth* [1930] A.C. 171 where a suspended injunction was granted against the corporation with reference to its operation of an electricity generating station.

161. *Supra*, p. 70.
162. [1895] 1 Ch. 287.
163. Ibid., p. 300.
164. Ibid., *per* Lindley L. J., p. 313.
165. Ibid., p. 316.
166. *Supra*, p. 70.
167. [1918] A.C. 498n.
168. Ibid., *per* Lord Sumner, pp. 499–500.
169. *Pennington* v. *Brinsop Hall Coal Co.* (1877) 5 Ch.D. 769.
170. *Cf. Stollmeyer* v. *Trinidad Lake Petroleum Co.* [1918] A.C. 485, 497 and *Stollmeyer* v. *Petroleum Development Co.*, ibid., 498n., 500.
171. *Cf. Frost* v. *King Edward VII Welsh & Assoc.* [1918] 2 Ch. 180 and *Reinhardt* v. *Mentasti* (1889) 42 Ch.D. 685.
172. In *Jones* v. *Llanrwst Urban District Council* [1911] 1 Ch. 393, 411, it is clear that the plaintiff did not ask for damages.
173. *Cf.* Mishan, 'Pangloss on Pollution,' in Bohm and Kneese (eds.), *op. cit., supra*, note 31, at p. 66; Leff, 'Economic Analysis of Law—Some Realism about Nominalism' (1974) 60 Virg. L.R. 451; Horn, *supra*, note 14, at pp. 314–15.
174. Freeman, Haveman and Kneese, *op. cit., supra*, note 31, p. 290, ch. 4; Johnson, *supra*, note 42, p. 292; Dales, *op. cit., supra*, note 31, p. 290, ch. 4; Hamill, 'The Process of Making Good Decisions About the Use of the Environment of Man' (1968) 8 Nat. Res. J. 279.
175. Ogus and Richardson, *supra*, note 19, at pp. 467–72.
176. Calabresi and Melamed, *supra*, note 43, at p. 119.
177. Ibid. pp. 119–20.
178. A problem recognized by the House of Lords Select Committee on Noxious Vapours 1862 (*supra*, note 96), which reported that nuisance actions were difficult 'partly in consequence of the expense such actions occasion, partly from the fact that where several works are in immediate juxtaposition, the difficulty of tracing the damage to any one, or of apportioning it among several, is too great as to be all but insuperable. . . .' See also Ogus and Richardson, *supra*, note 19, at p. 469.
179. The system is not likely to be adopted in the U.K.; *cf. Wallersteiner* v. *Moir* (No. 2) [1975] 1 All E. R. 849. Another device used in the U.S.A. to circumvent the problem of a plurality of victims each suffering minor damage has been the class action. As regards federal actions, however, fundamental procedural

difficulties have recently been encountered: see *Eisen* v. *Carlisle and Jacquelin*, 94 S. Ct. 2140 (1974), where the Supreme Court held that there was an obligation on the plaintiff to contact the estimated two million members of the class. More generally on class actions, see Krier, *op. cit., supra*, note 17, at pp. 226–230; Note, *supra*, note 46; Homburger, 'Private Suits in the Public Interest in the U.S.A.' (1974) 23 Buff. L.R. 343; Note, 'Managing the Large Class Actions' (1974) 87 Harv. L.R. 426. In the U.K. the closest analogy is the representative action but a combination of the Rules of the Supreme Court (Ords. 12 and 15) and common law principles has effectively restricted its potential by insisting on common relief: *Smith* v. *Cardiff Corp.* [1954] 1 Q.B. 210.

180. Legal aid applicants must satisfy the rigorous means test, and substantial contributions may be required. For current limits, see the Legal Aid (Financial Conditions) Regulations 1976, S. I. 1976 No. 1895. Each application is also scrutinised by a local committee who may dismiss it on the grounds that there is no probability that the action will succeed: Legal Aid Act 1974, s. 7 (5).

181. Generally the winner is awarded 'costs' against the loser, but these are usually on the 'party and party' basis which typically accounts for only two-thirds to three- quarters of actual legal fees and excludes all other disbursements: Rules of the Supreme Court, Ord. 62, r. 28 (2).

182. Epstein, 'A Theory of Strict Liability' (1973) 2 J. Leg. Studies 151 and 'Defences and Subsequent Pleas in a System of Strict Liability' (1974) 3 J. Leg. Studies 165, though Posner himself is sceptical: 'Strict Liability, A Comment' (1973) 2 J. Leg. Studies 205. An effort has been made to calculate the savings in judicial resources by substituting a strict liability on manufacturers of defective products in place of negligence: Ver Steeg, 'Strict Liability and Judicial Resources' (1974) 3 J. Leg. Studies 217.

183. *Cf.* Ogus and Richardson, *supra*, note 19, at pp. 471–2, and Pearce, *op. cit., supra*, note 17, at pp. 84–93. For a penetrating sociological analysis, see Gessner, 'Soziale Voraussetzungen des Selbstschutzes gegen Umweltschäden' (1976) 40 *Rabels Zeitschrift* 430. Questionnaires sent to all *Landgerichten* and *Oberlandgerichten* revealed details of only 73 civil suits against polluters in 1970. The plaintiffs in only 47 of the cases were individuals, and of these only one was a tenant: 14 of the actions were brought by anglers' associations.

184. The problem is fully documented in Winter, *Das Vollzugdefizit im Wasserrecht* (1975). See also Ellickson, *supra*, note 23, at p. 725.

185. Mill, *Utilitarianism* (Fontana edition, 1962), pp. 256–321; Stone, *Human Law and Human Justice* (1965), chs. 4–5; Rawls, *op. cit., supra*, note 16, § 30.

186. Rawls, *ibid.* § § 27–28; Lyons, *The Forms and Limitations of Utilitarianism* (1965); Miller, *Social Justice* (1976), pp. 31–40.

187. *e.g.* Allen, *Aspects of Justice* (1958); Hart, *Concept of Law* (1961), ch. 8; Perelman, *The Idea of Justice and the Problem of Argument* (1963); Ginsberg, *On Justice in*

Society (1965); Honoré, 'Social Justice,' in Summers (ed.), *Essays in Legal Philosophy* (1968); Rawls, *op. cit., supra*, note 16; Miller, *op. cit., supra*, note 186; Eckhoff, *Justice* (1974).

188. These issues are fully considered in Eckhoff, ibid., Part III.
189. Atiyah, *op. cit., supra*, note 4, at pp. 492–4; Dworkin, 'Hard Cases' (1975) 88 Harv. L. R. 1057, *infra*, p. 81–2.
190. *Op. cit., supra*, note 16, at p. 75.
191. Cunningham, *op. cit., supra*, note 29.
192. Freeman, Haveman and Kneese, *op. cit., supra*, note 17, at pp. 143–8.
193. Rehbinder, *supra*, note 33, Lutz, *supra*, note 17, p. 287; Baxter, 'The SST: From Watts to Harlem in Two Hours' (1968) 21 Stan. L. R. 1, 39–43; Roberts, 'The Right to a Decent Environment' (1970) 55 Cornell L. Q. 674. The U.K. Government is giving wide publicity to the view: see 'Pollution, Nuisance or Nemesis,' a Report on the Control of Pollution (1972), paras. 47–50, and the Third Report of the Royal Commission on Environmental Pollution, Cmnd. 5054 (1972), para. 16.
194. Lipsey, *An Introduction to Positive Economics*, 4th edn. (1975), ch. 7.
195. *Cf.* McAuslan, *op. cit., supra*, note 84, at p. 73.
196. [1965] Ch. 436.
197. Ibid., p. 447.
198. [1930] 1 Ch. 138. See also *Miller v. Jackson and Another* [1977] 3 W.L.R. 20.
199. Ibid., p. 165.
200. Ibid., p. 167.
201. *Supra*, p. 54–5 and see Hart, *op. cit., supra*, note 87, at pp. 159–61.
202. Ellickson, *supra*, note 23, at pp. 758–76; Posner, *op. cit., supra*, note 40, at pp. 20–21; Michelman, *supra*, note 13, at pp. 1229–34.
203. *Supra*, p. 60–1.
204. *Supra*, p. 64.
205. *Supra*, p. 65–6.
206. *Cf.* McAuslan, *op. cit., supra*, note 84, at pp. 48–73.
207. Fletcher, *supra*, note 16; Burrows, 'Justice and Efficiency in Pollution Control: A Different View of the Cathedral' (unpublished).
208. *Supra*, p. 54.
209. *Supra*, p. 76.
210. Rawls, *op. cit., supra*, note 16, p. 60.
211. Ibid., pp. 75–80.
212. Fuller, *The Morality of Law* (1964).
213. Stein and Shand, *Legal Values in Western Society* (1974), pp. 89–90.
214. *Supra*, note 89.
215. Ibid., pp. 1074–1078.
216. [1952] 1 All E.R. 1326, *supra*, note 106.
217. *Cf. supra*, note 44.

218. For surveys of existing legislation see Bigham, *op. cit., supra*, note 74, and McLoughlin, *Law and Practice Relating to Pollution Control in the United Kingdom* (1976).
219. In Japan there is a compensation fund for victims of environmentally harmful activities: Japan Environment Agency, *Quality of the Environment in Japan* (1972), pp. 110–13. The Dutch Air Pollution Act 1970, art. 64, established a similar fund for the victims of air pollution who are unable to obtain compensation elsewhere.
220. Linden, 'Tort Law as Ombudsman' (1973) 51 Can. Bar Rev. 155. See also Sax, *Defending the Environment: A Study of Citizen Action* (1971), p. 115.
221. Although in theory any person may institute criminal proceedings in the case of regulatory offences, it is in practice undertaken by the relevant enforcement authority which alone may possess access to the necessary information and to the required powers of entry. In some instances the public may even be prohibited from bringing prosecutions without the consent of the Attorney-General: see, *e.g.*, Rivers (Prevention of Pollution) Act 1961, s. 11 and Prevention of Oil Pollution Act 1971, s. 19 (1). The Control of Pollution Act 1974 will alter the position as regards rivers but at the time of writing is not fully in force.
222. Linden, 'Is Tort Relevant to the Automobile Accident Compensation Problem?' (1969) 47 Tex. L. R. 1012, 1021.

Structural Bias in Regulatory Law Enforcement: The Case of the U.S. Environmental Protection Agency*

PETER C. YEAGER†

Abstract

In this paper I demonstrate the utility and importance of merging two distinct yet related lines of inquiry that have been pursued in connection with illegal business activity. One tradition has sought to isolate the organizational and/or financial characteristics that may lead to such behavior on the part of firms. The other has investigated the political economic relations that influence legislation and enforcement efforts directed at business behavior. Using data on the Environmental Protection Agency's enforcement of the Federal Water Pollution Control Act, I analyze a structural model that links firm and regulatory characteristics to determine whether systematic biases operate in regulatory law enforcement. The results suggest that ostensibly neutral legal structures necessarily tend to favor more powerful businesses and to burden smaller companies disproportionately. Smaller firms appear more frequently on official lists of violators, indicating that regulatory law reflects and reproduces systemic inequalities.

The study of illegal business behavior is no longer in its infancy (cf. Dinitz, 1979). A flurry of research activity since the mid-1970s has improved our data bases, strengthened our analyses, and generally increased the intellectual vitality in this important field of inquiry. The public focus on corporate misbehavior in the wake of the Watergate events in the early 1970s and the first substantial government funding for such analyses initially stimulated work in this area.[1] This research has maintained its momentum to the present, despite disappearing funding and a relative shift of public and governmental attention away from the issues of social welfare and toward matters of economic growth and national security.

In general, investigative work on illegal business behavior has pursued two different yet inherently related lines of inquiry. The first research tradition began with Sutherland's (1949) pioneering study of corporate illegalities, and continued with the major investigation by Clinard and his colleagues of the noncompliance records of the Fortune 500 corporations (Clinard et al., 1979; Clinard and Yeager, 1980). Research in this tradition has been conducted not only by sociologists, but also by economists, management analysts, and journalists (e.g., Ross, 1980), and has largely been concerned with establishing the extent and correlates of corporate wrongdoing, with a view toward developing theoretical explanations of the behavior (see Yeager, 1986).

The second line of investigation reaches at least as far back as the work of Marver Bernstein (1955), passes through that of Gabriel Kolko (1963) into such recent contributions as Barnett (1979, 1981), Calavita (1983), Coleman (1985), Curran (1984), Donnelly (1982), Shover (1980), and Szasz (1984). These researchers have focused mainly on the political economic relations that influence legislation and enforcement directed at business activities. Their findings have directed attention to factors that limit the state's ability to regulate powerful business enterprises in the public interest.

The purpose of this paper is to demonstrate the utility and importance of merging these two lines of inquiry. My interest in this sort of merger grew out of earlier research on the infractions of the Fortune 500 companies (Clinard et al., 1979; Clinard and Yeager, 1980). In that work, we found it necessary to base indicators of corporate wrongdoing on official data regarding the enforcement actions taken by the various federal regulatory agencies. The consequent problem for analysis is familiar to sociologists who study deviance. Official lists of violators reflect the outcomes of two sets of processes: (1) etiological processes that determine which companies in fact violate laws; and (2) social reaction processes that shape the selection of targets for legal action from the universe of regulated enterprises. A more integrated theoretical approach to processes of law-breaking and legal regulation not only might clarify the law's limits as a regulatory mechanism, but also shed light on how regulatory law reproduces the prevailing social order, including patterns of business infraction. Indeed, as I will show here, the patterning of both the occurrence and the discovery of corporate illegality is contingent on the relation between the economic system and the regulatory apparatus.

The analysis I present here is based on my research into the federal Environmental Protection Agency's (EPA) efforts to regulate industrial water pollution through enforcement of the Federal Water Pollution Control Act (also known as the Clean Water Act) in the 1970s. Although the act was first passed in 1948, it, and a series of subsequent amendments, provided a weak and generally unsuccessful framework for regulation until 1972 (Yeager and Clinard, 1979). That year, dramatic growth in public concern for environmental protection influenced Congress to pass amendments to the law that radically altered the government's stance toward industrial water pollution. Among other things, the new legislation required industries for the first time to make expensive capital investments in pollution control technology, established major criminal penalties for serious violations of the law, and provided for citizen lawsuits against both violators of the act and the EPA in the event it failed to enforce the law. Thus, given the relative stringency of the 1972 amendments and the widespread support for them during the remainder of the decade, examination of the statute's implementation permits an assessment of the nature of a regulatory law's impact under relatively favorable conditions for enforcement.[2]

In the discussion below, I first present the theoretical arguments that inform my research. Second, I describe the data and methods used to examine my hypotheses. I then present the findings from the analyses, and conclude with a discussion of the implications of the results for theory, policy, and research.

Theory and Model

Most criminological research takes the nature of law as unproblematic, investigating violations of law as 'pure' behavioral phenomena unconfounded by the form of law or processes of its enforcement. For studies of conventional or 'street' crime, this position was challenged in the 1960s by research in the labeling tradition which highlighted the role of politics and law enforcement in the production of such offenses. More recently, developments in theories of state functioning, the sociology of law, and organizational theory have similarly underscored the importance of the relationship between state and economy for a fully-rounded analysis of illegal business activity. In sum, this argument suggests that the constraints embedded in the prevailing socioeconomic system generally determine the nature and content of legal activity—i.e., activity both in the legal subsystem and in its relation with the subjects of law—which in turn tends to reproduce the system and its social relations.

Theorists in the structuralist tradition argue that the state—and the legal system as one of its components (see, e.g., Balbus, 1977; Beirne, 1979; Chambliss and Seidman, 1982; Jones, 1984)—serves its reproductive function by being 'relatively autonomous' from particular socioeconomic interests (e.g., O'Connor, 1973; Poulantzas, 1973; Therborn, 1978).

While in the short term some state activities are costly to (and often strongly resisted by) some fractions of capital, structural theorists argue that the state in fact organizes and implements the long-term interests of capital as a whole by securing the stable and predictable social and economic conditions requisite for private capital accumulation.

According to this analysis, the true class character of the state is generally shrouded by its efforts to establish what might be called a 'technocratic neutrality' in its decision-making (cf. Gold et al., 1975; Offe, 1973a, 1973b). For example, recent studies of regulatory agencies have underscored efforts to establish legitimacy in turbulent, often highly politicized environments. To blunt the political opposition of potentially powerful opponents, the agencies translate their legal mandates into a series of apparently neutral, technical decisions, often made under elaborate procedural rules of due process—e.g., advance notice of rule changes, predecision hearings on all relevant issues, internal adjudicative processes (Anderson, 1980; Salamon and Wamsley, 1975).[3] However, such decision-making systems have the effect of favoring certain interests over others. In at least three ways, they are 'loaded' in favor of parties possessing the financial and technical resources necessary for negotiating with agency decision-makers (cf. Balbus, 1977; Gold et al., 1975; Sabatier, 1975; Schattschneider, 1960).

First, to the extent that agencies embrace a technical and professional orientation, the legal process may 'disenfranchise' concerned publics with too few resources to participate in the myriad decisions that ultimately determine the degree of regulatory rigor. For example, EPA's appellate procedures in water pollution cases, although formally open to all sides, typically involve only agency and corporate experts. Thus, public interest voices are silenced in effect by a lack of monetary and technical resources (Yeager, 1981). Second, the costs imposed by regulatory requirements may further entrench the dominant sector of large corporations by imposing higher relative unit compliance costs on smaller companies (Barnett, 1981; Lilley and Miller, 1977), thus reducing their ability to compete. Finally, this reproduction of inequality may similarly operate within the regulatory apparatus itself. For example, due to their differential size and resources, firms vary in their ability to avail themselves of legal avenues of appeal with regard to rules and regulations, and may therefore experience greater or lesser risks of violation.

Taken together, these arguments point to the likelihood that structural biases are 'built into' apparently neutral regulatory organizations. Figure 2.1 presents a schematic model of the operation of such biases. As in other

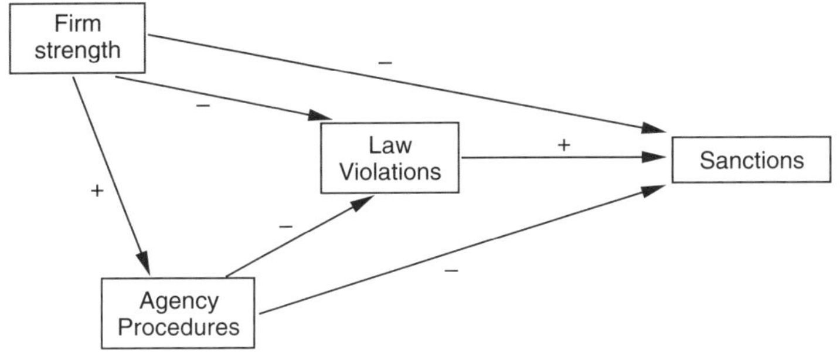

Fig. 2.1. A Structural model of Regulation

studies of business offenses, it links a firm's economic strength directly with illegal behavior, and also with sanctioning patterns. However, it elaborates these relationships by incorporating the mediating effects of regulatory agency procedures on subsequent violations and sanctioning experience. Therefore, the economic characteristics of the firm not only *directly* influence violation and sanctioning rates, but they also *indirectly* shape these rates through the intervention of agency processing. In sum, the model treats the interpenetration of state structure and the economy as central to the production of corporate illegalities.

The model includes the straightforward assumption that firms with greater numbers of detected violations will experience more sanctions and more serious penalties than companies with fewer infractions. In addition, I hypothesize that a firm's economic strength will directly and negatively affect the number and severity of sanctions received, holding constant the rate of violations. This argument is in line with research which shows that federal agencies are often reluctant to engage powerful corporate adversaries in legal battles, preferring instead to negotiate with them and administer symbolic penalties, if any (see, e.g., Clinard and Yeager, 1980). For lack of political and economic muscle, smaller firms may be more likely to feel the 'full force of the law.'

The model also includes the expectation that greater company strength is negatively related to violation rates. This follows from the argument that large, oligopolistic corporations are better able both to absorb and to pass on regulatory costs than are smaller companies, particularly those in more competitive economic environments. Therefore, the former should manifest greater legal compliance than the latter because regulatory burdens evenly applied in fact fall 'unevenly.'

The model also predicts that larger, more powerful corporations—because of their greater stock of legal and technical expertise—will more often use formal legal procedures to negotiate favorable terms of imposed regulations. To the extent that such terms are negotiated with agencies, these larger firms will have fewer infractions than companies less successful in procedural politics. Other things held constant, the latter will generally face relatively harsher restrictions than the former. Moreover, the use of administrative procedures may also provide an indirect advantage in terms of sanctioning experiences. For example, an agency cannot proceed against violators of requirements imposed by federal water pollution discharge permits when those requirements are under appeal. Thus, the model again predicts that larger companies will experience fewer sanctions than smaller firms for a given level of violations, not simply because the agency is reluctant to take on powerful opponents, but also because these latter are more often able to use ostensibly neutral legal procedures to suspend enforcement.

Data and Methods

I collected the data for the analyses at EPA's Region II headquarters in New York City. These data tracked the agency's enforcement of the Clean Water Act against industrial polluters in New Jersey from 1973 through early 1978. I chose this venue to obtain relevant data while keeping the scope of the project manageable. There is considerable variation in the quality of recordkeeping across the 10 EPA regional headquarters, where the data are compiled. The most sophisticated and complete data tracking system had been instituted by Region II, which has responsibility for New Jersey, New York, Puerto Rico, and the Virgin Islands. Region II data on pollution discharge permit characteristics, appeals and modifications of permit requirements, violations, and the agency's response to them were recorded for each industrial plant in a single computer file. The data systems in the other regions were more fragmented.

In addition to its data advantages, Region II also covers a heavily industrialized section of the country—one which contains a wide spectrum of industrial activity and which has experienced some of the most serious water pollution problems in the country. Despite covering only two states, Region II had the sixth largest number of private water pollution dischargers (2,474) among the ten regulatory regions, and had the *second* largest number of major dischargers (547). The Region is also responsible for numerous public waste dischargers such as municipalities.

I analyzed New Jersey data because I wanted to concentrate on *federal* enforcement of the Clean Water Act. Under the terms of the statute, EPA could delegate enforcement of the law to the individual states under particular conditions, and by the end of the decade the agency had done so to more than half the states, including New York. While a comparison of federal and state enforcement of the law would be instructive on its own terms, an effort to unravel and compare differences in both recordkeeping and enforcement policies would be complicated and beyond the scope of this study.

The Sample

I began with almost 600 private facilities in New Jersey with EPA-issued permits limiting their water pollution discharges, and then further limited the sample in several ways. First I confined the analysis to *manufacturing* plants—those with Standard Industrial Classification codes ranging from 20 to 39, inclusively. Among businesses discharging wastes into the nation's waterways, manufacturing facilities constitute the major source of waste and are the focus of regulatory attention. Second, I excluded plants that processed their wastes through a municipal treatment works, rather than building their own treatment facilities. The EPA does not regulate such plants directly; rather, it regulates them indirectly through permits issued to the municipal treatment works. Third, I omitted plants owned by non-American corporations to avoid potentially extraneous factors, such as those related to international relations and foreign trade. Fourth, I dropped some plants from the analysis due to incomplete data. Information on firm size was unavailable for 105 plants; and for approximately 40 plants, government regulatory data were incomplete. Finally, ownership changes, plant closings, and other such miscellaneous reasons justified the omission of a few facilities.

So specified, the final purposive sample consisted of 214 plants discharging wastes into the waterways. Of these, 87 (41 per cent) were classified as 'major' dischargers, defined by EPA documentation as having 'large' discharges 'and/or a high potential to violate applicable water quality standards' (U.S. Environmental Protection Agency, 1978). These are the facilities the agency has typically targeted for priority regulatory effort. The remaining 127 plants are classified as 'minor' dischargers.

Variables

As illustrated in Figure 2.1, the key theoretical variables included in the analysis are: (1) firm economic strength; (2) utilization of agency appellate procedures; (3) violations of the Clean Water Act permits; and (4) sanctions imposed for violations. As the indicator of economic strength, I used firm size measured in terms of a company's annual sales, both because this is a commonly assumed convention (cf. Clinard et al., 1979), and because other indicators (e.g., market share) are not available for large samples. In these data, the range in annual sales is from $325,000 to more than $32 billion, with a mean of $2.5 billion. Companies with more than $1 billion in annual sales own two out of every five plants.[4]

The appellate procedure I examined is EPA's formal adjudicatory hearing process, through which companies can challenge the restrictions contained in their pollution discharge permits. To invoke this process successfully, a company must marshall substantial legal and/or technical expertise in defense of its position. Therefore, I expect the hearing procedure to be more accessible to the larger, more resource-rich firms. The advantages of utilizing this process are two-fold: (1) significant changes in the firm's favor can be made in permit requirements; and (2) violations of challenged permit conditions regarding such matters as levels of discharge and pollution control construction requirements cannot be enforced while the hearing is pending. Thus, the ability to mobilize adjudicatory hearings may have a salutary effect on both violations and sanctions experience. As there was typically no information in the available data as to which aspects of their permits companies had challenged, I analyzed the process using a dummy variable—plants for which such hearings were either pending or settled were coded as having successfully invoked the process, while nonapplicants and those denied hearings comprised the comparison group.

I separately analyzed two types of pollution control violations.[5] First, I calculated a plant's total number of effluent discharge violations. These are infractions in which the plant has exceeded its permitted limits in one or more types of effluent. To avoid trivial matters that are unlikely to reflect poor compliance behavior by the firm, I excluded from this count any discharge violations the EPA record indicated had been of a minor nature. Second, I calculated the number of compliance schedule violations which involve failures to keep to the EPA-mandated schedule for installing pollution abatement equipment. Because these schedules were critical to the eventual reduction of water pollution, enforcement of them was a top priority of the agency in the 1970s (Yeager, 1981). On the other hand, these requirements often mandated costly capital outlays which provided ample incentive for businesses to appeal their permit requirements and often caused them to fall behind their schedules.[6]

Finally, I analyzed two sanctions variables corresponding to the two violations measures. These are measures of a plant's total number of sanctions for (1) effluent violations, and (2) compliance schedule offenses. I employed these measures for two reasons. First, these EPA data are unusual in that they include violations for which the agency determined that it would issue *no* sanction. This permits investigation of whether such 'nonresponses' are systematically related to characteristics other than the offense itself.[7] Second, the sanctions used by the agency consisted almost entirely of warnings and orders to comply; very few cases (six) had been referred to the Justice Department for civil or criminal prosecution. Thus, the only distinction meaningful for analysis is how many times the firm was sanctioned at all.

It may appear that formal warnings and orders to comply constitute rather meaningless sanctions, and that the difference between these actions and no enforcement at all is therefore trivial. However, as I have argued in greater detail elsewhere (Yeager, 1987), this is not the case. Once the EPA begins issuing formal sanctions of any kind to a company for ongoing violations of the law—in contrast to the option of bargaining 'no enforcement action' responses to engender 'good faith' efforts at compliance—it tends to commit itself to an escalating course of penalties in the face of continued noncompliance, or to a loss of institutional face, clearly an unacceptable outcome. Internal agency enforcement memoranda suggest that the decision to issue formal warnings rather than engage in quiet diplomacy can affect both the agency and the violator in precisely this way. Therefore, it is reasonable to conclude that the distinction between formal warnings and no enforcement action is both real and meaningful.

Control Variables

I also used five measures that are logically related to the violations and sanctioning experience as controls throughout the analysis. Two of these are proxy indicators of the relative stringency of the permit requirements imposed on polluting industrial firms. The first is simply a dummy variable indicating whether or not a plant's permit contained a compliance schedule for construction of pollution control facilities. The absence of such a schedule indicates that a plant needed to make relatively few changes to comply with pollution discharge limits. On the other hand, a required construction schedule indicates a plant for which compliance required a significant, often costly effort. The second indicator is the frequency with which a plant was required to make self-monitoring compliance reports to the EPA. This frequency reflects the seriousness of the discharge relative to the pollution control requirements imposed. The assumption here is that the greater the reporting frequency, the greater the stringency of the permit conditions, and thus the higher the likelihood of violation. The reporting frequency varied over the categories of monthly, quarterly, semiannually, annually, and no reports required (coded 1, 3, 6, 12 and 13, respectively).

The third control is the length of time a facility has been under permit requirements (in months). Because the EPA issued individual permits over time as the regulatory program was phased in, some plants had been under permit requirements for several years, while others had been permitted for only a year or less. Other things being equal, the former can be expected to have more reported infractions than the latter. The fourth control simply indicates whether or not the facility is a major discharger of pollutants, as defined above. Finally, I employed a fifth control indicating whether or not a plant was operated by a subsidiary or a parent corporation. This measure controls for any compliance variation due to differences in intraorganizational structures and relations.

Findings

Tables 2.1 and 2.2 present the ordinary least squares estimates for the two sets of analyses. In general, all of the significant relationships are in the predicted direction, but not all of the predicted relationships are significant. Moreover, the two sets of findings produced patterns of relationships that differ in important respects.

Effluent Discharge Violations

Table 2.1 shows the results for effluent discharge violations and the accompanying sanctions. The findings suggest that for this violation type, the advantages of large firm size are only indirect, and act to insulate larger companies from some sanctions but not from a record of pollution infractions. That is, controlling for the number of discharge violations, larger firms are no less likely to be sanctioned by the EPA than are smaller companies, unless the former have successfully invoked the adjudicatory hearing procedure, and are no less likely than smaller firms to commit these offenses in the first place.

The results in the first column show that an industrial facility's violations record is the most important determinant of the number of times the EPA administers formal sanctions to it and as indicated, the measure of firm strength is not a significant predictor of sanctioning. This suggests that the EPA tends to apply the law in an evenhanded fashion. On the other hand, it is altogether possible that any reluctance on the part of the agency to engage in legal grapples with the more powerful enterprises would only appear in connection with those sanctioning options for which agency resources are often overmatched by those of large companies—civil or criminal court cases. While these data cannot speak conclusively to this possibility, there are indications in my research that this may be the case (see Yeager, 1987). It is noteworthy that the few civil and criminal referrals were typically used against the violations of smaller firms—four of the six cases involved companies with annual sales of $10 million or less. In these data, such referrals were never used against companies with annual sales greater than $1 billion, even when the violations were similar in magnitude.

For example, the EPA considered a company's failure to file for a discharge permit under the Clean Water Act as very serious. Of the three such offenses committed by small companies in these data, two received administrative orders to comply and the third was referred to the Justice Department for prosecution. In contrast, of the two non-filer violations committed by large corporations, one received 'no action' and the other a warning letter. This comports with the spontaneous observation of a long-term EPA water pollution enforcement official in Washington that the agency was afraid to prosecute the most powerful corporations, preferring instead to concentrate its enforcement resources and most serious sanctions on smaller companies (conversation with author, 1978).

Moreover, as hypothesized, the results in column three indicate that larger companies more often invoke the EPA's formal hearing procedure successfully than do smaller businesses. In addition, major dischargers with compliance schedules were more likely to invoke the procedure successfully. Subsidiaries of larger corporations were also slightly more likely to employ the procedure.[8] As indicated in the first column, this ability to appeal regulatory conditions provides a degree of insulation from EPA sanctioning, holding the level of violations constant. That is, companies that successfully appealed their pollution control permits were not sanctioned by the agency for violations of discharge limits that were being legally challenged. Thus, larger firms tend to have some advantage over smaller companies in that they can delay compliance because of their

Table 2.1. *Regression Results for Nonminor Effluent Violations and Sanctions (N = 214)*[a]

Independent Variables	*Dependent Variables*		
	Total Sanctions	*Total Violations*	*Adjudicatory Hearing*
Total Violations	.66***		
Adjudicatory Hearing	−.12*	−.10	
Firm Strength	−.10	.02	.20**
Major Discharger	−.02	.24***	.15†
Compliance Schedule	−.02	−.19**	−.17*
Reporting Frequency	.01	−.30***	−.10
Age of Permit	.06	.16**	.03
Parent/Subsidiary	.01	.09	.12†
Adj. R^2	.43	.38	.17

Notes:
a. Standardized regression coefficients are reported.
†p < .08
*p < .05
**p < .01
***p < .001

greater access to ostensibly neutral legal procedures, and this enforcement advantage can be substantial. In New Jersey at the time I collected the data, most of the hearings were pending and had been so for two-to-three years and longer.

Finally, column two indicates that the controls were the only significant predictors of facilities' records of total pollution offenses. Facilities that were major dischargers, had construction schedules and greater reporting frequency requirements, and had been under permit longer were more likely than their counterparts to have longer violations records. Firm strength is unrelated to offense records which suggests that the incidence of these infractions may be determined less by a company's ability to afford regulatory compliance than by its commitment to the adequate operation and maintenance of pollution abatement technology once it is in place. If there has been a generalized reluctance on the part of industry to make full compliance with the environmental laws of the 1970s a priority (see Yeager, 1986), then the distribution of violations reflecting daily operations may be relatively 'random.' The result that adjudicatory hearings are unrelated to violations records is linked to the agency's regulatory policy in Region II—for companies that had successfully invoked the hearings procedure, violations of the originally-established pollution limits were listed in the agency's record but not enforced while the appeal was pending.

Compliance Schedule Violations

Table 2.2 presents the findings for compliance schedule violations and the accompanying sanctions. These offenses involve failure to meet mandated construction schedules for pollution abatement equipment. The construction requirements often involved large capital expenditures by firm, and given their importance to ultimate pollution reduction, they were targeted for top priority enforcement by the EPA.

The findings for these violations contrast with those for effluent violations discussed above. First, as indicated by the much larger coefficient for total violations (.95 as against .66), compliance schedule violations were more likely to meet with agency sanctions than were effluent violations. The results in the first column indicate that firms' violations records explain almost all of the variation in the number of sanctions they experienced; none of the other variables in the equation had any effect whatsoever, including firm strength. This suggests that the EPA was indeed implementing its policy that schedule violations were to be met with consistent pressure to comply, in contrast to its relative patience with periodic violations of the discharge limits.

Second, in contrast to the result for effluent violations, larger companies were slightly less likely than smaller businesses to have committed

Table 2.2. *Regression Results for Compliance Schedule Violations and Sanctions (N =14)*[a]

	Dependent Variables		
Independent Variables	*Total Sanctions*	*Total Violations*	*Adjudicatory Hearing*
Total Violations	.95***		
Adjudicatory Hearing	.01	−.18*	
Firm Strength	−.01	−.12†	.20**
Major Discharger	−.02	.07	.15†
Compliance Schedule	−.02	−.33***	−.17*
Reporting Frequency	−.01	−.13†	−.10
Age of Permit	.01	.03	.03
Parent/Subsidiary	.01	.09	.12†
Adj. R^2	.91	.17	.17

Notes:

a. Standardized regression coefficients are reported.

†p < .08

*p < .05

**p < .01

***p < .001

construction schedule offenses in the first place (column two). Although the magnitude of this effect is small, it nonetheless suggests that larger companies enjoy some 'regulatory economies of scale,' and can therefore more easily absorb legal demands requiring large expenditures of capital. In addition, large oligopolistic corporations may be better able to pass on such regulatory costs in the form of higher product prices than smaller companies in more competitive environments. In combination with the finding for discharge violations discussed above, this result suggests that larger, more powerful firms are able to make a better show of compliance with expensive construction requirements, but are no more committed to ongoing discharge compliance than are smaller businesses, due perhaps to the very low risk of serious sanction.

Third, the results again show that larger firms are more likely than smaller enterprises to use the hearings procedure successfully (column three; this is the same equation as in Table 2.1). And again this utilization results in regulatory advantages for the companies, only in this case the advantage takes the form of reduced violations records rather than reduced sanctioning (column two). Inspection of individual case records suggests two possible explanations for these results. For hearings cases that had been settled, some companies had succeeded in having the EPA modify the construction schedule requirements so that they were subsequently easier to meet. For those cases in which companies' appeals were still pending, the hearings often had the effect of staying the requirements of the original construction schedules while the terms of these requirements were under negotiation. In effect, the agency treated the contested schedules as nonbinding while they were under appeal. In the situations of both pending and settled appeals, then, the results are typically identical—the relaxation of regulatory requirements through a legal procedure that tends to be differentially available to firms depending on the level of resources they command.

Finally, as for effluent violations, the two indicators of permit stringency are related to compliance schedule offenses in the expected way (column two). Facilities with compliance schedules and more frequent compliance reporting requirements tended to commit these infractions more often. Again, where the legal requirements are most substantial, violations are more common. This is perhaps particularly likely in areas of regulation such as this, where the law encounters resistance from powerful producers who claim that regulation often hampers economic growth, an argument the Reagan administration came to use in defense of its deregulatory policies.

Discussion

Taken together, these findings carry a number of implications for theory, policy, and research. In terms of theorizing the relations between state structures and socioeconomic organization, my research suggests that regulatory legislation of this sort simultaneously reflects and reproduces the inequality in power and wealth of the social system of which it is part. In other words, even in capitalist democracies, ostensibly neutral state structures tend to reproduce existing relations of power even as they seek to regulate powerful entities.

In the case of environmental regulation, technology-forcing standards such as those required under the Clean Water Act tend to be regressive, disproportionately burdening the smaller companies with expensive implementation criteria. It is in this sense that large corporations may enjoy regulatory 'economies of scale,' to the extent that they are able to amortize compliance costs over larger volumes of production. Moreover, such an advantage is only enhanced to the extent that oligopolistic corporations are relatively more successful at avoiding price competition in their markets than are the smaller firms, permitting the former higher rates of profit.

In addition, the process of regulation itself reproduces inequality to the extent that it proves to be more accessible to organizations with greater resources for mounting legal challenges to it. Because such state regulation further strengthens the economic position of what O'Connor (1973) has labeled monopoly-sector corporations at the expense of competitive sector enterprises, it only reproduces the conditions that produce a structural bias in law, and in socioeconomic relations more generally.

The question remains whether these findings represent general processes in the regulatory apparatuses linking state and economy. The evidence, both historical and contemporary, suggests that they do, particularly with respect to what has widely been called 'social' regulation—i.e., those forms of state intervention that address the negative effects of production relations on consumers, workers, communities, and the general environment. Perhaps less certain—and beyond the scope of this discussion—is the general applicability of these conclusions to forms of 'economic' regulation, which seek to stabilize market relations by establishing the rules of exchange—e.g., securities, antitrust, and interstate commerce laws.[9]

For example, Kolko's (1963) analysis of the federal Meat Inspection Act of 1906 indicates that competition within the meatpacking industry played an important role in the passage of the law. In particular, the largest corporate meatpackers supported the law in part because they saw it as an opportunity to disadvantage the smaller meatpacking companies by bringing them under federal regulatory controls that would be more expensive for them to implement per unit of production.

Recent research on the enforcement of 'social' regulations suggests an additional advantage at law for major producers—enforcement agents consider the larger corporations more likely to be socially responsible, and to make good faith efforts at compliance. For example, in their study of the federal Office of Surface Mining Reclamation and Enforcement, Lynxwiler and his colleagues (1983) found that the agency inspectors operated on the basis of two assumptions—that larger mining companies were more responsive to and cooperative with regulatory demands than smaller firms, and that the former were also more likely to challenge violation citations in formal legal hearings (also see Shover et al., 1986). These assumptions were grounded in inspectors' experiences in the field—in particular, their interactions with large companies' technical experts whose own knowledge rivaled their own (thus eliminating the leverage of the government's regulatory expertise), and with whom the inspectors could negotiate professional and technical (i.e., 'nonpolitical') definitions of violations and remedies. On the other hand, the inspectors were more likely to see smaller companies—those without such expertise—as less cooperative and technically less able to comply with their environmental responsibilities. As a result of these working assumptions, inspectors tended to report the violations of smaller firms as more serious offenses, quite apart from more objective measures of the harm occasioned by them, and the agency tended to assess these smaller operations higher fines than those issued to larger corporate violators.

On the basis this evidence, then, it appears that processes of structural or systemic bias regularly attend the 'social' regulation of business. From standards carrying regressive impact to enforcement perceptions that larger companies are both more socially responsible and more likely to resist harsh legal treatment, regulatory law tends in important ways to reproduce existing relations of inequality in the economy.

It is important to note what these arguments and conclusions do not imply. First, I do not mean to suggest that environmental regulation—in this case water pollution control—has been entirely ineffective in achieving its stated aims. To the contrary, important progress has been made in some areas, both in improving water quality and in preventing further deterioration (e.g., Yeager, 1981). Nor do I claim that regulators always avoid legal confrontations with major corporate polluters. As suggested by the $13 million fine in 1976 against the Allied Chemical Corporation for the Kepone pollution of the James River, regulatory agencies are more likely to challenge particularly egregious corporate offenses, both because such violations often outrage regulators as well as citizens, and because failure to so respond would discredit the agency and ultimately threaten the legitimacy of the sitting administration if not that of the state as a whole. However, what the findings reported here do suggest is that such regulation may benefit one fraction of the Capitalist class at the expense of other fractions, even as it regulates industry more or less successfully in the pursuit of the public interest. To the extent that regulatory law contributes in some measure to the further concentration of economic power in the hands of fewer, larger corporations, it raises questions regarding whose interests are ultimately being served.

But the recognition of such a possibility does not amount to support for deregulation, whether in general, or for smaller producers, which do indeed produce much debilitating pollution. Rather, considerations of ecological and economic well-being, as well as of legal justice, suggest such solutions as progressively structured tax incentives and legal/technical assistance to reduce the inequalities otherwise inherent in such regulatory schemes. If both a clean, usable environment and economic vitality are widely valued social goals, then citizens may agree to help underwrite some of the costs of compliance, particularly for the smaller firms that account for a substantial share of employment and a disproportionate share of industrial innovation in the United States. Similarly, funding mechanisms that increase the resources of public interest environmental groups would enhance their ability to raise appropriate arguments and challenges in regulatory negotiations, many of which are presently conducted as technical matters between regulators and the regulated, without the adequate representation of informed citizens' concerns.

Finally, in terms of research implications, my findings indicate that the systemic nexus linking law and economy produces both real and discovered rates of regulatory law violations. That is, such rates are jointly determined by business and legal operations in the context of a historically-situated political economy. The result is that researchers need be cautious when relying on official sanctioning data in the study of corporate lawbreaking. To the extent that larger companies are treated more favorably than smaller ones, regulatory data will be systematically distorted. Making sense out of regulatory offense patterns thus requires that we take into account the nature and degree of such distortion for the specific period and place under investigation.

Notes

* I presented earlier versions of this work at the 1985 annual meetings of the Society for the Study of Social Problems, Washington, DC, and in a 1983 presentation at the Center for Criminal Justice, Harvard University Law School. For their insightful critiques, I am indebted to Harold Barnett, Neal Shover, and three anonymous *Social Problems* reviewers. Correspondence to: Department of Sociology, Boston University, Boston, MA 02215.

† Boston University

1. The now-defunct Law Enforcement Assistance Administration of the U.S. Department of Justice funded two major projects on business offenses and their regulation in the mid-1970s—one at the University of Wisconsin at Madison and the other at Yale University. Results of the former are reported in Clinard et al. (1979), and Clinard and Yeager (1980). The Yale studies include Wheeler et al. (1982) and Shapiro (1984).
2. These favorable conditions were not only evident in the results of public opinion polls and the monitoring activities of such recently-established public interest law groups as the Natural Resources Defense Council and the Environmental Defense Fund, but also within the agency itself. During my field research at the EPA in the late 1970s, I was impressed with the level of commitment to the law's enforcement expressed both by agency officials (in many formal and casual conversations) and in formal policy (as stated in the agency's series of enforcement memoranda).
3. These researchers have generally approached agencies as complex organizations adapting strategies for survival in uncertain environments. Thus, many of these studies are cognate with the institutional school of organizational analysis (e.g., Perrow, 1972). The congruence of the conclusions independently reached by these studies and recent theoretical approaches to the state is, I think, a particularly nice instance of linkage between abstract theory and middle-range explanation.
4. I compiled the annual sales data for firms from two types of sources. First, for the 143 cases this data base had in common with the earlier Clinard et al. (1979) study of Fortune 500 firms, I simply extracted values from the study's data file. For the remaining cases, I consulted standard business references, including *Moody's Industrial Manual, Dun and Bradstreet's Million Dollar Directory* and *Middle Market Directory*, and the *New Jersey State Industrial Directory*. The firm-size data from these two sources differed somewhat in form. The Clinard et al. measure had been calculated in terms of average annual sales for the five-year period 1971–1975. The supplementary data, on the other hand, were single-year figures for 1977. The difference is not substantial, however, inasmuch as the supple-

mentary data were typically for firms significantly smaller than the Clinard et al. companies.

The measure of skewness on this variable, measured in terms of thousands of dollars, was 3.85; therefore a long transformation was performed (skewness $= -.623$). Using the transformed indicator, I conducted multiple regression analyses parallel to those reported here. The results proved to be robust, with no significant change in the findings.

5. These data share with other sets of officially generated violations records the problem of bearing an uncertain relation to true rates, levels, or profiles of lawbreaking. The major question here, then, is whether the EPA data present a systematically biased profile of offense rates and offenders (e.g., by size of company) that would render my findings spurious. Because of the way the agency's records are generated, I believe they do not. EPA's compliance monitoring program for the Clean Water Act is based principally on a self-reporting system, supported by periodic inspections that focus on likely 'trouble spots' among major polluters. From all indications, such reported violations are faithfully recorded in the computerized files, even those infractions for which the agency decides to issue no sanction at all (see below). Thus, bias in the data would be due to systematic differentials in reporting honesty by type of company. While there is no substantial a priori reason to believe such differentials exist, the logic of my analysis—that larger, more powerful firms have greater resources with which to negotiate favorable resolutions with government agencies in terms of both regulations and sanctions—suggests that *smaller companies* would perhaps have more to gain by such misrepresentation (cf. Lynxwiler et al., 1983), a result which would run counter to my hypotheses. In any event, my analyses control for violations when investigating sanctioning responses by the agency, and control throughout for such compliance relevant matters as whether the plants are major polluters, are frequently required to report to the agency, etc.
6. This research faced a problem not uncommon to the study of business illegalities—that of counting the number of violations (see, e.g., Reiss and Biderman, 1980). For instance, pollution discharge violations may often be continuous, occurring over a period of months because the plant does not have its abatement equipment operating properly. In cases of such continuous violations, the plant that is required to make monthly compliance reports to the EPA may be found in violation each month in the official compliance data. The discharger with an annual reporting requirement may experience a similar violation, but because of reporting periodicity the infraction may only appear once in the official data. In addition, companies were also required to send 'notices of noncompliance' to the EPA soon after violations had been discovered at the plant. Because the same violations could also be recorded in the companies' separate periodic compliance reports, they could therefore appear twice in the agency's compliance data base. Thus, the information contained in the data base

was often too scanty to distinguish between: (1) continuous and discrete offenses; and (2) discrete offenses and a single violation recorded twice on the record.

I employed two safeguards in the analysis to control for these problems. First, I made the decision generally to record only one effluent discharge violation per reporting period, unless the data clearly indicated two distinct offenses (e.g., an oil spill from a holding tank on site, and an illegal discharge of a different substance from the company's regular discharges). Second, the frequency with which companies are required to make self-monitoring compliance reports to the EPA (e.g., monthly, quarterly, annually) was used as a control variable throughout the analyses to control for bias against frequent reporters.

7. Violations for which EPA regional officials took no enforcement action were added to the official data in the Spring of 1977. Thus, 'no action' determinations are recorded only for violations listed during the final year covered by the official data analyzed here.
8. Polluting plants were given a score of 1 if they were major dischargers as defined by the agency; otherwise they were scored 0. Plants with construction schedules were scored 0, while those without were scored 1. Plants of parent corporations were scored 0, while those of subsidiary firms were scored 1.
9. The distinction between 'social' and 'economic' regulation, while conventional, is quite imperfect because 'economic' regulations clearly affect 'social' well-being in terms of such factors as the cost-of-living and fully-informed participation in various markets, and because 'social' regulations can importantly affect market relations, as my findings suggest. Nonetheless, inasmuch as 'social' regulation seeks to intervene in aspects of production relations while 'economic' controls address exchange relations, the forms of political struggle which each type reflects and occasions can be expected to be different, with important consequences for the ultimate role of law in socioeconomic relations.

References

Anderson, Douglas D. (1980) 'Who owns the regulators?' The Wharton Magazine 4: 14–21.

Balbus, Isaac D. (1977) 'Commodity form and legal form: an essay on the "relative autonomy" of the law.' Law and Society Review 11: 571–88.

Barnett, Harold C. (1979) 'Wealth, crime, and capital accumulation.' Contemporary Crises 3: 171–86.

——(1981) 'Corporate capitalism, corporate crime.' Crime and Delinquency 27: 4–23.

Beirne, Piers (1979) 'Empiricism and the critique of Marxism on law and crime.' Social Problems 26: 373–84.

Bernstein, Marver H. (1955) *Regulating Business by Independent Commission*. Princeton: Princeton University Press.

Calavita, Kitty (1983) 'The demise of the Occupational Safety and Health Administration: a case study in symbolic action.' Social Problems 30: 437–48.

Chambliss, William and Robert Seidman (1982) *Law, Order and Power*. Revised edition. Reading, MA: Addison-Wesley.

Clinard, Marshall B., Peter C. Yeager, Jeanne M. Brissette, David Petrashek and Elizabeth Harries (1979) *Illegal Corporate Behavior*. Washington, DC: U.S. Government Printing Office.

Clinard, Marshall B. and Peter C. Yeager (1980) *Corporate Crime*. New York: The Free Press.

Coleman, James William (1985) 'Law and power: The Sherman Antitrust Act and its enforcement in the petroleum industry.' Social Problems 32: 264–74.

Curran, Daniel J. (1984) 'Symbolic solutions for deadly dilemmas: an analysis of federal coal mine health and safety legislation.' International Journal of Health Services 14: 5–29.

Dinitz, Simon (1979) 'Economic crime.' Unpublished paper.

Donnelly, Patrick (1982) 'The origins of the Occupational Safety and Health Act of 1970.' Social Problems 30: 13–25.

Gold, David A., Clarence Y. H. Lo, and Erik Olin Wright (1975) 'Recent developments in Marxist theories of the capitalist state.' Monthly Review 27 (October): 29–43; 27 (November): 36–51.

Jones, Kelvin (1984) *Law and Economy: The Legal Regulation of Corporate Capital*. New York: Academic Press.

Kolko, Gabriel (1963) *The Triumph of Conservatism: A Reinterpretation of American History, 1900–1916*. New York: The Free Press.

Lilley, William, III, and James C. Miller III (1977) 'The new "social regulation".' The Public Interest 47: 49–61.

Lynxwiler, John, Neal Shover and Donald A. Clelland (1983) 'The organization and impact of inspector discretion in a regulatory bureaucracy.' Social Problems 30: 425–36.

O'Connor, James (1973) *The Fiscal Crisis of the State*. New York: St. Martin's Press.

Offe, Claus (1973a) 'Class rule and the political system: on the selectiveness of political institutions.' Unpublished translation of chapter three of *Strukturprobleme der kapitalistischen Staaten*. Frankfurt: Suhrkamp.

——(1973b) 'The abolition of market control and the problem of legitimacy.' Kapitalistate 1, 2.

Perrow, Charles (1972) *Complex Organizations: A Critical Essay*. Glenview, IL: Scott, Foresman.

Poulantzas, Nicos (1973) *Political Power and Social Classes*. London: NLB.

Reiss, Albert J., Jr., and Albert D. Biderman (1980) *Data Sources on White-Collar Lawbreaking*. Washington, DC: U.S. Department of Justice, National Institute of Justice.

Ross, Irwin (1980) 'How lawless are big companies?' Fortune (December 1): 57–64.

Sabatier, Paul (1975) 'Social movements and regulatory agencies: toward a more adequate—and less pessimistic—theory of "clientele capture".' Policy Sciences 6: 301–42.

Salamon, Lester B., and Gary Wamsley (1975) 'The federal bureaucracy: responsive to whom?' In Leroy N. Reiselbach (ed.), *People vs. Government: The Responsiveness of American Institutions*. Bloomington: Indiana University Press.

Schattschneider, E. E. (1960) *The Semi-sovereign People: A Realist's View of Democracy in America*. New York: Holt, Rinehart and Winston.

Shapiro, Susan (1984) *Wayward Capitalists*. New Haven, CT: Yale University Press.

Shover, Neal (1980) 'The criminalization of corporate behavior: federal surface coal mining.' pp. 98–125 in Gilbert Geis and Ezra Stotland (eds.), *White-Collar Crime: Theory and Research*. Beverly Hills, CA: Sage.

Shover, Neal, Donald A. Clelland and John Lynxwiler (1986) *Enforcement or Negotiation: Constructing a Regulatory Bureaucracy.* Albany, NY: State University of New York Press.

Sutherland, Edwin H. (1949) *White Collar Crime*. New York: Holt.

Szasz, Andrew (1984) 'Industrial resistance to occupational safety and health legislation: 1971–1981.' Social Problems 32: 103–16.

Therborn, Goran (1978) *What Does The Ruling Class Do When It Rules?* New York: Schocken Books.

U.S. Environmental Protection Agency (1978) 'Definition of terms used with the permit compliance system.' Washington, DC. Mimeo.

Wheeler, Stanton, David Weisburd and Nancy Bode (1982) 'Sentencing the white-collar offender: rhetoric and reality.' American Sociological Review 47: 641–59.

Yeager, Peter C. and Marshall B. Clinard (1979) 'Regulating corporate behavior: a case study.' pp. 62–82 in P. J. Brantingham and J. M. Kress (eds.), *Structure, Law, and Power: Essays in the Sociology of Law.* Beverly Hills, CA: Sage.

Yeager, Peter C. (1981) *The Politics of Corporate Social Control: The Federal Response to Industrial Water Pollution*. Unpublished Ph.D. dissertation, University of Wisconsin, Madison.

——(1986) 'Analyzing illegal corporate behavior: progress and prospects.' pp. 93–120 in James E. Post (ed.), *Research in Corporate Social Performance and Policy*, Vol. 8. Greenwich, CT: JAI Press. (1987) 'The social production of environmental offenses: a case study.' Unpublished paper.

PART II
Environmental Law and Science

Holes in the Ozone Layer

A Global Environmental Controversy

MICHAEL S. BROWN AND
KATHERINE A. LYON

In the early 1970s the U.S. government evaluated building a fleet of supersonic jets (SSTs), and the aerosol industry was selling more than 2.9 billion spray cans a year.[1] These seemingly unrelated activities became linked when scientists raised concerns that both would disturb the earth's protective ozone layer and threaten public health and the environment. Though the United States never built a fleet of SSTs, chlorofluorocarbons (CFCs), a class of chemicals used in aerosols and in products ranging from refrigerators to insulation, became the focus of a long and bitter debate.[2]

High above the earth's surface, the stratosphere contains a thin layer of ozone, a colorless, unstable gas that protects ecosystems and humans from excess ultraviolet (UV) radiation. Although small amounts of UV reach the surface, greater exposures are expected to cause increases in skin cancer, loss of agricultural productivity, and severe disruptions to marine ecologies.

Early assessments of the environmental effects associated with CFCs suggested little cause for concern. Researchers who looked at typical effects, such as smog and adverse health consequences from direct exposure, were convinced that the chemicals were safe because they did not have a significant degree of toxicity and did not break down readily.

That very stability prompted Mario Molina and F. Sherwood Rowland, two atmospheric chemists at the University of California at Irvine, to investigate the long-term fate of CFCs. Without a known mechanism for removing the CFCs from the lower atmosphere (the troposphere), they presumed that the compounds would rise over a long period to the stratosphere, where higher intensities of ultraviolet radiation would break the chemical bonds of the molecule. Basing their judgement on the affinity of the free chlorine with ozone, the researchers suggested that a complex set of chemical reactions would reduce the amount of ozone in the stratosphere. When they analyzed CFC production, they found that the amount of ozone loss and the potential for significant amounts of ultraviolet radiation reaching the earth's surface was staggering. Their results, published in mid-1974,[3] soon made ozone depletion and CFCs into front page news.[4]

While the scientists called for a ban on nonessential uses of CFCs, industry ridiculed the dangers as theoretical while emphasizing that CFCs were critical to industrial economies. Policymakers faced tough political choices in trying to pass judgment on complex scientific and technical issues while balancing environmental and economic interests. The initial policy response to Molina and Rowland's findings was limited to a few countries restricting the use of CFCs as aerosol propellants.[5] It wasn't until the late 1980s that ozone depletion once again took center stage on the national and international policy agenda. Policy changes over the ensuing decade and a half reflected a myriad of issues, including the nature of scientific discourse, the influence of technological developments and economic considerations, global diplomacy, and costs and benefits to present and future generations.

The Policy Conundrum

Never before had policymakers confronted an environmental issue with characteristics quite like the matter of ozone depletion. This was an issue that required policy be tied to the predictive capability of science, rather than 'body counts' or measurable pollution. Acidified lakes and acid rain could be measured; air pollution could be seen and felt; cancer clusters could be counted; and epidemiological evidence of exposure to toxics could be assessed. However, until the mid-1980s, the only 'data' available to policymakers on ozone depletion were scientific theories and computer models.

There were also unusual temporal and spatial characteristics to the issue. Molina and Rowland predicted that depletion would not be measurable until long after releases had occurred. In effect, current generations would gain the economic and quality-of-life benefits, while future generations would suffer the harms. Moreover, CFCs released in one geographic location diffuse globally, creating a worldwide phenomenon, since emissions from the United States are as likely to affect people in Australia as emissions from India are to affect Americans. Under these conditions, a jurisdiction acting alone could not achieve a significant reduction of the health risks to its population, since CFC production capability and use were rapidly expanding through the industrial world and extending to developing countries.

Until the mid-1970s the United States, several European countries, the Soviet Union, and Japan manufactured nearly all the world's CFCs. However, production began increasing in a few developing countries, starting in the mid-1970s. They wanted to produce such consumer goods as refrigerators and foams for car seats and bedding, provide air-conditioning for commercial and industrial space, and establish manufacturing centers for electronics and other high-tech products. Was the ozone depletion issue a means by which the industrialized world would limit the ability of developing countries, particularly India and China, to raise their standard of living and become significant competitors in the world economy?

Further complicating the unusual scientific issues was the commercial appeal of CFCs, which seemed ideal for many applications. As a refrigerant, CFCs possessed positive characteristics for heat transfer and safety; similar characteristics made their use in insulating foam superior to available alternatives. One CFC was an effective industrial solvent and had the added benefits of compatibility with a wide variety of materials and a relatively low degree of toxicity. Producers of CFCs argued that the cost of developing replacement chemicals was enormous; users of CFCs were concerned about energy efficiency and safety of redesigned refrigerators and air-conditioning systems.[6] Could policymakers require innovations that did not have significant and clearly defined environmental, energy, or economic consequences? In light of the uncertainty, what process could policymakers use to decide if the short-term costs were worth the risks?

All of these issues combined to increase both the complexity and the degree of controversy surrounding the ozone depletion debate. In this chapter, we discuss the evolution of national and international policies in light of these scientific and technological controversies. We conclude with our view on the implications of the ozone depletion debate for other global environmental issues, such as global warming.

Science and Prediction

Predicting the effects of human activity on the earth's atmosphere is never simple. Even predicting the weather more than 2 or 3 days in advance is difficult. Modeling long-term climatic changes requires scientists to identify thousands of chemical reactions, define global air circulation patterns, and account for influences as diverse as solar flares and volcanic eruptions. The resulting uncertainties in any model of atmospheric change vastly complicate predictions about the influence of human activities, such as the production of CFCs.

Concerns about global climate change had led scientists to a search for appropriate chemicals that could be used to track global air patterns. Because of their stability, CFCs were a useful tracking chemical. Analyzing their dispersion in 1973, Dr. James Lovelock found that almost all CFCs produced to date appeared to be present in the lower atmosphere.[7] Lovelock's findings piqued Molina and Rowland's curiosity and led to their research. If there was a negative effect of the use of CFCs, the ubiquity of these chemicals would have significant implications.

Basing their opinion on the slow pace of CFCs' rise to the stratosphere, Molina and Rowland posited that even if emissions ceased in 1974, CFC-induced ozone destruction would surpass natural destruction levels in the mid-1980s, peak in 1990, and remain at elevated levels for up to 200 years. Debate quickly arose between atmospheric chemists, who were convinced that CFCs catalyzed ozone depletion, and meteorologists, who argued that global air movement would not increase stratospheric CFC concentrations and that other interactions would affect results.[8]

Reducing uncertainty might have been an academic exercise were the potential for ecological and public health damage less significant. The scale of potential harm from ozone depletion, however, forced policymakers to take notice. Given the scientific uncertainties during the 1970s, policymakers could either act on uncertain yet alarming predictions, or wait for incontrovertible evidence. This was a particularly difficult choice; for by the time scientists could actually measure ozone depletion, so many tons of CFCs would have been produced that serious depletion levels could not be avoided.

In response to a federal task force review,[9] the federal government requested a full analysis of the issue by the National Academy of Sciences. Although the chemical manufacturers industry began an intensive lobbying campaign to discredit the theory, the Academy's 1976 reports confirmed the conclusions of the Molina-Rowland hypothesis. However, the Academy panel was reluctant to call for a ban on the chemicals, recommending that further research be done before regulating the industry.[10]

The reports did little to resolve the growing conflicts between the industry, which was seeking to protect its economic interests, and the scientists and environmental groups, who were pressing for rapid action. A Congressional Science Fellow characterized the disagreement by remarking that industry representatives 'refer to it [the ozone depletion theory] disparagingly as "the theory." To a scientist, a theory is sort of the pinnacle of intellectual accomplishment. To industry, theory meant nothing more than your speculation versus my speculation.'[11]

Throughout the ozone depletion controversy, however, it was the economics of the industry that played the pivotal role. By 1974 CFCs and their associated products accounted for $8 billion in annual trade in the United States,[12] and even the White House had taken notice of the significance of the industry.[13] DuPont, the largest manufacturer of CFCs in the world,[14] helped organize the attack on the scientific models, using a well-funded advertising and lobbying campaign. Industry spokespeople argued that regulatory action was not justified without empirical evidence of CFC-caused ozone destruction and assurances that natural phenomena, such as air currents and volcanic activity, were not affecting the conclusions.[15]

Despite the 1978 ban on U.S. aerosol uses, CFC producers remained skeptical of the validity of the theory and increased their marketing efforts for nonaerosol uses. When there was no further federal action, producers increased output and, by the mid-1980s, worldwide CFC production exceeded that produced prior to the aerosol ban.[16] Moreover, research on alternatives all but stopped during this period. Although industry remained concerned about potential regulation, the lack of empirical evidence supporting the theory, and fluctuations in depletion predictions bolstered their inaction.

Things began to change in 1984 when British scientists reevaluated weather satellite data and found that a gaping hole in the ozone layer—a 40% reduction—had opened during winter over Antarctica.[17] Some scientists in and out of industry continued to present competing theories to explain this phenomenon, but the majority began to see it as the first evidence supporting the basic theory. However, scientists could not either conclusively link CFCs to the Antarctic ozone hole or provide an explanation for the increased ozone losses in winter. Thus, continuing controversy allowed the industry to claim that ozone depletion was not due to CFCs.

While research in Antarctica continued in an attempt to resolve uncertainties, laboratory scientists began to develop evidence that suggested a mechanism for the role of CFCs.[18] In 1987 scientists conducting NASA's Airborne Antarctic Ozone Experiment found that high levels of chlorine were present at the lowest measured levels of ozone.[19]

Confirmation of the Molina-Rowland hypothesis came in 1988, just after the signing of an international treaty to control the production of CFCs (the Montreal Protocol). The NASA-sponsored Ozone Trends Panel found an average 2.4% year-round depletion of global ozone levels and suggested that chlorine-containing chemicals were the cause.[20] DuPont, which had just recently restated its disbelief in the evidence linking CFCs with ozone losses, capitulated and became the first manufacturer to announce it would phase out CFCs as substitutes were developed.[21]

Although the links between CFCs and related chemicals and ozone depletion have been identified, depletion measurements continued to change. In early 1991 the Environmental Protection Agency (EPA) released new data, showing higher than expected depletion levels, and suggested that an additional 200,000 cases of skin cancer would result in the United States, 20,000 of which would be fatal.[22]

Researchers are improving methods of detecting depletion, and a decade and a half after publication, Molina and Rowland's theory has proved robust. Yet it is difficult to determine if science could have moved faster to support or disprove the theory, or if policymakers should have acted on less evidence. Without available alternatives for CFCs, the uncertainties surrounding the theory assumed major significance.

Technological Fixes

DuPont's development of CFCs in the early 1930s was rapidly applied to commercial uses. Initially, the refrigerant qualities of several CFCs were exploited for use in refrigerators, freezers, and air-conditioning equipment. As the characteristics of the chemical family became well understood, their use expanded into plastic foams, aerosol propellants, and cleaning applications. Unusual uses, such as fast freezing of delicate fruits and vegetables, chilling agents for medical injuries, and whipped frozen toppings, have come to the market.

By the mid-1970s ozone-depleting chemicals were produced in more than 24 countries.[23] Estimated production in 1973 was 900 million pounds for the United States and at least 1.7 billion pounds worldwide, although actual figures are likely to be substantially higher.[24] At that time, approximately 50 per cent to 60 per cent of U.S. production of CFCs went into aerosols, about 30 per cent went to refrigeration, 10 per cent went to plastic foams, and less than 5 per cent went to solvent cleaning.

Following the U.S. ban in 1978 on nonessential aerosol uses of CFCs, production shifted dramatically and declined by about one-third.[25] Since few countries followed the United States in banning aerosol uses, worldwide production grew substantially, primarily for nonaerosol uses. By 1985 the United States produced nearly 1 billion pounds; estimated worldwide (including U.S.) production of just two kinds of CFCs grew to at least 2 billion pounds.[26] Not until the implementation of the Montreal Protocol in 1989 did production level off and show signs of declining.

Uses of CFCs

Prior to the availability of CFCs, mechanical refrigeration relied on chemicals that were flammable, explosive, or toxic if the refrigerant leaked from the system. Since 1946 home refrigerators have used CFCs exclusively. It is still possible to have a non-CFC commercial refrigeration system in refrigerated warehouses since exposures can be more tightly controlled.

Vehicle air-conditioning first became available in luxury cars in the 1940s. Since then, CFC-based air-conditioners are standard equipment in cars, trucks, enclosed farm vehicles, buses, trains, and planes. Air-conditioning of residential, commercial, and industrial buildings has also become an expected standard. Some uses, particularly home air-conditioning and smaller commercial uses, rely on HCFC (hydrochlorofluorocarbon) compounds that affect ozone less than CFCs. Although other cooling methods are available, much of the air-conditioning in large facilities relies on the use of CFCs with a high ozone-depleting potential.

Foam products, such as cushions used in seats, bedding, and packaging and insulation used in refrigerators, construction, and packaging, have been made with CFCs since the 1950s. Unlike air-conditioning and mechanical refrigeration, which did not exist as a product category prior to the early part of the century, CFC-based foams replaced a variety of alternative products. CFCs' ease of use, hygienic qualities, thermal efficiency, and low weight created massive inroads in the market share of comparable products.

Along with their use in refrigeration and foam manufacturing, CFCs and related ozone-depleting chemicals came into wide use as solvents for a number of applications. Effectiveness and tolerable toxicity characteristics[27] led to applications in dry cleaning of clothing, degreasing of electronic components and metal parts, removing contaminants from computer circuit boards, and cleaning of plastic medical equipment. Because the compounds do not contribute to the formation of smog, they were exempted from air quality regulations in areas where solvents with a high VOC (volatile organic compound) content were prohibited. Ease of use and cleaning performance prompted the Department of Defense to require military contractors to clean with several ozone-depleting compounds, and the Food and Drug Administration to establish good manufacturing practices based on the use of the chemicals. The availability of these government requirements led a variety of commercial industries to specify the use of ozone-depleting chemicals when other cleaning standards did not exist.

The development of medical devices using plastic and electronic parts led to the use of ethylene oxide in industry, hospitals, and doctors' offices as an alternative to steam sterilization. Because ethylene oxide is explosive and flammable, it is usually used in combination with a CFC. Traditional practices resulted in venting of the ethylene oxide/CFC mixture to the atmosphere following evacuation of the sterilizing chamber.

CFCs and other ozone-depleting chemicals also became popular in consumer items, particularly products that were delivered from acrosol cans. CFCs replaced flammable propellants, such as isobutane and pentane, because they did not create a fire hazard, had relatively low toxicity, and were not very expensive. Personal products such as hair sprays and deodorants, specialty uses such as photographic dust-removal sprays, and toys such as sprayed party streamers used CFCs; other ozone-depleting compounds were commonly found in spot-cleaning products and a wide variety of paints and coatings.

Alternatives to Ozone-Depleting Chemicals

Most of the analysis that followed publication of Molina and Rowland's paper focused on the ozone depletion theory, the potential effects of increased UV, and the uses of ozone-depleting chemicals. Since substitutes for CFC aerosol propellants and for aerosol products themselves were readily available, regulatory analysis focused on this area. CFC refrigeration and air conditioning uses were considered to be irreplaceable, and industry did not even bother to investigate alternatives to other uses.

In considering substitutes for nonaerosol uses of CFCs, EPA turned to the RAND Corporation, which produced a report that reflected current conditions in the industry.[28] RAND concluded that the prospects for substantive technological advancements were not bright and that for a variety of uses, CFCs would remain the only feasible alternative. EPA's failure to regulate ozone-depleting chemicals after Reagan's election in 1980 prompted industry to suspend the development of alternatives. Not until the resurgence of interest in the ozone depletion issue later in the decade did firms provide substantial resources to finding alternatives.

Despite the quiescence of federal regulators, a small group of academics, environmental activists, and state agencies began advocating prevention of 'pollution at its source, whether through changes in production or by reducting reliance on environmentally harmful materials.'[29] This novel attitude began to take hold in the industrial community. Without looking for substitutes for ozone-depleting compounds in particular, companies began developing alternatives for processes that resulted in toxic solvent wastes. Novel methods of cleaning, degreasing, and drying metals, plastics, and electronic parts and assemblies began to appear on manufacturing shop floors. By the end of the 1980s, dozens of mostly small companies began supplying products that could eliminate the use of ozone-depleting compounds in a variety of industrial operations.[30]

While smaller companies were busy identifying new products that would eliminate the use of these chemicals, individual manufacturers were experimenting with their production processes, and chemical vendors began banding together to promote finding alternatives to CFCs.[31] Manufacturers evaluated the need for cleaning in some electronics applications, and some of the bigger chemical companies pushed forward on the development of chemicals that had low ozone depletion potential for use with existing technologies.[32]

Other applications, such as foams and refrigerants, have followed different paths. Manufacturers and users of foam food service packaging responded to public pressure by switching to non-CFC-based products, but foam products such as insulation continue to rely on CFCs for their thermal value. Manufacturers and servicers of home and commercial refrigerators and air conditioners have directed their initial efforts at recovering and recycling coolant, although several vehicle manufacturers expect to produce non-CFC air conditioners within a few years. Manufacturers of home and commercial refrigerators and air conditioners continue to struggle with energy efficiency requirements and do not expect to have alternative products available until the mid-1990s.

Technical Trade-Offs

Significant constraints continue to limit the ability to minimize use and emissions of CFCs and encourage alternative products and manufacturing processes. Penalties in the form of higher costs of production, loss of energy efficiency, higher toxicity, and greater occupational health and/or environmental problems are not fully addressed. Some alternatives are still ozone depleters, albeit at a reduced level. At best, some trade-offs are likely to be made between eliminating the global health and environmental effects of ozone-depleting compounds and accepting economic dislocations and environmental and occupational health risks.

Regulatory constraints, such as occupational health standards and restrictions on air pollutants, may limit the use of some alternatives. Others will pose significant risks to workers and surrounding communities, raising questions for policymakers as to what types of risks should be tolerated and who should bear the burden of the risk. In some jurisdictions different regulatory entities have different goals. Thus, air pollution agencies, struggling to minimize smog in urban areas, exempt several ozone-depleting compounds from emission restrictions and encourage their industrial use. Without a holistic approach,[33] public health risks may increase for some communities as overall risks from ozone depletion decline.

In addition to public health concerns, the search for alternatives challenges public policy goals of improving energy efficiency and promoting market competition. All currently available substitutes for CFCs in refrigeration and insulation systems carry an energy efficiency penalty. Research on new technologies may result in efficiency improvements, but are likely to come at a significant economic cost. An unfortunate result of the restrictions on CFC use in manufacturing operations may be a reduction in competition. Small organizations generally do not have the resources to identify and test alternatives, and lack the capital necessary to switch to alternative cleaning systems. Some of these require large investments in equipment, but cost substantially less than CFC-based systems to operate. Larger organizations that can afford the initial investment may become the low-cost producers, driving out smaller competitors who cannot afford the new equipment.

There are also noneconomic costs associated with alternative technologies. Changing specifications for military equipment, civilian aerospace suppliers, and biomedical products may increase the risks to ultimate users. New cleaning methods may alter failure rates and create reliability problems during use by military personnel, airline passengers, and patients. Issues, such as who must bear the burden of risk and at what cost, are only partially addressed in the drive to establish new manufacturing processes.

Policy Responses

Although the international community, including the United States, can easily be criticized for a certain amount of foot-dragging on the issue, in general the U.S. government took Molina and Rowland's thesis seriously. The U.S. policy response to the issue was to split the control of CFCs into two phases—aerosol and nonaerosol uses. Initial action focused on eliminating aerosol uses of CFCs, since this would immediately reduce emissions, and alternatives seemed readily available. However, regulating aerosols required the cooperation of at least three federal agencies: EPA controlled air quality, the Consumer Product Safety Commission (CPSC) oversaw aerosol consumer products, and the Food and Drug Administration regulated the use of aerosols for delivery of drugs, foods, and cosmetics. The Interagency Regulatory Liaison Group for CFCs was established as a mechanism for agreeing on a single rule.

The agencies jointly issued a rule that prohibited the use of CFC propellants in nonessential applications and identified several alternatives, including hydrocarbon propellants and pump sprays.[34] By the 1978 effective date of the rule, EPA estimated that CFC propellant use in the United States was less than 5 per cent of the pre-ban level. World reaction to the U.S. action was limited. Although Canada and several Scandinavian countries limited aerosol use, most did not see the need for immediate controls. Norway, Finland, and Sweden proposed a global ban on all aerosols, but did not receive much of a response.

The United States continued to work on a regulatory approach for nonaerosol uses. In October 1980 EPA issued a notice that it was considering regulating nonaerosol uses of CFCs.[35] EPA indicated that it was interested in applying market incentives to the control of CFCs, since few alternatives could be identified, and invited comments on the alternatives, the potential costs and benefits, administrative and compliance issues, and the need for regulation. The Agency got an unexpectedly large response: DuPont's customers submitted more than 2,500 comments, which were overwhelming negative about the need for action and the market incentive approach. DuPont itself submitted a stack of documents, approximately 3 feet high, which included nearly every journal article on CFCs and ozone depletion published through 1980. Only a handful of comments, primarily from environmental groups and schoolchildren, supported strong regulatory action.

The notice generated little media coverage, even though it proposed regulating uses that were synonymous with the quality of life enjoyed by industrialized countries. Most likely EPA's notice seemed insignificant, coming in the midst of the 1980 presidential election and running counter to the philosophy of the front-running Reagan campaign.

With Reagan's election, the ozone depletion issue quieted down. Although EPA's officials thought a market-based approach would be consistent with the new administration's philosophy, Reagan's appointees shelved a draft regulation and sided with industry in its belief that there was no need for immediate action, that it was too costly to control CFCs especially with economic incentives, and that resolution of the issue required global co-operation.[36] Except for continuing to monitor scientific developments, EPA stopped working on ozone depletion for the first half of the decade.[37] Only a few environmental organizations, particularly the Natural Resources Defense Council and Friends of the Earth, kept the ozone depletion issue from being completely ignored.[38]

Much of the policy focus shifted at this time to the international arena. During the mid-1970s, the United Nations Environment Programme (UNEP) had coordinated international action on CFCs and had produced a plan for encouraging further research on atmospheric processes and ozone depletion through existing international organizations. UNEP also established a committee to study policy issues that included governments and selected non-governmental organizations. The ozone depletion theory remained intact, and the government members of the committee began seeking a global agreement for the protection of the ozone layer.[39]

Four years later, participants at the Vienna Convention agreed to cooperate on research, policy development, and information exchange, establishing a precedent for international action on a problem with future consequences. Although the European Economic Community (EEC) and 22 countries signed the Convention, few ratified the treaty to impose mandatory action. UNEP reconvened the Vienna group of legal and technical experts to begin the process of drafting an international treaty controlling CFCs.

Differences in national approaches to the significance of the issue, regulatory measures, and equity considerations were raised and addressed in a series of meetings prior to the Montreal Conference scheduled for September 1987. By this time, scientific developments combined with political changes within the Reagan administration and EPA prompted an aggressive U.S. approach to the issue.[40] During one of these meetings the United States proposed to phase out the chemicals, while Japan and Europe, with smaller and more vulnerable producers, would only discuss a freeze on current production levels. Japan refused to consider any cuts in CFC-113, used primarily as a solvent by its electronic industry, and along with the EEC and the Soviet Union, opposed eliminating the use of ozone-depleting chemicals in fire extinguishers.

As more evidence demonstrating depletion became available, participants united in support of the need for action. Unresolved were issues involving the degree of control (ranging from a freeze at current levels to total elimination), the types of ozone depleting chemicals targeted, and differences in access to production rights between industrial and developing countries. This was a difficult issue for nonindustrialized nations because CFCs have become synonymous with the quality of life available in the developed nations of the world. Developing countries perceived the world concern about ozone depletion as a bias against efforts to improve their standard of living.

India and China, in particular, made a concerted effort to develop the capacity to produce CFCs and the products, such as refrigerators, that rely on them. They wanted assurance that if they went along with worldwide efforts to eliminate CFCs, they would receive assistance in developing alternative industries. However, industries in the developed countries feared that they would be unable to recoup the large sum spent on developing new production methods for CFC replacements and products that use those replacements. Moreover, if countries such as India and China were to develop their own industries, the market for alternative products would be smaller.

Hastily arranged technical meetings prior to the September meeting resolved most of the issues. Several questions almost scuttled the agreement,[41] but on September 15, 1988, 23 countries signed the Montreal Protocol on Substances that Deplete the Ozone Layer. Approximately 60 additional countries have signed and at least 50 have ratified the Treaty, revising their national laws and implementing the required controls.

The Protocol became effective in January 1989 and required a freeze in production and consumption equal to 1986 levels, a further 20 per cent reduction by July 1994, and an ultimate 50 per cent reduction. Developing countries were allowed a certain amount of growth, if warranted by a need to improve their standard of living. The Protocol also established a mechanism for further action to restrict production.

Negotiations of the Protocol were exceptionally delicate. Nongovernmental participants, particularly the environmentalist National Resources Defense Council and industry's Alliance for a Responsible CFC Policy, played as important a role in defining its terms as the designated government representatives. Although the environmental community achieved its goal of establishing an international mechanism for controlling CFC use, industry succeeded in avoiding a total phaseout and the inclusion of less-significant ozone-depleting chemicals (HCFCs and methyl chloroform). Given the available science at the time, the treaty reflected the distance the world community was likely to go in the absence of intense pressure to protect the world from global catastrophe.

Following U.S. ratification of the Protocol,[42] Congress imposed a tax on ozone-depleting chemicals,[43] and EPA issued regulations freezing CFC production.[44] Producers and importers had to have a permit, obtained either through an initial distribution by EPA or bought on the open market. Over time, the quantity of CFCs that could be produced under each permit would be reduced to meet the Protocol requirements.

About the same time, DuPont announced that its CFC production would cease by 1995. Finally conceding that the science was strong enough to support elimination of CFCs, this announcement sparked a rush to promote alternatives. In addition, concerns that the Montreal Protocol and federal actions were not strong enough to protect the ozone layer prompted cities and states in the United States and Canada to pass laws restricting a variety of uses of ozone-depleting chemicals.[45] Some of the legislative actions banned the use of CFC-based foam food packaging; other cities and states focused on preventing emissions of CFC refrigerants from vehicle air conditioners.

One of the most comprehensive laws originated in the City of Irvine, California. In August 1989 Irvine restricted the use of CFCs and other ozone-depleting compounds in manufacturing and cleaning activities, banned product and food packaging made with CFCs, and required recovery and recycling of refrigerants.[46] Limited exemptions were allowed if substitutes were infeasible. Although industry opposed the ordinance, it quickly found ways to reduce use and emissions. To some extent, Irvine's ordinance demonstrated that in some applications, industry could move faster than previously thought possible, placing greater pressure at the national level for faster action.

By 1990 evidence continued to accumulate that ozone depletion was increasing at an alarming rate, particularly over the South Pole, and that many ozone-depleting chemicals also contributed to global warming. Despite conflicts between the industrialized and developing countries, a meeting of the signatories to the Montreal Protocol in June 1990 led to an agreement to eliminate CFCs and other major ozone-depleting chemicals by 2000 and others by 2005.[47] Conflict was reduced when the participants voted to establish an international fund for developing countries' use in switching to compounds that would not deplete the ozone layer.[48]

Later that year the U.S. Congress revised the Clean Air Act for the first time since 1977.[49] Debates on revisions to the statute during the 1980s focused primarily on ambient air quality standards, regulation of electric power utilities, acid rain protection, and motor vehicle emission controls. Conflicts over stratospheric ozone protection language focused on the degree to which the United States should surpass international action, the need for control of ozone-depleting chemicals other than CFCs, and whether federal authority should preempt state and local actions on ozone depletion. General agreement on the scientific issues prompted complicated debates about relative cost-effectiveness, regulations requiring new technology, and the need for sufficient regulatory certainty to justify multibillion-dollar investments in new chemical production plants.

In the Clean Air Act Amendments of 1990, Congress adopted a national policy timetable roughly equivalent to that of the international agreement and established a long-term phaseout program for HCFCs (less ozone-depleting versions of CFCs). At the same time, Congress distrusted EPA's ability to act aggressively and spelled out detailed actions that the Agency must take to implement the statute's intent. Congress also allowed local jurisdictions to continue more stringent controls on the use (but not production) of ozone-depleting chemicals.

Further restrictions are likely to occur. At the Protocol's follow-up meeting, participants decided to consider a faster phaseout. The 1991 announcement by EPA Administrator Reilly, that ozone depletion was worse than expected, included the statement that the United States would seek more stringent international controls. At this point, the discussions clearly have moved from assessing the need for action to the speed with which the international community can eliminate the use of ozone-depleting chemicals.

Implications

The concern about potential damage to the earth's protective ozone layer began more than 20 years ago. In some aspects, it is remarkable that global consensus has been achieved on an environmental problem when the effects are not experienced by the current generation, but by their grandchildren. This case involves the interplay of science and technology development, the formation of consensus, and the subsequent role of local authorities in problems with global effects. Ultimately it has important implications for other global environmental problems.

In this example, the varying views of policymakers, scientists, environmentalists, and industry about the importance of scientific 'certainty' reflect the differences in their perception about the credibility of scientific evidence and the nature of risk. For instance, in 1974 DuPont representatives testified to Congress that if 'credible scientific data developed in this experimental program show that any chlorofluorocarbon cannot be used without a threat to health, DuPont will stop production of these compounds.'[50] The manufacturers assured the public that they would act when the model was 'proven,' but continued to insist over the next 15 years that proof did not exist.

Confronted by possible severe negative consequences, and lacking plausible alternative theories to explain ozone depletion, policymakers were faced with acting on the basis of incomplete information and extrapolations from current knowledge. Scientists viewed the development of theories as part of a continuing process toward the expansion of knowledge, while policymakers demanded conclusive evidence as a basis for decisions. For example, during early congressional hearings on ozone depletion, Senator Dale Bumpers asked a scientist for a definitive answer to the need for regulating CFCs. 'I am not trying to put you in a box of any kind,' said Senator Bumpers, 'Just give me a yes or no answer.'[51] Although reluctant to state that the science provided definitive support for banning CFCs, the scientist expressed his personal view that some regulatory action was justified. The absence of certainty leaves policymakers open to charges that they acted prematurely or, conversely, failed to act prudently. While the conduct of good science requires a healthy dose of skepticism and a willingness to challenge proposed theories, political actors are more likely to fit equivocal evidence into their strongly held beliefs.[52]

During the 1970s the uncertainties inherent in the ozone depletion theory—Molina and Rowland recognized that empirical evidence would not be available for years—meant that a decision to control ozone-depleting chemicals would have to be made without definitive evidence of harm. If the theory proved true and action was delayed until substantial proof became available, an unknown amount of harm would be irreversible. Nevertheless, it was difficult for U.S. policymakers to justify action, since if the theory could not be substantiated, they feared they might eliminate industrial practices that were critical to the economy and the American standard of living.

Manufacturers and users of ozone-depleting chemicals pressured policymakers to consider CFCs 'innocent until proven guilty,' highlighting the potential for substantial costs to their economic interests in exchange for very uncertain benefits. Countervailing pressures were also placed on policy-makers. The environmental community portrayed CFC propellants in hair care products and spray paints as a global threat to human health that was an unnecessary convenience, generating unaffordable risks.

Both policymakers and laypeople find it difficult to address risks of future harm, placing significant value on present-day benefits.[53] Unwilling to face the issue of balancing future risks and present-day costs, policymakers initially chose to act where costs could be minimized by substitute technologies. Thus, aerosol uses of CFCs were regulated quickly, but control of nonaerosol uses languished because of a lack of substitutes. When empirical evidence of harm became available, the lack of technologies posed less of a barrier to action at both the national and international levels.

The reluctance of policymakers to act on the CFC issue suggests that policymakers will hesitate on the issue of global warming as well. Here the controversy is similar, but the stakes are even higher. Predicted changes in global temperatures, due to the use of fossil fuels and the destruction of forests, even more than ozone depletion, appears to be linked inextricably with modern industrialization. Responding to the problem of global warming will require more than substitute chemicals. Industrialized nations dependent on fossil fuels have already cleared large tracts of land, yet they are seeking to limit similar activities in developing countries. Altering the effects of global warming may cost billions; reversing the expected trend will require a radical change in the nature of industrialization.

Scientists may develop sophisticated techniques to predict the global consequences of human activities, but policymakers will continue to struggle with balancing national development, private economic interests, the global ecosystem, and human health. Lessons learned in the ozone depletion case suggest that, despite early warnings, global environmental issues will remain difficult to address quickly.

Notes

1. Lydia Dotto and Harold Schiff, *The Ozone War* (New York: Doubleday, 1978), p. 146.
2. Although the billion-dollar price tag was the main impetus behind cancellation there was some concern over ozone effects. See Lydia Dotto and Harold Schiff, *The Ozone War*, pp. 63–4.
3. Mario J. Molina and F. S. Rowland, 'Stratospheric Sink for Chlorofluoromethanes Chlorine Atom-Catalyzed Destruction of Ozone,' *Nature* 249 (1974), pp. 810–12.

4. Walter Sullivan, 'Tests Show Aerosol Gases May Pose Threat To Earth,' *The New York Times* (September 26, 1974), p. 1.
5. Canada, Sweden, Denmark, and Norway joined with the United States on controlling aerosol uses.
6. Industry's arguments were based on regulatory bans of particular products. See discussion in U.S. Environmental Protection Agency, 'Ozone-Depleting Chlorofluorocarbons, Proposed Production Restrictions,' *Federal Register* 45 (1980), pp. 66726–34. In contrast, RAND researchers suggested that controlling production of CFCs would result in less economic dislocation and few other penalties as uses would be allocated more appropriately. See Adele R. Palmer and Timothy H. Quinn, *Economic Impact Assessment of a Chlorofluorocarbon Production Cap* (Santa Monica, CA: The RAND Corp., 1981).
7. J. E. Lovelock, R. J. Maggs, and R. J. Wade, 'Halogenated Hydrocarbons In and Over the Atlantic,' *Nature* 241 (1973), pp. 194–6.
8. For example, see *Geophysical Research Letters* 13 (1986).
9. Council on Environmental Quality and the Federal Council for Science and Technology, 'Fluorocarbons and the Environment,' Report of the Federal Task Force on Inadvertent Modification of the Stratosphere (IMOS) (June 1975), p. 3.
10. Committee on Impacts of Stratospheric Change, *Halocarbons: Effects on Stratospheric Ozone* (Washington, DC: National Academy of Sciences, 1976); and Committee on Impacts of Stratospheric Change, *Halocarbons: Environmental Effects of Chlorofluoromethane Release* (Washington, DC: National Academy of Sciences, 1976).
11. S. Roan, *Ozone Crisis: The 15-Year Evolution of a Sudden Global Emergency* (New York: John Wiley, 1989), p. 45.
12. Ibid., p. 36.
13. Dotto and Schiff (1978), p. 182.
14. DuPont's domination of the CFC market is reflected in the use of its trade name, Freon®, as a synonym for CFCs in general.
15. Kaiser Aluminum & Chemical Company, *At Issue: Fluorocarbons* (Oakland, CA: 1975).
16. J. K. Hammitt et al., *Product Uses and Market Trends for Potential Ozone-Depleting Substances: 1985–2000* (Santa Monica, CA: RAND Corp., 1986).
17. J. C. Farman, B. G. Gardiner, and J. D. Shanklin, 'Large Losses of Total Ozone in Antarctica Reveal Seasonal ClO_x/NO_x, Interaction,' *Nature* 315 (1985), pp. 207–10. Although the satellite data had been available for years, NASA scientists had not detected the ozone hole because the measured values were below the range predicted by models, and the values had been discarded by the computer program. Farman et al. spent 2 years checking the data because it was so far out of the range of expected values and were very concerned about accusations of sloppy work.

18. Mario Molina, Tai-Ly Tso, Luisa T. Molina, and Frank C-Y. Wang, 'Antarctic Stratospheric Chemistry of Chlorine Nitrate, Hydrogen Chloride, and Iee: Release of Active Chlorine,' *Science* 238 (November 27, 1987), pp. 1253–57; and Margaret A. Tolbert, Michel J. Rossi, Ripudaman Malhotra, and David M. Golden, *Science* 238 (November 27, 1987), pp. 1258–60.
19. J. S. Barrett et al., 'Formation of the Antarctic Ozone Hole by the CIO Dimer Mechanism,' *Nature* 336 (1988), pp. 455–8; and Robert T. Watson, 'Present State of Knowledge of the Ozone Layer,' in Robin Russell Jones and Tom Wigley, Eds., *Ozone Depletion: Health and Environmental Consequences* (Chichester, England: John Wiley, 1988), pp. 43–58.
20. Robert T. Watson and the Ozone Trend Panel, NASA, *Present State of Knowledge of the Upper Atmosphere 1988: An Assessment Report* (June 1988).
21. 'DuPont to Halt Chemicals that Peril Ozone,' *The New York Times* (March 25, 1988), p. 1.
22. At the September 1987 meeting in Montreal, scientists had not observed any depletion over the United States. By the June 1990 London meeting, 1.5% depletion over the United States had been measured. In April 1991 Administrator Reilly announced that 4.5% depletion had been observed over the United States and that near-term depletion of 10% to 12% could be expected. See USEPA, Office of Atmospheric and Indoor Air Programs, OAR, 'Stratospheric Ozone Protection Update: Disturbing New Data' (April 2, 1991).
23. IMOS (1975), p. 80.
24. Ibid., pp. 83–8. U.S. figures include HCFC-22, but do not include production of 1,1,1 trichloroethane or carbon tetrachloride. Worldwide figures include CFC-11 and CFC-12 only.
25. Katherine Wolf, *Regulating Chlorofluorocarbon Emissions: Effects on Chemical Production* (Santa Monica, CA: RAND Corp., 1980), pp. 11–15.
26. William E. Mooz, Katherine Wolf, and Frank Camm, *Potential Constraints on Cumulative Global Production of Chlorofluorocarbons* (Santa Monica, CA: RAND Corp., 1986), pp. 9–12.
27. CFC-113, a common ozone-depleting solvent, is typically listed in reference books as being low in toxicity and having a higher permissible exposure limit than most chlorinated solvents. However, deaths from cardiac arrhythmia and asphyxiatioa have occurred. See National Institute for Occupation Safety and Health, *NIOSH Alert: Request for Assistance in Preventing Death from Excessive Exposure to Chlorofluorocarbon 113 (CFC-113)* (Cincinnati, OH: USDHHS, PHS, CDC, 1989), DHHS Pub. No. (NIOSH) 89–109.
28. Adele R. Palmer et al., *Economic Implications of Regulating Chlorofluorocarbon Emissions from Nonaerosol Applications* (Santa Monica, CA: RAND Corp., 1980).
29. U.S. Environmental Protection Agency, 'Pollution Prevention Strategy,' *Federal Register* 56 (February 26, 1991), pp. 7849–64.
30. Some of these companies are listed in *CFC Alternatives*, available from the City of Irvine, P.O. Box 19575, Irvine, CA 92713.

31. Known as the Industry Cooperative for Ozone Layer Protection (ICOLP), the group started out with about a dozen of the largest users in the world, primarily in the electronics industries. ICOLP established several research and education programs plus OZONET, an electronic database of alternatives to ozone-depleting chemicals.
32. DuPont, Allied-Signal, ICI, and Dow, the major suppliers of ozone-depleting solvents, focused most of their efforts on alternative solvents that still resulted in generating hazardous waste. They sought to reassure customers that production could continue without major changes by using a 'drop-in' replacement chemical for their ODCs. Other, generally smaller, companies took the lead on less hazardous chemicals.
33. Cross-media, pollution prevention programs are slowly being developed. However, they have not permeated regulatory programs and encouraged interagency coordination. See USEPA (1991) for a discussion of EPA's proposed pollution prevention approach.
34. U.S. Department of Health, Education, and Welfare, Food and Drug Administration, 'Certain Fluorocarbons (Chlorofluorocarbons) in Food, Food Additive, Drug, Animal Food, Animal Drug, Cosmetic and Medical Device Products as Propellants in Self-Pressurized Containers: Prohibition on Use'; U.S. Environmental Protection Agency, 'Fully Halogenated Chlorofluoroalkanes'; U.S. Consumer Products Safety Commission, 'Fully Halogenated Chlorofluoroalkanes as Propellants in Aerosol Consumer Products,' *Federal Register* 43 (March 17, 1978), pp. 11301–26.
35. USEPA (1980).
36. See DuPont Co., 'Comments on the Advanced Notice of Proposed Rulemaking' (January 5, 1981) for a summary of industry's position. The opposition of CFC manufacturers and users to market-based regulatory schemes surprised Agency officials since they assumed that industry would prefer the least-cost regulatory option. See Michael Shapiro and Ellen Warhit, 'Marketable Permits: The Case of Chlorofluorocarbons,' *Natural Resources Journal* 23 (1983), pp. 576–91.
37. See U.S. Environmental Protection Agency, 'Report to Congress on the Progress of Regulation to Protect Stratospheric Ozone' (April 1983).
38. In 1984 NRDC sued EPA to force the Agency to take action protecting the ozone layer. EPA's response was to argue that unilateral action would not make a difference. When evidence of depletion became available several years later, EPA's commitment to action changed and the suit was settled. See U.S. Environmental Protection Agency, 'Stratospheric Ozone Protection Plan,' *Federal Register* 51 (1985), pp. 1257–9; and Paul Brodeur, 'Annals of Chemistry: In the Face of Doubt,' *The New Yorker* (June 9, 1986), p. 85.
39. Peter Usher, 'The Montreal Protocol on Substances that Deplete the Ozone Layer: Its Development and Likely Impact,' in Robin Russell Jones and Tom Wigley, eds., *Ozone Depletion: Health and Environmental Consequences* (Chichester,

England: John Wiley, 1989). The discussion that follows is taken primarily from this source.

40. When Lee Thomas took over as EPA Administrator, he made ozone protection a principle focus of the Agency. In contrast, other members of the Reagan administration downplayed the issue, with the Secretary of the Interior going so far as to suggest that the appropriate policy response was to adopt personal protection devices—sunscreen, hats, and sunglasses. EPA combined with the State Department to unite around a policy of eliminating CFCs.
41. Usher (1989).
42. Ratification occurred on April 21, 1988.
43. PL 101–239, 1989. See Sections 7506 et seq.
44. U.S. Environmental Protection Agency, 'Stratospheric Ozone Protection,' *Federal Register* 53 (1988), p. 30598.
45. In the United States at least 30 cities, regional governments, and states have passed restrictions, and there are many more under consideration.
46. City of Irvine, Code of Ordinances, No. 89–21, Title IV.Q-101 et seq.
47. United Nations Environment Programme, London Agreement (1990).
48. See U.S. Congress, House of Representatives, Committee on Science, Space, and Technology, Subcommittee on Natural Resources, Agricultural Research and Environment and Subcommittee on International Scientific Cooperation, *CFC Reduction—Technology Transfer to the Developing World* (Washington, DC: Government Printing Office, 1990).
49. Clean Air Act Amendments, PL 101–549, 1990.
50. Cited in Dotto and Schiff (1978), p. 180.
51. Cited in Roan (1989), p. 120.
52. Simon, H. A., 'Human Nature in Politics: The Dialogue of Psychology with Political Science,' *The American Political Science Review* 79 (1985), pp. 293–304.
53. For more detailed discussion, see William Rowe, *An Anatomy of Risk* (New York: John Wiley, 1977); Paul Slovic, Baruch Fischhoff, and Sarah Lichtenstein, 'Rating the Risks,' *Environment* 21 (April 1979), pp. 14–39; Roger E. Kasperson, 'Acceptability of Human Risk,' *Environmental Health Perspectives* 52 (1983), pp. 15–20; G. T. Gardner and L. C. Gould, 'Public Perception of the Risks and Benefits of Technology,' *Risk Analysis* 9 (1989), pp. 225–42.

Cross-National Differences in Policy Implementation*

SHEILA JASANOFF†

Like a genie emerging from a bottle, the framework of an international agreement on global warming is beginning to take shape, although its exact contours remain as yet ill defined. Policymakers and the scientists who advise them speak with surprising unanimity of an initial decision to stabilize greenhouse gas emissions, followed by further agreements to cut back to levels 20% to 30% below current discharges. Many view the 1992 United Nations conference as a reasonable target date for a draft agreement. For most global warming strategists, the absorbing concern of the moment is how to craft an agreement that will command wide international support and bring the largest possible number of industrializing as well as industrialized nations to the bargaining table.

Yet in a policy domain fraught with long-term uncertainties, a framework agreement to reduce emissions will mark little more than the first step on the policy high road. Once the broad outlines of such an agreement are in place, environmental regulators worldwide will have to turn their attention to the complex problems of implementation. In this more down-to-earth phase of policy-making, significant cross-national differences may resurface, for policy implementation, as we know from other areas of environmental decision making, is a culturally conditioned exercise. Even in Western democracies with very similar environmental objectives and governmental traditions, regulatory authorities have approached the tasks of implementation with different presumptions, procedures, and philosophies. These national policy styles (Vogel 1986) have the potential to drive wedges into an apparent international consensus long after a framework for emission reductions is formally in place.

What do we know at present about the factors that differentiate national approaches to policy implementation? And what impact will these differences have on the attempts of nation states to agree on specific measures for controlling global warming? For preliminary answers to these questions, I draw in this article on prior research comparing the regulation of chemical hazards in Europe and the United States.

Patterns of Convergence and Divergence

Comparative policy studies during the 1980s disclosed remarkable disparities in the way that industrialized countries approach the regulation of toxic substances in the environment (Gillespie, Eva, and Johnston 1979; Badaracco 1985; Brickman, Jasanoff, and Ilgen 1985; Jasanoff 1986).[1] Although chemical control strategies in Europe and North America were driven by similar political, scientific and economic concerns, styles of decision making diverged from one country to another, leading at times to substantial differences in policy approach. One area where systematic divergences and convergences were clearly observable was in the design of policies for regulating chemical carcinogens. As illustrated in Table 4.1, the United States, West Germany, and Britain differed strikingly in their processes of decision making with respect to these substances. Table 1 summarizes the differences under four headings: (a) policy formulation, (b) public participation, (c) enforcement, and (d) oversight.

Policy Formulation

Policy-making for carcinogens diverged along four principal dimensions in the countries compared in Table 4.1: (a) the selection of regulatory targets, (b) the basis for regulation, (c) the level of analysis, and (d) the choice of regulatory instruments. In the United States, the range of regulatory targets was initially the broadest, encompassing thousands of chemicals already in the marketplace as well as hundreds of new chemicals about to enter the stream of commerce. The rationale for regulatory action was expressed in highly formalized and quantitative terms through methods such as cost-benefit analysis and risk assessment. The level of analysis tended to be generic; that is, regulators sought a principled basis for evaluating classes of chemicals instead of single substances. Finally, regulatory instruments were selected with an eye to ease of legal enforcement. Preference was given to numerical safety standards that could be uniformly applied across industries and geographical regions.

Britain, in spite of close historical and cultural ties with the United States, displayed a diametrically different approach to policy formulation.

Table 4.1. *Controlling Chemicals: National Policies*

	Policy Formulation						*Oversight*	
	Targets	*Instruments*	*Basis*	*Approach*	*Participation*	*Enforcement*	*Legislative*	*Judicial*
United States	'old' plus 'new'	formal (regulations, numerical standards)	cost-benefit analysis, risk assessment	generic	unrestricted (pluralistic) open adversarial	legal action	continuous aggressive programmatic hearings	yes
Federal Republic of Germany	new (old only when special new information)	formal (regulations, numerical standards)	expert advice	case-by-case	corporatist closed (to others) negotiating	legal action (but avoided)	intermittent parliamentary questions	no
United Kingdom	new (old only when special new information)	informal (voluntary)	expert advice	case-by-case	elitist *or* corporatist closed (to noninvitees) negotiating	negotiation	intermittent parliamentary questions	no

British health and safety legislation focused primarily on new chemical hazards, and regulatory controls developed case by case, through negotiation and compromise rather than through formal scientific or economic analysis. Unlike U.S. regulatory agencies, British authorities openly tolerated plant-by-plant differences in safety standards within the same industry. Tellingly, Britain in the late 1970s regulated pesticides under a voluntary scheme agreed to by industry and government rather than by formal legislation; subsequently, statutory controls were adopted in compliance with European Community requirements.

The German style of policy formulation fell between the American and British extremes. Germany, like other European countries, focused mainly on new chemicals and favored a case-by-case, negotiated approach to risk management. Neither the scientific nor the economic basis for standard setting was made as explicit as in the United States. Safety standards, however, were expressed in numerical terms to facilitate monitoring and legal enforcement.

Participation

Again, Britain and the United States illustrated opposite polarities in their styles of providing public access to regulatory decision making. Avenues of participation were least restricted in the United States. Not only did interested parties have opportunities to express their views to government agencies, but the agencies were obliged by law to respond meaningfully to public comment. U.S. law also sought to ensure that the public would have broad access to information pertaining to regulatory decisions, excepting chiefly confidential commercial information and information essential to the effective workings of government. The politics of participation in the United States conformed to the classic pluralist model, with opposing interests confronting each other in adversarial settings such as regulatory hearings and courtrooms. In this process, even small and scattered interests were able to make themselves heard and to influence policy at some level.

Britain's participatory traditions, by contrast, provided access only to well-established political interests and favored negotiation over confrontation. British decision makers relied heavily on a loosely defined elite (informally dubbed 'the great and the good'), which consisted of individuals exceptionally well qualified by social status or technical and professional experience to act in the public interest. Frequently invited to serve on Royal Commissions or other expert committees, this trusted advisory community articulated the intellectual foundation for many controversial regulatory policies.[2]

Beyond this privileged circle, information pertaining to policy was tightly controlled. The British Official Secrets Act, which provides criminal penalties for unauthorized disclosure, represented a philosophy of government intrinsically opposed to the principles of openness embodied in America's freedom of information legislation.

In Germany, participation followed the neocorporatist model, which bore numerous points of resemblance to Britain's elitist approach. Powerful political interests, such as industry, labor, and major environmental groups, were represented by peak organizations at the apex of a decision-making pyramid. Interests not important enough to be embraced within the corporatist hierarchy were excluded from participation except through the chancy channels of electoral politics. As in Britain, however, procedures within the inner circles of decision making were largely informal, and policy generally emerged from a concurrent negotiation of technical as well as political differences.

Enforcement

Similar general patterns characterized the enforcement strategies of the three nations. Having defined safety obligations by means of legal standards, U.S. authorities viewed lawsuits as the appropriate vehicle for enforcement. German authorities, too, considered standards to be the most effective mechanism for establishing binding rules of conduct. Prosecution of violators, however, was rare in Germany, not only because industry generally chose to comply with applicable legal norms, but because lawsuits were perceived as an impermissible breakdown of that country's highly consensual approach to policy implementation. British authorities likewise viewed litigation as an evil to be avoided wherever possible. Prosecutions were launched only where other means of persuasion, such as 'improvement notices,' had failed and where the government could be absolutely confident of winning a conviction.

Oversight

A final major difference among the three countries had to do with oversight of regulatory agencies. In the United States, agencies were subjected to continuous, public, and systematic supervision by a critical and well-staffed Congress. Substantial agency resources were committed to explaining, and often defending, entire regulatory programs against legislative branch accusations of inefficiency or incompetence. Parliamentary oversight in Germany and Britain by contrast was sporadic, ad hoc, and issue-specific rather than programmatic. Parliamentary questions, not full-blown oversight hearings, provided the primary procedural channel for holding ministers accountable. In attempting to call executive officials to account, European legislators were hampered by inadequate staff support and the dearth of independent technical resources such as those provided by the Congressional Office of Technical Assistance in the United States.

U.S. agencies, moreover, were answerable to the judiciary in a manner totally unknown in Europe. Well into the 1980s, it was virtually impossible for U.S. chemical regulations to be implemented without first undergoing searching judicial review. Corresponding administrative decisions in both European countries were insulated against challenge either by political tradition or by law. For example, the mere promulgation of an environmental standard could not give rise to a citizen suit in Germany; litigation had to be founded on a direct infringement of an individual's protected rights. Industry-initiated lawsuits were likewise essentially unknown. Companies that had gained most of what they wanted through negotiation with government officials saw no need for subsequent recourse to the law. As a practical matter, therefore, judicial oversight of chemical policies was essentially nonexistent in both Germany and Britain.

The Paradox of Risk Assessment

The pattern of convergences and divergences described above accounted for what I shall call here the paradox of risk assessment. As used in the policy literature, the term *risk assessment* refers to the objective, scientific component of evaluating technological risks (National Research Council 1983). Such assessments serve as one major input to the process of *risk management*, in which technical considerations are combined with economic and political judgments to produce policy.

Looking cross-nationally, one would expect a priori to find considerable similarities in the risk assessments produced by different countries. In Western industrial nations, assessments generally are based on the same body of technical information and the analytic process is designed to be scientific and exact, hence presumably free of cultural predispositions. Correspondingly, one would expect to see greater disparities in the results of risk management, reflecting national differences in the social and political dimensions of decision making. With respect to toxic chemicals, however, comparative research uncovered interesting divergences in the assessment of risk, whereas management decisions tended to converge, at least over time.

Risk assessors in U.S. regulatory agencies, for example, generally were more willing to characterize substances as possible human carcinogens than were their counterparts in Britain or Germany. Thus pesticides such as DDT and aldrin/dieldrin (Gillespie, Eva, and Johnston 1979) were found to be carcinogenic only in the United States. Formaldehyde, which several U.S. agencies regarded as a potential human carcinogen, was considered to be only an animal carcinogen in Germany and was deemed not to present a risk to humans in Britain (Jasanoff 1986). Yet all three countries banned DDT and strictly regulated the use of aldrin/dieldrin and formaldehyde. More generally, most substances regarded as hazardous in one country eventually came under regulatory control in others. Looking across the field of potential carcinogens, it was difficult to say that any of the three countries adopted a significantly laxer or more stringent control regime than did the others (Brickman, Jasanoff, and Ilgen 1985).

Why Assessments Differ

Explanations for these paradoxical findings have begun to emerge from recent work in the social and political studies of science, particularly in the sociology of scientific knowledge. Scientific claims, we have learned, rest on a foundation of negotiated understandings amongs scientists as to how nature should be observed and how physical observations should be interpreted (Kuhn 1970; Collins 1985; Latour and Woolgar 1979). Science, in this sense, is a product of social activity among scientists; we can say that science is socially constructed (Johnson and Covello 1987).

The constructs of science appear especially unstable when science is used as a basis for policy (Nelkin 1984). The professional and disciplinary factors that generally promote consensus in science are largely missing in the policy context (Collingridge and Reeve 1986). Political contention tends to highlight areas of ambiguity or uncertainty in the evidence, leading to disagreements among experts. Resolution of these controversies ultimately depends on contextual factors that operate with different force in different cultures of decision-making.

Who sits on a country's scientific advisory panels, for example, may exercise profound influence on how the evidence on risk is interpreted.

Thus Britain's strong tradition of epidemiological research has correlated with a predisposition among that country's scientific advisory committees to discount nonhuman evidence (Jasanoff 1987b). British regulatory authorities, in contrast to their American and German counterparts, have generally regarded animal test results as inadequate to trigger regulatory action unless they are supported by data from studies of human populations.

Political and legal cultures also condition the interpretation of science. Controversies over policy-relevant science arise more frequently in some countries than in others. The adversarial political culture of the United States is known to provide exceptionally fertile ground for nurturing such disputes. In an environment that polarizes lay as well as expert participants, scientific claims align themselves along the cleavages created by social and political interests. Thus risk assessments became a favorite focal point for U.S. regulatory conflict in the 1980s. The seemingly objective, yet infinitely malleable, nature of these analyses made them a potent resource for political actors who sought to capture the authority of science in furtherance of their immediate policy objectives.

In a related development, mathematical modeling of risk gained wide currency in the United States because Congress and the courts insisted on action based on the possibility of harm—that is, *risk*—rather than on harm itself. U.S. regulators, who are unusually vulnerable to political pressure (see Table 4.1), embraced these techniques, recognizing that their decisions would seem more credible if justified in quantitative terms pursuant to 'objective' predictive models.

In turn, commitments to particular ways of dealing with uncertainty color how regulators evaluate different categories of evidence. The U.S. preference for generic decision making—reflected in the policy of assessing all carcinogens by the same principles—helps explain why regulators in this country proved relatively resistant to incorporating mechanisms of cancer causation into their risk assessment models. By contrast, European regulators, who are used to reviewing chemicals individually, saw nothing problematic in assuming that carcinogens behave differently from one another or that such differences should be factored into standard setting. In several instances, the notion that a particular carcinogenic compound affects human health only above a certain threshold of exposure was easily accepted in Europe (Jasanoff 1988). Confronted by the same data, U.S. agencies determined that the evidence was insufficient to overcome the generic no-threshold hypothesis that they applied to all carcinogens (Jasanoff 1988; Graham, Green, and Roberts 1988, 57–9).

Why Decisions Converge

How then do we account for the second component of our paradox, namely, that risk management decisions show greater cross-national consistency than do the underlying risk assessments? Although cultural and institutional considerations introduce disparities in the evaluation of scientific evidence, there are equally important forces that push risk management decisions toward convergence across national boundaries. The five most significant are as follows:

Scientific factors clearly promote some degree of convergence. New findings about technological risks tend to trigger similar political demands and policy responses in industrialized democracies, accounting for a broad parallelism of regulatory agendas. The pivotal role of climate researchers in arousing worldwide political concern over global warming is but one example of this phenomenon.

Economic factors also push toward regulatory convergence over time. Companies doing business across political boundaries sometimes find it more expedient to market a single product or process everywhere, even if this requires compliance with the most stringent of the applicable national standards. For example, many pharmaceutical manufacturers target their products to the U.S. market in spite of this country's stringent safety and efficacy requirements.

Bureaucratic factors, such as limited expertise or resources for scientific research and assessment, likewise militate in favor of convergence. Thus a chemical-importing country lacking independent risk assessment capabilities may decide for the sake of administrative convenience to ban products deemed unreasonably dangerous by regulators in exporting countries. Controversies involving attempted U.S. exports of pesticides (DDT and others), contraceptives (Depo Provera), and the flame retardant Tris illustrate this dynamic.

Political factors, too, are a force for convergence in an increasingly interdependent world. Modern mass communications have helped foster similar expectations of safety and health among people of different cultural backgrounds. The cross-national literature on risk management documents numerous instances in which interest groups successfully pressured their governments to model their policy priorities, and even their actual policies, on the actions of other countries.

Accidental factors, finally, are immensely important in forcing risk decision making into parallel paths across countries with divergent institutions and traditions of policy-making. Ripple effects from catastrophic events such as the methyl isocyanate explosion at Bhopal and the nuclear disaster at Chernobyl easily transcend geopolitical boundaries. Convergent national policies, such as the virtually simultaneous adoption of hazard notification requirements in Europe and the United States, are among the tangible results.

Implications for Risk Management

With so many powerful forces operating to neutralize discrepancies in the technical assessment of risk, is it reasonable to expect that countries will differ significantly in implementing policies dealing with the risks of global warming? If so, where are the differences most likely to occur?

Lessons from other areas of environmental regulation, as well as our experiences with global warming to date, suggest that cross-national convergence will be most complete in the early agenda-setting phases of policy-making. When an issue is as economically and politically salient as climate change, we should not be surprised to see it rise to the status of a public problem almost simultaneously in countries as disparate as Brazil, Britain, or Bangladesh. However, to translate an expressed commitment to reduce risk into detailed prescriptive requirements is quite another matter. We recall that general agreement about the need to control environmental carcinogens in the 1970s led nevertheless to nontrivial variations in policies aimed at particular chemicals. Although substances such as saccharin, formaldehyde, DDT, and asbestos were universally recognized as needing control, policy decisions ranged from outright bans in some countries to continued use in others under more or less restrictive regulatory conditions.

The timing of regulatory decisions, in particular, can be expected to vary across national boundaries in spite of pressures for convergence. Substantial policy differences can persist for a decade or two, far longer than the time scales pertinent to most political action. The case of unleaded petroleum is an instructive example. By 1990 many European governments had adopted at least a voluntary scheme for encouraging consumption of lead-free fuels. Under pressure from green political interests, major European automobile manufacturers, too, began switching over to cars with catalytic converters, thereby cutting into the demand for lead in gasoline. But these European developments trailed U.S. policy by more than a decade. Using its authority under the 1970 Clean Air Act, the Environmental Protection Agency (EPA) had mandated a nationwide shift to unleaded fuel by the mid-1970s. The EPA's policy forced American automobile manufacturers to adopt catalytic converter technology years ahead of their European counterparts.

Methods of control, as already noted, can vary across national policy frameworks even when there is general agreement about the need for regulation. The United States, for example, has adopted disclosure and right-to-know provisions for hazardous chemicals on a wider scale than have countries in Europe. The popularity of such policies in the 1980s can be traced to a widespread disenchantment with command-and-control regulation and more generally to a loss of faith in federal agencies in the aftermath of the Reagan administration's deregulatory reforms. Underlying the U.S. right-to-know movement is the sense that an informed public can best decide how to protect itself against risk. Countries with a less deeply ingrained tradition of grassroots activism and local political autonomy (Almond and Verba 1963) may be less inclined to follow along this particular regulatory path.

Attitudes toward new technologies may also prove resistant to some of the forces of convergence outlined earlier. When a technology is in its infancy and its benefits are not fully established, economic considerations play a less significant role in pressing countries toward a convergent policy outcome. National disparities in the perception and assessment of risk accordingly are especially likely to prove controlling in shaping policy for new technologies.

Cultural differences could assume large significance in the decisions of individual countries to accept particular new technologies as part of their implementation strategy against global warming. Within the European Community today, for example, some countries appear cautiously accepting of biotechnology—Dickson (1987) called these the 'yes-but' countries—while others—the 'no-but' countries—are much less favorably inclined. The former understandably would be more receptive than the latter to reducing greenhouse gas emissions with the aid of products based on biotechnology, such as genetically engineered alternatives to agrochemicals or fossil fuels.

Risk Perceptions of Developing Countries

Persistent differences among industrialized countries in the implementation of risk policies leads us to speculate about the consequences of implementing an environmental risk management program of truly global dimension. Should we expect to see divergences multiply at the expense of convergences as increasing numbers of developing countries—with their individual histories, political structures, decision-making traditions, and cultural biases—enter the bargaining process on global warming? The answer, I think, is a cautious negative, although the relative paucity of research on the risk policies of developing countries means that our responses at this stage must necessarily be tentative.

Discrepancies in risk assessment, to start with, are not likely to proliferate in direct proportion with the number of actors drawn into the global warming negotiations. New entrants for the most part will have neither the scientific and bureaucratic resources nor, as I suggest below, the political incentives to mount their own independent risk assessment programs. At least for the foreseeable future, developing nations will more probably function as a gigantic tuning fork, amplifying particular resonances in the risk controversies generated by countries with more elaborate infrastructures for scientific and technical analysis.

Which resonances will be so favored? One widely endorsed view about risk preferences holds that poor nations (like poor individuals) tolerate more risk than do rich nations because they recognize that risk is a necessary price of development (Lave 1978, 134–35; but see Douglas and Wildavsky 1982, 11–12). Yet some of the risk positions adopted by developing countries seem to contradict this bare assertion. Third World nations have in many instances accepted the views of relatively risk-averse analysts in the industrialized world. An illuminating example was the effort mounted in the United Nations to regulate the export of products such as pesticides, drugs, and toxic wastes that were deemed unreasonably hazardous in the country of origin. Unless there is a clearly established market for a hazardous product, as for example in the case of DDT and malaria control, importing countries are often loath to override an exporting country's official judgment that a product's risks outweigh its benefits.

Perceptions of risk, moreover, are known to be closely correlated with the perceiver's sense of control over the sources of risk (Fischoff, Slovic, and Lichtenstein 1983; Laird 1989). The lack of trust that pervades north-south relations undermines feelings of control and is likely to foster heightened awareness of risk in developing countries, particularly with regard to hazards originating outside their borders. The nexus between risk and distrust could well influence how developing countries select among competing risk assessments produced by political actors in industrial nations. Just as the U.S. public looks askance at official assurances of safety, so developing countries may be skeptical of corporate and governmental assessments that seem to understate risks to the Third World. The accounts of environmental and public interest groups, by contrast, may be perceived as disinterested, and hence more reliable, even if experts in industry or government dismiss them as alarmist and unscientific.

The risk communication practices of actors in industrialized countries will also have an obvious bearing on the way developing countries perceive risks. Western nongovernmental organizations (NGOs) have long favored open information policies and have cultivated close ties with the media to get their viewpoints across to a global audience. Corporate risk assessors, by contrast, have traditionally been more reluctant to take public stances on risk for fear of disclosing confidential commercial information or creating negative publicity. Accordingly, risk messages produced by technically expert NGOs, such as the U.S. Natural Resources Defense Council (NRDC), encounter relatively little opposition as they are transmitted worldwide. Research on the popularization of science suggests that such assessments even gain authority in the course of dissemination, for they are shorn of the reservations and limitations that accompanied the original statements (Gusfield 1981; Hilgartner n.d.). As far as the credibility of science is concerned, Collins (1987, 692) observed that 'distance lends enchantment.'

Thus in writing about the dangers of chemical pesticides in India, the mainstream periodical *India Today* identified daminozide, a controversial American-made plant growth regulator, as a carcinogen. This was consistent with the position adopted by U.S. environmental groups, including NRDC, although EPA scientists had questioned the data and the product's manufacturer had rejected the finding of carcinogenicity (Jasanoff 1987a). The layers of argument and ambiguity surrounding the determination of daminozide's risks in the United States clearly were lost in transmission.

Consequences for Global Warming Policy

As developing countries begin to participate more fully in discussions of global warming, political weight can therefore be expected to accumulate on the side of those who see the risks as real and severe. Climate models that predict devastating drought in the Sahel or disastrous floods in Bangladesh will present few surprises to citizens of those chronically fragile regions. Where natural hazards are a way of life, the prospect of worse yet to come will not seem improbably remote.

Moreover, as relatively minor contributors to greenhouse gas emissions, developing countries generally will have little incentive to contest the bleakest predictions of climate researchers. Instead, Third World political strategists may find it advantageous to enlist experts from other countries who will supply cognitive validation for their own perceptions of risk. Such cross-national 'epistemic communities' (Haas 1990) may begin to play an increasingly important role in future deliberations on global environmental hazards.

Disputes between north and south are more likely to multiply with regard to methods and strategies for controlling risk. In other words, risk management rather than risk assessment seems increasingly likely to emerge as the arena on which the countries of the world will play out their sharpest conflicts over global warming. The lessons we have learned from comparative policy research and the sociology of knowledge will remain highly relevant to this debate, for the displacement of controversy from assessment to management will very probably bring in its wake a similar displacement of expert conflict from the natural to the social sciences. In an era of globalized contention about risk, the economic theories and models that form the basis for global warming policies will be subject to criticism and deconstruction much as theories of chemical carcinogenesis were in earlier pollution controversies centered in the West.

Cross-national studies of policy implementation suggest, finally, that players in the global warming game will be able to choose between two fundamentally different political strategies, neither of which would accord well with the dictates of good decision making. For countries with substantial reservoirs of expertise, whether in climate research or social impact analysis, it will be tempting to define the issues as far as possible in technical terms. By monopolizing the production of risk and cost estimates, they would be able to exclude many players and to limit the terms of debate for others. For countries with fewer analytical resources, it may be more appealing to follow a strategy of 'decentering' expertise by exposing the uncertainties and disagreements that underlie technical assessments. Knowledge disputes among political adversaries in countries such as the United States would fuel any such effort. By denigrating the centrality of technical knowledge, developing countries could hope to secure a level playing field where their moral and political arguments would not be regularly trumped by claims of superior expertise.

Conclusion

Cross-national studies of policy implementation in industrialized countries have established that both the interpretation of policy-relevant science and strategies for linking scientific information to policy are profoundly affected by such factors as the competitiveness of the political system, its reliance on legal instruments, the openness of its information policies, and the methods by which the public participates in governmental decisions. Among similarly situated countries, the paradoxical result is that risk assessments diverge more strikingly than do corresponding decisions to manage risk. The socially constructed character of science provides wide latitude for varying interpretations of the same observations and claims. Over time, however, the macroforces of economic interdependence and mass communication bring about substantial convergence in policy outcomes.

I have suggested in this article that the paradox of risk assessment is unlikely to replicate itself exactly in the context of global warming policy, although my observations on this score necessarily remain speculative. Experience indicates that developing countries will gain little advantage in the short run by focusing their energies on risk assessment. They will serve their interests as well, if not better, by debating the validity of relevant economic models and the moral and social costs of divergent approaches to risk management.

Two major challenges will confront the international community as this discussion proceeds. The first is to create an inclusive framework for negotiation, whether or not all participants subscribe to the shared technical epistemologies of industrialized societies. The second is to ensure an appropriate use of science, so that the fragile baby of reliable knowledge is not thrown out with the bathwater of technical deconstruction.

Notes

* Existing research comparing regulatory processes for environmental and health hazards in Europe and North America indicates that there are considerable differences in the ways that countries with quite similar legal and political traditions approach both the scientific evidence on which policy is made and the frameworks that are used to implement such policy. Such differences may be even more extreme between countries with vastly different cultures and political traditions. This article describes and accounts for such differences in political, legislative, administrative, regulatory, and judicial systems that may present obstacles to reaching international accord.

† Director of the Program on Science, Technology, and Society at Cornell University. She is author of *Risk Management and Political Culture* and coauthor of *Chemical Regulation and Cancer: A Cross-National Study of Policy and Politics* and numerous other works. She is a Fellow of AAAS, a contributing editor of *Science, Technology, & Human Values*, and a panel member for the Ethics and Values Program of the National Science Foundation. Her research interests include comparative policy analysis, the use of risk assessment in regulatory decision-making, and interactions between science and the legal process.

1. The account I give of cross-national similarities and differences in policy implementation is consistent with the findings of all the studies cited here. The most comprehensive of these is Brickman, Jasanoff, and Ilgen (1985). I have drawn most of my specific examples of policy convergence and divergence from this work.
2. The work of the Royal Commission on Environmental Pollution has been particularly significant on issues related to the subject of this article. For example, the commission's reports on lead in the environment and the planned release of genetically engineered organisms were critically important in shaping government policy.

References

Almond, G. A., and S. Verba. 1963. *The Civic Culture*. Princeton, NJ: Princeton University Press.

Badaracco, J. 1985. *Loading the Dice: A five-country study of vinyl chloride regulation*. Boston: Harvard Business School Press.

Brickman, R., S. Jasanoff, and T. Ilgen, 1985. *Controlling Chemicals: The politics of regulation in Britain and the United States*. Ithaca, NY: Cornell University Press.

Collingridge, D., and C. Reeve. 1986. *Science Speaks to Power*. New York: St. Martin's.

Collins, H. M. 1985. *Changing Order: Replication and induction in scientific practice*. Beverly Hills, CA: Sage.

—— 1987. 'Certainty and the public understanding of science: Science on television'. *Social Studies of Science* 17:689–713.

Dickson, D. 1987. 'Europe splits over gene regulation'. *Science* 238:18–19.

Douglas, M., and A. Wildavsky. 1982. *Risk and Culture*. Berkeley: University of California Press.

Fischoff, B., P. Slovic, and S. Lichtenstein. 1983. 'The "public" versus the "experts": Perceived versus actual disagreements about the risk of nuclear power'. In *Analysis of Actual Versus Perceived Risks*, edited by V. Covello, G. Flamm, J. Roderick, and R. Tardiff, 235–47. New York: Plenum.

Gillespie, B., D. Eva, and R. Johnston. 1979. 'Carcinogenic risk assessment in the United States and Great Britain: The case of aldrin/dieldrin'. *Social Studies of Science* 9: 265–301.

Graham, J., L. Green, and M. Roberts. 1988. *In Search of Safety: Chemicals and cancer risk*. Cambridge, MA: Harvard University Press.

Gusfield, J. 1981. *The Culture of Public Problems: Drinking-driving and the symbolic order*. Chicago: University of Chicago Press.

Haas, P. M. 1990. *Saving the Mediterranean: The politics of international environmental cooperation*. New York: Columbia University Press.

Hilgartner, S. (n.d.) *Science as a Symbol: Cognitive authority in the diet-cancer debate*. Typescript.

Jasanoff, S. 1986. *Risk Management and Political Culture*. New York: Russell Sage.
—— 1987a. 'EPA's regulation of daminozide: Unscrambling the messages of risk'. *Science, Technology, & Human Values* 12:116–24.
—— 1987b. 'Cultural aspects of risk assessment in Britain and the United States'. In *The Social and Cultural Construction of Risk*, edited by B. B. Johnson and V. Covello, 359–97. New York: Reidel.
—— 1988. 'Reasoning about Risk'. In *Risk Assessment of Chemicals in the Environment*, edited by M. L. Richardson, 92–113. London: Royal Society of Chemistry.
Johnson, B. B., and V. Covello, eds. 1987. *The Social and Cultural Construction of Risk*. New York: Reidel.
Kuhn, T. 1970. *The Structure of Scientific Revolutions*. 2nd edn. Chicago: University of Chicago Press.
Laird, F. N. 1989. 'The Decline of Deference: The political context of risk communication'. *Risk Analysis* 9:543–50.
Latour, B., and S. Woolgar. 1979. *Laboratory Life*. Beverly Hills, CA: Sage.
Lave, L. 1978. 'Health, Safety, and Environmental Regulations'. In *Setting National Priorities: Agenda for the 1980s*, edited by J. A. Pechman. Washington, DC: Brookings Institution.
National Research Council. 1983. *Risk Assessment in the Federal Government: Managing the process*. Washington, DC: National Academy Press.
Nelkin, D., ed. 1984. *Controversy*. 2nd edn. Beverly Hills, CA: Sage.
Vogel, D. 1986. *National Styles of Regulation*. Ithaca, NY: Cornell University Press.

PART III
Government Regulation: Implementation and Impact

Compliance Strategy*

KEITH HAWKINS†

Compliance

Enforcement behaviour in pollution control is determined by the play of two interconnected features: the nature of the deviance confronted and a judgment of its wilfulness or avoidability. Field staff draw a distinction in practice between deviance which is continuous or episodic (*'persistent failures to comply'*) and that which consists of isolated, discrete incidents (*'one-offs'*). Because the persistent failure to comply is open-ended deviance, it is more amenable to detection. The one-off, on the other hand, is an unexpected discharge of relatively short duration, and hence less open to detection. It may be accidentally caused, but its unpredictability carries with it hints of attempts to evade detection.

Detectability is linked with avoidability. The field officer's common sense suggests that where a pollution is persistent, its perpetrator is easily detectable. Yet this ready detectability only rarely suggests wilful persistence. Instead the persistent failure to comply prima facie implies that the rule-breaking is unavoidable, the result of inadequate resources or knowledge. Where deviance is unavoidable, a strategy of compliance is called for to repair problems.

A one-off is a more sinister matter. The intimation of possible wilfulness, the suggestion that a pollution is preventable, prompts a penal response: there is no problem to repair, simply rule-breaking to punish. The one-off pollution, in other words, has the potential for resembling a traditional criminal act, making a conciliatory style of enforcement inappropriate, for there is a suspicion of 'trying to get away with it'. Its limited duration means that, compared with the persistent failure to comply, it is more difficult to discover the deviance, more difficult to detect an offender, and more difficult to establish that offender's motivation. Discerning cause here acquires considerable significance, since it is only a judgment about blameworthiness which distinguishes a preventable one-off from an 'accident'. Whether a pollution is regarded as 'accidental' or as something more ominous depends upon an image of the polluter. Such imagery 'explains' pollution.

Yet this is not to suggest that a penal response is never made to persistent failures to comply. Where an agency prosecutes in these cases, however, it is for a failure of the compliance process, a sanction for the irretrievable breakdown of negotiations.[1] Here, the failure of the compliance process suggests a persistence in wrong-doing whose wilfulness aligns the case with a deliberate one-off.

A notion of efficiency is the field man's major concern. The expeditious attainment of his given objectives means securing compliance at least cost to his future relationships with the polluter. With a persistent failure to comply, he must clean up a regularly dirty effluent. And though the one-off can prompt a punitive response, a concern for efficiency is expressed in the preventive work done to forestall recurrence—whether or not the incident is judged 'accidental'. In both cases the active co-operation of the polluter is required for the success of an enforcement strategy aimed at conformity.

What an enforcement agent understands by 'compliance' depends on the nature of the problem he is regulating. Persistent failures to comply are the episodic or continuing pollutions which are frequently or consistently above consent limits, either owing to inefficient treatment plant or inadequate attention to pollution control. The nature of this deviance is open-ended and persisting. It often comes to agency notice through proactive enforcement by routine monitoring and may have long been going on and only recently discovered or recently defined as pollution. Such pollutions are typically not regarded as 'serious' (most 'serious' persistent failures to comply have now been cleaned up), though field men may be anxious about their cumulative impact; indeed they are a classic embodiment of deviance as a state of affairs rather than as an act. The normal control response is to prescribe remedial measures to be applied in the course of the continuing relationship between officer and polluter.

Field staff sometimes describe persistent failures to comply as 'technical' as opposed to 'drastic' pollutions, a term reserved for serious 'one-off' cases.[2] The use of the word 'technical' aptly indicates a discharge above consent to which blameworthiness does not attach. Most such deviance is treated as routine, uneventful: 'I think people see discharges as outside consent conditions, and have been for a long time, and people don't take that much notice'. The enforcement response is modest; 'We would', said an area supervisor, 'just tend to niggle away at the bloke.' A persistent failure to comply will be treated as a more serious matter only where the discharge is regarded as substantially beyond consent limits and the pollution is noticeable.

The responses of the persistent polluter are, however, carefully monitored by field men. Here enforcement is a continuing, adaptive process. Persistence allows the construction of a career assembling past problems and past efforts at remedy made by the agency, interlinked with the polluter's responses to them.[3] To think in terms of an enforcement career is a useful device for the officer, structuring his expectations and moulding his responses. Present conduct has meaning and significance conferred upon it by past history; career creates context.

The one-off pollution is potentially of much greater significance. Almost by definition it will be serious simply because it is less open than a continuing pollution to detection through routine monitoring. The one-off pollution is a discrete event; it may be momentary or longer-lasting, but it is bounded in time with a finite beginning and end (its end sometimes the result of enforcement work). It is critical rather than chronic deviance; an 'incident', where a persistent failure to comply is a 'problem'.

The one-off normally comes to agency attention as a result of complaint from a third party; sometimes, though, it is difficult to detect: a discharge can be turned off or an effluent diluted before a field man arrives on the scene. And where a persistent pollution has overtones of the (for now) 'unavoidable', or possibly the 'careless', the one-off prompts a different moral categorization. It may be 'accidental'—a spillage, a leakage, a breakdown of treatment plant—or, more ominously, 'deliberate'—acid baths being emptied or settlement tanks flushed out.

Enforcement activity with one-offs is directed towards correcting damage done, preventing its recurrence, and deterring others. Because the one-off pollution by definition implies the existence of a discharge which is not normally made, or the presence of a pollutant in a normally clean discharge, compliance is relatively simple to secure where the effluent is still running. Field staff will demand a stop to it, and the more serious the pollution appears to be, the sooner they will expect effective remedial action. Compliance here can be instant: taps can be turned off, an effluent pipe blocked off, polluting liquid diverted or disposed of in waste tankers.[4]

Where persistent failures to comply or preventive work with one-offs are concerned, compliance is a continuing process, an organized sequence of requests and demands placed upon the regulated. Compliance here is elastic, and depends on the apparent 'progress' made by the polluter and other exigencies affecting his relationship with the field officer. The issue is not usually the discrete one of whether or not the discharger will take action, so much as whether he will act as quickly as the officer wishes and to the extent required. The stance adopted by the field man during negotiations and the sorts of demands made of the polluter will be influenced as much by interpretations placed upon the polluter's response as by the nature of the 'problem' to be remedied and the resources available for tackling it. The technical implications of the behaviour addressed by law require this fluid conception of compliance in practice. The nature of the problem has to be diagnosed, a remedy prescribed, installed, and made to work efficiently. This obtains even where the remedy may be a simple matter of digging a hole to serve as a settlement pit, for effective action is the central concern. In some cases compliance may involve installation of complex treatment plant requiring heavy expenditure of money and time. Elaborate apparatus often demands regular attention and maintenance to produce an acceptable effluent. Because compliance has an unbounded quality and is subject to constant negotiation, field men do not work to a notion of instant conformity when dealing with persistent problems. Instead compliance in one sense is measurable in months or years, and in the sense that discharges subject to continued monitoring may deteriorate or standards change, compliance is 'for now'. Where states of affairs are concerned compliance strategy requires constant vigilance.

Since water use is a continuing activity it is difficult for a field officer (unlike a policeman: Bittner, 1967b: 281) to think in terms of cases being 'closed', which has implications for what he may regard as 'compliance' and for the ways in which he is able for organizational purposes to demonstrate a successful outcome to his enforcement activities. One of the important features of 'compliance' for the pragmatic field man is the existence of some visible evidence of the consequences of his enforcement activity: a cleaner effluent, a new treatment plant, or a discharge diverted from watercourse to foul sewer. Such evidence provides a considerable sense of professional accomplishment:

> We drove to a colliery, whose discharges had in the past caused a great deal of trouble, to see two settlement lagoons designed to reduce the level of suspended solids in the effluent. Both had been installed at the field officer's insistence, one at a cost of £80,000, the other at £60,000. The officer thought the lagoons had greatly improved the quality of the effluent and there was no longer a 'problem'. 'I'm bloody proud of that,' he said, pointing to the larger of the lagoons. 'I look at those settlement lagoons and I think "That's me what's done that."'

The field officer's evaluation of satisfactory compliance is not geared to legal output measures.[5] So far as the one-off pollution is concerned, he will be satisfied if the discharge is stopped and precautions to prevent repetition are taken. If a one-off is categorized as accidental, the preventive work is often nothing more than some good advice about the need for greater care. A less conciliatory stance is only called for in the rare cases of major spot discharges, which are qualitatively important for their symbolic significance. The pollution which may have occurred as the result of negligence, and especially the persistent failure to comply, require a different approach. Negotiations over the introduction of new or improved pollution control facilities may take months or even years before the officer is satisfied that the discharger has 'complied'. And then compliance must be maintained.

Compliance, then, is much more than conformity, immediate or protracted, to the demands of an enforcement agent. The continuing relationship between officer and polluter, the open-endedness of problems encountered, and the pragmatism of field staff encourage a focus upon the deviant's efforts at compliance, an opportunity denied the deviant in breach of a rule in the traditional criminal code where an act committed is over and done with and beyond repair. A polluter who displays an immediate willingness to take whatever action is necessary may well discover that the gravity of the pollution itself is accorded less importance by the officer: 'it can become a secondary feature,' said one field man, 'if co-operation from the firm is complete.'

Compliance, in short, has a symbolic significance. Enforcement agents need, as much as a concrete accomplishment, some *sign* of compliance. Planning is as important as building; intention as important as action. Assessments of conformity thus tend to be fluid and abstract, rather than concrete and unproblematic. 'Attitudes' are judged as much as activities:

KH How important is the attitude of the other person?
FO Oh, I think that's the most important thing, is his attitude. Because the pollutions themselves can be so variable. . . . If he's trying to solve it, I go along with him. If he's not interested in it and thinks 'Well, it will go away in time anyway,' then obviously I'm going to press him harder then. Yeah, it is *the* most single important parameter I think, his attitude. [His emphasis]

The discharger who does what the field man asks—even though he may still be polluting—will be thought of as compliant. Compliance in practice is a continuing effort towards attainment of a goal as much as attaining the goal itself. The extent to which pollution is controlled is no more significant in a compliance strategy than the extent of the polluter's good faith (Goldstein and Ford, 1972:38; Holden, 1966). How 'good' the faith is, however, depends on the kind of polluter encountered.

Images of Polluters

It is possible to discern four working categories employed by pollution control staff, of dischargers. Their images are broadly drawn and depict both their individual contacts and the larger organization employing them. These working categories embody impressions of 'typical' kinds of polluter, as well as 'typical' kinds of problem. Polluters are identified by characteristics such as occupation, size, demeanour, and responsiveness. The characterization settled upon is important in contributing to a judgment whether a discharger can be held 'responsible' for causing a pollution (Hawkins, 1984, 161–71).

Most are regarded as '*socially responsible*'.[6] Polluters here comply as a matter of principle, manifesting a 'personal disinclination to act in violation of the law's commands' (Kadish, 1963:437) which spills over into the corporate identity of the firm. Profitable companies and most large undertakings, including the nationalized concerns, form part of this group (see also Katona, 1945:241; Lane, 1954: 95; Staw and Szwajkowski, 1975). They are generally viewed as helpful and responsive to the enforcement activities of the agency. The epitome of the 'essentially law-abiding' or 'public-spirited' discharger was said to be one well known company which gives its employees a course on pollution work and its significance, and assigns them precise jobs if a spillage occurs. Though it may impede economic interests, compliance with the law is for some firms a fundamental tenet of company policy. 'Large industries', said an area supervisor, 'have a policy of "We conform with the law—however much it costs".'[7] Similarly, nationalized concerns are expected to be 'socially responsible' because they are particularly concerned about their reputation and also possess the resources to afford whatever remedial action is thought necessary.[8] In a large organization the presence of personalities committed to a policy of compliance in senior positions is regarded as significant. It is not that the socially responsible do not cause pollution, rather that when pollution occurs it is likely to be defined as an accident, for it will almost certainly be an isolated instance of deviance. The socially responsible discharger in these circumstances will alert the agency, co-operate fully in clearing up, and take steps to prevent a repetition.

Socially responsible dischargers, however, rarely possess unblemished virtue. Most are regarded as reluctantly law-abiding and have to be talked into cleaning up their effluents or taking preventive action. One of the arts of pollution control is to persuade polluters to bear costs in ways which are rarely justifiable commercially, hence the use of the term 'dead money' by field staff to describe expenditure on treatment plant. The image of water users as essentially law-abiding comes with field men's claims of success in achieving compliance in the majority of cases.

Most polluters, however, are half-hearted in their resistance to the demands of the water authority. Those dischargers who cause serious difficulties are in a small minority. This was not always so. The more experienced field staff have discerned a greater pollution consciousness among dischargers and public alike which has been growing since the 1950s. Staff regard this shift as helpful to the task of control. This is not to suggest that dischargers are incapable of deviance, but that serious pollution as a result of negligence or deliberate misconduct is believed now not to be widespread or to occur regularly.

The result at field level is a dual image of dischargers. Staff still expect a measure of resistance to their enforcement efforts.[9] It is portrayed as almost a ritual response to an enforcement agent. For dischargers to 'try it on' or 'try to pull a fast one' is entirely normal behaviour. Disclaimers, evasiveness, and delay are common moves in the enforcement game. Dischargers are expected to 'drag their heels': 'usually people are pretty slow to spend money,' said an area man, 'no matter which sector of the public they come from'. This is true even of those who comply in principle, because delay admits the possibility that one might not have to do what one ought (Silbey and Bittner, n.d.:9). Their hesitancy is not questioned, but is taken for granted to be a desire to avoid commercially unjustifiable costs recoverable only by higher prices. Polluters have nothing to gain from treatment measures: 'It's no skin off his nose if it carries on going downstream. It's one less problem off his mind. He's got less slurry or less whatever to deal with. Or he hasn't got another soakaway to dig.' Many dischargers regard compliance, in the words of an industrialist, as 'doing as little in the way of treatment as they [can] get away with' (Barrett, 1977).

The three remaining categories embrace cases where compliance is less than ideal. First is a group held to be '*unfortunate*'. These dischargers find it difficult to comply completely with the agency's demands, owing to technical inability or to physical or economic incapacity. Agencies recognize that many purification processes are only imperfectly understood and effective treatment is sometimes beyond the competence of available expertise. They also acknowledge that some dischargers do not possess the physical resources (in the form of available land and appropriate topography) to permit effective pollution control—quite apart from the economic costs in terms of capital outlay or potential unemployment which could be the consequence of over-zealous enforcement. Economic incapacity is recognized by field men as a 'genuine' reason for non-compliance, perhaps because for that very reason many of the agencies' own sewage works perform badly. Enforcement in these circumstances produces a feeling of resignation, even of impotence: 'I know before I get there the effluent's going to be bad, and all I'm doing is producing figures so that maybe we can present them at the end of the year. It does seem rather a waste of time in some cases.' Moral inferences as to the willingness of the polluter to comply are not drawn here, in contrast with the two remaining categories.

The third group is comprised of the *'careless'*. Many dischargers find it difficult to adapt to new ways. Many old industries, in existence long before the water authorities or their predecessors, continue to behave as they have always behaved, only to find that the invention of new regulation recasts them as deviants. Then there are other dischargers who, through sloppy management, incompetence, inadequate internal sanctions, or a negligent labour force, regularly fail to maintain their effluents to an acceptable standard, or from time to time cause pollution incidents (cf. Kagan and Scholz, 1979). For field staff the worst form of carelessness amounts to outright negligence, and is particularly exemplified by the discharger whose failure to take preventive measures recommended by them results in pollution. Such negligence is both a symbolic disdain for conformity to the law, and a predictive construct: 'It implies an attitude that will determine whether they will meet our standards and whether I need to be strict with them,' as one officer put it. It is sometimes difficult in practice to distinguish an 'accidental' pollution from a 'careless' one. Sometimes the images of the polluter which 'explain' the deviance are sharpened in the course of negotiations. Sometimes the image will be redrawn, leading to a shift in 'theory', hence in enforcement practice. Indeed it is possible for a polluter to repair by the extent of his remedial work a previously unfavourable impression, leading to redesignation of the original incident as 'accidental'.

Finally, the *'malicious'* are those who quite deliberately pollute watercourses either to avoid the costs of treatment or disposal, or in symbolic rejection of the agency's authority. Where the careless are ignorant or irresponsible, the malicious are purposive and calculating. They are capable of both isolated and persistent instances of misconduct, but are not now regarded as numerous.

While these characterizations address the reasons for any pollution, another set treat the likely response of a polluter to the process of enforcement. A field man implicitly categorizes polluters into those more able and less able to comply, the effect of which is to shape his stance in the enforcement relationship. Those thought more able to comply are treated with greater stringency and less tolerance of delay or evasion. This categorization is based on a common-sense assessment of the financial well-being of a polluter and a technical judgment about the possibility of compliance.

A more important categorization, however, one cutting across evaluations of a polluter's ability to pay, and one continually open to redefinition, is a judgment of a polluter's co-operativeness. To regard a discharger as 'co-operative' or having a 'good attitude', or, in contrast, as 'unhelpful' or 'bolshie' informs an officer's expectations about the nature of his relationship with that polluter. Co-operativeness is welcomed for facilitating the job of enforcement and for encouraging principled compliance: 'If you get on well with them, they're more likely to look at the moral issue [of complying] than the economics.' The suggestion of willing compliance from the 'co-operative' polluter announces a respect for the officer's authority and reassures him that his demands are not only reasonably put, but *legitimate*. Besides, a show of compliance is a means of coping with uncertainty, as 'something is being done'.

Characterizations emerge in everyday work and are shared (and thus transmitted to new recruits) in the area office. Informal contact with colleagues creates opportunities to learn what kinds of pollutions and what kinds of polluters 'cause trouble'. The tendency for a label applied to one polluter to be generalized to others defined as falling into the same class is recognized by some: 'You don't trust one of them and it rubs off on the others.'

Past experience is also a source of characterization, favourable or otherwise. The polluter who generates an unfavourable reputation in the agency or who has regularly been in trouble is accorded greater scrutiny and less tolerance when assessments are made: 'You know, if the guy's got a previous history you tend to look on him a bit more harshly than somebody else.'

Officers' characterizations also embody assumptions about a discharger's incentives for complying with the law. It is for this reason that larger companies, with reputations to protect, are expected to be 'co-operative' and 'socially responsible'. Some of the signs emerge from a field man's comments about a large oil company. Responsiveness and willingness to act are important: '[They are] very co-operative because they implement any suggestions we care to make, and they've got a turbo-aerator plant costing £25,000 to improve their effluent. Any suggestions you might make—they'll take note. They'll get things done which they think are necessary.'

But in smaller companies, where margins are narrow and resources meagre, it is assumed that the dictates of commercial rather than legal norms are more likely to be obeyed. Here are found the 'fly-boys' or the 'fly-by-night' polluters who are 'here today, gone tomorrow'. They fall into the 'careless' or 'malicious' categories, whose response will be expected to be 'unco-operative'. These terms are most likely to be employed of small industries in urban areas, especially where 'self-made men' are involved. Such people (it is believed) are motivated solely by profit: in contrast with those who work in large companies who are 'very interested in their image, ... with a little firm they'd just say, "Oh, sod it".' Some rural field men say the same about farmers: 'I find the people with money, that have not been born into it—that are jumped up to it—they're the people that hang on to it and are the most difficult.' The expectation of an 'unco-operative' attitude will be strengthened if the polluter happens to be engaged in a business which produces large quantities of effluent, or effluent which is treatable only at considerable cost, such as the wastes from metal plating:

> Small companies tend to be a problem, the ones that employ ten people, operate on very tight budgets, have no money for effluent treatment, have no technical people to operate what little treatment they may afford. They can be the troublesome ones, I think ... they're the ones that you're constantly going back to and badgering. ... It often is enhanced by a very small site. Effluent treatment and land availability often go hand in hand, so you find that small firms in ... conurbations where they're restricted as to what they can do are the worst polluters I think, without doubt.

Farmers are an occupational group regarded by officers with rural patches as particularly troublesome, partly because of lack of resources, partly because of a characteristic stubbornness born of decades of water-use unencumbered by the attentions of any regulatory agency. They have a culture of their own which sometimes impedes the officer in doing his job: 'they're a tight-knit community,' said an officer of long standing from a large rural area, 'and they won't inform against one another. There's a lot of cover-up.' Indeed, of all the occupations regularly encountered, the farmer is the most consistently described as difficult to handle, as an area supervisor's question, posed with deliberate ingenuousness, acknowledges: 'Farmers, in particular where you get an unco-operative one, are [some] of the worst customers that we come across. I don't know whether you've heard that before?'

The officer's understanding of the reasons why particular kinds of polluters comply helps shape his choice of enforcement tactics, especially in those cases where the field man expects or is already experiencing 'trouble'. One assumption, with profound implications for enforcement behaviour, is that dischargers are sensitive creatures whose feelings may be easily bruised if urged to do too much, too soon. To 'use the big stick' or 'crack the whip' too zealously may be counter-productive (similarly Kagan, 1980; Stjernquist, 1973). To be too eager or abrasive in enforcement work is to risk encouraging in polluters an unco-operative attitude or even downright hostility. This is a major foundation of the commitment to a conciliatory style of enforcement relying on negotiation as a means of securing compliance; 'co-operation can not be established in the atmosphere of suspicion and distrust that rigid application of the law generates.' (Nicholson, 1973:4).[10] In practical terms this assumption supports two related imperatives for field staff aimed at preserving relationships: 'be reasonable' and 'be patient'. Rather than explicitly seeking to secure compliance at the outset by coercion, officers must demonstrate an understanding of the polluter's problems by discussion and negotiation. Enforcement takes time.

Another assumption is premissed on a belief in the efficacy of individual and general deterrence for organizations concerned with their business prospects and public image. Since businesses and other organizations are regarded as rational institutions which act purposively, they are held to be ultimately amenable to law as a form of control. In practice, the working concept of deterrence is perhaps broader than that contemplated by the law, which is presumably founded on a belief that compliance occurs because those tempted to cause a pollution will be deterred by the threat of the legal sanction. During the research period the maximum fine available to the courts for each pollution charge was £100 on summary conviction in a magistrates' court, £200 on conviction on indictment in the Crown Court.[11] These sanctions were universally regarded by staff of all ranks as inadequate, indeed derisory, deterrents for all polluters except the most impecunious of farmers.

This did not, however, lead to an abandonment of general deterrence as a principal stated rationale for prosecution. Deterrence, rather, resides in the threats which precede use of the formal law, or in the informal sanctions which accompany it (Hawkins, 1984, 129–54). Because field staff intuitively perceive one-off pollutions in cases which are not satisfactorily attributable to 'accidental' causes as the outcome of rational, purposive, or negligent behaviour, they assume that dischargers are susceptible to other kinds of deterrence than the criminal sanction. Where a polluter is being less than co-operative and compliance has clear, easily-quantifiable economic costs attached to it, field staff negotiate by generating contexts in which deterrence will take on significant meaning. They draw attention, for example, to some of the difficulties which the discharger will bring upon himself if he is prosecuted. An individual's or an organization's public reputation is displayed as at risk if non-compliance continues. That aspect of the use of formal law believed to be most important for industrialists ('farmers are a different kettle of fish') is the publicity associated with court appearance. Few officers suggest that there is a stigma with economic implications reflected in damage to sales and profitability which attaches to a manufacturer found guilty of polluting a watercourse. Instead it is assumed that a company will seek to protect its reputation as a good-in-itself. Some, however, believe a company's motives to comply are linked with a generalized desire to avoid the 'trouble' stemming from public embarrassment. Publicity implies the construction of reputation, and companies do not want to be seen as 'trouble-makers', since the label will encourage others—especially public authorities which may have benefits to confer—to lay blame for other problems at their door. Other industrialists, it is believed, will not do business with those who engage in sharp practices. The publicity of prosecution can cause all sorts of 'trouble', as an experienced area man suggested:

> It's not so much public relations and the consumer, it's the . . . people who live in that particular area who kick up trouble about [certain kinds of industry], for example . . . In general, the public attention is focused on them. They start ringing their MP and all of the rest. . . . Every firm likes to give an outward impression of responsibility to the public . . . I don't think it affects their sales, y'know, unless it gets to the point of national press campaigns. But . . . locally they're very aware of it because they know jolly well if they want to expand, if they want to make alterations and all the rest of it, they're going to get public enemies all the time. . . . [The authorities] have got to investigate all public complaints. . . . They know jolly well that if they don't satisfy the public, he's going to bring in his local councillor and his MP. [With some firms] you hint about publicity and, boom, that'd be done straight away, that. They're very conscious of it, it's a very useful weapon.[12]

Another kind of 'trouble' may also encourage management to comply. Internal mechanisms of control may well be an effective constraint against carelessness or misconduct in large organizations, both for senior staff and those at junior levels. 'There's a tendency for any adverse publicity to reflect on the management personally,' said one officer, who had worked in industry before joining the water authority. In other words, individuals likely to be held 'responsible' for a company's prosecution have a substantial incentive to protect their personal reputations and positions (Dickens, 1974). The favourable characterization of the large organization is again supported, as a young officer explained: 'Big companies will jump on their employees. We went round to a big American firm and the Manager said "If we don't get that interceptor within the week, I'll get the sack". So he jumped.' Although talk of the sack in this case may be an exaggeration designed to impress the officer of the urgency with which the firm was complying with his request, the sense of an internal sanctioning system to be taken seriously is clearly conveyed. Indeed, in many firms shopfloor workers held responsible for a pollution which leads to prosecution risk the sack.[13]

The important feature in all of this is the threat of public stigma associated with prosecution for pollution. It is believed to be a more powerful incentive to compliance in more suburban and rural areas where greater value attaches to reputation, and where adverse publicity is more readily transmitted, when, in the familiar phrase, 'the local paper will go to town.' Companies will go to considerable lengths, it is thought, to keep their names out of the papers. The concern about reputation can be exploited by ensuring that maximum publicity is generated about prosecutions, a supervisor explained, to assist enforcement and control in other troublesome cases:

> What you would do is you'd make certain the newspapers were there–being a bit naughty. I've done this time and time again, y'know, a little tip-off to the local newspapers to go along. That used to help a lot. There used to be a splash there. You know, it helps your cause.

The real value of the stigma, however, is more symbolic than concrete. Prosecution in a compliance system is valuable not as a sanction, but as a threat, because (as Hawkins, 1984, ch. 7 shows) the threatened sanctions can be made to appear more serious than they are.

The Enforcement Game

A major assumption shaping an officer's enforcement strategy and moulding his relationships with dischargers is that most polluters will ultimately do what he wants them to do.[14] Yet most polluters are expected to display reluctance and disingenuousness at the outset. Neutralization (Sykes and Matza, 1957) by way of disclaimers and evasiveness is regarded as a normal response to pollution control work, especially early in an enforcement relationship. The enforcement of regulation, in short, is conceived of in ritual terms. The metaphor of the game is frequently invoked for descriptive purposes (cf. Edelman, 1964: 44 ff.; Ross, 1970:22). 'Everyone tries it on, at least to begin with. Even the big firms who will do what we want eventually,' said a field man from a mixed catchment. 'They will all say "It wasn't us", or "It was an accident".' Asked how often dischargers tried to pull the wool over his eyes, he replied:

> Very regularly, very regularly. Nearly everyone to more or less a degree will try to kid you about something. Either the nature of the cause of the pollution, or how long it's been going on, or they 'weren't aware that there was a pipe there', or 'Is it really? I've never been down and looked at that watercourse for the last 20 years, I didn't realize we were causing a problem.' But nearly everyone tries some minor deception. . . . They will all have a go . . . even the biggest companies where you're going to get the perfect response, but they will still try to kid you that they 'weren't aware that this was happening', or 'it was while they were on leave' or, y'know, they 'weren't doing it at all'.

Unless, however, the discharger is defined as belonging to a class considered more prone to pollute, or has otherwise displayed himself as unco-operative, his ritual reluctance will be expected to yield ultimately to compliance.

Compliance is not usually achieved without a struggle. Most enforcement problems are caused by a small number of malicious polluters and another larger group of unco-operative dischargers who continue to conduct their affairs as they wish, despite the attentions of pollution control staff. When efforts are made to have them stop or clean up their effluents they adopt protective strategies akin to those which delinquents employ to affect the outcome of their cases (Emerson, 1969: 101 ff.). These 'bolshie types' are few in number but occupy disproportionate amounts of field officers' time.

Bolshie polluters employ a variety of strategies to resist, delay, or avoid enforcement. Most officers encounter dischargers who seek to evade detection, or if discovered, attempt to deflect their attentions by resort to various forms of deceit. It is all part of the game. Some polluters go to considerable lengths to pull a fast one: 'They have a man on the look out,' said one officer from a highly industrialized area, 'and as soon as you appear on the horizon, he's off. Or they dump the stuff on a Sunday evening because they know we don't work on a Sunday evening.' A colleague from a mixed catchment gave another kind of example:

> I've had a certain amount . . . of y'know making discharges when they think you're not about. I had a farmer who kept me talking and feeding me with tea and biscuits while the farm labourers were emptying the silage tank that had been overflowing into the brook. And then [he] took me along to show me this tank and [said] 'Well, you see it couldn't be me, it's empty'—and it was still dripping wet!

Perhaps the tactic most familiar to field staff is for their admission to premises to be delayed so that incriminating evidence can be disposed of. 'The standard thing', said a supervisor, '. . . was . . . when the [officer] arrived, to keep him hanging about while they turned on the fire mains and all sorts of things so they diluted the effluent. So when he took a sample it was perfectly alright.'

A commoner source of difficulty for the enforcement officer, however, is to persuade dischargers to overcome their reluctance to take effective remedial action, once their pollutions have come to light. Delay is the commonest ploy adopted here. Delay is routinely expected, but difficult to establish, especially where technical questions are concerned, or the polluter has to rely on others for the manufacture or supply of equipment to enable him to comply. Yet an officer cannot afford to overplay his hand; efforts to speed things up may prove to be counter-productive:

> There are always delaying tactics. . . . We may be talking here about a method of treating a difficult waste, so the question is how on earth do you treat it? . . . Now this can go on for ages and ages [but] they just keep on saying 'Oh well, we've written to these manufacturers and the experiments have been going on, but it broke down.' . . . But you can't prove they're not getting on very quick with it. . . . People are very wily and very clever and if they think they're over pushed there is a chance of . . . well, slightly delaying and procrastinating on a thing. They always come up with a story of 'Well, we haven't got planning permission yet'.

A supervising officer described another kind of delay:

> You come across the technique of never really being able to . . . get a decision because you're always chasing the elusive man who can make the decision. . . . Some of [the local authorities] are much more adept at playing this game than an industry is. You get a planning committee going. They always *do* something; they're always doing things—working parties, consultants, new committees. And you go round and round and round, and in the end you just have to turn round and say 'Look you've got to do something now—or else'. [His emphasis.]

And so far as industry is concerned:

> You've always got works and things going on and you're always digging the place up... they always employ consultants and they're always looking into problems, they have lots and lots of meetings and things and you can never really screw them down to a day when something is actually going to be finished.... Some of the big firms do use [the] technique of hiding the person responsible.... Once you've got as far as you possibly can go with one person and it's obvious that you're getting a bit shirty... then someone else will appear in the chain of command and you go and see them. And it is a job to find who was really responsible. You know, they... play this... managerial game....

In some cases the use of delaying tactics is bolstered by the polluter's attempt to display himself as the blameless victim of *force majeure*: 'They have all sorts of excuses: delay in arrival of spares and breakdowns and this and that; the factory being on holiday and not being able to produce the goods. There's stacks of that; I think that's all part of the game really.'

The use of excuses to deflect accusations of blame suggests some familiarity on the part of dischargers with field staff's conception of the rules of the game. Extensive dealings with pollution control officers make available to polluters a sense of the features of any problem which officers define as significant. The more frequent the involvement with pollution control staff, the more the polluter acquires the awareness of the 'repeat player': he learns the ropes and the procedures, and develops counter-strategies (Galanter, 1974). For instance, the officer who receives a report of a pollution from the polluter himself will be much more favourably disposed than if the pollution came to light as a result of complaints from third parties or even following routine monitoring. The polluter accordingly learns that his own early warning of the pollution is highly valued, from the requests field staff put routinely to dischargers to report any trouble to the agency immediately (Brittan, forthcoming). By alerting the agency when the pollution (however caused) occurs he has a good chance of avoiding the possibility that blame will be attributed to him: favourable moral evaluations lead to more tolerance on the part of field men and a greater reluctance to sanction misconduct (Hawkins, 1984, 161–71).[15] Someone who does not alert the agency of a noticeable pollution will be treated prima facie as 'trying to pull a fast one'. On the other hand, a polluter who presents himself as well intentioned may well be able to slow the pace at which he is brought into compliance (but if he subsequently finds himself in trouble, he may discover that his earlier reluctance is now characterized as evidence of a basic unco-operativeness, prompting a less sympathetic approach).

There are, of course, other games, of greater or lesser sophistication:

> You get the attempt to use muscle on a personal level, and you get attempts to use muscle on a political level. You get both. And it works. One sees it working where there is clearly pressure being brought to bear, up in the dizzy heights, and as a result you're restricted in the things that you can do with... either individuals or companies. Similarly one gets intimidation on a personal level, more so from our agricultural friends than from industrialists.

In the case which is partly described in Chapter 3:

> the officer had received a report of a pollution of a small stream in a public park in the city. The water was cloudy and foul-smelling. The pollution was traced to a small ice-cream manufacturing company, where the manager claimed that a vat had accidentally overturned, spilling the contents down a drain. The officer found the man extremely hostile and aggressive and for this reason decided not to take a formal sample, though in his view there was every reason to do so. The officer thought the manager was lying: the vat had been deliberately overturned, because the ice cream was substandard and tipping it down the drain was the most convenient way of getting rid of it.

Discussing this case later, the officer suggested the firm had probably escaped prosecution because of the manager's belligerence, which made him think first of his personal safety:

> FO It wasn't that we didn't want to take a stat; we were anxious to do so, but because this gentleman had been throwing [his product] at us and threatening other forms of physical violence, it was just impossible to get onto his premises to take a statutory sample. In cases like that, one is advised by the authority not to get a broken nose but to retire gracefully and seek a magistrates' warrant, and return. Which is fine if it's a long-term problem, but in the case of a one-off then the intimidation works, and by the time you return then the problem has passed.
> KH ... If you are sufficiently belligerent following a one-off pollution then it's very difficult for the officer to enforce the law in effect?
> FO Yeah, yeah, ... it can be made virtually impossible if you have to enter land to get the sample.

The bribe is doubtless the best known means of evading law enforcement, though as a taboo subject it is difficult to research (cf. Blau, 1963: 187–93). Subtly employed, it can be a useful delaying tactic: 'We used to think that a good lunch would put if off for another three months,' said an officer who had worked, before joining his authority, in an industry notorious for its pollution problems. Sometimes, it seems, polluters are less discreet and attempt to persuade field officers to accept a gift in return for favourable treatment:

I was once taken to a showroom of a very reputable company when dealing with a pollution. I'd just taken legal samples, and my biggest problem was to get out of the showroom and get on with dealing with the pollution, when he said to me, 'Is there anything you want?' Y'know he didn't say 'Is there anything you want to drop the prosecution or throw away the samples?', or——he just said, 'Is there——if you want anything, just say'. And he put it as simple as that. And the cheapest thing . . . they made was about £400. . . . He made it perfectly clear that, y'know, I could have had what I wanted.

Bargaining

The voluntary compliance of the regulated is regarded by the agencies as the most desirable means of meeting water quality standards. For the agencies it is not only viewed as the most effective strategy, it is a relatively cheap method of achieving conformity.[16] For agency staff it is a means of promoting goodwill, a matter of profound importance in open-ended enforcement relationships which must be maintained in the future. Compliance takes on the appearance of voluntariness by the use of *bargaining*.[17] Bargaining processes have 'a graduated and accommodative character' (Eisenberg, 1976: 654, italics omitted) which draw their efficacy from the ostensibly voluntary commitment of the parties. The more legalistic style of penal enforcement with decision-making by adjudication and the imposition of a sanction risks, according to agency staff, continued intransigence from the guilty polluter. Bargaining is central to enforcement in compliance systems; control is buttressed for it is derived from some sort of consensus (Schuck, 1979: 31). Bargaining implies the acquiescence of the regulated, however grudging. And it inevitably suggests some compromise from the rigours of penal enforcement.

The essence of a compliance strategy is the exchange relationship (Blau, 1963: 137 ff.), a subtle reminder of the mutual dependence which Edelman (1964: 47) regards as central to the conception of the game. The polluter has goodwill, co-operation and, most important, conformity to the law to offer. The enforcement agent may offer in return two important commodities: forbearance and advice.

The offer of forbearance is the opportunity for another display of the officer's craft. He will not ask for costly remedies unless the problem is a major one or the polluter is undoubtedly wealthy. He will recognize inherent constraints facing the polluter, such as lack of space. He will respect a previously co-operative relationship. Most important, he will offer a less authoritarian response than that legally mandated. He offers the polluter time to attain compliance, for bargaining strategies 'are based on the principle that success in pollution control is 'bought' by giving up some of the demands that are fixed in the legal norms to be implemented' (Hucke, 1978: 18).

Bargaining is possible, then, only *because the law need not be formally enforced*. Rules are a valuable resource for enforcement agents since, as Gouldner has observed (1954: 174), they represent something which may be given up, as well as given use. The display of forbearance is valuable in obliging the polluter to take action in response to the show of leniency:

> . . . instead of leaving the impression that you're some jumped-up little upstart from an office using the law to tell him what he must do, if you talk to him right, you finish up leaving him with the view that 'Well, he's a damn good chap. . . . I could've been prosecuted for this. I'm breaking the law, but he's obviously going to shoot it under the carpet and let me get away with it.' So . . . he does what he has to do, with goodwill, and everybody's happy.

Or, again:

> I've said 'Alright, well, look, I've got this stat sample here and this could be used against you in legal proceedings, but provided that you play ball with me and get done what I want to get done, then I'll get rid of it.' And [I've] very often poured it out in front of his eyes. And you'd be amazed. This has done the trick on every occasion that I've ever dealt with. They're *so grateful*. . . . [His emphasis.]

Discreetly coercive bargaining is equally useful in preventive work:

> You can say 'If you build this bund wall or you take these steps, we'll drop the stat.' You can achieve a lot with this–*they* feel they've got you off their back, and *we've* got them to do something. [His emphasis.]

A sense of mutual trust is important in sustaining the bargaining relationship: trust that the polluter will not 'pull a fast one', trust that the officer will not penalize theoretically illegal conduct. Field staff generate a sense of trust by showing how 'reasonable'—that is forbearing—they are, polluters by displaying a willingness to conform and a readines to report 'problems'. Forbearance aids the detection of pollution by encouraging self-reporting whenever there is an escape of effluent. The polluter himself is, after all, in the best position to discover and control the pollution and prevent it from becoming a public matter. 'You do tend to learn an awful lot more,' said a supervisor based in a major conurbation:

particularly if they know what your actions are going to be. And also if they realize that when things do go wrong, if they tell you . . . you're going to react in a sensible sort of way. And when something goes wrong that they could be prosecuted on, they would still tell you because they know that . . . you're going to be more reasonable with them, because you know that they haven't hidden things in the past.

The field man will do all of this in recognition of the belief that without forbearance, compliance is the more difficult to attain. What he will demand in return for his forbearance is some show on the polluter's part of compliance with his requests:

FO I always explain to them . . . that they can do it in active co-operation with us, with us showing forbearance, and we give them as much advice and help as possible. Or they can be awkward and they can do it having been prosecuted . . . and with us watching them like a hawk forever afterwards. Which option would they choose? And when I sell it to them that way which way would anyone choose? They are obviously going to opt for the easier option. Now they might try back-sliding, but they can procrastinate once, but then we put dates on them. And legal samples are taken.
KH When you say you put dates on them——?
FO Dates for them to meet the standards. If they say 'Yes, we'll gladly spend the money required' and time goes by and they keep coming up with excuses and it is *clear that they are not in earnest*, then in that case you put a date by which they are required to meet the consent. And if they do not then I feel no compulsion in taking a legal sample. After all, I have tried my best to get them to do it the easy way. And with good feeling all round. [My emphasis.]

The symbolic properties of compliance are clear in these remarks: what is important is the display of good faith.

Since compliance enforcement is practised in a continuing relationship, 'fixing dates' by which a certain degree of compliance must be displayed provides a method of assessing the polluter's degree of conformity. If a period of time is fixed by the field officer (or, better, agreed upon with the polluter) and articulated in the form of a calendar date, the polluter is presented with an unambiguous target by which he should have stopped the discharge, dug a hole, installed equipment or replaced existing plant. Time is a good, exact index of compliance, more useful for enforcement purposes than the prescription of work to be done which is inherently open to negotiation. Deadlines can nevertheless be made flexible to provide the appearance of a softening of demands. Since compliance is often a lengthy and costly process, the field man may spin out the time allowed and present his demands in stages (cf. Kaufman, 1960: 225; Thompson, 1950).

Deadlines aid an enforcement officer's appreciation of the polluter's career as deviant. A deadline met is an index of progress, of headway, while a polluter who fails to meet a deadline can be mutually recognized as a rule-breaker, even as unco-operative. In presenting such unambiguous evidence of non-compliance the field man inevitably casts most polluters into a defensive posture, forcing them to account for their failure to live up to their side of the bargain. If the field man can convincingly portray himself as having been generous in the amount of time he has allowed, he can increase the polluter's sense of obligation to comply with future demands. At the same time, failure to meet a date is a breach of the implied bargain and gives the officer grounds to be less forbearing towards the polluter, if this is tactically desirable, unless the latter can offer some plausible account for his failure. What constitutes a plausible account usually involves establishing financial or technical impediments to compliance; thus, to quote an example frequently treated as plausible by field staff, if the polluter can claim the late delivery of equipment he is usually freed from imputations of fault, and has an 'excuse' demanding forbearance from the officer.

The realization that in pollution matters conformity with the law involves more than simply refraining from proscribed conduct is reflected in the second commodity a field man can offer in bargaining. An officer's willingness to act as expert consultant recognizes the often costly and complicated business of compliance. Technical advice will be given whether the field man is dealing with persistent polluters, where the advice will be about the suitability of particular remedial measures, or with one-off cases, where he will want to prevent a recurrence. Advice is always given tentatively, since the officer must protect himself and his agency against any repercussions which may follow heavy expenditure to little effect. Field agents' preoccupation with ends ensures that advice is realistic and negotiable. The remedial action suggested will not simply depend on technical issues centred around the nature of the 'problem', but will also be geared in particular to the officer's perception of the abilities of the polluter to pay. Industrialists are considered to be economically capable of supporting more elaborate measures than other dischargers: 'I think the expensive jobs are loaded on industry and I think industry can bear the cost.' By 'industry' is normally meant companies with large numbers of employees; minor concerns are regarded as 'small men' and *ipso facto* assumed less capable of bearing the costs of control. This categorization between rich and poor is an important distinction, for it provides the officer with a means of establishing whether the troublesome discharger has reasonable grounds for dragging his heels. As most dischargers are not large private companies or nationalized industries, field staff are accustomed to offering advice about remedial action which is as cheap to effect as possible. The more modest the remedy, the more reasonable the demands seem, and the easier the task of enforcement: 'With those that can't afford it I'll say, "Look, just dig a bloody hole in the ground—that'll serve the purpose." I don't like people's money being used needlessly.' And the cheaper the action proposed, the less embarrassing it will be for the officer if his suggestion proves less than successful. The following conversation nicely illustrates the officer's stance, focused as it is on getting the job done 'for now':

FO If there is a problem, a problematical discharge at the site and there are a variety of solutions, one invariably tends to lean towards the least costly, providing it does the job . . . simply because you want the industrialist to go along with you and if you go for the most expensive one, you're less likely to get a satisfactory response. The pollution's going on longer while he's umming and ahing and perhaps at the end of the day you've got to take a stat and go through all that machinery, whereas perhaps at the first or second meeting you can agree on a much cheaper, but perhaps equally satisfactory solution. So . . . the primary consideration is stopping a pollution as quickly as possible, and if by demonstrating that there is a cheap and effective way of doing it as well as putting an expensive plant in, then in the long-term perhaps it's not as desirable, but by getting that in and getting it cleaned up, you've got breathing space to then keep wearing at them and trying to get them to improve that facility. And in the long-term maybe getting the better plant.

KH So you are saying then that to do your job it's important to know the financial state of a firm?

FO Well you need to know two things really. It's very necessary to be, within a few pounds, aware of the cost of treatment facilities, so that you're not asking for the ridiculous, as well as being able to assess whether the company can afford it, so that you know where to pitch. If there's a plant costing £50 and a plant costing £500 and a plant costing £5000, it helps to know those three costs and to know which one the company can afford, so that you get the right response when you say, 'This is necessary to improve your effluent, you really ought to put this in or put that in.' [You tell them to] get the stuff organized and get it in. But again you're thinking of financial constraints and consultants' fees and, without committing the authority, if you can in general terms give an indication of the plant that they need, give them an on-the-spot consultation if you like, for free, and get them moving . . .they're more disposed to doing it than if you say, 'Well, if you ring a consultant he'll come and see you in a fortnight and he'll charge you £200 for driving in through your gate,' and this sort of thing. It's all adding to cost. Obviously one doesn't—can't—give clearly defined guidelines as to treatment facilities because ultimately if the treatment facility fails, then you can't go back to them and say 'It's not good enough,' because they'll say, 'Well it was put in subject to your recommendations.'

Postscript

Compliance is often treated as if it were an objectively-defined unproblematic state (e.g. Nagel, 1974), rather than a fluid, negotiable matter. Compliance, however, is an elaborate concept, one better seen as a process, rather than a condition. What will be understood as compliance depends upon the nature of the rule-breaking encountered, and upon the resources and responses of the regulated. The capacity to comply is ultimately evaluated in moral terms, and is of utmost importance in shaping enforcement behaviour. A greater degree of control is likely where a discharger is regarded as able to bear the expenditure for compliance; this issue is still a moral one, fundamentally, not one of economics.

Compliance is negotiable and embraces action, time, and symbol. It addresses both standard and process. It may in some cases consist of present conformity. In others, present rule-breaking will be tolerated on an understanding that there will be conformity in future: compliance represents, in other words, some ideal state towards which an enforcement agent works. Since the enforcement of regulation is a continuing process, compliance is often attained by increments. Conformity to this process itself is another facet of compliance. And when a standard is attained, it must be maintained: compliance here is an unbounded, continuing state. It is not simply a matter of the installation of treatment plant, but how well that plant is made to work, and kept working. And an ideal, once reached, may be replaced or transformed by other changes—in consent, in water resource or land use, for example—which demand the achievement of a different ideal (Hawkins, 1984, 32–5). Central to all of this is the symbolic aspect of compliance. A recognition of the legitimacy of the demands of an enforcement agent expressed in a willingness to conform in future will be taken as a display of compliance in itself. Here it is possible for a polluter to be thought of as 'compliant' even though he may continue to break the rules about the discharge of polluting effluent.

A strategy of compliance is a means of sustaining the consent of the regulated where there is ambivalence about the enforcement agency's mandate. Enforcement in a compliance system is founded on reciprocity, for conformity is not simply a matter of the threat or the rare application of legal punishment, but rather a matter of bargaining. The familiar discrepancy between full enforcement and actual practice is 'more of a resource than an embarrassment' (Silbey and Bittner, n.d.:5). Compliance strategy is a means of sustaining the consent of the regulated when there is ambivalence about an enforcement agency's legal mandate. The gap between legal word and legal deed is ironically employed as a way to attaining legislative objectives. Put another way, bargaining is not only adjudged a more efficient means to attain the ends of regulation than the formal enforcement of the rules, bargaining is, ultimately, morally compelled.

Notes

* Chapter 6 in *Environment and Enforcement: Regulation and the Social Definition of Pollution*, Oxford, Clarendon Press, 1984.

† Keith Hawkins is Reader in Law and Society, and Fellow and Tutor in Law of Oriel College, Oxford.

1. About half the prosecutions brought in the southern authority are for persistent failures to comply (agency communication).
2. Similarly Ross and Thomas (1981:12) report that housing inspectors regard violations as 'chickenshit' or 'important'.
3. The concept of career is treated in Rock (1973b) and Roth (1963).
4. Stopping (rather than cleaning) the discharge is sometimes the ultimate (but not the immediate) aim with persistent failures to comply: some polluters are encouraged to recycle waste water or dispose of it to foul sewer.
5. So far as the agency is concerned, the nature of the behaviour to be regulated and the realities of the enforcement strategies adopted mean, in effect, that it is difficult to display 'compliance' or other measures of success or impact in any meaningful fashion (cf. Wilson, 1968:57). River surveys will indicate broad changes in water quality over the years which agency staff may attribute to more extensive and efficient enforcement. But it is extremely difficult to sustain this claim with any precision owing to problems in disentangling enforcement practices from other shifts which have had an impact on water quality, such as changing patterns in land use or changes in public expenditure on sewage treatment.
6. Similarly, businesses are regarded in the consumer field as essentially law-abiding (Cranston, 1979:29). Principled compliance may be commoner in Europe than the USA, as Kelman's data seem to suggest (1981). See, generally, Anderson, 1966. Brittan's study of discharges (forthcoming) supports the perception of a majority given to principled compliance.
7. Field staff assume that larger businesses have a reputation to protect and are thus 'better' or 'more responsive', a notion suggested by Lane (1953).

8. Brittan (forthcoming) suggests that officers' assumptions about large companies and nationalized industries are correct.
9. Compare the unquestioning compliance which police can expect in regulating traffic behaviour (Bittner, 1967a: 702)
10. Kagan and Scholz (1979:15) observe that legalistic enforcement 'seems to have been a primary factor in stimulating political organization by regulated firms and attempts to attack the agency at the legislative level', while a more legalistic approach by the California Occupational Safety and Health authorities has led to an increased number of appeals (ibid., 14). See also Barrett (1979); Kagan (1980); Kelman (1981).
11. These penalties have since been increased by the Control of Pollution Act 1974 and the Criminal Law Act 1977—but the sanctions are still generally regarded as modest by field men despite the provision for terms of imprisonment. Most officers, however, only had a very hazy notion of the availability of this sanction.
12. In the USA, the Environmental Protection Agency has consciously used adverse publicity as an enforcement tool: Gellhorn (1973:1401 ff). See also Rourke (1957).
13. See further Brittan, (forthcoming). Cases have been known to occur in which shop-floor workers have manipulated the system of internal organizational control to encourage an unwilling management to comply. They have acted in a deliberately unco-operative manner, ultimately forcing the field officer to threaten the company with prosecution. This is normally enough to ensure that management make the resources available to improve their pollution control arrangements.
14. The proportion of discharges presumed to be utterly unco-operative varies according to the nature of the field officer's patch, with those working in urban industrialized areas expecting more deviance and greater reluctance to comply than those whose areas are predominantly rural. This is despite the view of the farmer as 'troublesome'. The apparent contradiction may possibly reflect the fact that farm effluents, in contrast with many industrial discharges, are all relatively familiar and easily traced. One supervising officer from a largely urban area suggested that about 70 per cent of dischargers were 'co-operative, willing to comply'; about 20 per cent were 'slow to comply'; the remaining 10 per cent or so he classified as 'having to be forced to comply'.
15. This raises the question of the techniques adopted by field staff for categorizing dischargers into those 'genuinely' reporting a pollution, and those taking unfair advantage of pollution control staff, an issue addressed in Hawkins, Environment and Enforcement, Oxford, Clarendon Press, 1984 ch. 8.
16. A former Chairman of the Illinois Pollution Control Board has observed that 'if no one complied until prosecuted, enforcement costs would surely strangle the program' (Currie, 1975:390).
17. Bargaining is one of the central characteristics of legal processes: see Hagevik (1968); Holden (1966); Jowell (1977a); (1977b); Ross (1970); Silbey (1978); Stjernquist (1973: 149); and, generally, Gouldner (1960); Strauss (1978).

References

Anderson, James E. (1966) 'Public economic policy and the problem of compliance: Notes for research' *Houston Law Review* 4: 62–72.

Barrett, J. W. (1977) 'We're good boys now but can we stay in business' *Product Finishing* March.

——(1979) 'Prosecution may soon make cowboys of us all' *Product Finishing* 32:12/14.

Bittner, Egon (1967) 'The police on skid-row: A study of peace keeping', *American Sociological Review*, Vol. 32, 699–715.

Blau, Peter M. (1963) *The Dynamics of Bureaucracy: A study of interpersonal relations in two government agencies* (Chicago: University of Chicago Press).

Brittan, Yvonne (forthcoming) *The Impact of Water Pollution Control on Industry*, Oxford: Centre for Socio-Legal Studies.

Cranston, Ross (1979) *Regulatory Business: Law and consumer agencies*, (London: Macmillan).

Currie, David P. (1975) 'Enforcement under the Illinois pollution law' *Northwestern University Law Review* 70: 389–485.

Dickens, Bernard M. (1974) 'Law making and enforcement—a case study' *Modern Law Review* 37: 297–307.

Edelman, Murray (1964) *The Symbolic Use of Politics* (Urbana, Ill.: University of Illinois Press).

Eisenberg, Melvin Aaron (1976) 'Private ordering through negotiation: dispute-settlement and rulemaking' *Harvard Law Review* 89: 637–81.

Emerson, Robert M. (1969) *Judging Delinquents. Context and process in juvenile court* (Chicago: Aldine).

Galanter, Mark (1974) 'Why the "haves" come out ahead: Speculations on the limits of legal change' *Law and Society Review*, 9, 95–160.

Gellhorn, Ernest (1973) 'Adverse publicity by administrative agencies' *Harvard Law Review* 86: 1380–441.

Goldstein, Paul and Ford, Robert (1972) 'The management of air quality: legal structures and official behavior' *Buffalo Law Review* 21: 1–48.

Gouldner, Alvin W. (1954) *Patterns of Industrial Bureaucracy* (New York: Free Press).

Hagevik, George (1968) 'Legislation for air quality management: reducing theory to practice' *Law and Contemporary Problems* 33: 369–98.

Holden, Matthew jun. (1966) 'Pollution control as a bargaining process: an essay on regulatory decision-making' (Ithaca, NY: Cornell University Water Resources Center).

Jowell, Jeffrey L. (1977a) 'Bargaining in development control' *Journal of Planning and Environmental Law*: 414–33.

——(1977b) 'The limits of the law in urban planning' *Current Legal Problems* 30: 63–83.

Kadish, Sanford H. (1963) 'Some observations on the use of criminal sanctions in enforcing economic regulations' *University of Chicago Law Review* 30: 423–49.

Kagan, Robert A. (1980) 'The positive uses of discretion: the good inspector', paper presented to the 1980 Annual Meeting of the Law and Society Association, Madison, Wisconsin, June.

—— and John T. Scholz (1979) 'The criminology of the corporation and regulatory enforcement strategies' paper presented to the Symposium on Organizational Factors in the Implementation of Law, University of Oldenburg, May.

Katona, George (1945) *Price Control and Business. Field studies among producers and distributors of consumer goods in the Chicago area, 1942–44* (Bloomington, Ind.: Principia Press).

Kaufman, Herbert (1960) *The Forest Ranger. A study in administrative behavior* (Baltimore: John Hopkins University Press).

Kelman, Steven (1981) *Regulating America, Regulating Sweden: a Comparative Study of Occupational Safety and Health Policy* (Cambridge: MIT Press).

Lane, Robert E. (1953) 'Why business men violate the law' *Journal of Criminal Law, Criminology and Police Science* 44: 151–65.

Nagel, Stuart (1974) 'Incentives for compliance with environmental law' *American Behavioral Scientist* 17: 690–710.

Rock, Paul (1973b) *Making People Pay* (London: Routledge & Kegan Paul).

Ross, H. Laurence (1970) *Settled Out of Court: The social process of insurance claims adjustment* (Chicago: Aldine).

Ross, H. Laurence and Thomas, John M. (1981) 'Blue-collared bureaucrats and the law in action: housing code regulation in three cities' unpublished paper.

Roth, Julius A. (1963) *Timetables: Structuring the passage of time in hospital treatment and other careers* (Indianapolis: Bobbs-Merrill).

Rourke, Francis E. (1957) 'Law enforcement through publicity' *University of Chicago Law Review* 24: 225–55.

Silbey, Susan S. (1978) 'Consumer justice: the Massachusetts Attorney General's Office of Consumer Protection, 1970–74' Ph.D. dissertation, University of Chicago.

Silbey, Susan S. and Egon Bittner (n.d.) 'The availability of legal devices' unpublished paper.

Staw, Barry M. and Szwajkowski, Eugene (1975) 'The scarcity-munificence component of organizational environments and the commission of illegal acts' *Administrative Science Quarterly* 20: 345–54.

Stjernquist, Per (1973) *Laws in the Forests. A study of public direction of Swedish private forestry* (Lund: C.W.K. Gleerup).

Strauss, Anselm (1978) *Negotiations. Varieties, contexts, processes, and social order* (San Francisco: Jossey-Bass).

Sykes, Gresham M. and David Matza (1957) 'Techniques of neutralization: a theory of delinquency' *American Sociological Review* 10: 132–39.

Thompson, Victor A. (1950) *The Regulatory Process in OPA Rationing* (New York: King's Crown Press).
Wilson, James Q. (1968) *Varieties of Police Behaviour* (Cambridge, Mass.: Harvard University Press).

The Political Economy of Environmental Regulation: Towards a Unifying Framework*

ROBERT W. HAHN†

Abstract

There are several theories that attempt to explain various aspects of environmental policies. Building on insights from this theoretical work, and recent advances in our understanding of instrument performance, this chapter constructs a more complete theory of environmental regulation. There are two primary contributions of this research. The first is to provide more satisfactory explanations for a number of observed patterns of environmental policy. For example, there is, as yet, no satisfactory theory about the emergence of incentive-based mechanisms, such as marketable permits and effluent fees. The second contribution of this paper is to develop a parsimonious framework for understanding many important aspects of environmental policy. This framework suggests the outputs of environmental policy emerge from a struggle between key interest groups.

Introduction

During the last two decades, there has been tremendous growth in the scope of environmental regulation. More chemicals are regulated than ever before. The stringency of regulation has also increased over time, particularly in densely populated areas. Despite the increase in the level of environmental regulation, the dominant approach to regulation has changed very little. In most places, a central regulatory authority sets standards. These standards vary in type, but they typically place stringent emission limits on individual sources.

In addition to standards, governments have made liberal use of subsidies to help promote environmental quality. For example, the U.S. federal government provided large subsidies, in the billions of dollars, to aid in the construction of municipal waste treatment plants. States often provide subsidies and tax incentives to aid in the control of pollution. Indeed, both standards and subsidies have enjoyed widespread use in most developed countries.

Less widespread, but growing in popularity, is the application of tools that economists find more appealing from an economic efficiency perspective. Examples include effluent fees and marketable permits. While the implementation of these instruments tends to depart substantially from the textbook versions, the application of these tools has had a marked impact on environmental quality and the costs of achieving environmental goals (Hahn, 1987).

Given the vast array of different approaches to environmental regulation, it is only natural to ask how their selection might be explained or rationalized. The first step in searching for a deeper understanding is to identify patterns in environmental regulation. The second step is to examine underlying forces that might help explain these patterns. The purpose of this chapter is to provide simple rationales for many of the patterns that are observed in environmental policy. An understanding of the basic forms that environmental regulation takes will help provide insights into the potential and conditions for regulatory reform.

Several scholars have attempted to understand different aspects of environmental policy using positive political theories. This research will review and build on the insights which have been developed. There are two primary contributions of this chapter. The first is to provide more complete explanations for a number of patterns in environmental policy which have not been satisfactorily explained. For example, there is, as yet, no satisfactory theory about the emergence of incentive-based mechanisms, such as marketable permits and effluent fees. This chapter develops some formal models which shed light on these issues. The second contribution of this chapter is to develop a simple framework for understanding many important aspects of environmental policy. This framework views the outputs of environmental policy as emerging from a struggle between key interest groups.

Positive theories pertaining to the application of environmental regulation is critically examined in Section 2. Section 3 presents a formal analysis aimed at identifying key factors which affect policy design. A series of models is presented which provides insights into the existing standard-setting process, new regulatory approaches, and dominant patterns in environmental policy. Section 4 raises some broader issues related to the construction of a theory of instrument choice. Finally, Section 5 reviews the key conclusions and suggests areas for future research.

Theories and explanations: A critical appraisal

Before discussing existing positive theories of environmental regulation, it is useful to identify suitable goals for a positive theory. These goals, taken in conjunction with the existing state of the art, will help to suggest a research agenda. Ideally, what would we want from a positive theory of environmental regulation? Like any positive theory, we would hope that it has predictive power. Moreover, it should be able to explain what gets regulated, the methods chosen for regulation, and the likely winners and losers from regulation. While some insights from political theory can be brought to bear on these questions, our knowledge of what will get regulated is quite limited.

In contrast to our rudimentary understanding of what is regulated, our understanding of how things are regulated, and the associated distribution of benefits and costs, is relatively advanced. Indeed, virtually all of the positive theories which have been developed are based on some notion of net benefit maximization either by a single agent or in the context of a mathematical game. Often the single agent represents an interest group. For example, Buchanan and Tullock (1975) argue that firms will prefer emission standards to emission taxes because they result in higher profits. Emission standards serve as a barrier to entry for new firms, thus raising profits of existing firms. Charges, on the other hand, do not preclude entry by new firms, and also represent an additional cost to firms. This argument is based on the view that industry is able to exert its preference for a particular instrument because it is more likely to be well-organized than consumers. Since this seminal article by Buchanan and Tullock, several authors have explored the instrument choice problem using this basic framework (Coelho, 1976; Dewees, 1983; Yohe, 1976). The basic insight of this work is that the preference for standards over taxes depends crucially on the precise nature of the instruments being compared. It also depends on the amount of power that particular interest groups have, and how this power is wielded in the political process.

The influence of different interest groups has been modeled in several ways. Perhaps the most popular (and also the most tractable) is to assume that a single agent, such as a legislator, chooses policies to maximize net benefits. The initial framework for this maximization problem was suggested by Peltzman (1976) in the context of regulation. Recently, Campos (1987) has adapted this framework to the instrument choice problem. He assumes that a legislator chooses the most preferred instrument from a distinct number of alternatives. Campos examines the motivation underlying the choice of price supports or quotas in agriculture. He shows that the answer will, in general, depend on both the demand for the commodity and the nature of the constituency support that the legislator attempts to nurture. In another application of Peltzman's approach, Magat, Krupnick and Harrington (1986) attempt to explain how different groups affect the stringency of standards at different points in the rulemaking process.

A somewhat more abstract approach is taken by Becker (1983) who assumes that groups compete for influence in an attempt to redistribute 'the pie' to their benefit. Becker (1983) has argued that governments will tend to choose mechanisms which are more efficient over those which are less efficient in redistributing revenues from less powerful to more powerful groups. One feature of existing environmental regulation is that it appears to result in high degrees of inefficiency. However, this does not necessarily refute Becker's theory since the inefficiencies may result from interest group pressures. If there is no more efficient means for redistributing revenues given interest group preferences, then Becker may be right. One problem with Becker's theory, however, is that it may not be testable in its current form because of the difficulty in specifying the influence functions.

While some theories of instrument choice are based on direct redistribution from one group to another, there are others which build on the political decisions to delegate power, and the form of the power which is delegated. Both Fiorina (1982) and McCubbins (1985) have focused on Congress, and attempted to identify conditions under which policies will be delegated. These models are important because they accentuate the role of the legislature in determining the nature of policy. McCubbins and Page (1986) illustrate how many of these ideas can be applied to environmental policy. The authors argue that economic incentive schemes may not be selected because they tend to increase conflict and uncertainty among politicians by providing firms with greater flexibility. While this may be true, there are many instances where the government has opted to use economic incentive schemes for both social and economic policies. Moreover, the use of these approaches is becoming more widespread. Thus, some further explanation about the emergence of these schemes would be helpful.

There have been several stories and theories about the winners and losers from environmental policy. Tucker (1982) argues that the environmental movement in the U.S. primarily serves to enhance the wealth of the privileged class. Ackerman and Hassler (1981) paint a somewhat different picture. Studying the emergence of regulations which required power plants to install scrubbers, the authors argue that a coalition formed among environmentalists and Eastern coal interests. The resulting regulations were very expensive and may actually have lowered environmental quality. The case study is important because it provides evidence that environmental groups may be more concerned with symbols, such as forced scrubbing, than actual environmental outcomes. It also shows how interest groups can form coalitions which yield seemingly bizarre outcomes, yet are perfectly sensible from the viewpoint of the interest groups involved.

There is a debate in the published literature about the extent to which new regulations benefit well-organized interests. Stigler (1971) argues that producers will generally be the beneficiaries of regulation. Rolph (1983) takes issue with this finding, arguing that the existing distribution of property rights is important in shaping new policies, but not finding a systematic trend for new regulations to favor well-organized interest groups, such as producers. Certainly in the area of environmental regulation, the verdict on this issue is out. Welch (1983) and Hahn (1987) argue that the current distribution of property rights strongly affects the design of new incentive-based policies. However, the major beneficiaries of these policies seem to vary from case to case. This should not be particularly surprising since the configuration of interest group influence can also be expected to vary.

Formal tests of theories about the beneficiaries of environmental regulation are just beginning to emerge. Perhaps, the best known theory involves the use of standards to enhance industry profits. After laying out the theory, Maloney and McCormick (1982) present some empirical support based on cotton dust standards and an air pollution ruling affecting smelters. While they argue that the results are consistent with the view that industry benefits from regulations, a detailed analysis of the cotton dust case by Hughes, Magat and Williams (1986) casts doubt on their conclusions.

This review of the state of our understanding of environmental policy choices reveals that virtually all the formal models are based on theories about redistribution and power. The simplest models assume that industry has all the power, and that there is a single decision-maker. More elaborate models relax these assumptions. The models help to explain some important stylized facts about the choice of standards over other instruments and the likely beneficiaries of environmental regulation. However, they provide few insights on the conditions under which incentive-based instruments will be chosen, the mechanics of the standard-setting process, and the choice of the form of environmental regulation. The next section adds to this theoretical foundation by addressing a variety of issues in environmental policy related to the selection of instruments and the choice of environmental targets.

Towards a more unified theory of environmental policy

Environmental policy is almost always at the source of a great deal of controversy. At the heart of this controversy lie two fundamentally opposing points of view. One, represented by 'industry', usually focuses on the impact of environmental policy on profits. A second, represented by 'environmentalists', is more concerned with the impact of policy on the environment. The reduction of the diverse range of interest-group perspectives on environmental policy into two distinct viewpoints is a gross oversimplification. The simplification is made purely in the interest of developing a parsimonious and elegant theory of environmental policy. The purpose of this section is to explore how this view of the world can enlighten many of the choices and patterns that are observed in environmental policy. The first part of the section will examine the logic of the standard-setting process. This will be followed by a discussion of the emergence of alternative regulatory mechanisms which address environmental problems. More general themes in the choice of what is regulated and the level of regulation are taken up in the third part of this section.

One critical simplification that will be used to facilitate the analysis is the assumption that environmental policy is made by a single decision-maker or decision-making unit, typically represented by a regulator or a legislator.[1] While this is clearly at odds with reality, it is again made in the interest of simplicity. Moreover, many of the examples presented here could be recast in the form of a mathematical game in which multiple interest groups compete. The unitary actor assumption is consistent with the models developed by Buchanan and Tullock (1975), Fiorina (1982), and Peltzman (1976). Nonetheless, it suffers from the fact that institutions are not explicity factored into the analysis. Typically, Congress is the institution which most scholars are concerned about including in the analysis (see, e.g., Fiorina, 1982; and Page and McCubbins, 1986). However, for many applications in environmental policy, various levels of bureaucracy also play an important role, and one which has not received the attention it deserves. In addition, in the United States, the courts have played a significant role in shaping environmental policy (Melnick, 1983).

Towards a theory of standard-setting

A useful starting point in addressing issues in instrument choice is to examine how the dominant instrument in environmental policy—the standard—is applied. Surprising as it may seem, there is no generally accepted theory of how regulatory standards are applied. Suppose that a regulator is charged with imposing standards on individual sources until a given environmental objective is met. The regulator must decide how standards will be applied. One way to think about this problem is that the regulator must balance economic objectives against political concerns. Suppose there are two types of standards which can be imposed, one which imposes low economic costs on individual firms, and another which imposes high economic costs. The decision in this case is relatively straightforward. Standards with the lower economic cost will be applied first.[2]

However, suppose that standards also have a political cost attached to them. This cost might result from standards affecting unemployment, plant closure, or environmental quality in the neighborhood of an important politician. Then the regulator needs to rank standards on two dimensions. Table 6.1 provides a two by two matrix representation of the various alternatives facing the regulator. His preference over these alternatives is reflected in the number in each box. The number '1' represents the most preferred alternative and the number '4' represents the least preferred alternative. Clearly, the regulator's first choice is to impose standards with low political and economic costs. Conversely, the least preferred alternative is represented by standards which impose both high economic and political costs. The remaining two cells in the matrix are more difficult to evaluate, and highlight the nature of the balancing problem. Here, it is assumed that political costs dominate economic concerns for the regulator, and thus, a standard with low political costs and high economic costs is preferred to one with high political and low economic costs. Whether this will always be true depends on the precise nature of the regulator's utility function.

This basic paradigm captures the notion that a regulator needs to balance different concerns; however, it does not explicitly introduce the

Table 6.1. *How standards are selected by a regulator*

	Low economic cost	High economic cost
Low political cost	1	2
High political cost	3	4

concerns of interest groups. To explore difference in viewpoints among interest groups, it is instructive to consider a concrete example. One persistent theme in environmental regulation is that new sources of pollution get regulated more stringently than existing sources. A simple reason often used to explain this observation is that new sources don't 'vote', while existing sources have access to political power. A slightly different, but complementary, way of looking at this problem is offered in Table 6.2. Suppose a legislator has to choose between low and high standards for new and existing sources of pollution. Instead of showing the preferences of the regulator, Table 6.2 shows the preferences of two interest groups. Each ordered pair represents the preferences of industry and environmentalists, respectively. Industry is assumed to prefer low standards across the board, because it reduces costs.[3] Environmentalists, on the other hand, prefer high standards across the board. As in the preceding example, the interesting comparisons arise in the low/high cells. For these two cells, both environmentalists and industry exhibit the same direction of preference. Stricter standards for new sources are preferred by both groups to stricter standards for old sources. Industry adopts this preference ranking because lower costs to existing firms are more important than lower costs for new firms. Environmentalists adopt this ranking because they take a long-term outlook on environmental quality and assume that ultimately, environmental quality will be improved by having stricter standards for new firms.

The legislator is expected to balance the concerns of industry and environmentalists in a way that maximizes net benefits. The choice of a particular cell by the legislator will depend on the utility function. Assuming that both environmentalists and industry have an important effect on this function, it is reasonable to expect that the choice reduces to the low/high cells, since the low/low and high/high are the least preferred

Table 6.2. *Choice of standards for new and existing sources*

		New sources	
		Low standard	*High standard*
Existing sources	Low standard	(1,4)*	(2,2)
	High standard	(3,3)	(4,1)

*For each ordered pair, the first coordinate represents industry preference, and the second coordinate represents environmental preference.

alternatives of one group. But if the choice reduces to the low/high cells, the choice is relatively simple for the legislator. The cell with a high standard for new sources and a low standard for existing sources dominates its competitor for both interest groups, and consequently will be selected.

The movement away from standards

The use of this basic framework can be formalized and used to derive testable predictions. One of the areas which has received very little attention until recently is the emergence of incentive-based mechanisms to address environmental problems. Theories on the political feasibility of these mechanisms and the likely form these mechanisms will take are just beginning to emerge. The early work of Buchanan and Tullock (1975) gave rise to a steady stream of research on explaining the choice of standards. The instrument against which standards were most frequently judged were emissions taxes in their pure form. As several scholars have noted, emissions fees are rarely implemented in ways even remotely resembling their pure form (see, e.g., Brown and Johnson, 1984). Consequently, this instrument choice comparison may not be terribly revealing.

To develop a more realistic theory of instrument choice, it is necessary to explore how actual instruments behave in practice. The actual performance of incentive-based mechanisms varies widely. For example, the market in lead rights for controlling lead levels in gasoline has performed quite well in terms of efficiency, while the markets for controlling emissions from air pollutants have not performed that well (Hahn and Hester, 1987). Is it possible to account for such differences in performance, and if so, how?

From a theoretical point of view, it is possible to ascribe these differences to several factors. Suppose that industry and environmentalists have preferences over both the nature of instruments used and the overall level of environmental quality. Let M be a variable which characterizes the nature of instruments, and let Q represent the level of environmental quality. Environmental quality is relatively easy to measure, but the nature of instruments needs to be defined. In this case, M represents a single dimension which denotes the degree to which a system is 'market' oriented. When $M = 0$, this corresponds to the case of conventional source-specific standards. When $M = 1$, this corresponds to a 'pure' marketable permits approach. Values of M falling between 0 and 1 represent varying 'degrees' of markets. This may seem like a peculiar concept in that either markets exist or they don't. However, markets are frequently governed by very different rules of exchange, and this variable attempts to capture the extent to which trading is restricted. For example, the market for lead rights would be associated with a value of M close to 1, while the markets for controlling air pollutant emissions would be associated with a value of M much closer to 0. As M increases, the efficiency of the instrument, measured in terms of aggregate reductions in cost savings, is presumed to increase.

The preferences of industry and environmentalists are given by the functions I(M,Q) and E(M,Q), respectively. The problem facing the regulator is to maximize utility, which is assumed to be a linear combination of the preferences of environmentalists and industry.[4] Thus, the regulator will choose M and Q to:

$$\underset{M,Q}{\text{Maximize}}\ a\,I(M,Q) + (1-a)E(M,Q). \tag{1}$$

In this problem, and in all subsequent variations of this problem, a is a weighting parameter which is assumed to vary between 0 and 1. The preferences of industry receive a high weight when a is close to 1.

The regulator's choice typically will be constrained by the requirement that the choice of M and Q be acceptable to both interest groups. Acceptability can be determined by whether the new policy is at least as good as the *status quo* for both groups. This requirement could easily be added to the formal constraint set. It is suppressed here in the interest of simplicity.

Assuming the function is differentiable, the first order conditions for an interior maximum are:

$$aI_1 + (1-a)E_1 = 0,$$

and

$$aI_2 + (1-a)E_2 = 0,$$

where the subscripts on the I and E variables denote partial derivatives with respect to the arguments of the functions. For example, I_1 denotes $\partial I/\partial M$. The first-order conditions state that a weighted sum of the marginal utilities will be 0.

Up to this point, nothing has been assumed about the precise form of the preferences of industry and environmentalists other than that they are differentiable. To understand how M and Q are affected by changes in exogenous parameters, such as *a*, it is necessary to specify the nature of interest group preferences. In this, and all cases which follow, both industry and environmental preferences are assumed to be 'well-behaved.' In particular preferences are assumed to be representable by strictly concave functions which are twice differentiable. This assumption is made in the interest of simplicity, and because it is plausible for the situations represented here. Strictly concave preferences for industry and environmentalists imply that the regulator's maximization problem, which is a linear combination of these preferences, is also strictly concave.

All that remains to be specified is the exact form of the utility functions. These will vary across the different cases presented here. For this particular case, industry and environmentalist preferences are characterized by the following set of partial derivatives:

$$I_1 > 0, I_2 < 0, I_{11} < 0, I_{22} < 0, I_{12} \geq 0, \text{and}$$
$$E_1 < 0, E_2 > 0, E_{11} < 0, E_{22} < 0, E_{12} \geq 0.$$

Industry is assumed to prefer a more market-oriented alternative because it saves money.[5] However, there are decreasing returns to further movements in this direction. Industry prefers lower environmental standards, but again there are diminishing returns. Environmentalists, on the other hand, are distrustful of market alternatives and prefer the current standard-based approach. As the market orientation is lowered (M decreases), the marginal gain from a unit decrease in M is lower. Unlike industry, environmentalists prefer higher levels of environmental quality, but this is also subject to diminishing returns. These assumptions are fairly standard. A critical assumption relates to the cross partial derivative of both of these functions. In this case, the cross-partial for industry is non-negative. This says that as the environmental quality standard increases, the marginal utility from using a market increases or remains unchanged. This results from the fact that higher levels of environmental quality are associated with higher gains from trade.[6] For environmentalists, an increase in the environmental standards is assumed not to decrease the attractiveness of using markets. Both of these assumptions are plausible, but not universally true. Thus, it will be necessary to discuss the implications of relaxing them.

Given these assumptions, it is possible to examine how M and Q will respond to changes in industry influence. This will provide insights into the conditions under which markets are likely to emerge. The basic result is given in Proposition 1:[7]

Proposition 1: An increase in industry influence will increase the market orientation of the instrument and reduce the level of environmental quality which is selected.

The intuition behind this result is that as industry influence increases, environmentalist influence decreases. Thus, we will tend to observe more of what industry likes, and less of what environmentalists like. In this case, industry is assumed to like market-oriented alternatives and lower levels of environmental quality, since both can result in higher industry profits.

If the cross partial derivatives are positive or of unknown sign, then Proposition 1 does not hold. However, it is still possible to say something about the effects of a shift in the relative importance of environmentalist and industry preferences. This is summarized in Proposition 2:

Proposition 2: If preferences are well-behaved, an increase in industry influence will result either in a decrease in environmental quality and/or an increase in the market orientation of the instrument.

A similar theory can be used to explain the use of emission fees. Emission fees are primarily used as a means of raising revenues. These revenues are almost always earmarked for improving specific environmental problems associated with the pollutants which are subject to the fee. Only in a few applications have emission fees been shown to have a marked incentive effect.[8] The choice about the type of fees which are selected can be succinctly modeled by assuming that interest groups have well-defined preferences over the size of fees, F, and how they are used, U. Higher levels of fees are associated with higher values of F. Greater earmarking for specific environmental improvements is associated with higher values of U. This yields the following maximization problem for the regulator:

$$\underset{F,U}{\text{Maximize}}\ a\, I(F,U) + (1-a)E(F,U) \tag{2}$$

To understand how choices change with different weightings, the preferences need to be defined. Industry and environmentalist preferences are characterized by the following set of partial derivatives:

$$I_1 < 0, I_2 > 0, I_{11} < 0, I_{22} < 0, \text{and}$$

$$E_1 > 0, E_2 > 0, E_{11} < 0, E_{22} < 0.$$

Industry prefers lower fees to higher fees because fees represent an extra cost of doing business. Environmentalists prefer higher fees because they will reduce pollution either directly, through their impact on firm decisions to pollute, or indirectly, through their impact on expenditures aimed at reducing pollution. Both groups prefer the earmarking of fees—industry, because it increases the credit they can claim for reducing pollution, and environmentalists because they are in favor of activities which promote environmental quality. Both functions reveal diminishing marginal returns in F and U. The cross partial effects are more difficult to predict, and again are key to predicting the effect of shifts in influence on the level of fees and the degree of earmarking. This results of a shift in the relative influence of industry are summarized in Proposition 3:

Proposition 3: An increase in the relative influence of industry will result in a decrease in fees if preferences are independent. An increase in the relative influence of industry will result in a decrease in fees and no change or an increase in earmarking if the cross partials are non-negative and the marginal utility of earmarking for environmentalists does not exceed the marginal utility of earmarking for industry.

If preferences are well-behaved, an increase in industry influence will result in a decrease in fees and/or an increase in earmarking.

Part of this proposition conforms to intuition. As greater influence is given to industry preferences, fees are reduced, since industry prefers lower fees and environmentalists prefer higher fees. The situation with earmarking is clear, since both groups prefer higher levels of earmarking. There are a variety of fees which are currently in use for activities ranging from aircraft noise to hazardous waste disposal. These fees exhibit wide variations in their effect. Even within particular categories of pollutants, fees vary widely across industries and jurisdictions. This model argues that part of this variation is attributable to the relative influence of industry and environmentalists.

It is worth noting that the structure of this model suggests that earmarking is a very stable feature of the political landscape. Economists have often criticized earmarking because it restricts the flexibility that the government has in allocating its budget. This argument is not likely to obtain when strong interest groups are interested in claiming credit for state expenditures, especially when the state chooses to impose a special tax on specific industries that are influential.

The two models of fees and market-based activities look at different aspects of choice within these two classes of activities. This provides insights on the nature of instruments that are likely to be chosen within these classes. Frequently, however, both classes of instruments may be considered in the actual application of instruments. An example will illustrate the nature of choices that are involved.[9] The state of Wisconsin is in the process of devising a plan to help address the ozone problem in the southeast portion of the state. The state has generated a surplus of emissions rights for hydrocarbons, one of the major contributors to the formation of ozone. The problem confronting the regulators and legislators is how to allocate this surplus. After considering charging a fee which reflects the marginal cost of a permit, or trying to create a market in permits, the state has opted for a regulatory strategy based on first-come first-serve, with a nominal one-time fee attached to the use of the permits.[10] The decision to adopt this approach can be understood in terms of political costs and benefits. Politicians in this region are very interested in creating jobs, and in particular, jobs which are quite visible. At the same time they are interested in promoting regulatory systems which appear to have a low cost to industry.

The choices open to regulators and politicians are summarized in Table 6. 3. The three basic instruments are presented in the table. The policy which was selected is denoted as first-come first-serve, since this is the most salient feature of the policy. The costs of this policy are not readily apparent to the population at large. They include the cost of generating surplus emissions reductions, and the efficiency cost associated with the fact that the mechanism does not induce firms to search for more efficient approaches to pollution abatement. While the policy does not do well when measured in terms of efficiency, it does quite well on the dimension of visible job creation. It is designed to help accommodate 'blockbuster' projects which would bring large numbers of jobs to a depressed economic region.

Table 6.3. *Instrument choice when jobs matter*

		Visible cost	
		Low	*High*
Visible jobs	Low		Marketable permits Emission fees
	High	First - come first - serve	

In contrast, marketable permits and an emissions fee which is based on the marginal cost of abatement share the opposite characteristics. The costs of these policies are quite visible in the sense that these costs fall directly on industry. Industry can readily identify these costs in terms of tax expenditures or expenditures for permits. The efficiency gains associated with these policies tend to be more diffuse. Moreover, relative to the case of first-come first-serve, job creation is not as visible. No state entity has to be consulted before using these pollution rights, and there is no explicit need to justify the use of these rights on the basis of employment impacts. To the extent that direct job creation occurs, much of it may occur through relatively small changes in the use of inputs such as pollution and labor.

In short, these two policies are associated with highly visible costs and jobs with low visibility. This is just what politicians don't want. On the other hand the first-come first-serve policy has the desired characteristics. It appears to be relatively low in cost and promotes the highly visible forms of job creation. The lesson to be learned from this example is that there may be strong forces working at the local level to impede the development of incentive-based alternatives. However, this is not universally true. Indeed, in cases where abatement costs and potential cost savings are relatively high, and jobs are relatively less important in the political calculus, the appearance of market-based alternatives is more likely.

Broader patterns in environmental regulation

While the preceding arguments highlight the use of various instruments in meeting environmental quality objectives, much of the struggle in the environmental area concerns the choice of an objective itself. Often, objectives are selected which are not met. For example, Congress once called for eliminating all discharges into navigable waterways by 1985. In addition, Congress has repeatedly mandated standards for air pollutants which were not met in the specified time frame. The Clean Air Act was amended in 1977 because it did not meet certain goals such as the standard for ozone. Over a decade later, the same act still needs to be amended because the target has not been met. The consistent pattern of falling short of the stated target suggests that legislators may not really intend for the target to be met in the specified time frame. It is worthwhile exploring the possibility that a key motivation for adopting such goals is rooted in their symbolic value.

The general importance of symbols in politics is well known (Edelman, 1964). They provide benefits for politicians who are interested in mobilizing specific constituencies. They can also provide benefits to those constituencies as well. These general insights still leave some important unanswered questions pertaining to the use of symbols in environmental regulation. For example, what motivates the consistent pattern of behavior where targets are frequently not met in the specified time frame? Alternatively, why are laws and regulations passed which appear to be quite stringent, but the incentive to comply with these laws based on existing monitoring enforcement capabilities is quite low?

A partial answer to these questions can be found by examining the payoff to different interest groups. Environmentalists may want a high symbolic value for environmental quality for several reasons. First, it may signify a long-term commitment to a goal. Thus, standards are set either at the limits of technological feasibility or beyond the realm of what is currently feasible. Implementation then proceeds at a much slower pace, and only a small fraction of resources are allocated to monitoring and enforcement activities. Another explanation is that symbols can help influence the preference structure and values of individuals. Thus, environmentalists may want future generations to be imbued with an environmentalist ethic. Industry, on the other hand, may be opposed to symbols, in the sense that symbols can affect actual targets over the long term; higher actual targets are frequently associated with higher costs.[11]

These contrasting attitudes towards symbols can be illustrated in a simple model. Consider a two period model where industry and environmentalists can negotiate over the level of environmental quality. They have two variables over which they can negotiate—the actual level of environmental quality level, Q, and the target level, S. Suppose, for simplicity, that the symbolic target in period 1 becomes the actual level in period 2. The regulator selects values for Q and S in the first period. These values then determine the actual value for Q in the second period. The value of S in the second period is assumed to be equal to the actual level achieved in the second period. Table 4 elaborates on this possibility. Each ordered pair gives the value of Q and S respectively. Two cases are examined in the table. The point is to compare a case where actual environmental quality does not vary across periods against one in which environmental quality increases with time. In the first case, the regulator sets $Q = Q^1$ and also picks a value of $S > Q^1$. This results in a second period actual value of S. In the second case, the regulator chooses a value for $Q = Q^2$ and $S = Q^2$, so the actual environmental quality does not

Table 6.4. *An example of the feedback effect between the stated target and the actual level*

Period 1	*Period 2*
$[Q^1, S]$	$\rightarrow [S, S]$
$[Q^2, Q^2]$	$\rightarrow [Q^2, Q^2]$

change in the second period. Now suppose that $S > Q^2 > Q^1$. Which option does the regulator choose? Again, this depends on the underlying preferences of industry and environmentalists. However, one could easily imagine values for the parameters which result in choosing the first strategy. A relatively low actual level in period 1 would result in lower costs for industry. These costs would have to be weighed against the higher costs in period 2. The low environmental quality in period 1 might not be of major concern to environmentalists if the ultimate level which was achieved was high. This is consistent with the view that environmentalists may implicitly choose to heavily discount the present in favor of the future.

Up to this point, the focus in this section has been on explaining specific aspects of instrument choice in environmental policy. One of the important themes that arises in the implementation of virtually all environmental policies is that they are multifaceted. Indeed, almost every incentive-based system involves the use of several instruments. For example, some type of standard lies at the heart of most environmental regulatory systems, even those which feature fees and marketable permits. Moreover, a system of monitoring and enforcement is required to ensure that most systems will achieve some degree of compliance. Given the pervasive use of multiple instruments, there is a need to explain this phenomenon. Perhaps, the simplest explanation for this phenomenon is that the implementation of most environmental policies requires several steps. These steps include defining the general problem, providing specific guidelines to firms and ensuring that firms will meet these guidelines (e.g., see Bohm and Russell, 1985; Hahn and McRae, 1982). It is unreasonable to think that a single instrument is likely to be suited to the myriad of tasks involved in implementing an environmental policy. This is true regardless of whether a philosopher-king implements the environmental policy or the policy is implemented by mere mortals governed by political forces. In both cases, the use of multiple instruments will tend to be the rule rather that the exception. A simply way of thinking about multiple instruments is adopting the conventional paradigm used in environmental economics. Imagine that there are benefits and costs associated with using different configurations of instruments. The regulator or legislator chooses a set of instruments to maximize a prescribed political objective function. This will involve trading off between the costs of using additional instruments and their marginal benefits (e.g., see Hahn, 1986). Thus, the problem of using multiple instruments can be conveniently described in terms of the conventional maximization calculus used here.

The preceding analysis has couched the instrument choice problem in terms of a regulator or legislator maximizing a political support function or balancing the competing claims of industry and environmentalists. This paradigm was helpful in three general areas. First, it added to our understanding of the standard-setting process by providing insights on how standards are likely to be implemented. Second, it was useful in identifying conditions under which incentive-based instruments will emerge, and identifying the type of incentive-based instruments that are likely to be adopted. Finally, it was useful in explaining some broader patterns in environmental regulation.

Modelling issues

The theory presented here has focused on some central aspects of environmental policy. It also has left out some very important parts of the problem. For example, the issue of subsidies was not explicitly addressed. The political motivation underlying subsidies is fairly well understood. Subsidies enable politicians and bureaucrats to take credit for supplying specific benefits to their constituencies. A good example from the field of environmental regulation is the huge subsidy for municipal sewage waste treatment plants (Arnold, 1979). While it is easy to understand the general use of subsidies in the political process, relatively little is known about the determination of subsidy levels and the geographic distribution of subsidies. Becker (1983) suggests a model for income transfer that sheds some light on the features of subsidies, but the model is not suited to answering questions about their observed levels. The problem of geographic distribution of political 'pork' such as subsidies is still the subject of heated debate (Ferejohn, 1974; Arnold, 1979). These unresolved questions about subsidies point out an important limitation of the modeling approach that has been adopted in this chapter. It does not take advantage of many of the important *institutional* features which shape regulatory policy (Noll, 1983; Weingast, 1981). Nonetheless, it can be helpful in addressing certain parts of the subsidy issue. In the case of municipal waste treatment plants, for example, there has been a marked tendency on the part of the federal government to provide major subsidies for capital expenditures, but to require states to shoulder the operation and maintenance costs. This can be modeled in terms of the payoff to a single congressman, who gets most of his credit up front, with the initial ground-breaking ceremony for the plant.

Providing a more comprehensive theory of environmental policy design will require a careful look at the institutions which shape this design. The importance of the organization of the Congress and comparable legislative institutions in other countries has been pointed out by several scholars (e.g., see Fenno, 1973; Noll, 1983). Other scholars have tended to focus on the importance of the bureaucracy and the courts (Melnick, 1983; Wilson, 1980). Relatively few studies have been done which examine how these organizations have helped shape the type of instruments discussed in this chapter. Hahn and Hester (1989) have argued that forces within the bureaucracy had a major impact on the development of the 'emissions trading' policies by the Environmental Protection Agency (EPA). In the case of market-based reforms, there appears to be an important role played by both academics and 'bureaucratic entrepreneurs' who are trying to take credit for new ideas.

Liroff (1986) has chronicled some of the divergent views that exist in the EPA. There is an important difference between parts of the agency dedicated to implementing programs (the 'program offices') and the part of the agency dedicated to evaluating policy (the 'policy office'). Program offices are interested primarily in implementing their regulatory mandate. Crudely speaking, they get evaluated on producing regulations. The policy office, on the other hand, does not have a specific regulatory mandate. Members of this office get evaluated on their attempts to produce more efficient regulation. Not surprisingly, the impetus for both major marketable permit programs has tended to come from the policy office and other parts of the government interested in promoting more efficient forms of environmental regulation (Hahn and Hester, 1987). Nonetheless, both the program office for managing air pollution and the policy office have had major impacts on actual rules regarding the trading of rights to emit air pollutants. This suggests that bureaucratic incentives can and do play an important role in affecting the emergence and design of policies.[12]

At the same time, it would be misleading to imply that bureaucracy shapes policies independently of either the Congress or key interest groups. Indeed, the bureaucracy is constantly trying to gather support for its actions from all of these groups. Analysis of actual applications of environmental instruments suggests that the bureaucracy is not necessarily best viewed as a passive agent that carries out the wishes of Congress.

The relationship between the bureaucracy and other political institutions may be critical for determining policy outcomes. Several scholars have commented on the differences in the importance and style of bureaucracies across countries (e.g., see Brickman, Jasanoff and Ilgen, 1985). While it is clear that bureaucracies differ, it is less clear how this substantively affects policy outcomes. However, bureaucracies that are seen as agents of the ruling party (when there is one) may develop quite different policies from bureaucracies that have to balance the interests of an executive and legislative branch dominated by different parties. The reason is that politicians will face different payoffs in the two cases. In the case where legislators and the executive are dominated by different parties, legislators may try to use the bureaucracy in ways that make the executive look bad.

There is another very important sense in which the bureaucracy matters in considering problems in instrument choice. The preceding formal analysis was built on the assumption that certain tradeoffs could be made among different dimensions of policy. Trading, and the nature of trading, are likely to be constrained by the design of political institutions. This includes the design of legislative institutions, the courts and bureaucracies. In the case of the EPA, for example, issues in monitoring and enforcement are carried out largely independently of standard-setting. This means that there is little opportunity to effect trades on these issues at the bureaucratic level. Thus, the principal opportunity for 'trading' in this area would be at the legislative level. This example illustrates that a careful analysis of organizational design can provide insights into the potential for bargaining as well as the likely arena in which bargaining will take place.

Another important issue related to the study of bureaucracies is that of delegation. There has been a great deal of study of legislative delegation of authority (Aranson, Gellhorn and Robinson, 1982; Fiorina, 1982). However, it is important to recognize that bureaucracies have choices in what they delegate to other bureaucracies. For example, the EPA's recent revision of its trading policies made it easier for state environmental agencies to develop programs with less federal oversight. Moreover, there is evidence that decreased levels of oversight are associated with increases in the efficiency of emissions trading (Hahn and Hester, 1989). It would be useful to have a theory of why bureaucracies delegate in some instances and not others, and the expected effects of delegation in terms of efficiency and equity. Such a theory could be built on existing legislative theories of delegation (e.g., see McCubbins, 1985).

The preceding discussion reveals that instrument choice, like many other political decisions, is driven by a wide array of interest groups both in and outside of government. Yet the formal modeling approach used here focuses on a single, or representative, decision maker. This is obviously a gross oversimplification. Nonetheless, it is useful for helping to understand some of the broad outlines of environmental policy. Moreover, more realistic attempts to include the interrelationships among key groups influencing instrument choice decisions quickly leads to an analytical quagmire. In the past, scholars have attempted to deal with this problem by modeling salient aspects of the institutional process that are analytically tractable, such as the committee structure in Congress. The institutionalist approach is quite useful when the institution being modeled is the driving force behind the problem. However, it can also be quite misleading if the institution represents only one of many key actors in the decision making process. For example, in many of the cases examined here, the bureaucracy was seen as the prime mover or a major participant in many of the key decisions. Thus, detailed modelling of institutions other than the bureaucracy may lead to only marginal gains in understanding these decisions. The point is not that institutional analysis is not needed, but rather that great care should be exercised in choosing the appropriate institutional focus.

This entire chapter has been devoted to constructing a more complete theory of instrument choice. This theory has been built using two important assumptions: First, that different policy instruments can be distinguished on the basis of their distributive implications; and, second, that the set of available instruments can be specified. Given the nature of the theory, it cannot be expected to distinguish between instruments that have similar distributive consequences. This observation points to an important limitation of existing theories of instrument choice. To the extent that instrument choice is motivated by reasons which do not have distributional consequences, the theory does not contribute to our understanding. However, there is a deeper problem with theories of instrument choice that relates to the second building block on which the theory rests. The assumption that the feasible space of instruments can be specified is problematic. Certainly, instruments that are being used can be identified. Sometimes, it is also possible to identify instruments that were considered at some point in the decision process, but were not selected. However, defining the entire feasible space of instruments is virtually impossible. At best, we can hope to get a reasonable grasp of political constraints that limit the choice of instruments.

This raises the question of how to judge a theory of instrument choice, and one on which surprisingly little has been written. Certainly, one would like a theory that predicts what instruments are likely to be chosen under different conditions. It would also be useful to know what instruments are not likely to be chosen. The real art in developing a theory of instrument choice enters in defining the choice set. Until recently, the choice set has been defined more by theory than by empirical realities. Thus, for example, Buchanan and Tullock (1975) choose to 'explain' the choice of standards by choosing what, upon closer inspection, appears to be an unlikely alternative. At a minimum, a theory of instrument choice should try to explain important characteristics of instruments that exist in the real world. To the extent possible, it should place instruments in the feasible space that are 'reasonable' competitors to existing instruments.

Related to the issue of defining the feasible set is the vexing problem of defining precisely what is meant by an instrument. For practical reasons, it would be useful to define instruments that are measurable, and which are likely to have systematic effects on policy outputs. From a theoretical standpoint, instruments can only be distinguished on the basis of their distributional properties. Consequently, in theory, it is often possible to design standard and tax systems that are indistinguishable. 'Different' instruments may have similar political payoffs, and therefore may not be different in terms of their theoretical properties. The point is that words like 'standard' and 'tax' have meaning in terms of the theory only to the extent that they imply a particular distributional outcome. While it is useful to retain the general terminology, I also believe it is important to be very clear about the precise nature of the comparisons. For example, Buchanan and Tullock (1975) do not show why industry has a marked preference for standards over taxes. They show why industry has a marked preference for a very specific standard over a very specific tax.

In addition to being careful about instrument definition within a particular class, such as standards or taxes, problems can arise in making distinctions among classes. For example, to what extent should instruments such as standards and taxes be distinguished from monitoring and enforcement mechanisms? Ideally, it would be nice to merge many of these classes to do more global comparisons of instruments. Unfortunately, in many cases, the problems become analytically intractable. Thus, it is necessary to break the problem of instrument choice into manageable cases. The advantage of doing this is that it enables us to clearly understand the political and economic forces acting on one particular part of the problem. The disadvantage is that the separation may be artificial. Monitoring and enforcement mechanisms are inextricably linked to the choice of using pricing and quantity approaches for regulating pollution. In constructing theories of instrument choice, it is important to be cognizant of how these linkages can affect the validity of the theory.

Conclusions and Areas for Future Research

This chapter has illustrated that some relatively simple models of instrument choice can help explain important elements of environmental regulation. While developed primarily to explain themes in environmental policy, many of the theories have broader applicability. For example, the theories of standard-setting are relevant to the general field of regulation. The basic framework using competing interest groups was helpful in explaining the process of standard-setting, the emergence of new regulatory approaches, and some broad patterns in environmental regulation.

The theory of instrument choice is still in its infancy. There are many ways in which it could be extended. Earlier, the issue of why bureaucracies choose to delegate certain types of tasks was suggested as an area for study. A more general question that has intrigued economists relates to the relative efficiency of policy choices made by political institutions. At present, there is widespread agreement that there is no reason to presume that government policies will be efficient (Becker, 1983; Shepsle and Weingast, 1984). However, very little is known about the degree to which government policies are likely to deviate from an efficient solution (assuming such solutions can be defined) in specific instances.

This chapter has suggested one vehicle through which efficiency can enter into the choice of incentive-based instruments. However, this is an area that needs a great deal more elaboration. One important factor affecting the efficiency of various regulatory approaches is the ability to monitor and enforce sidepayments. For example, in the case of health and safety, it may not be possible to induce labor unions to agree to broader regulation which is less stringent because there is no way of effecting the necessary payoffs. In the case of environmental problems, there may be no way to get industry to agree to a broader scope for toxic substance policy because they have no assurances that the resulting regulations will not be draconian. Political constraints on law makers will impose substantial barriers towards moving to more efficient short-run policies. For those scholars interested in fashioning more efficient policies, the challenge still remains to identify conditions under which such policies are likely to emerge. The models on this subject to date are very general and also lead to highly ambiguous results. Perhaps, it is necessary to trade off some generality for a better understanding of the performance of specific policies. Hopefully, this chapter represents a first step towards this end.

Notes

* This research was supported by the National Science Foundation. I would like to thank Gordon Hester for helpful comments. Responsibility for the final product rests solely with the author.

† Council of Economic Advisers, Executive Office of the President, Washington, DC 20500

1. The motivations of regulators are rarely the same as elected officials. Nonetheless, elected officials can exert a great deal of control over regulators through a variety of oversight mechanisms such as budget allocations and hearings. In the subsequent analysis, the objectives of the two groups are assumed to be identical.
2. In the interest of simplicity, the distribution of economic costs across firms is ignored. One view of environmental regulation that has achieved some popularity in the economics literature is that firms use this regulation to increase industry profits or raise rival's costs. There is no question that some firms and industries will try to use the regulatory process in a strategic manner (Maloney and McCormack, 1982; Owen and Braeutigam, 1978). For example, recently the automobile companies and oil companies have been engaged in an argument over who should be required to install control equipment related to reducing automobile emissions. In the interest of brevity, I have chosen not to explore these strategic issues in detail. However, they are certainly important, and they do help to explain some differences between old and new source regulation.
3. To the extent that new source standards serve as a barrier to entry, industry might value the option more highly. However, this switching of industry preferences does not change the basic analysis.
4. In the formal analysis which follows, the word 'regulator' will be used. However, it should be understood that the regulator could be a politician or a bureaucrat at any level of government.
5. This is clearly an oversimplification. It assumes that the degree of market orientation is a good proxy for cost savings, and does not address distributional issues. For example, the distribution of savings across firms could be important for strategic reasons, and could have a tremendous impact on how individual firms feel about a proposed change. Moreover, it is reasonable to assume that industry will prefer systems that are more familiar, even if their expected cost is higher.
6. This assumption is consistent with most simulation studies I have seen over the region of interest (e.g., see Hahn and Noll, 1982). Note, however, that as the

overall level of emissions approaches 0, then industry will probably feel differently. To see this consider the extreme case where the emission limits are 0. Then all firms have the same emission standard, and a market adds no flexibility in this case.

7. All proofs are provided in the appendix.
8. See Hahn (1987) for a review of the literature on fees and an assessment of their effects.
9. This section draws heavily on analysis contained in Hahn (1988).
10. Interestingly, first-come first-serve is used quite frequently in the initial allocation of many types of property rights. For example, businesses locating in relatively clean areas are typically allowed to locate there without purchasing emission rights until the surplus in emission rights is exhausted. These businesses do have to comply with existing state and federal standards.
11. A third possibility not captured here is that the symbol itself may have intrinsic value, separate from its effects on preferences or physical outputs. This possibility is not considered explicitly in the formal analysis though it could easily be incorporated.
12. It is also quite possible that the training of the individuals charged with developing policies can affect their form. Indeed, some scholars have argued that the general use of command and control approaches as opposed to incentive-based approaches can be explained, in part, by the fact that lawyers, and not economists, typically exert greater control over policy outputs. Lawyers see command and control as a concrete way of addressing environmental issues (Kneese and Schultze, 1975). I think this argument has merit. Professional training clearly affects the way we approach problem solving. Within the context of the models considered here, this would suggest that the utility function of the hypothetical decision maker depends on his or her profession.

References

Ackerman, B. and Hassler, W. (1981). *Clean Coal/Dirty Air.* New Haven, CT: Yale University Press.

Aranson, P., Gellhorn, E. and Robinson, G. (1982). 'A theory of legislative delegation'. *Cornell Law Review* 68: 1–67.

Arnold, R. (1979). *Congress and the Bureaucracy.* New Haven, CT: Yale University Press.

Becker, G. (1983). 'A theory of competition among pressure groups for political influence'. *Quarterly Journal of Economics* 47: 371–400.

Bohm, P. and Russell, C. (1985). 'Comparative analysis of alternative policy instruments'. In A. Kneese and J. Sweeney (eds.), *Handbook of Natural Resource and Energy Economics*, Volume 1, 395–461. New York: Elsevier Science Publishers.

Brickman, R., Jasanoff, S. and Ilgen, T. (1985). *Controlling Chemicals: The politics of regulation in Europe and the United States.* Ithaca, NY: Cornell University Press.

Brown, G., Jr. and Johnson, R. (1984). 'Pollution control by effluent charges: It works in the Federal Republic of Germany, why not in the U.S.' *Natural Resources Journal* 24: 929–966.

Buchanan, J. and Tullock, G. (1975). 'Polluters' profits and political response: Direct controls versus taxes'. *American Economic Review* 65: 139–147.

Campos, J. (1987). *Toward a Theory of Instrument Choice in the Regulation of Markets*. Mimeo. California Institute of Technology, Pasadena, California, 26 January. 30 pp.

——(1989). *Legislative Institutions and the Endogenous Choice of Regulatory Instruments: A political economy approach to instrument choice*. Working Paper, Wharton School, University of Pennsylvnia, February. Forthcoming in the *Journal of Economics, Law and Organization*.

Coelho, P. (1976). 'Polluters' profits and political response: Direct control versus taxes: Comment'. *American Economic Review* 66: 976–978.

Dewees, D. (1983). 'Instrument choice in environmental policy'. *Economic Inquiry* 21: 53–71.

Edelman, M. (1964). *The Symbolic Use of Politics*. Champaign, IL: University of Illinois Press.

Fenno, R. (1973). *Congressmen in Committees*. Boston, MA: Little, Brown and Co.

Ferejohn, J. (1974). *Pork Barrel Politics*. Stanford, CA: Stanford University Press.

Fiorina, M. (1982). 'Legislative choice of regulatory forms: Legal process or administrative process?' *Public Choice* 39: 33–66.

Hahn, R. (1986). 'Tradeoffs in designing markets with multiple objectives'. *Journal of Environmental Economics and Management* 13: 1–12.

——(1987). *Economic Prescriptions for Environmental Problems: Not exactly what the doctor ordered*. Working Paper, School of Urban and Public Affairs, Carnegie-Mellon University Pittsburgh, PA. Forthcoming in the *Journal of Economic Perspectives*.

——(1988). 'Jobs and environmental quality: Some implications for instrument choice'. *Policy Sciences*, 20: 289–306.

——and Hester, G. (1987). *Marketable Permits: Lessons for theory and practice*. Working Paper, School of Urban and Public Affairs. Carnegie Mellon University, Pittsburgh, PA. Forthcoming in the *Ecology Law Quarterly*.

—— and —— (1989). 'Where did all the markets go?: An analysis of EPA's emission trading program'. *Yale Journal on Regulation* 6: 109–153.

Hahn, R. and McRae, G. (1982). 'Applications of market mechanisms to pollution'. *Policy Study Review* 1: 470–476.

Hahn, R. and Noll, R. (1982). 'Designing a market for tradable emissions permits'. In W. Magat. (ed.), *Reform of Environmental Regulation*, Cambridge, MA: Ballinger.

Hughes, J., Magat, W. and Williams, R. (1986). 'The economic consequences of the OSHA cotton dust standard: An analysis of stock price behavior'. *Journal of Law and Economics* 29: 29–50.

Kneese, A. and Schultze, C. (1975). *Pollution, Prices and Public Policy.* Washington, DC: TH Brookings Institution.
Liroff, R. (1986). *Reforming Air Pollution Regulation: The toil and trouble of EPA's bubble*, Washington, DC: The Conservation Foundation.
Magat, W., Krupnick, A. and Harrington, W. (1986). *Rules in the Making: A statistical analysis of regulatory agency behavior.* Washington, DC: Resources for the Future.
Maloney, M. and McCormick, R. (1982). 'A positive theory of environmental quality regulation'. *Journal of Law and Economics*, 25: 99–123.
McCubbins, M. (1985). 'The legislative design of regulatory structure'. *American Journal of Political Science*, 29: 721–738.
—— and Page, T. (1986). 'The congressional foundations of agency performance'. *Public Choice* 51: 173–190.
Melnick, R. (1983). *Regulation and the Courts*, Washington, DC: Brookings Institution.
Noll, R. (1983). 'The political foundations of regulatory policy'. *Zeitschrift für die gesamte Staswissenschaft* 139: 377–404.
Owen, B. and Braeutigam, R. (1978). *The Regulation Game.* Cambridge, MA: Ballinger.
Peltzman, S. (1976). Toward a more general theory of regulation. *Journal of Law and Economy* 19: 211–240.
Rolph, E. (1983). 'Government allocation of property rights: Who gets what?' *Journal of Policy-Analysis and Management*, 3: 45–61.
Shepsle, K. and Weingast, B. (1984). 'Political solutions to market problems'. *American Political Science Review*, 78: 417–434.
Stigler, G. (1971). 'The theory of economic regulation'. *Bell Journal of Economics*, 2: 3–21.
Tucker, W. (1982). *Progress and Privilege: America in the age of environmentalism.* Garden City, NY: Anchor Press.
Weingast, B. (1981). 'Regulation, reregulation, and deregulation: The political foundations of agency clientele relationships'. *Law and Contemporary Problems* 44: 147–177.
Welch, W. (1983). 'The political feasibility of full ownership property rights: The cases of pollution and fisheries'. *Policy Sciences*, 16: 165–180.
Wilson, J. (ed.) (1980). *The Politics of Regulation.* New York: Basic Books, Inc.
Yohe, G. (1976). 'Polluters' profits and political response: Direct control versus taxes: Comment'. *American Economic Review* 66: 981–982.

Appendix

This appendix contains formal proofs of the three propositions.

Proof of Proposition 1: An increase in industry influence is represented by an increase in a. It suffices to show that $\partial M/\partial a > 0$ and $\partial Q/\partial a < 0$. Total differentiation of the first order conditions resulting from (1) yields:

$$\begin{bmatrix} aI_{11}+ & (1-a)E_{11} & aI_{12}+ & (1-a)E_{12} \\ aI_{12}+ & (1-a)E_{12} & aI_{22}+ & (1-a)E_{22} \end{bmatrix} \begin{bmatrix} \mathrm{dM} \\ \mathrm{dQ} \end{bmatrix} = \begin{bmatrix} (E_1 - I_1)\mathrm{d}a \\ (E_2 - I_2)\mathrm{d}a \end{bmatrix}$$

This problem can be solved by inverting the matrix. The assumptions on the preferences of environmentalists and industry ensure that the matrix of second-order derivatives is negative definite. Inversion yields the following sign pattern:

$$\begin{bmatrix} \mathrm{dM} \\ \mathrm{dQ} \end{bmatrix} = \begin{bmatrix} - & +/0 \\ +/0 & - \end{bmatrix} \begin{bmatrix} -\mathrm{d}a \\ +\mathrm{d}a \end{bmatrix}$$

This sign pattern implies $\partial M/\partial a > 0$ and $\partial Q/\partial a < 0$.

Proof of Proposition 2: The proof relies on the fact that the function being maximized is negative definite. Note that the effect of a change in a on industry utility is given by the expression:

$$\frac{\partial I}{\partial a} = \mathrm{I}_1 \frac{\partial M}{\partial a} + \mathrm{I}_2 \frac{\partial Q}{\partial a}$$

Since $\mathrm{I}_1 > 0$ and $\mathrm{I}_2 < 0$, it suffices to show that $\partial I/\partial a > 0$.

Define 'det A' to be the determinant of the matrix of second order partials. Solving explicitly for the effects of a change in a yields:

$$\frac{\partial M}{\partial a} = (1/\det \mathrm{A})\ [(a\mathrm{I}_{22} + (1-a)\mathrm{E}_{22})(\mathrm{E}_1 - \mathrm{I}_1) - (a\mathrm{I}_{12} + (1-a)\mathrm{E}_{12})(\mathrm{E}_2 - \mathrm{I}_2)], \text{ and}$$

$$\frac{\partial Q}{\partial a} = (1/\det \mathrm{A})[(a\mathrm{I}_{12} + (1-a)\mathrm{E}_{12})(\mathrm{E}_1 - \mathrm{I}_1) + (a\mathrm{I}_{11} + (1-a)\mathrm{E}_{11}(\mathrm{E}_2 - \mathrm{I}_2)]$$

Multiplying $\partial M/\partial a$ by I_1 and $\partial Q/\partial a$ by I_2, and adding gives the following expression for $\partial I/\partial a$:

$$(a/\det \mathrm{A})\{\mathrm{I}_2(\mathrm{E}_2 - \mathrm{I}_2)\mathrm{I}_{11} - [(\mathrm{E}_1 - \mathrm{I}_1)\mathrm{I}_2 + (\mathrm{E}_2 - \mathrm{I}_2)\mathrm{I}_1]\mathrm{I}_{12} + \mathrm{I}_1(\mathrm{E}_1 - \mathrm{I}_1)\mathrm{I}_{22}\}. \quad (3)$$

Since I is strictly concave and twice differentiable, the quadratic form associated with the Hessian of I is negative definite. This implies that the associated quadratic form is negative. Through suitable manipulation, (3) can be related to a quadratic form. The first order conditions associated with (1) imply:

$$\mathrm{E}_j = [a/(a-1)]\mathrm{I}_j \text{ for } j = 1, 2.$$

Substitution into (3) yields:

$$[a/((a-1)\det \mathrm{A})]\{\mathrm{I}_2^2\mathrm{I}_{11} + 2\mathrm{I}_1\mathrm{I}_2\mathrm{I}_{12} + \mathrm{I}_1^2\mathrm{I}_{22}\}$$

after factoring $(1/(a-1))$. The first expression, $[a/((a-1)\det \mathrm{A})]$, is less than 0 since $a \epsilon (0, 1)$ and det A > 0. The second expression is a quadratic form. To see this define the vector $(\mathrm{h}_1, \mathrm{h}_2) = (\mathrm{I}_2, -\mathrm{I}_1)$. Then the bracketed expression takes the form $h_1^2 I_{11} + 2h_1 h_2 I_{12} + h_2^2 I_{22}$. Since $(h_1, h_2) \neq 0$, and the quadratic form is negative definite, this implies that the expression in brackets is less than 0. Multiplying the two negative expressions together yields the result that $\partial I / \partial a > 0$.

Proof of Proposition 3: The first part of the proposition can be derived by totally differentiating the first order conditions. The results, not shown here, are the same as for Proposition 1, except that M and Q are replaced by F and U. Assuming the cross partials for industry and environmentalists are 0 yields the following sign pattern:

$$\begin{bmatrix} dF \\ dU \end{bmatrix} = \begin{bmatrix} - & 0 \\ 0 & - \end{bmatrix} \begin{bmatrix} + & da \\ ? & da \end{bmatrix}$$

This implies $\partial F / \partial a < 0$.

Assuming that the cross partials are non-negative and the marginal utility of earmarking for environmentalists does not exceed the marginal utility of earmarking for industry yields:

$$\begin{bmatrix} dF \\ dU \end{bmatrix} = \begin{bmatrix} - & +/0 \\ +/0 & - \end{bmatrix} \begin{bmatrix} + & da \\ -/0 & da \end{bmatrix}$$

This sign pattern implies $\partial F / \partial a < 0$ and $\partial U / \partial a \geq 0$.

The proof used to show that an increase in industry influence will result either in a decrease in fees and/or an increase in earmarking is precisely analogous to the proof used for Proposition 2 and will not be repeated here.

Can Social Science Explain Organizational Noncompliance with Environmental Law?

JOSEPH F. DIMENTO†

Abstract

Noncompliance with environmental law is an immense problem whether evaluated from its incidence or its consequences. Noncompliance often results from the activities of large corporations and agencies and their interactions. This paper presents a theoretical perspective on organizational compliance in the environmental field. It first reviews and analyzes the leading bivariate relationships between compliance and independent variables, including communication of regulations, enforcement, and characteristics of actors in the compliance event. Single factors can be influential in promoting compliance; however, only in rare cases will one psychological, organizational, or economic factor explain business response. Since regulatory systems attain compliance through a variety of routes, a multivariate perspective is offered that integrates several literatures and empirical studies.

Some of the behaviors that create problems of environmental degradation shock the conscience. Corporate executives decide to use the city sewers to dispose of substances that they know kill all forms of life. Small businessmen hire maverick truck drivers to spread toxics along nearby scenic highways. A Fortune 500 company falsifies reporting information about its hazardous waste site. Other environmental violations are less reprehensible. A 'big three' automaker fails to observe one of several thousand performance standards that apply to its products. A farmer unknowingly violates a new water quality standard. A fisherman exceeds a quota by counting his catch differently from the agency official who drafted the rule on counting.

As these examples suggest, environmental violations do not always result from the behaviors of individuals. Rather, they are outcomes of collectivities, small and large, and their interactions—sometimes when those interactions are not even known or knowable to involved individuals. In the movement to bring about environmental quality and to promote environmental protection, the complex organization has a central place. Certainly individual citizens and small ad hoc environmental groups play important parts in strategies for environmental protection, but large agencies and corporations are responsible both for much of the activity that creates environmental degradation and for attempts to remedy it. One must consider the organizational level to understand compliance with the numerous and complicated environmental mandates of the last two decades.

How can the dramatic variations in organizational responses to environmental law be explained, and what role do the social sciences have in that explanation? This paper presents some of the major theoretical work on compliance as it relates to these questions. Further, it integrates that work in a theoretical framework that aims to explain compliance and noncompliance. An important, but not exclusive, focus is on the organization.

Noncompliance is an immense problem. Violations result from the acts of innocent individuals, from the refined plans of sophisticated criminal groups, and from the actions of governmental entities whose other activities promote environmental protection. Statistics come from many sources, but they converge in describing a great incidence of environmental degradation in many different sites, ranging from municipal water systems to domestic fishing vessels (Environmental Quality Council, 1980, 1981; *Inside EPA*, 1983; South Coast Air Quality Management District, 1983). The range of behaviors involved in non-compliance is similarly wide—from falsifying compliance reports to the Environmental Protection Agency (EPA), to dumping copper, nickel, and zinc into a sewer system (the New Bedford case, which led to a 41-count federal indictment of a shoemaking firm and resulted in a million dollar criminal fine).

What does it mean to comply? This seemingly simple question has generated a large literature. In part, variety in definition exists because (a) the literature addresses different dependent variables, and (b) the pursuit of compliance is an imprecise enterprise.

A basic distinction exists between specific compliance and general compliance. *Specific compliance* refers to the response of the entity (business or individual) targeted by a specified incentive or sanction, when the response is believed consistent with societal objectives or regulations. *General compliance* refers to responsive behavior of the universe of businesses (or other target entities) whose law-abiding performance government aims to effect—i.e., the overall reaction of an industry.

But definitional variation results from several other complicating phenomena. Interest groups promote different interpretations of what it means to comply because of the significant financial, environmental, and philosophical implications of choice of meaning. In fact, Stone (1985) reports speculation that fines may be set at levels to promote *non*compliance because, from a societal welfare perspective, compliance is not (economically) justified. Definitions often are derived by those most skilled in the process of aligning meanings in order to fit their clients' interests: the lawyers. Furthermore, words have ambiguous and multiple meanings in most contexts; and in the world of legislation, those concerned with policy on the environment actively strive to introduce their interpretations of words into statutes, regulations, and judicial opinions. Issues of interpretation are not limited to legal analysis. For example, by one method of statistical analysis, compliance may be demonstrated; by another, a violation may be found. (An EPA policy document identified ten different 'yardsticks' for establishing compliance with water quality regulations, ranging from a ratio of populations served by differing qualities of water to the existence of valuable fish species—Sutinen & Anderson, 1985).

Compliance has a timing dimension—e.g., how long will industry be given to come into compliance? It also has a dimension of completeness—should good-faith efforts be equated with legal compliance? Should the standard be 'substantial compliance,' 'some reasonable probability of noncompliance,' 'tolerable noncompliance,' or should no discretion be left to administrators—'total compliance all of the time'?[1] Definitional variation makes compliance scholarship either highly refined and only marginally useful from a policy perspective, or more general but less precise scientifically.

Noncompliance does not result from a lack of imagination and creativity in devising approaches and incentives for effecting compliance. On the contrary, the range of approaches covers a wide continuum, from imprisonment of individual perpetrators of what are classified as environmental crimes, to policy decisions to provide incentives for environmentally responsible behavior or to establish markets that aim to induce compliance. Furthermore, an extensive literature addresses the efficacy of individual regulatory strategies and attempts comparative evaluations.

Theoretical Framework: The Factors

Several factors promote compliance by organizations with environmental law. The literature focuses attention on enforcement of regulatory policy,

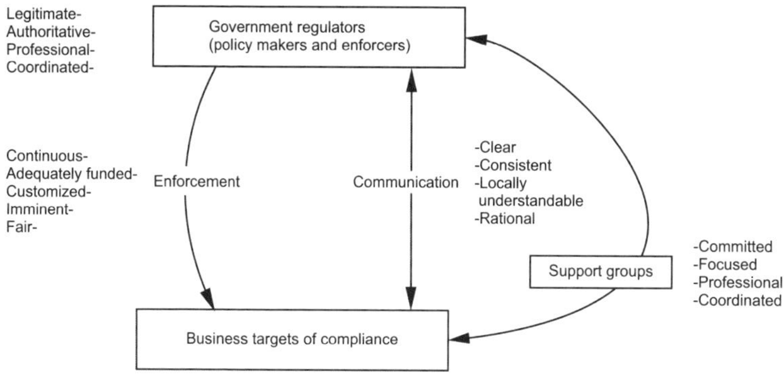

Fig. 7.1. A framework for understanding compliance with environmental law. Arrows denote compliance-promoting dynamics.

Source: DiMento, 1986b

on communication of regulations, and on characteristics of actors in the compliance event—government regulators, business firms that are targets of environmental law, and groups that take a special interest in environmental quality. Within each of these categories, there is a long list of variables; each has some explanatory power, but none stands out as singularly important. This paper focuses attention on only a sample of them, and the sample is not based on a criterion of greatest explanatory power, for the framework shown in Fig. 7.1 is too preliminary to make such a claim. The aim here is to present a sense of the dynamics of compliance, at the expense of comprehensiveness. (For a more comprehensive presentation, see DiMento, 1986b).

I focus here first on bivariate relationships and then present a multivariable context, which is illustrated in Fig. 7.1. The state of the literature does not allow quantitative conclusions that changes in a given independent variable of a certain amount produce changes in a dependent variable of a specified quantity. But it is possible to report on directionality and nature of influence.

Enforcement

As in many areas of the criminal justice system, the almost unavoidable conclusion is that efforts to achieve compliance with environmental law fail because of a weak enforcement approach. Not enough violators are identified; when identified, not enough are sanctioned; and when they are sanctioned, penalties are too weak to communicate that violations will not be tolerated.

This perception is partially accurate. A sound enforcement policy is necessary to affect corporate and small-business behavior. But enforcement is here understood to mean a system. A full enforcement system encompasses the sanction, the resources of the enforcing agency, the severity and certainty of a punishment being imposed or an incentive being awarded, the manner in which the regulated business perceives the enforcement policy, and the enforcement agency's relationship with other branches of government.

Enforcement and the Utility Function

The sanction must affect the firm's complex cost-benefit calculations (Brown & Stover, 1977; Downing & Watson, 1974; Marlow, 1982), for business more often complies when information about the meaning and importance of rules and about enforcement indicates that costs of noncompliance will exceed benefits of noncompliance. However, the firm does not just evaluate its compliance decisions as a simple utility function in purely economic terms (Byrne & Hoffman, 1985). Complex organizations have a variety of corporate goals (Stigler, 1970; Wilson, 1980). They may emphasize status (both of the firm and of individuals within the firm), goodwill, or reputation (again of corporate executives individually and of the company). The cost-benefit analysis is but a skeletal summary statement of the firm's forecasts, decisions, and responses (Likens & Kohfeld, undated). Diver (1980) and Fisse (1978) identify the following among the costs considered by the firm: potential tort liability, business losses following adverse publicity, future litigation costs, and costs incurred in coming into compliance.

To be effective, a regulatory agency needs access to information about the firm's subjective and shifting calculations of costs and benefits as well as the company's competitive profile (Diver, 1980). Perceptions of cost also vary with other factors in the compliance framework. Activity by enforcers and outside groups can influence the 'baseline' of cost calculations that the firm employs. As Roberts and Bluhm (1981, p. 337) found: 'What appeared to be cheap or expensive to each organization depended heavily on their expectations, which changed over time.' In considering the cost-benefit balance, the target may take the long run into consideration. For instance, a company may seek a precedent-setting victory, which would remove any threat of future prosecution.

The Sanction Itself

Social science makes one of its most important contributions to a public policy on environmental protection in explaining that the route to compliance may take different paths. Conversely, there is no one strategy or tool that will assure compliance in the absence of attention to other factors that are part of the context for compliance.

The nature of the sanction itself is less important than other factors in explaining compliance. No enforcement strategy, when considered alone, universally motivates *corporations* to behave. For example, there has been increased attention on use of criminal sanctions in environmental law. But the deterrent effect of criminal sanctions is by no means clear in relation to corporate bodies or small businesses. Furthermore, counterproductive aspects of using this tool have been identified.

Research suggests that severity of punishment deters criminal behavior (Bean & Cushing, 1971; Erlich, 1973; Gibbs, 1968; Gray & Martin, 1969; Tittle, 1980; Tittle & Logan, 1973), and theory posits a deterrent effect of punishment in the organizational setting (Braithwaite & Geis, 1982; Chambliss, 1966; Packer, 1968). This work indicates that criminal sanctions may have an important place in promoting environmental compliance for at least a subset of violators. Chambliss considers white-collar criminals as eminently deterrable because their actions are often based on calculated risks, not on passion, as is the case for many other criminal behaviors. Braithwaite and Geis (1982) conclude that the reorientations required by punishment-based deterrence are more easily made by organizations than by individuals: 'A new internal compliance group can be put in place much more readily than can a new superego' (p. 310).

But some researchers disagree (Paternoster et al., 1983; Schwartz, 1968; Waldo & Chiricos, 1972). Paternoster and Iovanni (1986) found that 'perceived severity has no deterrent effect on later deviant behavior' (p. 751). In their work, peer behavior, moral beliefs, and social disapproval were more strongly related to criminal behavior than was the fear of formal sanctions. However, this work dealt with direct and immediate effects on the commission of minor offenses, and thus, as the authors caution, it may not generalize to larger offenses. (Severe sanctions may trigger informal mechanisms of social control, a point covered below in the section on support groups as actors in environmental regulation.) Also, application of most research results to organizations as targets is not direct, for empirical findings rarely involve corporate violators (Braithwaite & Geis, 1982).

Moreover, business leaders have pointed out several counterproductive outcomes of the use of criminal sanctions. Criminal sanctions can jeopardize the regulatory cooperation of business and industry. Industry representatives, for example, are proud of their relationships with moderate community members in activities geared toward local cleanups, environmental education programs, and financial support of nonprofit organizations, but these activities could be jeopardized by the hostilities that legal actions generate. Sanctions can also raise the cost of violations to the point at which businesses choose to oppose regulations. Business people consider criminal sanctions for environmental violations, though acceptable in the abstract, rarely appropriate and rarely applicable to their situations (Clay, 1983; DiMento, 1986b). Criminal sanctions may chill a legitimate and useful challenging of environmental rules and counter a learning process about effective regulations.

The degree of business opposition to the use of criminal sanctions raises concern over efficient use of enforcement resources: such sanctions may engender business objections to enforcement efforts based on unyielding principles rather than on cost-benefit considerations. Offenses that might be admitted and resolved quietly if classified as a civil wrong may become a *cause célèbre* if classified as criminal.

The literature underscores a regulator's dilemma. Although a sanction must threaten high costs to a firm, if a large percentage of the target group considers penalties excessive, government's ability to foster general compliance will be jeopardized. Business will fight sanctions considered unfair by litigating, by using political influence to limit regulatory agency powers, and by challenging the rationality of rules through propaganda campaigns (DiMento, 1986b; Scholz, 1984).

The nature of the incentive or the penalty, rather than its legal source, may most strongly determine the deterrence-and compliance-promoting power of regulatory enforcement. A series of civil suits can be costly to a company's image. A well-publicized administrative order can be timely in a given economic environment. Conferences and conciliation with the new management of a firm can also be influential if professionally undertaken by top agency administrators, as can several forms of alternative dispute resolution (Susskind & McMahon, 1985). Central to compliance are the costs that the firm associates with an enforcement approach, the consequences to a business person for non-compliance, and the attitude of the regulated toward the overall regulatory policy. Attitudes in turn are mediated by several characteristics of enforcement policy, which are addressed next.

Perceptions of Fairness of the Enforcement Policy

Executives evaluate the fairness of enforcement policy in conscious and deliberate decisions about compliance (Roberts & Bluhm, 1981; Rodgers, 1973; Skolnick, 1968; Stigler, 1970). For example, if business perceives that government chooses enforcement targets in a systematic and equitable way, both general and special compliance are fostered. But when government prosecutes only vulnerable firms (e.g., small companies or those uncommonly profitable) in order to meet enforcement quotas, business takes note.

Perceptions of Certainty and Imminence of Enforcement

Communication of the enforcement policy has a time dimension (Chambliss, 1966; Ermann & Lundman, 1975; Gibbs, 1968; Horai & Tedeschi, 1969; Rodgers, 1973). Complex organizations will discount the costs of enforcement when they are projected into some uncertain future. Thus, regulatory activity must be perceived as imminent.

Imminence is promoted if the regulator has good information about the firm's behaviour and about the agency's other activities and priorities. Institutional barriers to the flow of information can weaken enforcement threats. Some agency decision rules formally impede information gathering—e.g., rules that promote societal objectives other than compliance, such as protection of proprietary information and privacy. Industry itself can create an information overload in legislative, administrative, and judicial activities, and thus lessen the regulator's ability to apply sanctions quickly. Industry can supply immense amounts of data, some irrelevant, which the regulator (or other decision-maker) must formally and systematically process. Administrative records of several thousand pages are not uncommon in environmental cases. The need to react to information, no matter what its quality, impedes enforcement. Furthermore, because of the unrealistic design of some compliance objectives, government enforcement proceedings are often long, laborious, and inefficient.

Imminence of Sanctions and White-Collar Regulatees

Information considered irrelevant in other areas of law may counter the threat of a sanction. For example, in determining penalties for environmental violations, courts generally consider the community status of white-collar defendants (in some cases, by literally counting unsolicited letters praising the defendant) and how punishment may affect the defendants' families. The business sector is aware of this history of sympathetic judicial treatment.

Mann, Wheeler, and Sarat (1980) conducted interviews with federal court judges and concluded that, in sentencing white-collar criminals, judges are primarily interested in general deterrence. Judges consider the process of indictment to be punishment enough for the white-collar criminal, and they wish to limit the harm done to innocent parties, including the relatives of the convicted. Thus they often add an element of compassion and understanding in cases of environmental compliance—an unusual factor in criminal cases. In one Los Angeles area case (DiMento, 1986b, p. 99), the judge, declaring that 'the time for any danger to the community has long since passed,' excused the defendant from probation and dropped a contempt of court citation. The court emphasized whether a general outcome, the cleanup of hazardous acids and contaminated soils, had been achieved, rather than whether deadlines established for that outcome had been met, and it suspended the original sentence to allow the owner of the company to clean up the site. The defendant's lawyer declared the judge's action a 'complete vindication' of his client's behavior.

Some studies have found, in contrast, that 'white-collar offenders appear to be sentenced more harshly than other persons convicted of felonies,' according to Geis's (1985, p. 76) review of the literature. However, Geis noted methodological deficiencies in these studies, and also, they may not be relevant to the complex organizational crimes that typify many environmental violations. Furthermore, these studies are notable because they counter intuitive notions of the treatment of regulation violators, including those held by targets of compliance strategies.

Personnel movement within the company and diffusion of responsibility for the firm's actions can also make threats of sanctions and promises of rewards meaningless. Prosecution can fall outside the time frames according to which personnel operate, or enforcement efforts may not be directed to appropriate parties. In addition, government often reduces the credibility of enforcement threats by extending compliance deadlines (Marcus, 1980), as has been typical for electroplating operations, which have consistently failed to meet standards under the Federal Water Pollution Control Act regarding discharges of heavy metals (*Wall Street Journal*, June 29, 1984).

Other organizational behaviors and characteristics that diminish the credibility of enforcement action include issuing of variances and extensions by regulators (sometimes dressed up as part of an innovative enforcement policy); inadequate resources for surveying likely noncomplying sites; agency inexperience in law enforcement and in use of sophisticated testing equipment; publication of enforcement strategies that inform violators of the probabilities of being inspected, sued, or prosecuted (Diver, 1980); and rules and practices of the judiciary that make even well-lawyered regulatory cases difficult to win in some courts. Especially in the lower courts, judges often lack the background to assess arguments of causation and proof. For example, this is apt to be true in cases where health effects of pollutants are at issue, when experts differ strongly about the relevance or meaning of a scientific study or about the cumulative significance of many studies, or when the intricacies of risk assessment are being presented.

Continuity and Consistency of Enforcement

To promote compliance, the enforcement or incentive policy must be perceived as continuous (Schwartz & Orleans, 1967; Skolnick, 1968)—that is, not subject to change with shifts in the economy or in administrative personnel. Business may judge continuity by reference to enforcement of a particular mandate, or it may evaluate a total enforcement program (Erickson & Gibbs, 1975). Business generally knows whether the legislature has ceased its oversight function, leaving follow-up to an indifferent, understaffed agency or to one hostile to the law. Industry also monitors whether the judiciary has interfered with an agency's enforcement approach. Whether priority items under one administration will remain so under another is important intelligence for a regulated firm, as is the degree of agency consensus about the significance of an individual prosecution or negotiation. The private sector will comply with many regulations only if government cares whether it complies.

On the practical side, business people typically conclude that an agency that demonstrates a long-standing commitment to achieving compliance will withstand industry attempts to erode the agency's influence. Nonetheless, the effects of continuity derive from other dynamics in addition to practicality. Continuity in orientation to achieving the goals of a regulatory program leads to a kind of social contract that industry enters with government. In a sense, regulatory programs become another cost of doing business—equivalent to complying with a well-known, although thoroughly disliked, tax law.

However, there are opposing views of the effects of inconsistency in policy under certain conditions. Absence of consistency prevents a firm from behaving in a rational and self-protective manner. In a sense, a firm is forced to be on guard constantly, making noncompliance much more risky. This effect is probably most relevant for companies prone to avoid regulations in stable regulatory environments (G. Geis, personal correspondence, May 20, 1986). Sax (1976, p. 753) has argued, 'Probably nothing is more urgently required in environmental management than institutions for controlled instability. . . .The old idea of a stable and predictable regulatory agency, patiently negotiating solutions that will then be fixed and unquestionable for years, or even decades, is hopelessly outdated. A mixture of legal techniques—designed to destabilize arrangements that have become too secure—is precisely what is needed for a milieu in which rapid change is the central feature.'

Communication

It also is totally unrealistic to assume that more than a fraction of the persons and entities affected by a regulation—especially small contractors scattered across the country—would have knowledge of its promulgation or familiarity with or access to the Federal Register. (Justice Powell in *Adamo Wrecking Company* v. *United States*, 434 U.S. 275, 290, 1978)

In this section I focus on communication of the law, but communication of enforcement is important as well. Whatever the sanction, it must be communicated continuously; otherwise, enforcement messages lack credibility (Erickson & Gibbs, 1975; Schwartz & Orleans, 1967; Skolnick, 1968). Yet the regulatory agency must achieve a balance between demonstrating to business that its enforcement policy is fair and intelligent (e.g., based on a systematic analysis of costs and expected results of legal actions) and giving so much information as to undermine the surprise element of effective enforcement.

Nonetheless, no matter how fully supported and professional, enforcement cannot ensure compliance with law. Poorly conceptualized, badly drafted, and incompletely articulated regulations counteract positive responses to environmental goals.

The Simple Elements of Communication

Most obviously, business must understand statutes, ordinances, regulations, and judicial opinions. Rules will fail if they are either vague or overly specific. Diver (1983, p. 69) discusses the 'transparency' of law and states that rule makers should 'use words with well-defined and universally accepted meanings within the relevant community.' Often this is not true in environmental law. Nor are regulations generally accessible—that is, 'applicable to concrete situations without excessive difficulty or effort' (Diver, 1983, p. 67). As one executive put it, review of regulations is 'like learning the Koran.'

The generality or ambiguity of the legislation that is the basis of regulations may be at fault. Legislators' compromises ('I'll support your standard if you support my exemption'), interest group pressures, and advocacy of ambiguity by potential regulatees all contribute to legislation's impotence. Political scientists have explained why ambiguity characterizes some reform laws (Jones, 1977; Lindblom, 1959). If clear articulation of rules and standards were required at the legislative phase, interest groups might act to thwart reform or dilute regulatory action. By keeping parts of the control strategy unspecified and granting some discretion to administrators, legal change can often bypass scrutiny by targets of control.

The ambiguity of law also must be understood in light of the delicate nature of some highly complex law. A case in point is the 1986–1987 Clean Water Act, which passed unanimously in 1986 at the close of the congressional session. President Ronald Reagan then pocket vetoed it. When Congress returned in January 1987, now dominated by the opposition party, its leaders wished to ensure that the bill would become law as soon as possible, for one objective was to embarrass the president. However, the bill contained a glaring exemption allowing four Louisiana companies to dump pollutants into the Mississippi River. Some congressional leaders, wary of reopening consideration of the bill, preferred to leave the exemption in and try to explain it away on the House and Senate floors; they would create a legislative history indicating that the intent of Congress was to give the EPA administrator discretion in enforcing the law vis-à-vis the four polluters. The explicit statutory language would allow the exemption, but the 'real meaning' of the law would confine it substantially.

Environmental law can communicate sufficiently without detailing all the activities required or precluded. The law of public nuisance is an example: business defendants have argued that the language of this law is unconstitutionally vague because 'detriment' and 'natural tendency to cause harm' are not narrowly enough defined to inform business of the standard to which it will be held. Courts, however, have disagreed.

A risk of detail in regulation is that even a comprehensive statute may not specifically mention some actions that the legislature intends to control. Companies may find ways of distinguishing their behaviors from any of those proscribed and thus avoid prosecution even though they clearly fall within the range of targeted activities (Kagan, 1984). As a practical matter, articulation of all potential violations in all definitions of compliance is not possible. As Kagan (1984, pp. 3–4) put it:

> No maker of protective rules can fully envisage the diversity of technologies and the countless ways things can go wrong in a complex and dynamic economy, or the inexhaustible capacity of workers and managers to slip into previously unspecified modes of inattention, stupidity and heartlessness.

Continuity of Communication

To promote compliance, the regulatory message must be consistently and constantly communicated (Krislov, 1972; Pfeffer, Salancik, & Leblebici, 1976; Schwartz & Orleans, 1967; Skolnick, 1968). In the organizational sphere, this dimension may be even more important than message clarity. For example, an investigation of the compliance of lower courts with Supreme Court libel law (Gruhl, 1981) concluded that consistency, more than clarity of a policy statement, had the greatest influence on lower courts. Ongoing articulation acts as a reminder and an expression of commitment to implement the law and contributes to a stable business environment. Constancy of the message also has its limits; if government indicates that it will occasionally temper enforcement with flexibility, business respect for regulation will be greater than when messages are constant but unnecessarily rigid.

Law can be clear and appropriately specific but fail because of inconsistency in its articulation. Especially under conditions of uncertainty, social influence, rather than universalistic statements of general criteria, is apt to affect decision making in complex organizations (Pfeffer et al., 1976). In environmental policy, the political environment is typically highly uncertain; without consistent communication of the law, the business target will probably not be convinced that the same standards will apply over time (DiMento, 1986b, Interviews C and D). Administrative changes, personnel movement, and shifting societal priorities all predict otherwise.

A desire for constancy can reflect different corporate concerns. One company may seek it, even above favorable regulations, to allow for a stable commercial environment; another company may desire it because it helps maintain a superior competitive position within an industry.

Inconsistency as an Organizational Outcome

Organizational factors can create inconsistency in regulations even when the actors responsible for compliance seek consistency. Government's environmental activity derives from a group of quasi-independent units with different organizational objectives. This is the case not only across agencies, but also within agencies and within departments or divisions of agencies. For any potential case, differences may arise over whether there actually is a significant violation, whether the violator should be pursued, which strategies should be employed to prosecute or litigate, and which sanctions work best. Differences are both technical and ideological. The classic case may be in administrative giants such as EPA and the Department of Justice, with decision makers ranging from conservative appointees of one administration through career civil servants who espouse very liberal views of environmental protection; but similar differences are found on a smaller scale in other levels of government.

Bureaucratic processes produce results that may deviate from outcomes that legislators and regulators contemplated. Conybeare (1982) has noted that:

> a complex regulatory environment will lead to a complex organizational structure in the regulatory bureau.... Complex structures may inhibit the ability of the organization to follow a coherent regulatory goal ... standard operating procedures for processing information and making decisions may inhibit the ability of the organization to respond to problems with appropriate policy. (pp. 36–37)

It is not surprising, then, that some of the most effective environmental programs are administered by counties and state agencies with few employees. (The Los Angeles Hazardous Waste Strike Force is one example.)

Organizational obstacles of several kinds block information flow among agencies and between government and business targets. These obstacles are found in agencies that articulate environmental rules, in the regulated industry itself, and in government units that monitor or enforce rules. Excessive organizational differentiation, absence of coordination within bureaucracies, and disruption caused by litigation are among the most important factors.

Lawmaking Irrationality

> And you'll never tell me ... this process of running around the hall in and out of a conference committee at 11 o'clock at night deciding whether it should be .41 or this or that or other thing is a rational process. The people bartering on what the emission levels should be on automobiles wouldn't know a hydrocarbon if they tripped over it (DiMento, 1986b, Interview C)

Several criticisms of environmental lawmaking center on its dubious rationality (Bardach & Kagan, 1982; Foss, 1985; Levin, 1977; Rodgers,

1973; Sabatier, 1977; Skolnick, 1968). Rationality has both objective and subjective dimensions. It is one test by which business decides whether government cares about the quality of rules or whether rules reflect primarily value or policy positions that are objectively nondefensible (DiMento, 1986a, b).

A frequent criticism of the rationality of environmental regulations concerns the science that forms the background for standard setting. Debate centers on both specific standards and the very need to regulate. Challenges to the information base of environmental controls are several: data are lacking, biased, incomplete, or irrelevant (DiMento, 1986a). Adversaries conclude that scientists 'on the other side' deliberately distort the meaning of findings and results (Brooks, 1975). Recent examples include analyses of the need for acid rain legislation, of the health effects of pesticides such as malathion, and of whether formaldehyde should be strictly regulated.

The Gaps in Science

For policy and political reasons, government regulates with insufficient information. Several questions that must be answered to convince industry of the soundness of regulation are transscientific; that is, they are not subject to resolution through the normal procedures of science (McGarity, 1979). Here are some examples. Animal experiments to test a suspected substance at an ambient level may be prohibitively costly. As in the classic 'mega mouse' case, employing the number of mice necessary to reach statistically significant conclusions may be logistically impossible (McGarity, 1979). Extrapolation of animal results to humans is not always convincing, and extrapolation of high-dose laboratory data to low-dose ambient levels can employ many different mathematical assumptions. Resulting predictions of the incidence of health effects of a suspected substance differ by orders of magnitude. A related issue concerns the relevance of data generated from high doses over short periods of time to the effects of comparatively low doses over a lifetime.

Even when answers are practically achievable through scientific means, much work remains before scientists and regulators reach consensus. For many health problems, theories of causation are multiple; only a few involve environmental contamination. Researchers cannot always identify suspected contaminants and model their streams in air, water, and land, nor specify routes within these media in which the pollutant travels. We have only elementary knowledge about interactions with other forms of the suspect substance and with other substances in the environment (for example, of alcohol with formaldehyde), about pathways in the body, and about biochemical reactions in various routes of entry. Within the body there are numerous potential combinations with other toxic or hazardous materials, and with naturally occurring substances that are benign at lower levels (Report, 1984). Cigarette smoking and other social behaviors confound analyses of effects; and cultural, psychological, and individual responses to disease complicate the environmental sciences (Levine, 1982).

Most fundamentally, the structure of science itself invites attacks on results used in regulation because the scientific process is basically one of rejecting hypotheses rather than asserting causation. Thus, the same characteristics of science that promote sincere charges of irrationality also provide business with opportunities for tactical strikes at the information base of environmental law. Industry finds standard setting under conditions of great uncertainty particularly disturbing. Since the science of detection is outpacing the science of causation, business fears the prospect of control being extended to parts per trillion of emissions (DiMento, 1986a). If agencies regulate to the point at which pollution is identifiable, there will be no limit to potential controls (Efron, 1984). When science is unable to give unambiguous results or clear direction, a regulatory dilemma arises: the issue, crudely put, is whether to wait for a dead-body count before one regulates. However, some potentially regulatable entities probably will never demonstrate ill effects. Time is not the issue; rather, causation is. Science can only speculate on actual outcomes of people's environmental exposure (DiMento, 1981).

In sum, looking to science for objective referents to acceptable controls can assist at the margins and in some special cases, but scientific conclusions will not generally satisfy those affected by expensive regulations. Indeed, science will be used to generate alternative understandings of what is rational. It is facile to say that good science will prevail and, over time, policymakers will have unbiased information. But even in situations where this is true, one must keep in mind that industry response to regulations is as real an obstacle to compliance as is the absence of consensus in the scientific community about the basis for controls.

The Actors

To understand compliance, one must understand variation among the individuals and groups involved in the regulatory process. Variations among people who fill roles in government, in the business firm, and in advocacy groups are especially significant when norms are both divergent and in transition. This is the case in environmental law.

The Firm's Perception of the Regulator

The firm's information about the regulator influences compliance. The business target evaluates, sometimes systematically and often less formally, the status of the regulatory agency. This information is a barometer of the regulatory threat. The relationship between the status of the communicator of a requirement and the degree of compliance is positive (Faley & Tedeschi, 1971; Hall, 1977; Stone, 1978; Tapp & Levine, 1972; Wilson & Rachal, 1978). Legislative acts carry more weight than judicial opinions, and administrative agency directives carry still less influence (Faley & Tedeschi, 1971; Horai & Tedeschi, 1969). Environmental commands to highly paid, highly respected corporate executives are often created, communicated, and enforced by people with lesser status—the so-called faceless bureaucrat (Wilson & Rachal 1978). Roberts and Bluhm (1981) found that the more professional the agency, the more responsive was the firm to its directives.

Administration that appears informed, fair, efficient, and smooth generates respect for the regulator (Bardach & Kagan, 1982; Kagan, 1984). Several types of performance impress those being regulated. The integration of scientific information into rule making enhances legitimacy when the agency uses qualified experts, requires or sponsors quality research (Kagan, 1984), yet recognizes the need to take action even when knowledge gaps exist. Agency stakeholders also appreciate the careful and balanced consideration of a variety of points of view in regulatory matters. Agencies are more highly regarded if their procedures are understandable and accessible, and not subject to endless continuances. Clear and unequivocal articulation of rules and enforcement decisions promotes compliance. Some of the evidence for these propositions is qualitative, and observers differ on assessments of legitimacy and effectiveness, but general classifications can be made. In recent years former EPA Administrator William D. Ruckelshaus's decision on lead was well respected, whereas the EPA failure to list formaldehyde as a carcinogen and the 1970s conclusions of the EPA Community Health and Environmental Surveillance System ('CHESS') were actions that weakened the agency's reputation.

Professionalism. Industry personnel assess inspectors' professionalism, and the performance of agency personnel in the field influences the agency's reputation. The total regulatory process at times appears to be simply the official who comes into the plant. The inspector is 'a surrogate for the rule itself,' and Clay (1983) and Bardach and Kagan (1982) report that his or her professionalism is correlated with the efficacy of enforcement. In addition, industry regularly assesses an agency's lawyers, technical experts, and policymakers, and makes implicit and explicit determinations about probabilities of meaningful enforcement.

Ideology as a compliance obstacle. On the other hand, perceptions that decisions are ideology driven (as opposed to law directed) counteract compliance when they highlight and exaggerate general government-business differences over regulation. Attention to the value of specific rules—which themselves may be relatively noncontroversial—is then replaced with ongoing debates about political theory and government's proper function. Government can exacerbate the rift by failing to recognize that some decisions may be truly trivial and that flexible, pragmatic responses can win over potential adversaries.

When business views environmental agencies in adversarial terms, or government uses ideology to categorize regulated industries, communication obstacles to compliance result. The conflict is heightened through labeling, and there is an increased likelihood of incorrectly hearing the position of the other side. This is not to say that criticism of compliance activities (either of regulations or of reactions to them) has no place; that would assume a compliance framework that is far from the patchwork behavioral system we are describing. But non-professional, emotional reactions to messages from 'the other side' exacerbate miscommunication, and may lead to attempts to force compliance using poor or irrelevant information.

Agency organizational characteristics. Agency structure and organization are also important to the delivery of regulatory information. Since the quality and strength of the regulation and its enforcement greatly influence compliance, the capacity to generate effective rules is crucial. Agency deficiencies that are relevant here include agency overload, inadequate resources, limited access to business information, and technical deficiencies.

Support Groups

Collective concern is a necessary condition for government action. Called by many names (pressure, influence, political involvement), support for adherence to rules channels the activities of agencies in promoting compliance. On the other side, activity strongly supportive of opposing societal objectives has a negative impact on compliance with environmental laws.

The term *support group* does not precisely match the term *interest group* in political science; it covers both smaller and larger collectivities and those with shorter life spans. Both outside groups that support environmental objectives and, occasionally, company insiders can play central roles in implementation of environmental law (Ball & Friedman, 1965; Dolbeare & Hammond, 1971; Milner, 1971; Muir, 1967; Roberts & Bluhm, 1981; Sabatier, 1975). Groups that have strong, clearly formulated attitudes about compliance can influence regulatory action out of all proportion to their numbers (Roberts & Bluhm, 1981; Schwartz & Orleans, 1967; Wichelman, 1976), and potential victims of environmental violations are uniquely positioned to promote agency attention to violations (Kagan, 1984, citing Sabatier & Mazmanian, 1978). Support groups that influence compliance may be elite and long-standing, or ad hoc groups such as a determined committee or coalition that forms for a single issue involving an alleged violation.

The Dynamics of Support Groups

Political theory offers no convincing rationale for basing regulatory enforcement on support-group complaints. But socially, the modern state is so comprehensively involved in citizens' affairs, and guiding laws are so numerous, that government administrators must seek means of setting priorities. In the political and legal environment of pollution control, law enforcement is not a sure outcome of legal philosophy or government theory. Enforcement is more pragmatic, even in highly politicized administrations—responsive to growing and changing citizen demands.

Information is a major source of group influence. Environmental support groups describe to regulators the impacts of environmental violations. They help choose business targets in a context wherein comprehensive enforcement is seldom possible. They alert business to citizen concerns about compliance. Conversely, support groups for business tell government when enforcement is unwarranted or inappropriate in light of the benefits provided by an environmentally destructive enterprise.

Institutional channels modulate the strength of the compliance message delivered by support groups. For example, citizen suits can make concerns heard when they might be ignored in administrative or legislative proceedings. Support groups can join together to enhance the impact of information and to disseminate statements that are more influential than their separate backers. These coalitions also carry a symbolic message about the seriousness of environmental violations.

The quality of information sent varies, and the relationship between support-group influence and compliance is not always positive. Inaccurate information can complicate routine, standard agency approaches to inducing compliance. Fixating attention on a particular case or procedure can impede development of effective compliance strategies. Furthermore, communities in certain controversies may favor noncompliance. Environmental law enforcement based on national attitudinal support for compliance is often mitigated by local views of an offense (including its economic benefits) and familiarity with the defendants (Clinard & Yeager, 1980). Moving toward prosecution of some classes of violations is difficult, especially when would-be defendants are residents of tightly knit communities and when an environmental insult was not willful.

Characteristics of the Firm

Independent of the interplay among law, communication, and support, organizational variables such as size, economic profile, structure, and culture have all been linked with compliance performance and incidence of violations both in individual firms, and on an industrywide basis.[2]

Scholarship has reached various conclusions about the influence of size of the firm (Clinard & Yeager, 1980). Some of the differences result because scholars operationalize size in different ways: number of employees, average assets, gross revenues, number of divisions, and volume of production. In addition, some studies center on the actual commission of violations, whereas others describe government's motivation to uncover or pursue existing noncompliance.

Likewise, no clear linear relationship exists between compliance and organizational differentiation. For example, in American corporations differentiation often includes development of specialized legal divisions, and these units may see regulatory compliance as their *raison d'être* and favor responsiveness to law (Mitnick, 1981). On the other hand, firms with legal expertise may hear only discouraging news from counsel about the nature of regulations, and at times lawyers exaggerate the potential for government intervention. The legal department can thus become isolated (Gross, 1978). To many corporation managers, the lawyers represent an obstacle to business progress. Businesses may screen the bad news of legal requirements from managers at operating levels and even from corporate executives, thus disregarding the need to meet health and safety and environmental standards of increasing stringency. In this way a potentially compliance-promoting organizational department may become a source of surreptitious violation (DiMento, 1986a).

Because degree of compliance is fundamentally a legal determination, businesses with highly specialized regulatory law sections can create positive compliance records. In interactions with government, corporate lawyers can mold working interpretations of environmental law (Lund, 1977). They can lessen regulatory disruption of corporate activities by channeling and narrowing the law's impact. Simpler firms will not have this husbanding ability; they must rely on outside counsel in critical cases, putting the firm in a vulnerable position. Companies without an environmental law capacity may fail to employ a legal defense that is obvious to a specialist. Inexperienced counsel may not recognize technical definitions of compliance, whereas experienced lawyers can undermine even well-developed agency enforcement strategies.

In addition, company environmental lawyers can initiate informal communications with government, increasing the governmental cost of promoting compliance. Business counsel can unduly complicate an initially straightforward case (Diver, 1979). Requests for clarification, for conferences to share new information, for extensions, and descriptions of good-faith efforts to realize compliance may impede the timely realization of government's objective. Such demands by industry lawyers may lead an agency to put aside a prosecution in order to pursue other tasks that can readily be counted as agency victories.

The Factors Within a Compliance Framework

Policymakers concerned with business compliance with regulatory law do not have the luxury of viewing the issue of compliance, as in the above review, from a single-factor perspective. A regulator, an enforcer, a business person interested in compliance and its costs cannot 'hold other variables constant.' A theory of organizational compliance with environmental law must address enforcement, communication, support-group activities, and characteristics of regulators, enforcers, support groups, and firms all together. Figure 7.1 portrays the compliance activity in a multivariable manner, and suggests that compliance can result from several different paths. Support groups alone, for example, may influence a firm to comply. Enforcement strategies, even in the absence of good regulations, may foster compliance. Or combinations of forces may explain compliance—e.g., when the regulator seeks and obtains good information about the firm, when enforcement messages are clear and consistent, and when support groups within the firm and public interest groups converge on an understanding of acceptable behavior. Conversely, several different weaknesses in relationships among the government, the business sector, and environmental advocates can explain noncompliance.

While single factors can be influential, only in the narrowest band of cases will one psychological, organizational, or economic variable explain compliance. A system achieves compliance through a variety of routes and may be out of compliance because of numerous possible deficiencies. For example, clearly stated environmental regulations based on respected scientific research may promote compliance even when enforcement policy is not fully implemented and when the general population is indifferent to compliance. Or, as a different example, a strong enforcement policy that is fairly and predictably applied and backed by considerable resources may promote compliance even when environmental rules are inconsistent and lack scientific certitude.

Conclusion

As these examples suggest, public policy should consider the route to compliance and not simply the realization of compliance, since some routes are costly and undesirable. In reaching decisions about appropriate regulatory action, decision makers need to recognize the number and identity of parties involved, the diversity of their motivations, and the dynamics that result from interactions among the individual and organizational participants in successive steps toward regulatory compliance.

Further research can assist in making these decisions and choices of strategies less speculative. But the needed research is long range, complex, and will by necessity be limited in its prescriptive applicability. We need to know more about the classification of corporate environments and the interactions between types of organizations and coercive vs. cooperative strategies. We need to understand better how rationality is defined by actors in the compliance framework. We need to test propositions about the relationship of administrative procedures to organizational responses. We would benefit from additional studies about the characteristics and strategies of support groups and the long-term effects of their contributions. We need to operationalize and test alternative dispute-resolution techniques better, as they are increasingly used to foster compliance.

The next steps in research should include greater refinement of the factors included in the framework presented here (e.g., Port, 1988). Leading candidates include the dependent variable, compliance, and the communication factors. Also, testing of the bivariate propositions of the framework is needed, using different types of regulatory law and different organizational sizes and cultures. Going beyond tests of single factors, attempts to operationalize the multivariate framework in successive case studies should provide additional useful insights.

Such research will allow us to have greater confidence in our choice of regulatory strategies. But we will still remain far from confident prediction of organizational reactions to specific compliance strategies. This cautious conclusion is required in a study of phenomena where the targets vary from tiny dry-cleaning firms to mammoth multinational corporations, the laws vary from simply hortatory to statutes of several hundred pages, and support groups range from local pollution control task forces to the Sierra Club.

Notes

† Professor of Social Ecology and Management at the University of California, Irvine. He holds a Ph.D. (Urban and Regional Planning) and a J. D. from the University of Michigan. He has written extensively about issues relating to environmental law and policy, and his most recent book is entitled *Environmental Law and American Business: Dilemmas of Compliance.*

1. Industry reports that there is 'very little or no coal that will comply 100% of the time' with federal new-source performance standards (Nelson & Dragos, 1977, p. 41).
2. We leave aside entirely corporate and regulatory culture, factors that are receiving increased attention in the regulatory literature (Clinard & Yeager, 1980; Meidinger, 1986). Limited space in this article and the difficulties in operationalizing the variables sufficiently even to address the directionality of impact on compliance require this omission.

References

Ball, H. V., & Friedman, L. M. (1965). 'The use of criminal sanctions in the enforcement of economic legislation: A sociological view'. *Stanford Law Review, 17*, 97–223.

Bardach, E., & Kagan, R. (1982). *Going by the Book: The problem of regulatory unreasonableness*. Philadelphia, PA: Temple University Press.

Bean, F. D., & Cushing, R. T. (1971). 'Criminal homicide, punishment and deterrence: Methodological and substantive reconsiderations'. *Social Science Quarterly, 52*, 277–289.

Braithwaite, J., & Geis, G. (1982). 'On theory and action for corporate crime control'. *Crime and Delinquency, 28*, 292–314.

Brooks, H. (1975). 'Expertise and politics—Problems and tension'. *Proceedings of the American Philosophical Society, 119*, 257.

Brown, D. W., & Stover, R. V. (1977). 'Court directives and compliance'. *American Politics Quarterly, 5*, 465–480.

Byrne, J., & Hoffman, S. M. (1985). 'Efficient corporate harm: A Chicago metaphysic'. In B. Fisse & P. A. French (eds.), *Corrigible Corporations and Unruly Law* (pp. 101–36). San Antonio, TX: Trinity University Press.

Chambliss, W. J. (1966). 'The deterrent influence of punishment'. *Crime and Delinquency, 12*, 70–75.

Clay, T. (1983). *Combating Cancer in the Workplace: Implementation of the California Occupational Carcinogens Control Act*. Unpublished doctoral dissertation, University of California, Irvine.

Clinard, M. B., & Yeager, P. C. (1980). *Corporate Crime*. New York: Free Press.

Conybeare, J. A. (1982). 'Politics and regulation: The public choice approach'. *Australian Journal of Public Administration, 41*, 33–45.

DiMento, J. F. (1981). 'Making usable information on environmental stressors: Opportunities for the research and policy communities'. *Journal of Social Issues, 37*(1), 172–204.

——(1986a). 'Der consensus workshop: Ein geeignetes Forum für Grenzwertsetzung?' In G. Winter (ed.), *Grenzwerte* (pp. 103–9). Germany: Werner-Verlag.

——(1986b). *Environmental Law and American Business: Dilemmas of compliance*. New York: Plenum.

Diver, C. S. (1979). 'The assessment and mitigation of civil money penalties by federal administrative agencies'. *Columbia Law Review, 79*, 1435–1502.

——(1980). 'A theory of regulatory enforcement'. *Public Policy, 28*, 257–299.

——(1983). 'The optimal precision of administrative rules'. *Yale Law Journal, 93*, 65–109.

Dolbeare, K. M., & Hammond, P. E. (1971). *The School Prayer Decisions from Court Policy to Local Practice*. Chicago: University of Chicago Press.

Downing, P. B., & Watson, W. D. (1974). 'The economics of enforcing air pollution controls'. *Journal of Environmental Economics and Management, 1*, 219–250.

Efron, E. (1984). *The Apocalyptics: Cancer and the big lie*. New York: Simon & Schuster.

Environmental Quality Council. (1980). *Eleventh Annual Report, environmental quality*. Washington, DC: Author.

——(1981). *Twelfth Annual Report, environmental quality*. Washington, DC: Author.

Erickson, M. L., & Gibbs, J. P. (1975). 'Specific versus general properties of legal punishments and deterrence'. *Social Science Quarterly, 56*, 290–297.

Erlich, I. (1973). 'Participation in illegitimate activities: A theoretical and empirical investigation'. *Journal of Political Economy, 81*, 521–565.

Ermann, M. D., & Lundman, R. J. (1975). 'Deviant acts by complex organizations: Deviance and social control at the organizational level of analysis'. *Sociological Quarterly, 19*, 55–67.

Faley, T., & Tedeschi, J. T. (1971). 'Status and reactions to threats'. *Journal of Personality and Social Psychology, 17*, 192–199.

Fisse, W. B. (1978). 'The social policy of corporate criminal responsibility'. *Adelaide Law Review, 6*, 361–412.

Foss, R. D., (1985). 'Psychological factors in child safety restraint use'. *Journal of Applied Social Psychology, 15*, 269–284.

Geis, G., (1985). 'Criminological perspectives on corporate regulation: A review of recent research'. In B. Fisse & P. A. French (eds.), *Corrigible Corporations and Unruly Law* (pp. 63–84). San Antonio, TX: Trinity University Press.

Gibbs, J. P. (1968). 'Crime, punishment, and deterrence'. *Southwestern Social Science Quarterly, 48*, 515–530.

Gray, L. N., & Martin, J. D. (1969). 'Punishment and deterrence: Another analysis of Gibbs' data'. *Social Science Quarterly, 50*, 389–395.

Gross, E. (1978). 'Organizational crime: A theoretical perspective'. *Studies in Symbolic Interaction, 1*, 55–85.

Gruhl, J. (1981). 'The Supreme Court's impact on the law of libel: Compliance by lower federal courts'. *Western Political Quarterly, 33*, 502–519.

Hall, R. M. (1977). 'The evolution and implementation of EPA's regulatory program to control the discharge of toxic pollutants of the nation's waters'. *Natural Resources Lawyer, 10*, 507–529.

Horai, J., & Tedeschi, J. T. (1969). 'Effects of credibility and magnitude of punishment on compliance to threats'. *Journal of Personality and Social Psychology, 12*, 164–169.

Inside EPA. (1983, April 8). p. 14.

Jones, C. O. (1977). *An Introduction to the Study of Public Policy.* North Scituate, MA: Duxbury.

Kagan, R. (1984, June). *Regulatory Enforcement Styles*. Paper presented at the meeting of the Law and Society Association, Boston.

Krislov, S. (1972). 'The parameters of power: The concept of compliance as an approach to the study of the legal and political process'. In S. Krislov, K. O. Boyum, H. N. Clark, R. C. Schafer, & S. O. White (eds.), *Compliance and the Law: A multidisciplinary approach* (pp. 333–50). Beverly Hills, CA: Sage.

Levin, M. H. (1977). 'Crimes against employees: Substantial criminal sanctions under the occupational safety and health act'. *American Criminal Law Review, 14*, 717–745.

Levine, A. G. (1982). *Love Canal: Science, politics and people*. Lexington, MA: Lexington Books.

Likens, T. W., & Kohfeld, C. W. (undated). *Models of Mass Compliance: Contextual or economic approach*. Unpublished manuscript.

Lindblom, C. E. (1959). 'The science of "muddling through".' *Public Administration Review, 19*, 77–88.

Lund, L. (1977). *Corporate Organization for Environmental Policymaking*. New York: Conference Board.

Mann, K., Wheeler, S., & Sarat, A. (1980). 'Sentencing the white-collar offender'. *American Criminal Law Review, 17*, 497–500.

Marcus, A. (1980). 'Environmental Protection Agency'. In J. Q. Wilson (ed.), *The Politics of Regulation*. New York: Basic Books.

Marlow, M. L. (1982). 'The economics of enforcement: The case of OSHA'. *Journal of Economics and Business, 34*, 164–171.

McGarity, T. A. (1979). 'Substantive and procedural discretion in administrative resolution of science policy questions: Regulating carcinogens in EPA and OSHA'. *Georgetown Law Journal, 67*, 729–810.

Meidinger, R. (1986). *Regulatory Cultures*. Unpublished manuscript.

Milner, N. A. (1971). *The Court and Local Law Enforcement: The impact of Miranda*. Beverly Hills, CA: Sage.

Mitnick, B. M. (1981). 'The strategic uses of regulation and deregulation'. *Business Horizons, 24*, 71–83.

Muir, W. K. (1967). *Prayer in the Public Schools: Law and attitude change*. Chicago: University of Chicago Press.

Nelson, A., & Dragos, J. (1977, October). *Coal Variability and Sulfur Compliance*. Paper presented at the National Coal Association/Bituminous Coal Research Coal Utilization Symposium, Louisville.

Packer, H. L. (1968). *The Limits of the Criminal Sanction*. Stanford, CA: Stanford University Press.

Paternoster, R., Saltzman, L. E., Waldo, G. P., & Chiricos, T. G. (1983). 'Perceived risk and social control: Do sanctions really deter?' *Law and Society Review, 17*, 457–479.

Pfeffer, J., Salancik, G. R., & Leblebici, H. (1976). 'The effects of uncertainty on the use of social influence in organization decisionmaking'. *Administrative Science Quarterly, 21*, 245.

Port, T. (1988). *Hazardous Waste Facilities in Minnesota: A test of the effect of enforcement, communication, and personnel on corporate compliance with environmental law.* Unpublished doctoral dissertation, University of California, Irvine.

Report on the Consensus Workshop on Formaldehyde. (1984). *Environmental Health Perspectives*, 323–381.

Roberts, M. J., & Bluhm, J. S. (1981). *The Choices of Power: Utilities face the environmental challenge*. Cambridge, MA: Harvard University Press.

Rodgers, H. R. (1973). 'Law as an instrument of public policy'. *American Journal of Political Science, 17*, 638–647.

Sabatier, P. A. (1975). 'Social movements and regulatory agencies: Toward a more adequate and less pessimistic theory of clientele capture'. *Policy Science, 6*, 301–42.

—— (1977). 'Regulatory policy-making: Toward a framework of analysis'. *National Resources Journal, 17*, 415–460.

—— & Mazmanian, D. A. (1978). *The Conditions of Effective Implementation: A guide to accomplishing policy objectives*. Unpublished manuscript.

Sax, J. L. (1976). 'A general survey of the problem'. In *Science for a Better Environment*. Science Council of Japan.

Scholz, J. T. (1984). 'Voluntary compliance and regulatory enforcement'. *Law and Policy, 6*, 385–404.

Schwartz, B. (1968). 'The effect in Philadelphia of Pennsylvania's increased penalties for rape and attempted rape'. *Journal of Criminal Law, Criminology and Police Science, 59*, 509–515.

Schwartz, R. D., & Orleans, S. (1967). 'On legal sanctions'. *University of Chicago Law Review, 34*, 274–300.

Skolnick, J. H. (1968). 'Coercion to virtue: Enforcement of morals'. *Southern California Law Review, 41*, 588–641.

South Coast Air Quality Management District. (1983). *A Progress Report, 1977–1983*. South El Monte, CA: Author.

Stigler, G. J. (1970). 'The optimum enforcement of laws'. *Journal of Political Economy, 78*, 526–536.

Stone, C. (1985). 'Corporate regulation: The place of social responsibility'. In B. Fisse & P. A. French (eds.), *Corrigible Corporations and Unruly Law* (pp. 13–28). San Antonio, TX: Trinity University Press.

Stone, C. D. (1978). 'Social control of corporate behavior'. In J. D. Ermann & R. J. Lundman (eds.), *Corporate and Government Deviance: Problems of Organizational behavior in contemporary society* (pp. 243–58). New York: Oxford University Press.

Susskind, L., & McMahon, G. (1985). 'The theory and practice of negotiated rulemaking'. *Yale Journal of Regulation, 3*, 133–165.

Sutinen, J. G., & Anderson, P. (1985). 'The economics of fisheries law enforcement'. *Land Economics, 61*, 389–397.

Tapp, J. L., & Levine, F. J. (1972). 'Persuasion to virtue: A preliminary statement'. In S. Krislov, K. O. Boyum, H. N. Clark, R. C. Schaefer, & S. O. White (eds.), *Compliance and the Law: A multidisciplinary approach* (pp. 181–98). Beverly Hills, CA: Sage.

Tittle, C. R. (1980). 'Crime rates and legal sanctions'. *Social Problems, 16*, 409–423.

——, & Logan, C. H. (1973). Sanctions and deviance: Evidence and remaining questions. *Law and Society Review, 7*, 371–392.

Waldo, G. P., & Chiricos, T. G. (1972). 'Perceived penal sanctions and self-reported criminality: A neglected approach to deterrence research'. *Social Problems, 19*, 522–540.

Wall Street Journal. (1984, June 29).

Wichelman, A. F. (1976). 'Administrative agency implementation of the National Environmental Policy Act of 1969: A conceptual framework for explaining differential response'. *National Resources Journal, 16*, 263–300.

Wilson, J. Q. (ed.). (1980). *The Politics of Regulation*. New York: Basic Books.

——, & Rachal, R. (1978). 'Can the government regulate itself?' In M. D. Ermann & R. J. Lundman (eds.), *Corporate and Government Deviance: Problems of Organizational behavior in contemporary society* (pp. 309–22). New York: Oxford University Press.

PART IV
Alternative Methods of Environmental Regulation

Regulation and In-Company Environmental Management in the Netherlands*

MARIUS AALDERS

Abstract

This chapter addresses the relationship between preventive systems of social control and regulation of the behavior of public bodies and private organizations. Illustrated with material on new developments in self-regulation concerning environmental management in companies in the Netherlands, the author argues that a combination of stimulated (or 'regulated') self-regulation and stringent enforcement policies is feasible and should lead to company compliance with environmental regulation. The article discusses the assertion that to reduce the social distance between government and individual citizen, between regulator and regulated, a mixture of policy instruments is needed, ergo: by involving societal groups of interested people in policy formation and self-regulation, enhancing the creation of normative systems (involvement 'by association') on the one hand and the availability of adequate law enforcement procedures on the other, corporations, through responsive government regulation, could promote an adequate and successful preventive system of social control.

Introduction

Western industrial democracies are characterized by a great social distance between regulators and regulated. This creates a demanding and obstinate task for preventive systems of social control (Black, 1976; Horwitz, 1990: 237). These systems seem to be most effective within small, closely knit, homogeneous groups. Informal sanctions have considerable impact in such systems. Whenever the relational distance between regulators and the regulated increases, more formal sanctions will be used, as Black's general theory of law predicts (Black, 1976: 40–41, 65 ff.). Grabosky and

Braithwaite (1986: chap. 15), explaining variations in enforcement activity across ninety-six agencies in Australia, based one of their hypotheses on Black's theory. They found strong support for the hypothesized relationship between relational distance and enforcement activity.[1]

Law in modern societies may have lost much of its power to regulate effectively the conduct of individuals. However, it can regulate successfully the behavior of public bodies and private organizations (Horwitz, 1990: 237). What is ominously called the 'implementation gap' is just another way of conceding that regulation does not work without the use of other policy instruments. In social psychology it is alleged that command-and-control strategies are poor vehicles for changing behavior.

In the Netherlands the flaws in enforcing the relatively new environmental law became very apparent in the 1980s. From 1970 environmental law in the Netherlands developed into a vast system of legislative programs on matters ranging from surface water and sea pollution, to nuisance and noise abatement, to air pollution and soil protection. These laws pretend to be all-encompassing, but are best described as over-inclusive. They try to provide for such a wide array of possible cases that even the officials responsible for implementing them are sometimes at a loss what to do when they give permits or enforce regulations. Loopholes are being found and in practice the environmental legislative network appears to be flawed. Needless to say, the targeted group (industry and other potential polluters) has problems complying with all these regulations.[2] Moreover, the Dutch legislative process could be characterized as a very sophisticated system of policy formulation. Much formal and informal consultation, influence by private associations, and numerous possibilities for review may hold up decisions for a long time.

In spite of this vast body of legislation, with ample opportunity for appeal, there has been much scepticism about the impact of environmental regulation. In 1983, after a government committee analyzed and evaluated a case of deliberate water and soil pollution (The Netherlands, 1983), the time seemed to be ripe for strengthening the enforcement of environmental law. The central Environmental Health Inspectorate saw its duties enhanced. A financial program was set up to stimulate local government enforcement of environmental legislation. Staff was considerably increased, as compared to other fields of government care where economizing measures were the order of the day.

At the same time, though, as in other industrial democracies, there was a trend in Dutch politics toward deregulation, and also toward stimulation of industry self-regulation and 'internal enforcement.' These two tendencies—deregulation and promoting self-regulation on the one hand and developing a deterrence strategy by strengthening the criminal law organization on the other—initially appear to be contradictory. But in modern bureaucracies it comes as no surprise that the one hand does not know what the other is doing. Moreover, it is by no means certain that the two strategies, if proposed in a combination of policies, will not lead eventually to the stated policy goal, i.e. a change of behavior of corporations and individuals in the direction of compliance with the environmental law.

Beginning in 1980 the phrase 'overregulation breeds undercompliance' was widely used as an argument amongst policymakers to deregulate. But the repeatedly pronounced dictum that 'enforcement was the missing link in the environmental policy-chain,' requiring extended manpower and increased training for personnel, signalled a harder line in government policy towards polluters. Questions of how far the 'enforcement' policies may actually be implemented or whether they have mainly symbolic meaning (Edelman, 1964; Aubert, 1966; Aalders, 1984) are worth studying, but must be dealt with in another place.

In this article we raise the following questions and try to find an answer:

1. Are alternative regulatory strategies of stimulating companies to develop internal management systems the answer to regulatory problems with implementing environmental policy and enforcing environmental legislation?
2. Can we conclude from research data into styles of rule application and law enforcement in environmental regulation, especially from the few comparative studies that have been conducted, that eco-policy tends into the direction of compliance-oriented enforcement and self-regulating in business?

The analysis starts with a brief overview of theories of variations in social control (part II). This will be followed in part III by a report of research in the Netherlands in the field of environmental law enforcement. Special attention will be given to styles of environmental rule application by officials at local and provincial government levels. This phenomenon has been studied in the Netherlands and the Federal Republic of Germany as well as in the United States and the United Kingdom. The Dutch study was part of a research program on rule application by officials that was undertaken in 1980 at the University of Amsterdam by the Department of Sociology of Law. We conclude this section with a discussion of possible developments in environmental law enforcement and research into this matter.

In part IV some implications of the findings in Dutch as well as in other, notably English and American, research will be discussed exposing different styles and strategies of environmental law enforcement. The paradox of enforcement of environmental legislation leads us to the general conclusion that accommodative, conciliatory styles of enforcement by environmental law inspectorates are felt to be more effective than stringent, penal styles of enforcement. In this light we must understand the quest for alternative enforcement strategies.

The enforcement of environmental law is paradoxical. The findings of much research of regulatory enforcement point in the direction of flexible enforcement policies and more compliance-oriented strategies (part V). In this respect a recent development in Dutch government regulation strategy is worth considerable attention. Government is stimulating industry to adopt systems of Internal Company Environmental Management (ICEM; *bedrijfsinterne milieuzorgsystemen*). The implications of ICEM for government regulation and enforcement of environmental legislation will be dealt with in the last section. Problems of self-regulation, responsive regulation, internal enforcement, the emergence of environmental control structures in firms and companies, related to the (diminishing?) role of government control will be reflected upon in part VI.

Theories of Social Control

Regulation, i.e., rule application and enforcement of legislation, is a form of social control. Mannheim classified social controls as direct and indirect methods of influencing human behavior. These controls are always based on personal influence and work 'from near at hand,' meaning that the effect of this influence (of direct methods of social control) is always identified with the man who exercises it (Mannheim, 1940: 274). In that case the desired human behavior can be obtained 'by a single act of compulsion' (ibid.: 273). Indirectly influencing human behavior occurs by influencing the action, outlook, and habits of the individual by conscious or unconscious control of the natural, social, or cultural surroundings (ibid.: 274). Influencing the surroundings of regulated industries is one of the alternatives that governments of western democracies seem to consider, as a result of the ineffectiveness of direct compulsionary methods of regulation. Indirect social control can be seen in the accommodative, conciliatory, compliance-oriented enforcement styles adopted by inspectorates of socio-economic legislation in industrialized democracies, depending on the legal policy, the legal culture and the socio-political environment they are operating in.

Social control can also be established through organized bodies by means of rationalized behavior (Mannheim, 1940: 293). Intermediate organizations, or *associations* (Streeck & Schmitter, 1985) play an ever more important role in environmental policy implementation. This is in accordance with the emergence in Western societies of systems of bargained interest accommodation and concerned policy in the 1960s and 1970s (cf. Schmitter & Lehmbruch, 1979). It is important to focus on the social control of *industries* (i.e., not occupations or organizations) because it alerts us to the way that industry structure and composition, in turn, affect the control and regulatory process (Zald, 1978: 83).

On the basis of these complex societal developments we may distinguish a continuum of styles of social control. Horwitz, in his comprehensive study of social control, proposes four ideal types of social control: penal, compensatory, conciliatory and therapeutic styles (Horwitz, 1990). In terms of environmental law enforcement, social control means that environmental behavior can be controlled through the following styles:[3]

- a *penal* style; a moralistic style that aims to punish offenders who have broken some legal or extralegal standard of behavior (e.g., criminal law, coercion through imposed sanctions);
- a *compensatory* style; involving the payment of a debt from offenders to their victims; once restitution has been provided, the matter is settled (e.g., civil law, financial instruments);
- a *conciliatory* style; parties involved work together or with the aid of third parties to negotiate a mutually agreeable outcome (e.g., bargaining in the shadow of the law, communicative instruments).

Moreover, Horwitz distinguishes forms of social control, i.e., mechanisms that deal with problematic situations as conflicts, injuries, injustices, rivalries, discomforts, and irritations. Social control could be *unilateral*, *bilateral* and *trilateral*. This is important for the three elements of social control that govern Dutch societal relationships and that could also be discerned in matters of environmental policy: government, industry, and concerned citizens (for instance: trade unions and consumer as well as environmental organizations). It is significant that Braithwaite and Ayres in developing the idea of 'responsive regulation' mention the notion of 'tripartism': 'the process in which relevant public interest groups become fully fledged third players in the game,' so that they even 'have a seat at the negotiating table with the firm and the agency when deals are done' (1991: 25–39).

Another relevant distinction is the dichotomy between *deterrence* and *compliance* in law enforcement in which penal, compensatory and conciliatory styles are incorporated (Reiss, 1984: 23ff.; cf. Richardson, Ogus & Burrows, 1983; Hawkins, 1984). Of course these styles only operate in a unilateral form of social control. However, the more compliance oriented one gets, the more the conciliatory style will dominate.

Empirical studies give us a clue about styles of government social control which are, in principle, unilateral. For example, environmental health officers in Britain use *insistent* and *persuasive* strategies. Hutter devotes her study of environmental health officers in large part to a discussion of the variations within what she calls the 'accommodative framework' adopted by these officers (1988: 8, 189 ff.). Kagan (1978) observes a difference in *stringent* and *accommodative* rule application in an American regulatory agency. Grabosky and Braithwaite (1986: chap. 16) use the continuum conciliators to enforcers for developing a typology of Australian regulatory agencies, based on hierarchical clustering analysis. These range from 'conciliators,' 'benign big guns,' 'diagnostic inspectorates,' 'detached token enforcers,' 'detached modest enforcers' to 'token enforcers' and 'modest enforcers.'

To reach compliance, controlling officers have to *communicate* the law (DiMento, 1986); they have to make law *available* and even *negotiate* the law (Grace & Wilkinson, 1979). Compliance is promoted if the regulated persons consider regulations rational (Bardach & Kagan, 1982). Enforcement by indirect social control takes time. To be over zealous and overacting, to 'wield a big stick' and use repression and deterrence strategies too much, may in the end turn out to be counterproductive (Hawkins, 1984; Aalders, Korrel & Uylenburg, 1987). Deterrent law enforcement may be expected to shift towards proactive rather than reactive forms of mobilization (Black, 1973; Reiss, 1984: 34; see also Hawkins, 1984: 80–84, 90–96).

It should be clear though, that a shift to more conciliatory styles of enforcement does not mean a reduction of regulation, let alone abandoning regulation altogether. The former Dutch secretary of the environment, Pieter Winsemius, currently a consultant with the Dutch branch of McKinsey and Company, once stated that 'all that legislation about which business is complaining in fact exists because business wants it so badly; business has a stake in regulating and ordering the market.' State intervention may distort markets, just as the outcome of free contracts and competition may contradict state policies. At the same time, markets require a legal framework and the authoritative enforcement of contracts, and even the most etatistic states seem to require markets as supplementary mechanisms of allocation (Streeck & Schmitter, 1985: 2). Yeager (1991: 116) makes the point that the consolidation of federal environmental programs in the U.S.A. was driven jointly by public pressure for meaningful controls and by large corporate interests in the rationalization of environmental law in an increasingly turbulent political climate.

Theories of Social Control and Styles of Environmental Law Enforcement

In 1980, the Bonger Institute for Criminology at the University of Amsterdam published a research report on enforcement of the so-called 'Nuisance Act.' This law dates from 1875 and could be considered an environmental law *avant la lettre*. The report revealed that a harsh administrative sanction in the Nuisance Act, factory closure, was hardly ever imposed although, strictly-speaking, it should have been (Aalders, 1984). It was further discovered in research in a local government office that both environmental and building inspectors often use different styles of rule application, if 'application' is at all the appropriate word (Aalders, 1982). These officers use many informal ways of 'enforcing' the law, especially in consultation with the applicants for permits, both before the formal procedure starts, but also in stages where the polluters are in fact violating the law. The existence of preliminary informal bargaining in German formal regulatory procedures has been extensively documented by Mayntz, Bohne, et al. (1978; see also Bohne, 1980; Hucke, Mueller & Wassen, 1980).

In two Dutch studies it was found that styles of applying rules by local environmental and building inspectorates differed in many respects, often differing within the same bureau (see Aalders, 1982; Aalders, Korrel & Uylenburg, 1987). This research found that, although the environmental inspectors had greater discretionary powers, they nonetheless showed themselves rather stringent and legalistic in enforcing the law. Once they had produced 'a good permit' (which could take considerable time and be coupled with extended talks and bargaining), they would stick to the requirements they had so painstakingly established in cooperation with the applicant, rather than show a bit of leniency towards him. These officials took for granted that the effect of these decisions was often counterproductive. In the terminology of Kagan they hovered between *legalistic* and *retreatist* modes of rule application (Kagan, 1978).

In contrast, the building inspectors, who were much more bound by law and who did not have discretionary powers, in fact had an accommodative enforcement style and were inclined to assist builders and constructors when they acted against the law. These inspectors sometimes even 'looked the other way' when they saw something that could not bear the light of day. Later research into decision-making processes by environmental officials revealed a shift from rigid, self-binding styles of rule application to a more flexible, accommodative style. This was due to the inflow of younger and better-educated personnel and more frequent contact between inspectors and company officials.

Possible reasons for these different styles of building and environmental enforcement may be the following:

1. The environment is a relatively new area of legislation. In this situation, where structures are unknown, the culture of control (the controllers and the controlled) has yet to be developed. Where relationships with polluters are not well-established, to cling to the rules and go by the book is the safest way of avoiding criticism. As a result the inspector covers himself from both angles. Experiences with the American Environmental Protection Agency (EPA) have led to the conclusion that the theory of a life-cycle of bureaus (Bernstein, 1955) can be corroborated in the sense that inspectorates that begin from scratch tend to be very adversarial enforcers in the beginning but gradually take on a more conciliatory attitude (cf. Marcus, 1980: 267–303).
2. The shift from a stringent approach to a more accommodative strategy (and vice versa) may be explained by changes in the social and political environment within which the agency operates (Shover, et al., 1984: 140). As Bardach and Kagan state: 'If law is the medium of legalistic enforcement, it can also be the medium of legalistic contestation, and as the adversaries exhaust their energies in legal battles the basic goals of the regulatory process remain unattended' (1982: 117).
3. Interaction between controller and regulated may be seen as a dominant factor in making legislation work. In fact, inspectors get much satisfaction out of their work by educating and advising the regulated. Some controlling officers even consider themselves more or less 'social workers.'[4] The building inspector in particular has this type of relationship with the builder. Hutter found the same relationship between environmental health inspectors and industry (1988: 140).

On the basis of research that has been conducted on the issue of enforcement of environmental law, we may conclude that compliance-oriented styles are dominant in environmental regulation. Although in newly begun enforcement structures of environmental legislation inspectorates may adopt a deterrence-oriented enforcement style for a while, they will soon lean to a more accommodative style. The few comparative studies in the field of styles of regulation lead us to believe that in socio-economic regulation compliance-oriented enforcement styles are dominant over deterrence-oriented enforcement styles. Kelman (1980, 1984) makes a comparison of Swedish and American practices as regards enforcement of occupational safety and health regulations. It appears that there are dramatic differences in inspector attitudes in these countries. These attitudes parallel the differences between the way the inspection systems have been organized. The American enforcement system of the Occupational Safety and Health Administration (OSHA), set up after 1970, was designed to be enforcement-oriented, while the system in Sweden was cooperation-oriented (Kelman, 1984: 108). Kelman's research regarded OSHA, which concerns itself only indirectly with environmental issues. Nevertheless, his findings could very well hold for the environmental situation.

These differences become quite clear in Vogel's study where patterns of environmental regulation in Great Britain and the United States were compared. He also explains why these two nations have adopted such divergent approaches to controlling, as he calls it 'the externalities associated with industrial growth' (1986: 9). It is important to note Vogel's remark that many of the most critical differences in British and American regulatory practices have arisen only in the last two decades (ibid.: 226). In Britain the cooperative relationship between business and government has persisted through the present day. In America it atrophied.

Of course there are more explanations for the differences in regulatory and enforcement styles. Hutter found that the environmental health officers she studied regard their work as a job rather than a vocation (1988: 57). Whereas Hawkins, on the other hand, establishes that the newer recruits to the water authorities he studied have a higher level of formal education than their older colleagues and are especially marked by a sense of vocation and mission (1984: 39). This might explain different styles of enforcement.

In the Netherlands applying the rules of environmental legislation has become primarily the task of the Dutch provinces. Not only is most of the actual rule application delegated to regulation personnel, but it is the environmental inspector who eventually decides, in close interaction with company officials, 'what the rules are.' Accommodative, conciliatory styles of enforcement and stringent, adversarial styles of enforcement are to be found within the same office. The following example illustrates this:

A big steel factory was being controlled by officials who regularly visited the site and tried to find solutions for problems of air pollution in close cooperation with the environmental manager. They knew every tab, every flange in the factory. In fact they had been employed there themselves before joining the government service. The officials in this provincial environmental office who were especially designated to control waste regulation had a much more punitive style. They decided ad hoc on cases and didn't reflect much on possible outcomes of their actions in the future. Also they were not very much inclined to establish a good relationship with offenders. In fact, some of them were ex-police officers. They had a hard time getting acquainted with their working place and their colleagues who considered them as strangers in their organization. This phenomenon has been documented in other research. (Aalders, Korrel & Uylenburg, 1987 (translation by author); see also Hutter, 1988: 40)

Another important factor explaining differences in enforcement styles is the important fact that unlawful industrial environmental behavior, for instance air pollution, is much less 'criminally visible' than waste dump delinquency with its possible associated offenses like falsifying documents and other fraudulent behavior. The variety of environmental violations by industry is as striking as is the variety of violators. Violations result from the acts of innocent individuals and from the deliberate calculations of sophisticated corporations or organized criminal groups (cf. DiMento, 1986: 20–25).

An American study suggests that there is also regional variation in regulatory law enforcement. Local problems or structural arrangements within the same organization may produce substantial and important differences in the exercise of the regulatory mandate (Shover, Lynxwiler, et al., 1984: 122). The major determinants of these variations were found in enforcement styles of different regions of the Office of Surface Mining in the U.S. which can be grouped into regional differences in (1) employees' experiences with and beliefs about coal operators and state regulatory programs; (2) the political and regulatory environment; and (3) the regulatory task (ibid.: 130 ff.). Results of Dutch research in a provincial office, where several environmental laws are being applied, give rise to the same conclusion (Aalders, Korrel & Uylenburg, 1987).

Given the fact that different styles or strategies of enforcement are to be discerned,[5] it is plausible to suggest a continuum of legalistic, punitive, deterrence-oriented styles on the one hand and accommodative, conciliatory, compliance-oriented styles on the other (cf. Grabosky and Braithwaite, 1985; Hawkins, 1991). Movements of the regulatory style from the open and accommodative towards the closed and adversarial extremes and vice versa, are dependent on political factors, especially political organization. Kagan suggests that:

> if the United States employs a legalistic, adversarial style of social control and dispute resolution more often than other industrialized democracies, it is because American political structure encourages and enables politically organized groups to pursue their aims through legalistically cast programs and processes. (1988: 737)

In some instances, therefore, due to political pressure, deterrence strategies are being adopted as the more obvious means to achieve compliance. In other instances, where the power structure is not as open and fragmented as it is in the United States, a more accommodative stance is being taken towards polluters. Kelman, though a supporter of the accommodative Swedish enforcement system of occupational safety and health regulations, still believes that achieving high levels of regulatory compliance without extensive use of sanctions may remain an elusive task for the United States (Kelman, 1984: 117).

Compliance-oriented enforcement and accommodative styles of controllers seem to have more impact than deterrence-oriented and strict, legalistic enforcement styles in some circumstances. Of course it could be the other way around, as the American situation, in comparison with some Western European countries, proves to a degree. Although critics of the 'negotiation approach' and the 'compliance school' stress the importance of a tough, punitive approach toward polluters, most Western European enforcement officials seem to find the 'paradoxical' line more rewarding.

Towards Understanding the Enforcement Paradox

Although it is plausible that flexible, accommodative enforcement practices in environmental regulation are preferred by controllers over strict enforcement practices and that control systems are being built around compliance rather than deterrence strategies (see also Reiss, 1984: 34), nevertheless this empirical fact meets with considerable moral indignation from critics. For instance, Pearce and Tombs (1990) are extremely critical of what they call 'the compliance school.' In their debate with Hawkins they accuse the latter of an incorrect view of the determinants of business conduct. They assert that Hawkins misunderstands how the police deal with conventional crime and maintenance of order and that he contributes to a climate in which regulatory agencies are little more than consultants and business is increasingly trusted to regulate itself (Pearce & Tombs, 1991: 415).

This critique has been aptly refuted by Hawkins (1990, 1991), who rightly makes a stand against the notion that regulatory inspectorates, in contrast to the police for example, are opting for compliance styles of enforcement and that this should be a recommendable development. The ideological charge in Pearce and Tombs' suggestion is contrary to the many findings 'compliance' researchers have been reporting. Furthermore, there is virtually no difference between police and regulatory inspectorates in these matters. The idea of deterrence styles *versus* compliance styles is not so much one of polar opposites, but rather of shifting points on a continuum (Hawkins, 1991).

In understanding the enforcement paradox, Moore's theorem of 'semi-autonomous social fields' (Moore, 1973) might be helpful. Enforcement inspectorates as semi-autonomous social fields can produce and enforce rules. Regulating industry does not take place in a situation that is devoid of rules. New laws are thrust upon existing social arrangements in which there are already complexes of binding obligations. Semiautonomous social fields of administrative units that implement the law are 'loosely coupled' with firms as semiautonomous social fields, in which certain rules already exist (cf. Weick, 1976). This social field is not only a source of alternative regulation, of 'indigenous norms' (Galanter, 1981) responsible for the non-effectiveness of regulation, but it is also responsible for the degree and the way that regulation is effective (Griffiths, 1990: 33). Moore argues that 'an inspection of semi-autonomous social fields strongly suggests that the various processes, that make internally generated rules effective are often also the immediate forces that dictate the mode of compliance or non-compliance to state-made legal rules' (1973: 57).

From a neo-corporatist view Streeck and Schmitter (1985: 4) state that the fact that associative action may be dysfunctional for the community, the market and the state[6] does not by itself rule out the possibility that it may also contribute to order.

As an aside, a question could be raised regarding why environmental polluters are being treated differently from such ordinary criminals as robbers or even drunken drivers. This is frequently true for all offenders in the domain of socio-economic criminality, usually called white-collar crime; ordinary criminals are not given the treatment of prolonged bargaining over possible penalties and are not met with cooperative styles of law enforcement.

According to Weber (1954: 38), those who participate in the market intercourse with their own economic interests have a far greater rational knowledge of the market and interest in the situation than the legislators and enforcement officers whose interest is only abstract. Therefore it is difficult to effect successful legislative coercion in the economic sphere. Legislators depend upon private interested parties for the success of a legal measure in the marketplace. 'It is those private interested parties who are in a position to distort the intended meaning of a legal norm to the point of turning it into its very opposite, as has often happened in the past' (ibid.).

Lindblom (1977) notes that employers are not merely powerful, prestigious figures socially and politically. They are also the people to whom in market economies we have entrusted the vital tasks of investing and producing as we pursue such generally desired goals as full employment and economic growth. Errors of judgment or carelessness made in the execution of those duties are to be treated differently from carelessness or errors of judgment in general. Regulation is different because it embodies our veiled attempts to reconcile such supposedly sacred values as human life with what are, in practice, our equally strong commitments to economic growth, employment, and profits. On the other hand, Vogel (1986: 28) emphasizes that American industry has been forced to struggle harder to resist additional government restrictions on its prerogatives than in any other capitalist nation. In fact, companies being prosecuted for not complying with the law are often considered, most of all by their own counterparts, as 'bad apples' and are often treated with disdain (Bardach & Kagan, 1982). That is precisely why industry fears criminal law and its great publicity value (DiMento, 1986: 42–43). Precisely in the case of white-collar crime 'the process is the punishment' (Feeley, 1979).

We have seen that environmental regulation of industry and enforcement of environmental law are species of direct social control. Such control of industry is difficult to realize because of the intertwining of semiautonomous social fields of law-executing officials and regulated industry, a relationship in which frequent contacts are a necessity. Recognizing this fact leads us to varieties of indirect social control and of regulatory conduct. Indicative for differences in styles of regulation and social control are the regulated domain, the legal culture for regulators and regulated, the relational distance between controllers and industry, the discretionary value of the legal program, and the social environment.

Internal Company Environmental Management: an Alternative Regulatory Strategy

Bardach and Kagan, in their study of the problem of 'regulatory unreasonableness,' draw up their assessment of *legalistic enforcement* as follows:

> [R]egulatory toughness in its legalistic manifestation creates resentment and resistance, undermines attitudes and information-sharing practices that could otherwise be cooperative and constructive, and diverts energies of both sides into pointless and dispiriting legal routines and conflicts. (1982: 119)

The case for stringent, legalistic, deterrence-oriented styles of social control of companies in the application and enforcement of environmental legislation no longer seems strong in circumstances where the cooperation of industry is necessary. Penal styles are unlikely to provide effective responses to the problems that give rise to these sanctions. For reasons explained above, we are not pleading for deregulation and depenalization regarding environmental law. However, we deem it essential to recognize and, if necessary, to promote styles of compensatory and conciliatory control.

Basic to a more conciliatory style of social control is, as we have seen earlier, less relational distance and more frequency of contact between regulator and regulated. Commonly shared orientations towards a political solution of environmental problems should accompany increased contact, as should recognition of Moore's theorem that regulators and regulatees operate in semiautonomous social fields with their own characteristic norms and values.

If the structure of social relationships shapes the style, form, and effectiveness of social control, then fundamental changes in relational structures should, consequently, produce basic shifts in social control systems (Horwitz, 1990: 239). Several suggestions in this respect have been made. Bardach and Kagan propose forms of *indirect* regulation, for instance private regulation. Most of the regulation that takes place in the United States is already 'in the hands not of government officials but of the myriad individuals employed in the private sector,' for example, financial auditors, assembly line inspectors, quality control engineers and legal advisers. Government could take the initiative in 'stimulating private standards development,' 'mandating self-regulation,' or compelling enterprises to 'designate responsible officers' (Bardach & Kagan, 1982: 218 ff.). Other varieties of regulatory conduct have been suggested by Grabosky and Braithwaite (1986: 33 ff.), for example, state agreements, self-monitoring and mandatory self-reporting, public involvement in the regulatory process, and effluent charges.

One example of this shift in regulatory conduct may be observed in the development of a new strategy of environmental regulation by the Dutch government. In response to initiatives being taken by organized industry (*Bureau Milieuhygiene van de samenwerkende werkgeversorganisaties VNO en*

NCW), the government is stimulating the development of systems of Internal Company Environmental Management (ICEM). In ICEM the following elements are included:

a. environmental policy statement;
b. environmental programme;
c. integration of environmental management in business operation/ environmental coordinator;
d. measurements and registration;
e. internal monitoring;
f. internal information and training;
g. internal and external reporting/environmental reporting;
h. examination of total environmental management system/environmental audit. (The Netherlands. Parliament, 1989: 1)

The government considers environmental management to be an integrated part of corporate management and thinks that ICEM is a suitable tool to strengthen the compliance with environmental regulations by companies. Companies themselves should start looking for solutions to limit, and if possible, to prevent environmental impact with a view toward sustainable development. Currently, the Dutch government encourages the voluntary introduction and modelling of ICEM in companies, 'on the basis of initiatives from business and in accordance with intrinsic company responsibility.' In a special Note for the Dutch Lower House it says:

> Government objective is geared to reach integrated environmental management systems being available in 1995 in almost all [of the] 10.000 to 12.000 companies with (medium sized-) large environmental impact or specific environmental risks. This system must perform well and should be designed to deal with the nature, size and complexity of the individual companies. In addition the Government aims for clear steps to be taken in 1995 for the estimated 250.000 smaller companies with limited environmental impact in order to arrive at the introduction of an adequate environmental management system, taking into account the nature of the companies involved. To realize the proposed objectives in 1995 the Government deems it advisable to perform an interim evaluation at the end of 1992. Evaluation of results reached by that time, will possibly lead to policy adjustment. In case of insufficient progress this adjustment will also include the drawing up of additional statutory regulations for the introduction of environmental management systems as yet. (Ibid., 1989: 1–2)

The government paper makes it clear that 'the availability of an environmental management system does not in itself replace the requirement for an environmental permit.' The environmental permit indicates the framework for environmental activities within the company. But, by linking ICEM and environmental permits, regulations may be adapted in such a manner that will crete 'more maneuverability' for the company to shape the form and content of its ICEM. The ICEM will therefore become part of the permit as a side-effect of linkage.

Irrespective of whether companies have an ICEM, authorities will continue to inspect business regularly in the future. However 'governmental supervising will shift in future from purely inspecting the compliance of environmental regulations to supervising and testing the correct operation of the environmental management system within the company' (ibid.: 3). This creates an altogether different form of social control than in former days. The role of the supervisors (instead of inspectors) is focused more intently on getting insight into the *performance* of the ICEM and to see the company *internally checking* its ICEM itself in an adequate manner. The message remains clear:

> Companies which do not have an efficiently operating environment management system at their disposal will in the Government's view be sooner considered for intensified enforcement activities by competent enforcement authorities relative to companies which are trusted to have an efficiently operating environmental management system. (Ibid.)

The 'big stick' is still there, but the speech is smoother than ever.

What can be expected from the introduction of ICEM in relation to government regulation? The odds are that industry will tend to comply with environmental regulation sooner once a company has internalized the ICEM system, i.e. has structurally and culturally adopted the ICEM on a voluntary basis. This internalization will occur among the inner circle of an industry (or intermediate organizations or associations, like branches of industry) and on an individual basis. In the light of the earlier stated theory of the emergence of different styles of enforcement in relation to semi-autonomous social fields it looks as if governmental stimuli of ICEM fit very well as regulatory strategy regarding compliance with environmental rules.

Some critical notes, however, are not out of place here. First, it may be expected that the accommodative style of enforcement will be the dominant mode of rule application in such circumstances. However, it will take a lot of experience before officials adapt to this new form of 'enforcing' the law. An accommodative style of enforcement not only needs highly educated and professional personnel, but also requires the development of social relationships and bargaining skills.

Second, a really accommodative, flexible style of enforcement of environmental law will not be possible in all circumstances. Due to the changing significance of the permit (in fact it is reduced to a piece of paper which reflects a certain amount of self-reported performance by the firm in question) inspectors may become uncertain about the actual degree of compliance by that firm. Checking prescriptions in permits may become difficult and this could lead either to allowing firms to proceed uncontrolled, without the slightest obstacle in their way, or to regulatory unreasonableness.

Third, when deregulation sets in (and is the actual reason for accommodative enforcement) and informalism gets the upper hand on the regulatory scene, no sufficient remedy or review is left for third parties to protest against threats to their interests. Legal review of governmental decisions is no mere 'nuisance value.' Adjudication is anything but 'pathological'; it functions rather as an indicator of emergent political struggles for valued ends or as symptomatic of deeper social problems requiring structural change (Sarat, 1988: 700). The environment poses such a problem. Besides, formalism not only protects the powerless, it also allows the powerful to resist state control (cf. Abel, 1982: 11). So when industry proclaims that it does not thrive on regulation, its reasoning is short-sighted and contradicts its own interests.

According to Bardach and Kagan, if a legal basis of regulatory authority could be created that would be more independent of public accountability norms, regulators could operate with more discretion, flexibility, and reasonableness (1982: 217). Apart from the questionable legitimacy of distracting civilians from their legal rights, one may wonder, if industry in the long-run will not be worse off in these circumstances. State control will no longer be curbed, because public accountability norms would no longer hold for officials. The solution to this problem could be found in *tripartism* (Braithwaite & Ayres, 1991). This involves empowering public interest groups and guaranteeing their participation in the regulatory process (e.g., right-to-know-law, public involvement plans).

Fourth, more often than not officers will not only be supervisors of rule application, but they will also be expected to mediate and negotiate for a better environment. Although the relationship between an inspector and a company official will decreasingly be an adversarial one, it still is possible that the former will act 'unreasonably.' On the other hand, the danger of tolerating industry transgression, for reasons of harmony and social order, lurks even more when supervision of ICEM by officials depends on 'bargaining in the shadow of the environmental permit.' What is being argued about environmental dispute resolution, mediation, and negotiation holds even more for the relationship between officials and business representatives (cf. Abel, 1982; Amy, 1987; Sarat, 1988; Pearce & Tombs, 1990).

Fifth, the introduction of ICEM in the Netherlands anticipates the European Commission's initiative to establish environmental auditing in the Community. The European Commission's proposal for voluntary participation in an eco-audit scheme (1992 O.J. (C 76) 2) holds four important elements:

1. '[t]he Commission shall request the appropriate European standardization bodies to develop and adopt *standards for environmental management systems*' (art. 4);
2. '*environmental statement[s]* shall be prepared for each site participating in the Eco-audit scheme . . . written specifically for the public in a concise, non-technical form' (art. 5(1));
3. an 'accreditation system of *environmental auditors* shall be developed' (art. 7);
4. an *Eco-audit logo* 'may be used in relation to sites participating in the Eco-audit scheme' (art. 11) (author's emphasis).

By the end of March 1993, the European Council of Ministers—the decisive body in the Community legislative system—reached agreement on the Regulation. But it is expected that the introduction of the Eco-Audit Logo System in the Member-States will not be completed before 1995. (*Europa van Morgen*, 1993: 157)

From our review of the several regional and national differences in enforcement strategies and styles of regulatory conduct it will be clear that a one-sided arrangement by the Dutch government will not fit in with the policy of the European Community. The implications of the implementation of European law in the legislation of member-states is a widely discussed subject. Research into these phenomena has not even started yet, let alone comparative research into the various national legal programs and their respective legal cultures. Will Great Britain get into trouble if it maintains a non-legalistic style of environmental regulation in the European community (cf. Vogel, 1986: 103–6)? Or will the other countries adapt to the accommodative style of enforcement; and will different styles live in peaceful existence next to each other, as empirical data seems to indicate? The Netherlands indulges in a vast body of environmental legislation and Dutch environmentalists have been relatively successful in their pledge for more government constraint and strengthening of penal enforcement. However, the strong corporatist tradition of intermediate organizations in the Netherlands and the preference for government negotiation with interest groups[7] and for bargaining over government decisions may prove to be an important countervailing power.

Conclusion: the Polluter and Enforced Self-Regulation

The environmental regulation of industry is difficult to realize, although it is clear that regulation as an instrument for ordering the marketplace is indispensable. Some policymakers, and political scientists alike, do not want to compromise and flatly state that compliance-oriented strategies are no good, neither logically nor empirically.[8] There is nothing wrong in saying, though, that regulation works. But, like providence, it works in strange ways, often not productive, but not always counterproductive. In adopting conciliatory, accommodative strategies of regulatory conduct, officials attain policy targets sometimes more effectively than by 'going by the book.' Such is the paradox of enforcement. Precisely in these circumstances, a shift to stringent enforcement of environmental regulation, when some firms are violating the rules, will have a preventive impact. Variation in enforcement styles is a requisite for adequately provoking polluters to comply with the rules; this can be considered as *responsive* regulation (Braithwaite & Ayres, 1991).[9]

Law can regulate successfully the behaviour of public bodies and corporations. Regulators must succeed in involving them in 'enforced' or 'regulated' self-regulation (involvement 'by association') and, if necessary, they must act with stringent enforcement as a means of preventive social control when the rules are violated.

The Dutch regulatory strategy of urging and, if necessary, forcing industry to engender forms of self-regulation through the adoption of ICEM may function as an adequate preventive system of social control. Although we must look skeptically at alternative ways of social control, agreements and dispute resolution, this does not mean that they cannot be productive.

Notes

* This is a revised version of a paper presented at the joint meeting of the Law and Society Association and Research Committee on Sociology of Law of the International Sociological Association, held in Amsterdam, 26–29 June 1991.

† Senior research fellow at the Centre for Environmental Law at the University of Amsterdam. He received his Ph.D. in 1984 from the Law Faculty of the University of Amsterdam. His dissertation was on the symbolic uses of the Nuisance Act, a Dutch environmental law dating from 1875. His research topics are the enforcement of environmental legislation, the rule-applying process by inspectorates in regional and local communities, negotiating in environmental law and normative aspects of environmental management in corporations.

1. Incidentally, they found no support for 'capture' theories of regulatory behavior, which state that, over time, regulators come to be more concerned to serve the interests of the industry with which they are in regular contact, than the more remote and abstract public interest (cf. Bernstein, 1956; Stigler, 1975).
2. The fragmentation of environmental policy is not uncommon in other Western democratic systems. See, e.g., Yeager (1991: 114–18) who indicates the failure of the centralization of environmental regulation in the U.S.A. See also Marcus, 1980: 275–76.
3. The therapeutic social control strives to return patients to normality and changes the personalities of impaired individuals and is not relevant here.
4. Cf. the 'service style' and the 'watchman style' of enforcement of some police officers, as opposed to the 'legalistic style' of others, as observed by Wilson (1968: 188ff.).
5. Cf. styles of rule application, observed by Kagan, 1978; Aalders, 1982; Shover, et al., 1984; Knegt, 1986; Vogel, 1986; Hutter, 1988.
6. The three (other) institutional bases of social order.
7. Cf. the 'pillarization' of Dutch society in Lijphart, 1975.
8. See Pearce and Tombs, 1990, and their debate with Hawkins, 1990; Pearce and Tombs, 1991; Hawkins, 1991.
9. Cf. the concept of responsive or autopoietic law: Teubner 1988.

References

Aalders, Marius v. (1982) 'Styles of Rule Application in a Dutch Environmental Protection Office.' Paper presented at the annual meeting of the Law and Society Association, Toronto, 3–6 June.

—— (1984) *Industrie, milieu en wetgeving: De Hinderwet tussen symboliek en effectiviteit*. (Summary in English.) Groningen: Wolters-Noordhoff.

Aalders, Marius, Peter Korrel, and Rosa Uylenburg (1987) *Handhaving van milieurecht*. Meppel/Amsterdam: Boom.

Abel, Richard L. (1982) 'Introduction.' In *The Politics of Informal Justice*. Vol. 1, *The American Experience*, edited by R. L. Abel. New York: Academic Press.

Amy, Douglas J. (1987) *The Politics of Environmental Mediation*. New York: Columbia Univ. Press.

Aubert, Vilhelm (1967) 'Some Social Functions of Legislation,' *Acta Sociologica* 10: 98–120.

Bardach, Eugene, and Robert, A. Kagan (1982) *Going by the Book: The Problem of Regulatory Unreasonableness*. Philadelphia: Temple Univ. Press.

Bernstein, Marver H. (1955) *Regulating Business by Independent Commission*. Princeton, N.J.: Princeton Univ. Press.

Black, Donald J. (1973) 'The Mobilization of Law,' *Journal of Legal Studies* 2: 125–49.

——(1976) *The Behavior of Law.* New York: Academic Press.

Bohne, Eberhard (1980) 'Informales Verwaltungshandeln im Gesetzesvollzug.' In *Organisation und Recht: Organisatorische Bedingungen des Gesetzesvollzugs*, edited by E. Blankenburg and K. Lenk. Opladen: Westdeutscher Verlag.

Braithwaite, John, and Ian Ayres (1991) 'Convergence in Models of Regulatory Strategy.' Paper presented at the annual meeting of the Law and Society Association and Research Committee on Sociology of the International Sociological Association Law Conference, Amsterdam, 26–29 June.

DiMento, Joseph F. (1986) *Environmental Law and American Business: Dilemmas of Compliance*. New York: Plenum Press.

Edelman, Murray (1964) *The Symbolic Uses of Politics*. Urbana: Univ. of Illinois Press.

Europa van Morgen (31 March 1993) The Hague: EC-Bureau.

Feeley, Malcolm M. (1979) *The Process Is the Punishment: Handling Cases in a Lower Criminal Court*. New York: Russel Sage Foundation.

Galanter, Marc (1981) 'Justice in Many Rooms: Court Private Ordering, and Indigenous Law,' *Journal of Legal Pluralism* 19: 1–47.

Grabosky, Peter, and John Braithwaite (1986) *Of Manners Gentle: Enforcement Strategies of Australian Business Regulatory Agencies*. Melbourne: Oxford Univ. Press.

Grace, Clive, and Philip Wilkinson (1979) *Negotiating the Law: Social Work and Legal Services*. London: Routledge & Kegan Paul.

Griffiths, John (1990) 'De sociale werking van rechtsregels en het emancipatoire potentieel van wetgeving.' In *Recht en emancipatie: bondgenoot of barrière*, edited by T. Havinga and B. Sloot. 's-Gravenhage: VUGA.

Hawkins, Keith (1984) *Enforcement and Environment: Regulation and The Social Definition of Pollution*. Oxford: Clarendon Press.

——(1990) 'Compliance Strategy, Prosecution Policy, and Aunt Sally: A Comment on Pearce and Tombs,' *British Journal of Criminology* 30: 444–66.

——(1991) 'Enforcing Regulation: More of the Same from Pearce and Tombs,' *British Journal of Criminology* 31: 427–30.

Hawkins, Keith, and John M. Thomas (eds.) (1984) *Enforcing Regulation*. The Hague: Kluwer-Nijhoff.

Horwitz, Allan V. (1990) *The Logic of Social Control*. New York: Plenum Press.

Hucke, Jochen, Axel Müller, and Peter Wassen (1980) *Implementation kommunaler Umweltpolitik*. Frankfurt/Main: Campus Verlag.

Hutter, Bridget M. (1988) *The Reasonable Arm of the Law? The Law Enforcement Procedures of Environmental Health Officers*. Oxford: Clarendon Press.

Kagan, Robert A. (1978) *Regulatory Justice; Implementing a Wage-Price Freeze*. New York: Russel Sage Foundation.

Kagan, Robert A. (1988) 'What Makes Uncle Sammy Sue?,' *Law & Society Review* 21: 717–42.

Kelman, Steven (1980) 'Occupational Safety and Health Administration.' In *The Politics of Regulation*, edited by J. Q. Wilson. New York: Basic Books.

——(1984) 'Enforcement of Occupational Safety and Health Regulations: A Comparison of Swedish and American Practices.' In Hawkins and Thomas, 1984.

Knegt, R. (1986) *Regels en redelijkheid in de bijstandsverlening: participerende observatie bij een sociale dienst*. Groningen: Wolters-Noordhoff.

Lindblom, Charles (1977) *Politics and Markets: The World's Political Economic Systems*. New York: Basic Books.

Lijphart, Arend (1975) *The Politics of Accommodation: Pluralism and Democracy in the Netherlands*. 2d ed. Berkeley and Los Angeles: Univ. of California Press.

Mannheim, K. (1940) *Man and Society In an Age of Reconstruction: Studies in Modern Social Structure*, trans. E. Shils. London: Routledge & Kegan Paul.

Marcus, Alfred (1980) 'Environmental Protection Agency.' In *The Politics of Regulation*, edited by J. Q. Wilson. New York: Basic Books.

Mayntz, Renate, Eberhard Bohne, Hans-Ulrich, Derlien, B. Hesse, Jochen Hucke, and Axel Muller (1987) *Vollzugsprobleme der Umweltpolitik*. Stuttgart: Kohlhammer.

Moore, Sally Falk (1973) 'Law and Social Change: The Semi-Autonomous Social Field as an Appropriate Subject of Study,' *Law & Society Review* 7: 719–46.

The Netherlands (1983) Government report on Uniser Co.

——Parliament. Lower House. Documents (1989) *Internal Company Environmental Management: Summary of the Note*. 20633, nr. 3. 30 August.

Pearce, Frank, and Steve Tombs (1990) 'Ideology, Hegemony, and Empiricism: Compliance Theories of Regulation,' *British Journal of Criminology*, 30: 423–43.

——(1991) 'Policing Corporate "Skid Rows": A Reply to Keith Hawkins,' *British Journal of Criminology* 31: 415–26.

Reiss, Albert, J., Jr. (1984) 'Selecting Strategies of Social Control Over Organizational Life.' In Hawkins and Thomas, 1984.

Richardson, Genevra, Anthony Ogus, and Paul Burrows (1983) *Policing Pollution: A Study of Regulation and Enforcement*. Oxford: Clarendon Press.

Sarat, Austin (1988) 'The "New Formalism" in Disputing and Dispute Processing,' *Law & Society Review* 21: 695–715.

Shover, Neal, John Lynxwiler, Stephen Groce, and Donald Clelland (1984) 'Regional Variation in Regulatory Law Enforcement: The Surface Mining Control and Reclamation Act of 1977.' In Hawkins and Thomas, 1984.

Schmitter, Philippe C., and Gerhard Lehmbruch (eds.) (1979) *Trends Toward Corporatist Intermediation*. New York: Sage Publications.

Stigler, George, J. (1975) *The Citizen and the State: Essays on Regulation*. Chicago: Univ. of Chicago Press.

Streeck, Wolfgang, and Philippe C. Schmitter (eds.) (1985) *Private Interest Government: Beyond Market and State*. London: Sage Publications.

Teubner, Gunther (1988) *Autopoetic Law: A New Approach to Law and Society.* Berlin: de Gruyter.

Vogel, David (1986) *National Styles of Regulation: Environmental Policy in Great Britain and The United States.* Ithaca, N.Y.: Cornell Univ. Press.

Weber, Max (1954) *Max Weber on Law in Economy and Society,* edited by M. Rheinstein, trans. E. Shils and M. Rheinstein. Cambridge: Harvard Univ. Press.

—— (1967) *Rechtssoziologie.* Neuwied am Rhein: Luchterhand.

Weick, Karle E. (1976) 'Educational Organizations as Loosely Coupled Systems,' *Administrative Science Quarterly* 21: 1–19.

Yeager, Peter Cleary (1991) *The Limits of Law: The Public Regulation of Private Pollution.* Cambridge: Cambridge Univ. Press.

Zald, Mayer, N. (1978) 'On the Social Control of Industries,' *Social Forces* 57: 79–102.

Green Markets: Environmental Regulation by the Private Sector*

P. N. GRABOSKY

Abstract

This chapter begins with a review of recent trends in the devolution of state functions to nongovernment institutions, and discusses how private interests may be enlisted in furtherance of public policy. It then outlines a variety of institutions and instruments which might comprise a system of regulation for environmental protection, and suggests some of the forms of interaction between them.

The focus then turns to commercial activity which can further the interests of environmental protection. It summarizes eight emerging trends in 'green commerce' and concludes that in some settings, the constructive influence of commercial forces can exceed that wielded by government agencies.

Introduction

Although recently overshadowed by the economy as the major issue of contemporary public concern, the environment remains high on the policy agenda, and it is destined to remain so. At the same time, it is becoming widely acknowledged that the capacity of governments to achieve desirable social goals, among them protection of the environment, is not without limits. Continued pressures on governments to reduce public expenditures and to foster a climate favorable to business remain dominant facts of political life. This leads one to ask how nongovernmental resources may be mobilized in furtherance of environmental objectives.

The present article addresses one variety of nongovernmental resource: commercial activity within the private sector, which impacts upon regulated entities. As distinct from those regulatory devices which are commonly termed economic instruments (emission charges, taxes, and tradeable emission rights), commercial environmentalism already exists as a powerful institution of corporate social control. Its potential contribution is even greater.

The article begins with a brief and general discussion of nongovernmental interests and their relationship to public policy. In so doing, it reviews recent trends in the devolution of state functions to nongovernmental institutions. It then provides a broad outline of the regulatory landscape for environmental protection, introducing the basic elements of a regulatory ordering and discussing forms of interaction between institutions and instruments that might comprise such an ordering.

Next, the article turns to one corner of this broad canvas—the issue of 'green markets' or environmentally appropriate commercial activity.[1] Notwithstanding the extent of environmental degradation that may be attributed to market failure, it is suggested that there remains considerable potential for harnessing market forces in furtherance of environmental interests. The article will focus on naturally occurring market phenomena and on those occurring as by-products of regulation, as opposed to the direct application of economic instruments devised by governments as an adjunct to command and control regulation. It will become apparent that in some settings, the influence of market forces in furtherance of environmental protection can exceed that wielded by government regulators.

This article seeks to describe and to explain some of the considerable opportunities which now exist for those of entrepreneurial inclination to profit from environmentalism. In so doing, we shall enjoy the brighter side of the double entendre contained in the old adage, 'where there's muck, there's money.' At the same time, the article recognizes the pitfalls of commercial environmentalism and notes these where appropriate. The article concludes with a discussion of policy implications, noting which particular institutional orderings might best enhance the constructive operation of commercial forces in furtherance of environmental interests.

New Technologies of Government

Before the rise of the modern state, many functions that came to be regarded as core responsibilities of government were carried out by nongovernmental institutions or individuals. As the state grew in power and scope, it assumed an increasing number of functions, such as welfare, criminal justice, and education. But even at the high watermark of state influence, governments were hardly monopolists of social control and conflict resolution. Rather, governments shared many functions with various non-state institutions both formal and informal.

Law too has had its analogues outside the public sector. Observers, such as Ehrlich (1912), who came to be known as 'legal pluralists,' saw law as but the top stratum from which a web of quasi-legal rules and controls ordered everyday life. More recent scholars began to focus upon the interrelationship between state law and private forms of social control and conflict resolution. Fitzpatrick (1984) employed the term 'integral plurality' to refer to the reciprocal influence of state law and these private orderings: state law is shaped by substructures such as the family, and private sub-structures are simultaneously shaped by state law.

One of the seminal thinkers of the late twentieth century, Michel Foucault (1991), observed that the real practice of government was not through the imposition of law, but rather working with and through the constellation of interests, institutions, and interpersonal relations that are part of civil society. Burchell adds further texture to Foucault's outline when he refers to 'governing in accordance with the grain of things' (1991, 127) and the role of the state in guiding conditions so that interests may converge in furtherance of the public good.

Teubner (1983) has spoken of how, instead of imposing direct substantive controls on behavior, states might structure mechanisms for self-regulation. He refers to the fostering of a 'regulated autonomy' based largely on private orderings. The state facilitates the development of these self-regulating systems rather than engaging in direct intervention.

Rose and Miller (1992) refer to this as 'governing at a distance,' using 'new technologies of government' that harness energies resident outside of the public sector in furtherance of public policy:

> The question is no longer one of accounting for government in terms of the 'power of the state', but of ascertaining how, and to what extent, the state is articulated into the activity of government; what relations are established between political and other authorities; what funds, forces, persons, knowledge or legitimacy are utilized; and by means of what devices and techniques are these different tactics made operable. (Ibid., 177)

This line of argument has been popularized in the very influential North American book *Reinventing Government* (Osborne & Gaebler 1992).[2] Recognizing that government as traditionally configured has its constraints and limitations, the authors advocated that governments adopt the role of facilitator and broker, rather than that of commander. They suggested that governments 'steer' rather than 'row,' and that they structure the marketplace so that naturally occurring private activity may assist in furthering public policy objectives. Osborne and Gaebler (1992, 280) use the term 'leverage' to refer to this approach.

The Shrinking State

This idea of a 'hybrid space of government' combining public and private energies (Burchell 1991, 141) is receiving increasing recognition just as the traditional activities of the state have been called into question. Recently, western industrial societies have experienced a contraction in the role of the state (Crook, Pakulski & Waters 1992, ch. 3). Inspired in part by ideology, in part by chronic fiscal constraint, and in part by a recognition that some functions normally performed by the state can be performed by nongovernmental actors more effectively and at less cost, this transfer of state functions has taken numerous forms.

In some instances, state responsibilities have been shed upwards. Most nations today are bound by numerous international covenants and treaties that establish standards and define appropriate conduct in realms as diverse as the interdiction of illicit drug traffic and the protection of migratory birds (see, e.g., Chayes & Chayes 1991). Member nations of the European Community (EC) are bound by EC regulations. Other institutions, such as the World Bank, exercise considerable control over national economies.

In the domestic realm, the commingling of public and private resources in furtherance of social control has been accorded extensive treatment.[3] In one type of public/private interface, the state may conscript private institutions to perform functions in furtherance of public policy. In a number of western nations, banks are required by law routinely to report transactions over a certain threshold, as well as those transactions that are of a suspicious nature irrespective of their amount, to a governmental authority. Thus banks have become generally instruments of policy to combat tax evasion, drug traffic, and money laundering. Similarly, immigration authorities routinely require that international airlines screen passengers to ensure that they possess valid travel documents (Gilboy 1992).

In some cases, the state may simply abdicate its activities, and leave them to markets to provide. The demise of government business enterprises, such as transportation, insurance, and publishing, are but three examples. In other instances, private activity will emerge to meet a need that has been neglected by governments. Early efforts on behalf of victims of sexual assault and domestic violence were provided by 'grass-roots' collectivities precisely because public agencies of health, welfare, and criminal justice were regarded as unresponsive to victims' needs.

Other forms of devolution include contracting to private enterprise functions previously performed by public agencies and establishing mutual agreements between public and private sectors. Examples of the former are activities previously regarded as quintessential state responsibilities, such as the management of prisons. The latter includes agreements of varying degrees of formality. International air carriers cooperate with immigration authorities in processing and repatriating undocumented aliens (Gilboy 1992), and customs authorities enlist the assistance of major importers to report activities that may indicate movement of contraband.

Governments may invite routine contributions by private interests to public forums. To be sure, the invitation in part reflects democratic principles, and the need to maintain legitimacy. But one may also regard the contributions of interest groups as information resources, that might lie beyond the normal inclination or capacity of public authorities to generate.[4]

What, then, are the implications of the above trends for environmental protection?

On Regulatory Orderings for Environmental Protection

Although it is not uncommon to think of environmental regulation as the exclusive province of government, Shearing (1993) reminds us that the function of corporate social control is shared by a variety of institutions in the public, private, and nonprofit sectors.[5] Indeed, in light of the above discussion of governmental technologies, it could be argued that some of these control functions are performed more effectively, more efficiently, and with greater legitimacy (from the standpoint of the regulatee) by nongovernmental institutions than by government agencies.

A given regulatory domain, or 'policy space' (Harter & Eads 1985), will contain a variety of institutions that each possess a set of resources or instruments. At the most general level within the domain of environmental protection, these institutions may be categorized as follows:

1. Traditional regulatory standard setting and enforcement by government authorities;
2. Self-regulatory activity by individual companies and by industry associations; and
3. Influences wielded by third-party actors, including environmental interest groups and commercial, nongovernmental actors, such as banks and insurance companies.

The fact that state regulatory agencies do not exist in a vacuum, but rather in a framework of mutually constitutive interaction with nongovernmental institutions and actors, suggests that to focus on a single institution, in whatever sector, gives one a limited perspective on the regulatory process. Indeed, one of the most neglected areas of regulatory analysis is the interaction between sets of instruments within and between the three general categories specified above.[6]

On the Complementarity of Regulatory Institutions and Instruments

The interaction of regulatory institutions, and of the instruments that they command, may take numerous forms. The following section presents a typology of interactions and offers some tentative illustrations from the domain of environmental protection.

Neutralization

x negates y
x dilutes y

The term neutralization refers to the effect of one institution in negating or diluting the effects of another. Criticism voiced by a citizen's group about the polluting behavior of a large industrial corporation may be neutralized by a public relations campaign on the part of the company which portrays itself as a paragon of environmental stewardship.[7]

Catalysis

x facilitates the combination of y and z

The term catalysis refers to the effect of a given institution or instrument in initiating a reaction between two others. Pressure exerted by environmental interest groups in publicizing an actual or impending pollution problem may facilitate compromise between industry and regulatory authorities, who might otherwise be disinclined to reach agreement on a preferred course of action for prevention or abatement.

As will be discussed in greater detail below, consumer demand for environmentally friendly products may inspire retailers to exert considerable influence on manufacturers to conform to 'green' specifications.

Inhibition

x impedes the combination of y and z

Inhibitors are the opposite of catalysts. Rather than facilitate the regulatory equivalent of a chemical reaction, inhibitors drastically slow or impede such a process. For example, it might be argued that the law of libel, by deterring criticism of a particular polluter or of a regulatory authority, inhibits the influence that an environmentalist organization may have in pressing for more stringent regulatory enforcement against polluters.

Activation

x is a necessary condition for the operation of y

By activation, we refer to a situation whereby a particular institution or instrument is requisite to the functioning of another. The activating condition may be required in advance of, concurrently with, or following use of the other instrument.

For example, the provision of finance for a particular project may be conditional upon a satisfactory environmental audit and upon the implementation of a regular monitoring program. When the audit and monitoring program would not have occurred but for the requirements imposed by the financier, those requirements may be regarded as having activated the program.

Regulations regarding product safety and environmental protection in Sweden have inspired technological innovation and competitive advantage in a number of industries. Similar efficiencies have been achieved in the Netherlands (Porter 1990, 648; Huppes & Kagan 1989, 225). The regulations may be regarded as activators if the innovations would not otherwise have occurred.

Redundancy

x replicates y

Redundancy occurs when one institution duplicates the activities of another. One might envisage, for example, a federal agency and a state authority each undertaking a life cycle analysis of the same brand of washing machines. Redundancy may occur across jurisdictions in a federal system, or it may reflect duplication of effort by public agencies and private interests.

Redundancy is not necessarily an undesirable property of institutional orderings. For a citizen's organization to duplicate the research efforts of a public agency may be educationally enriching, or may contribute to feelings of competence and efficacy on the part of the citizen researcher. Redundancy in monitoring, particularly in relation to ultra-hazardous activities, may provide greater confidence in risk-management procedures. Replication of an agency's procedures or findings by a citizens' organization may enhance the agency's legitimacy.

Synergy

x and y enhance each other

Synergy refers to interactions in which each instrument enhances the effect of the other. The combined action of the two instruments is thus greater than that of their independent contributions added together. The institution of 'eco-labelling,' or formal certification of products as environmentally preferable, facilitates environmentally conscious purchasing behavior and amplifies the influence of consumers. The exercise of consumer purchasing power in turn enhances the legitimacy and credibility of the eco-label.

Proceeds from a tax on all lubricating oil purchases in Germany serve as the source of subsidies to firms engaged in the collection and the environmentally responsible disposal of waste oil (Russell 1988, 268). This combination of incentives succeeded in fostering a recycling industry and in creating a self-sustaining market. Consider also a decrease in the tax on unleaded petrol combined with an increase in the tax on leaded petrol. Each enhance the incentive provided by the other.

Complementarity

x replaces y

In this circumstance one institution functions to fill a gap left by the absence or inactivity of another. In the United States, the expansion of citizen litigation under the Clean Water Act in response to the perceived relaxation of enforcement by the Environmental Protection Agency (EPA) constitutes one example (Boyer & Meidinger 1985).

In recent years, marine insurance underwriters have been concerned about inadequate government inspection of maritime vessels, particularly those flying 'flags of convenience.' To compensate for this regulatory shortfall, and to ensure that the vessels that they insure are indeed seaworthy, underwriters have engaged their own marine surveyors to inspect the vessels of prospective clients.

Complementarity can, of course, be rationally coordinated. Divisions of labor can arise from design as well as from default. Cheit (1990, 222) has shown how comparative institutional advantages can flow from public and private efforts in furtherance of regulatory objectives.

Market Forces and Environmental Protection

To what extent can market forces arising from the exercise of individual preferences produce environmentally beneficial consequences? The parable of the commons should warn us of the potential conflict between private interest and the public good. And yet, economists maintain that in many settings, reliance on markets is more likely to result in cost-effective outcomes than in solutions imposed by command and control requirements (Schultze 1977; Moran 1990, 11).

Market opportunities for environmental protection reside in three categories: 'environmentally friendly' products, which appeal to consumer preferences; 'end-of-pipe' pollution-abatement technology; and process modification approaches, which achieve greater efficiencies in production by conserving raw materials and energy and by minimizing waste. In the words of the U.K. Environment Secretary:

> Those businesses that recognise these realities and respond to them will survive and prosper in the cleaner and greener markets of the future. Those that do not will find themselves lagging behind in the battle for global markets. (Howard 1992).

The Genesis of Market Opportunities for Environmental Protection

1. Regulation

Market opportunities arise from a number of influences. As noted above, environmental regulatory standards, by prohibiting or discouraging certain practices, may inspire a quest for more environmentally appropriate alternatives. Impending restrictions on the use of chlorofluorocarbon (CFC) aerosol propellants stimulated a search for substitutes; limits on permissible levels of lead in petrol encouraged the development of unleaded petrol and alternative automotive fuels.

Herein lies a significant irony: regulatory standards, often regarded as an economic burden, may actually create commercial opportunities. Even disasters can be profitable. Regulation can trigger innovation, rather than stifling economic activity, and thereby produce a competitive advantage to the innovator (Porter 1990, 585–8; Braithwaite 1993). It is by no means coincidental that the world's leading exporters of pollution control products are those Organization of Economic Cooperation and Development (OECD) countries with the most stringent environmental regulations.

Japan leads in air pollution control, Germany in water pollution abatement technology, the Netherlands in soil remediation, and the United States in the management of toxic waste (OECD 1992, 19). A range of impending directives and standards to be introduced by the European Community will further stimulate the environment industry. New industries have also emerged to assist production engineers in assessing the relative environmental impacts of particular materials and processes.

2. *Consumer Preferences*

Market opportunities are also created as a result of changing consumer preferences. Growing public sensitivity to environmental issues is reflected in consumer behavior. Consumers who are environmentally aware are inclined to purchase products that they perceive to be environmentally appropriate, and to favor products of manufacturers who have otherwise demonstrated concern for the environment. Companies that are in a position to demonstrate their credibility as environmentally responsible corporate citizens, and thereby to benefit from consumer preferences, will thus enjoy a competitive advantage (Stewart 1992). Indeed, consumer preferences may be more exacting than regulatory requirements. In the words of one Swedish pulp and paper operator, 'it would be easy if we only had to cope with the regulators: It is the consumer's pressure that challenges us most' (Beaucamp & Girgensohn 1992, 24). Substantial public relations and marketing advantages can flow from a legitimately earned reputation as an environmentally responsible company.

The influence of consumer preferences also extends to the financial industry. We discuss below how financial institutions are concerned about the image (and liability) of their corporate borrowers. Banks, in their pursuit of competitive advantage, are becoming increasingly sensitized to the importance of projecting a green image with regard to their own retail operations (Mechlin 1993).

Collaboration between companies can lead to mutual advantage. The U.S. computer manufacturer, DEC, converted fifteen tons of recycled computer plastic into roof tiles for two McDonald's restaurants in Chicago. Both companies are able to boast of an enhanced 'green image.'

Failure to anticipate changes in consumer demand can also be costly. The United States automobile industry paid a heavy price for its neglect of emerging preferences for more fuel-efficient vehicles. The more prescient Japanese industry seized the competitive advantage at the time of the 1973 oil crisis, an advantage that it has continued to enjoy for two decades.

3. Process-Driven Opportunities

A third factor influencing market opportunity is the profit potential arising from technology-driven efficiency. More efficient production can also be cleaner production. In many manufacturing processes, consumer preferences are gratuitous, since efficiencies in production will be inherently green. For example, improvements over the years in smelting technology have enabled more efficient processing of ore, which incidentally achieves reduction in emissions.

Simple efforts to reduce waste in organizations can combine favorable environmental impact with significant profitability (Schmidheiny 1992). Not only can waste minimization programs appeal to downstream purchasers and to an environmentally conscious public, they can also achieve substantial cost reduction. As a result of its 'Pollution Prevention Pays' program, the 3M Corporation claims to have saved $500 million over fifteen years (Berle 1991, 213). The Royal York Hotel in Toronto, through such measures as phasing out disposable cups and recycling other sources of solid waste, has achieved a 57 percent reduction in waste. Given landfill tipping fees of $140 per ton, this constitutes a significant reduction in waste removal costs (Haggett 1992).

Trends in Commercial Activity

The influence of regulation, consumer preferences, and process-driven opportunities have produced at least seven emerging trends in environmentally appropriate commercial activity.

1. Environmentally Appropriate Products Which Appeal to Consumer Preferences: Scrutiny of Suppliers and Buyers

The power of consumer preference is by no means wielded solely by the ultimate purchaser. Companies affect each others' behavior. Purchasers influence suppliers; in industry, the interchange between buyers and suppliers generates incentives to innovate (Porter 1990, 590).

Large retailers are in a position to register their product and process preferences with suppliers, and the awesome purchasing power that large retailers command often carries considerable influence. The influence of the retail sector in driving innovation is widely recognized (Porter 1990, 502; 523). Suppliers' practices can bear upon a retailer's public image, and buyers are increasingly sensitive to the risk of being tainted by a supplier's questionable environmental performance. To this end, buyers are tending increasingly to scrutinize products from a 'cradle to grave' perspective, noting such considerations as energy efficiency in manufacture, minimization and responsible disposal of waste, economical use of materials in packaging, and recyclability of product (Suart 1992). Anticipated purchasing power may also influence product design. Thus are producers of raw materials and manufacturers of basic ingredients such as cold rolled steel, normally beyond the reach of the average consumer, subject to the discipline of environmentally conscious purchasing.

In 1990, McDonald's restaurants began a program to purchase $100 million worth of products made from recycled materials each year. The British retail chemist, Boots, has set a goal to reduce the volume of packaging of merchandise by 75 percent by 1997 (Reuters 1992a). Another firm in the U.K. requires every supplier to have a company environmental policy, affirmed by an audit (Suart 1992). In addition, it has developed a comprehensive questionnaire to obtain information from prospective suppliers. Successful suppliers are required to sign codes of conduct and to manage their activity in accordance with specified principles. Noncompliance may lead the buyer to obtain a new source of supply.

Similarly, British Telecom encourages prospective suppliers to explain their own environmental programs and to be responsible for their products' environmental impact. A company questionnaire seeks information from prospective suppliers on the use of recycled materials in their products and the potential for reuse and recycling of the products. It further seeks to identify any environmental hazards that may arise during the course of the product's life, energy consumption entailed in manufacture, and the supplier's plans for improving its overall environmental performance. British Telecom also encourages supplier buy-back of products after their normal life. While larger suppliers command the resources and organizational infrastructure to develop environmental management programs, their smaller counterparts may not. Confronted with detailed requirements specified by the purchaser, small business may be unable to compete in the market. There are nevertheless other green purchasing strategies that may assist the smaller supplier.

A more cooperative approach to prospective suppliers is that taken by the Body Shop cosmetics retailer, which assists suppliers in self-assessment and works with them to improve their environmental performance. At other times, the Body Shop can be more adversarial, and more demanding. Recently, it advised a supplier that they would consider increasing their purchases if the supplier were to adopt a formal environmental policy, publish a comprehensive audit report, and end 'unnecessary confrontation with environmental groups' (Greenpeace 1993).

Wal-Mart, a large retailer in the United States, encourages its suppliers to reduce overpackaging, and actively seeks environmentally friendly changes to their products (Elkington, Knight, with Hailes 1992, 126). The retailer then actively publicizes their achievements. In the words of one sign, prominently displayed in retail stores:

> Our Commitment: Land—Air—Water
> Our customers are concerned about the quality of our air, land and water and want the opportunity to do something positive. Together with our manufacturing partners, we'll provide you with information on products which have been environmentally improved. (Berle 1991, 143).

The company is even developing prototype 'green' stores, which would be designed and managed consistent with principles of low energy consumption, low waste generation, and recyclability (Platt 1992). By calling public attention to their environmental policies and practices, retailers perform an educative function that extends well beyond the conventional marketing role (Schmidheiny 1992, 112). This in turn can help shape future consumer preferences.[8]

Scrutiny of suppliers is hardly the sole province of retailers. Manufacturers are also in a position to influence supplier behavior. Volvo, for example, asks that its suppliers comply with its environmental standards. Even financial institutions may work to improve the environmental performance of their suppliers. One large bank, in its invitations to tender for the supply of a variety of goods and services, asks whether the prospective supplier has an environmental policy, whether it has environmental management systems in place, and inquires about the company's philosophy of compliance with environmental regulations (Lury & Hatfield 1992).

Governments themselves are significant consumers of goods and services, and wield great potential influence in the market (Porter 1990, 127). As such, they may exercise their very considerable purchasing power in furtherance of environmental objectives. Just as large retailers can demand environmentally friendly products from their suppliers, so too can governments. Government purchasing power, no less than that of large buyers in the private sector, can stimulate innovation. By contributing to the demand for such products as recycled paper, governments may nurture a market, strengthen demand for new products, and assist emerging industries. In 1992, the Australian government, which spends about $10 billion each year buying goods and services, announced an environmental purchasing policy (Australia 1992). The policy seeks to identify and to promote environmentally sound products and to raise the awareness of buyers. In addition, it seeks to encourage industry to develop new products that are environmentally responsible, and to redesign existing products to reduce adverse environmental impact.

As is the case with private sector purchasing, government buyers may impose 'green standards' or work with suppliers in a more cooperative way to encourage them to improve their environmental performance. Although each approach may have its merits in particular settings, a more genuine market solution would entail appraising the supplier of the desired environmental outcome and allowing innovation to produce a product solution. The opportunity also exists for government buyers to team up with other buyers in the private and public sectors to increase their influence in furtherance of greener products and processes.

The very existence of supplier assessment sends signals to the marketplace. As upstream environmental vetting becomes even more common, these signals will be amplified. Of course, prospective suppliers are always free not to cooperate with 'green' purchasing policies. But in defying market forces, they run the risk of losing a competitive edge.

Market influence is by no means limited to the purchaser. Suppliers are also in a position to influence 'downstream' use of their products. The 'Product Stewardship' program in the chemical industry embraces concerns well beyond initial design and manufacture of products, to their sale, distribution, use and ultimate disposal. This program entails informing customers about known product hazards and providing advice on proper use, handling and disposal. In some instances it entails actual monitoring by the manufacturer of customer use (Elkington, Knight, with Hailes 1992, 120).

One anecdote which illustrates the virtues of product stewardship tells of a salesperson for a chemical manufacturer who, in the course of a sales visit, became aware that a customer was failing to observe proper storage and handling procedures with regard to one of the manufacturer's products. The salesperson called this to the customer's attention and even provided a safety video on proper handling, but to no avail; on subsequent visits, the misuse was seen to continue. Eventually, the salesperson suggested that unless the inappropriate procedures were modified within thirty days, he would no longer provide his company's product. At this point, the customer requested, and received, the manufacturer's detailed technical assistance in handling the product. Both parties were satisfied, the risk was abated, and sales continued (Morris 1991).[9]

Indeed, it has been suggested that opportunities exist for chemical industry firms to provide commercial consulting services, and to profit by marketing their knowledge and expertise to downstream customers. Any reduction in profit to the manufacturer resulting from the customer's more efficient use of the product could be offset by revenues from consultancy services (Wheatley 1993).

Contrasting with positive appeals to consumer preferences are those messages which are essentially defensive in character. Commercial appeals to environmentalism may be designed to preempt or to neutralize negative publicity. To the extent that appeals to consumer preferences raise awareness and inform consumer behavior, they are environmentally appropriate. To the extent that they obscure issues and contribute to false consumer consciousness, they can be counterproductive. Green marketing may, at times, be more of an advertising ploy than a productive commitment (Greenpeace 1992).

To cite yet another example of the greening of commercial relations, companies are now advised to choose their waste management contractors carefully. 'Don't hesitate, even after giving a waste management firm your business, to monitor periodically, and even to audit their waste management practices. A reputable firm with nothing to hide will welcome such scrutiny by its customers' (Kamlet 1992, 37). Companies are encouraged to require accurate disposal records from their waste disposal contractors.

2. *Boycotts*

The purchase of environmentally preferable goods and services entails implicit rejection of less acceptable alternative products. At times, this rejection can become explicit. The boycott, or concerted avoidance of certain purchases, may be mobilized against products or producers deemed to be environmentally harmful.[10]

One recent example of a consumer boycott in furtherance of environmental protection is the boycott of Norwegian fish products organized in 1993 by Greenpeace in protest against that nation's resumption of whaling. Boycott organizers maintained that the loss of foreign markets significantly exceeded the commercial value of Norway's whale catch.

Aside from their questionable legality in some jurisdictions, the boycott can be a double-edged sword. In 1989, representatives of the U.S. timber industry called for the boycott of a brewer that sponsored a controversial televison documentary on forests which had been produced by the National Audubon Society (Fahey 1991, 679).

3. 'End-of-the-Pipe' Pollution Abatement Technology

Environmental concerns have given rise to entire new industries, each with significant market opportunities. Innovations in pollution abatement tend to be driven by regulation. By contrast, process modification technologies, such as energy efficient plant and equipment, tend to be profit driven.

The main types of pollution abatement product are water and effluents treatment, waste management, air quality control, land reclamation, and noise reduction. The pollution abatement industry served a worldwide market estimated in 1992 at U.S. $200 billion per year. Already larger than the aerospace industry, this market is expected to grow at 5.5 percent per year through the turn of the century (OECD 1992, 4).

(a) Water Pollution

Citizen concern over water quality is common to most industrial societies (Beder 1989) and to developing societies as well. Municipal water and wastewater treatment facilities and effluent treatment for manufacturing industry constitute a significant market opportunity. Primary treatment equipment such as filters exists to remove solid particles; secondary treatment equipment, such as chlorination and biological treatment, counters bacteria, and tertiary equipment, such as chemical recovery systems and reverse osmosis, addresses chemical or metal compounds.

Problems of leakage from underground storage tanks, which exist by the hundreds of thousands around the world, have inspired innovations in monitoring technology and in improved tank construction. The challenge of remediating groundwater contamination has inspired the development of monitoring systems and methods to remove contaminants.

(b) Waste Management

Growing recognition of the problem of toxic waste has led to the development of specialized handling equipment and disposal technologies, such as chemical and biological degradation methods and incineration systems. One sees the emergence of entire new industries involved with the collection, transport, treatment and disposal of wastes. Commercial opportunities exist for the development of incineration, re-use and recycling methods, and techniques for the neutralization of waste products.

Landfill space in many western industrial societies is in short supply. It has been estimated that at current rates of waste generation, and barring further development, landfills in Australia's major metropolitan areas will be used up soon after the turn of the century (Australian Bureau of

Statistics 1992). Such pressures suggest an obvious market for alternative waste disposal services. Declining landfill space around the world has stimulated the development of incineration techniques and improved landfill management methods.

It is increasingly acknowledged that recycling will become an important part of the future global economy. Firms in the forefront of developing recycling technology and those in the development of recyclable materials or the production of recyclable products are well positioned to exploit future market opportunities. European automobile manufacturers, for example, have begun to produce vehicles from which 100 per cent recyclability is more easily achieved.

Air quality control equipment exists to remove pollutants from a gaseous stream, or to reduce their concentration prior to discharge. Air pollution control equipment may be designed to effect particulates, such as dust and ash, gases, such as carbon monoxide and sulphur dioxide, and liquids or liquid fumes.

Market opportunities for environmental protection have not been overlooked by some of the largest companies in those industries where one might expect to find awareness of pollution control problems—chemical, engineering and electronics. In recent years, Dupont established a subsidiary company for toxic waste management services. Dow, Bayer, and Hoechst are developing methods for recycling plastic.

Profit and environmental protection, far from being mutually exclusive, can be part of the same package. Improved production technologies generate fewer pollutants and make more efficient use of materials and energy. The relative merits of investing a given amount in pollution abatement technology and investing in new production facilities that would achieve more efficient production and generate less waste should be obvious.

4. Process Modification Technologies which Conserve Raw Materials and Energy and Minimize Waste

According to the OECD, market opportunities are shifting from 'end-of-pipe' abatement technologies to manufacturing process technologies. The design of production systems that are both environmentally friendly and more efficient will generate even greater competitive advantage. Integrated technologies for feedstock and process modifications, which combine low energy consumption with low emissions, are the most desirable. The emphasis of such an approach is on pollution prevention through production efficiency, rather than abatement. This industry will develop and exploit opportunities in energy conservation, and in environmentally appropriate materials and production processes. The company that can claim to be first with the greenest manufacturing technology will be ahead of the market.

Governments have actively sought to inspire the development and dissemination of clean technology. The Australian state of Victoria's Clean Technology Incentive Scheme provides grants to businesses for the introduction of innovative technologies to reduce waste (OECD 1992, 28). The Australian federal government makes ten-year interest-free 'cleaner production' loans to eligible companies. In Norway, subsidies to the pulp and paper industry have encouraged the introduction of new, cleaner production processes (Cramer et al. 1990, 49).

5. Renewable Energy Systems

A number of energy technologies exist as alternatives to fossil fuels. Some are already commercially viable, albeit on a small scale. Others have considerable potential which could be realized when technological developments permit.[11]

The most common technology is solar power. Solar collectors for water heaters have become a common feature on the roofs of houses from Japan to Australia. Telecom Australia has been using solar photovoltaic technology to power remote area telephone systems for nearly two decades. Prototype motor vehicles powered by solar energy have crossed the Australian continent; further refinements in the technology of collection and storage will extend the potential for solar energy considerably.

Whilst hydroelectric power generation on a massive scale tends to require a degree of environmental devastation, less intrusive technologies of micro-hydroelectric power generation entail no such cost. Small generators may be constructed on the banks of rapidly flowing streams, and the resulting power may be sufficient to support a small village. Such technology already exists, with considerable potential application in developing nations.

The windmill is a common feature of many rural landscapes, but the potential for wind energy extends well beyond pumping water. Wind energy technology has developed to the extent that it complements conventional electric power generation in some locations.

Other forms of alternative energy include: biomass, where organic matter is either burned or used in the production of alcohol or gas fuels; geothermal, where the earth's internal heat is harnessed as a source of energy; and wave or tidal power, where water movements can be used to drive turbines for the generation of electricity.

6. *Institutional Investors*

Environmental performance is increasingly regarded as an indicator of business health. Good environmental management reflects good management in general. To the extent that this perception is shared by financial markets, pressure on companies to improve corporate environmental citizenship will be that much greater.

Recent years have seen the emergence of specialized environmentally conscious investment funds (Smith 1990, 175–6). Such green institutional investors avoid companies and industries with poor environmental reputations and specialize in environmentally reputable companies. Beyond the influence of specialized 'green funds,' the potential influence of large institutional investors in this regard can be substantial. In 1991, the twenty largest pension funds in the United States controlled over $620 billion in assets. In a number of U.S. jurisdictions, state pension fund managers are required to give preference in their investment decisions to companies in compliance with the Valdez Principles (Elkington, Knight et al. 1992, 71). One trustee of the New York City Employees Retirement System, with $21 billion in assets, was quoted as saying:

> We hold the view that when corporations treat the environment badly, they treat their investors badly—by subjecting the company to harmful publicity and by exposing themselves to enormous liability. The pension funds have become activists in protecting our investments by working to protect the environment. (Reuters 1992b)

Market influence is further enhanced by regulatory requirements that shareholders and financial markets must be kept informed of potential environmental liabilities.[12]

7. *Banking and Insurance Companies as Co-Producers of Regulation*

In addition to their activities as institutional investors, banks and insurance companies are in a position to exercise considerable influence over their clients. Lenders and insurers now recognize the risk to their own commercial well-being posed by questionable environmental practices on the part of a borrower or policyholder. Beyond the lender's obvious interest in the commercial viability of the borrower, banks must now be concerned about the environmental risks posed by any assets that they might hold as security for a loan. In the event of foreclosure, banks could end up owning a liability rather than an asset.[13] The pressures that the banking and insurance industries can exert in furtherance of environmental citizenship can be considerable. Schmidheiny (1992, 64–5) predicts that an environmental audit report is likely to become an integral part of a loan application,[14] and that companies with an unfavorable record of environmental compliance 'will find it increasingly difficult and expensive to get insured.'

A note of caution is appropriate for those who would regard finance and insurance as fail-safe instruments for environmental protection. The influence of financiers and insurers may not always be beneficial. For example, purveyors of agricultural finance and crop insurance may specify the use of ecologically harmful fertilizers and pesticides as a condition of obtaining their product. Thus, where the scope of risk is narrowly defined, finance and insurance may be environmentally counterproductive (Hornstein 1993).

8. *Environmental Services Industry*

The OECD predicts that the market for environmental services will exceed that for equipment in the years ahead, and predicts that the environmental services industry, which delivers such auxiliary products as environmental monitoring, auditing, risk management and product testing, will become one of the growth industries of the 1990s, with growth estimated to be in excess of 7 per cent per year.

One of the more dynamic new industries is the provision of engineering services to assist in the selection and implementation of the improved process technologies referred to above. Another is that which undertakes life cycle analyses of particular products to better inform producers and consumers of the product's overall environmental impact.

The Environmental Adaptability of Business

Those companies that can anticipate consumer preferences and regulatory trends are in an advantageous position. Businesspeople with anything more than a very shortsighted view towards next quarter's profit figures will see significant opportunities in environmental stewardship. The framework of environmental regulation entails as many, if not more, opportunities than it does obstacles. Pressure from government, the public, and other commercial actors can be converted to commercial advantage.

Business culture reflects the wider culture within which it resides. In those societies where environmental awareness is relatively high, such as the Netherlands, business tend to integrate environmental considerations into all aspects of their operations. Business communities of many western nations are encouraged to emulate the Dutch, who have succeeded admirably at capitalism for most of the past five hundred years and incorporate environmental issues into their overall strategy development (Beaucamp & Girgensohn 1992).

It should also be recognized that, at least in western industrial societies, pressures that emanate from the market are likely to be regarded as more legitimate, and thus likely to encounter less resistance than directions issued by governments. As noted above in some sectors of industry, firms exert greater pressure on each other than governments could ever wield.

One of the ironies of life is that just as market failure has produced environmental despoliation, so too can market forces provide efficient means of environmental protection. The challenge is how best to intervene to prevent the former and how best to nurture the latter.

We noted above how small businesses may be disadvantaged by the lack of organizational resources with which to conform to 'green' buyer requirements. Similarly, the cost of abatement technology or of environmentally responsible waste management services may be prohibitive. Particularly during periods of recession, economic survival may be the dominant concern. It may be difficult to 'think green' when one is confronted by a rising tide of red ink. Nevertheless, adversity or constraint can be an energizing force for innovation (Porter 1990, 282).

The incorporation of environmental considerations into general business strategy may have a radiating effect throughout the entire economy (Cramer, Schot et al. 1990, 51).

Conditions that Foster Green Markets

The above discussion raises a number of policy implications for government as well as for environmental interest groups and for commercial actors. Like any other instrument for environmental protection, markets are no panacea. Markets in the environmental industry may still be vulnerable to failure. Profit-driven behavior may still result in cutting corners or opting for a cheaper and dirtier alternative. Markets may not always be conducive to recycling. As demand for recyclable material is driven in turn by consumer demand for products made from recyclable material, the value of materials recovered must exceed the cost of collection and processing. Many recycling initiatives worthy from the social or ecological standpoint have not been economically viable.

For this reason, markets should be regarded as but one strand, albeit a significant one, in the web of orderings for environmental protection. Non-market institutions can act to foster and strengthen markets; market forces themselves complement other institutions. In a real sense, green marketing may be regarded as a response to pressures from governments and from citizens. Far from being independent of the directive role of the state, commercial environmentalism is often a response to state direction, and an anticipation of further state influence.

What kind of institutional ordering might one envisage in order to enhance the effect of market forces in furtherance of environmental protection?

Governments and 'Green' Markets

Government influence on markets extends well beyond command and control regulation, although the entrepreneurial opportunities that flow from regulation have been widely recognized. We noted above the influence that government purchasing policies may have on establishing and maintaining markets and in fostering environmentally friendly industry practices. In addition, governments have an important role to play in contributing to the norms and culture of environmental citizenship. Beyond this, they bear an important responsibility for constituting and for nurturing green markets, as they do for markets generally.

Incentives and Technical Assistance

Governments can send strong signals to the marketplace in other ways. Although the market for environmental protection products may thrive even in the face of a 'hands-off' policy by government, state intervention may stimulate innovation and demand. Here we refer not to the stimulus that may be provided by strict regulatory standards, or to the influence of government purchasing power discussed above, but to other noncoercive involvement, such as the provision of information and the sponsorship of research and development. We have noted the selective use by governments of subsidies to encourage cleaner process technology. Nations whose governments regard environmentally friendly technology in strategic terms stand to benefit both environmentally and economically.

One of the more significant barriers to the diffusion of clean technology can be simple ignorance. Small firms in particular may be unaware of developments that could enhance their competitive position. Although the purveyors of green technologies may be competent in the marketing of their products, they may well benefit from governmental assistance.

The provision of information and technical assistance to industry is a common feature of industrial policy in advanced societies. By raising industry awareness of environmental issues, and by offering assistance to industry in achieving technical solutions to a variety of environmental problems, governments can contribute to both economic development and environmental improvement. Assistance may be informational or may entail a form of financial subsidy. The Swedish National Board for Industrial and Technical Development offered an award for the development of an energy-efficient refrigerator; included in the package was a guarantee to purchase a given number of units and subsidies to reduce the price of the product (Schmidheiny 1992, 238).[15]

Assistance to industry in furtherance of green productivity can thus be made a core element of industrial policy. Environmental care can become an integral part of business strategy. The Netherlands Ministry of Economic Affairs provides information, assistance, and training, and establishes regional demonstration projects for firms throughout the Dutch economy (Cramer, Schot et al. 1990).

For other illustrations of industrial policy and its environmental implications, one may look to Japan. There, the Ministry of International Trade and Industry (MITI), by commissioning reports that are given substantial publicity and by undertaking high profile campaigns, can prod industry to improve its environmental performance. This is characteristic of government-business relations in Japan, a style often described by the term 'administrative guidance.'

International organizations are also in a position to provide environmentally friendly industry assistance. We have already referred to the OECD report on trends in the environment industry. The United Nations Environment Programme (UNEP), through its cleaner production program established in 1989, seeks to increase awareness of cleaner production techniques around the world. It maintains an International Cleaner Production Information Clearing House (ICPIC) to promote the use of safe and clean technologies. UNEP publishes technical reviews and guidelines and convenes training courses and conferences.[16] Their efforts are particularly important in fostering environmentally friendly technology transfer to developing nations in order to minimize the environmental impact of such industries as metal finishing, tanning, textiles and pulp and paper.

Government investment in environmentally oriented research and development (R&D) may help the growth of an environmental protection industry. The strength of the U.S. aerospace industry in the decades since World War II owed a great deal to government R&D. Although driven primarily by considerations of national defence, the economic benefits were obvious. Environmental R&D could be given a similar stimulus, as it has in Japan, where the powerful MITI has established a Research Institute of Innovative Technology for the Earth (RITE) to coordinate research on environmentally appropriate technologies. Australia's Waste and Environmental Management Technology Program (WEMT) was funded at $12 million (Australian) over three years, as part of a larger Industry Research and Development Program (OECD 1992).

Information

The basis of a market is information. Yet another contribution that governments can make to enhance the influence of markets is to ensure that those markets are properly informed. Market failure often results from lack of information (Levačić 1991). By requiring a manufacturer to disclose the contents of a product, one facilitates the exercise of consumer preferences. Efforts, from whatever sector, to enhance the availability and quality of information about products will contribute to greener markets.

There are circumstances in which governments may compel disclosure of information relating to environmental implications of products and processes. Alternatively, such disclosure may be required by actors upstream or downstream in the course of a commercial transaction.

Governments may also play a role in ensuring the integrity of information that is made available to the marketplace. More generally, they can create and enforce laws that are conducive to the functioning of a healthy marketplace (Hayek 1991, 197). Governments, in tandem with more honest and responsible commercial actors, are responsible for protecting citizens against false marketing claims. The influence of markets may be further enhanced by the existence of criteria for the assessment of environmental compatibility. A product which can boast of a 'green seal' or 'eco-label' is likely to enjoy a decided advantage in today's market.

Claims of 'environmental friendliness' are easily made; not all are valid. The development of nationally or internationally recognized certificates of environmental appropriateness can reduce the risk of deceptive, misleading, ambiguous, or trivial claims. Governments can contribute to the development of labeling standards, to the accreditation of eco-labeling schemes, and thus to the legitimacy of markets for environmentally friendly goods and services (OECD 1992; Van Goetham 1992).[17]

The proliferation of such criteria within nations, and across international collectivities such as the European Community, has given rise to differences of opinion over the rigor and the appropriateness of various standards, and to discussions relating to the harmonization of various schemes. Significant regional variations may exist in the ability of the ecosystem to absorb a given environmental impact. While CFC emissions are harmful to the biosphere, the impact of phosphates may be more selective.[18]

Recognition

Governments and the private sector may also develop awards programs to encourage green business in general, to highlight new products that are most ecologically innovative, or publicly to praise suppliers that have made singular contributions to the environment. UNEP, in cooperation with the European Community, sponsors the European Better Environment Awards for Industry, and confers awards in the categories Good Environmental Management, Clean Technology, Eco-Product, and Environmental Technology Transfer. The Confederation of British Industry, as part of its 'Environment Means Business' program, sponsors Better Environmental Awards for Industry. These include a category devoted to encouraging technology transfer to the third world. Such awards, and the publicity that accompanies them, can be a significant incentive to innovation and a boon to marketing.

Interest Groups and Green Markets

Interest groups are well situated to help create and enhance environmentally appropriate commerce. Through their educative role, interest groups help raise public awareness and can play a crucial role in shaping consumer preferences.

Interest groups are in a position to engage in strategic collaboration with industry, and therefore directly contribute to improvement in corporate practices. Such collaboration may be general, with an entire industry, or with a particular industry association. In some cases, they may assist firms in developing environmentally beneficial products or procedures. The Environmental Defense Fund, for example, has assisted McDonald's restaurants in developing its recycling program (Elkington, Knight, with Hailes 1992, 16; Schmidheiny 1992, 88). Greenpeace had collaborated with German appliance manufacturers to produce a CFC-free refrigerator. A public utility and an environmental group in the U.S. have collaborated in an energy demand reduction program involving financial incentives to encourage consumer conservation.[19] One may expect a proliferation of collaborative ventures between interest groups and industry (Schmidheiny 1992, 86, 189).[20]

Environmental groups play an important educative role by calling public attention to specific environmental issues, generating information about products in the market, monitoring that information, and suggesting appropriate consumer behavior.

Interest groups may play a constructive role by identifying and by publicly criticizing environmentally deleterious market failures. Within the constraints posed by laws of libel, they are also in a position to maintain vigilance against spurious marketing claims (Sethi 1990; Schorsch 1990). Indeed, one organization makes 'Green Con' awards (Commonder 1990). Alternatively, by recognizing and publicly bestowing praise for good environmental citizenship interest groups help industry achieve a competitive advantage.

Third-party commercial interests and green markets

In addition to the influence of purchasing power, product stewardship, and the exercise of environmentally sensitive decisions regarding investment, lending, and insurance, there are other means by which commercial third parties may contribute to 'green markets.' Within the burgeoning environmental services industry there are those who advocate more open environmental reporting, and offer to assist clients in 'coming clean' (Deloitte Touche Tohmatsu International 1993). National and international standards organizations, commercial and nonprofit, can also play a central role in providing a normative and informational foundation for commercial environmentalism (Cascio 1994).

Conclusion

The ideal ordering for environmental protection cannot be envisaged as one grand machine, controlled as if through a master console or switchboard. Many aspects of what we would regard as an ideal institutional ordering are beyond the capacity of any government to dictate. Governments can, however, contribute to the climate within which nongovernmental instruments and institutions function effectively.

It would appear that the domain of environmental protection provides an excellent proving ground for new technologies of government as we approach the twenty-first century. The interests of industry can be guided at a distance by governments, and further conditioned by commercial and noncommercial third parties to produce outcomes more advantageous than might ever be achieved by directions imposed from above.

The power of market forces (with or without a boost from governments or third parties) should not be underestimated and may exceed the capacity of command and control regulation to improve environmental citizenship. In the words of Michael Howard, then British Secretary for the Environment, 'The penalties for poor environmental performance that the financial world will exact are likely to be far more swift and certain than anything governments have been able to achieve' (Howard 1992). Thus may private interest be harnessed for the public good. It is an interesting paradox that just as much environmental degradation is attributed to the profit motive, so too is a good deal of exemplary corporate citizenship.

Despite the promise of green markets, green technology, and their anticipated environmental impacts, they should be embraced with a degree of caution. Markets, at least until recently, have not been kind to the environment. Some of the orderings that we envisage, such as those relying upon environmental audit, may be no more successful in producing environmentally responsible conduct than were financial audits successful in preventing the corporate excesses of the 1980s. Some observers have suggested that the upstream influence of large purchasers of agricultural products can contribute not to stewardship of the land, but rather to environmentally irresponsible use of pesticides, fertilizer, and irrigation water (Burch, Rickson & Annels 1992). At the end of the day, much decision making about green marketing is still more a function of profitability than of commitment to higher ends. And a good deal of green commercialism is more commercial than green. One may easily be distracted from impending crises and lulled into a false sense of virtue by the evangelistic signs that emanate from green commerce.

Suffice it to say that despite continued progress in the technology of environmental protection, there will always be risks and there will always be room for improvement. What one can say with confidence is that those who recognize this and who position themselves to exploit these opportunities will be doing themselves, and the environment, a favor.

Notes

* This paper was prepared in the context of a larger research program that the author is conducting in collaboration with Neil Gunningham of the Australian Centre for Environmental Law, Australian National University. The author is grateful to the ANU Urban Research Program for its support, and to the Institute of Comparative Law in Japan at Chuo University for the use of its facilities during revision of the manuscript. In addition, the author wishes to

acknowledge the helpful comments of Tim Bonyhady, John Braithwaite, Bob Goodin, Max Neutze, and three anonymous reviewers on earlier versions of this essay.

1. It will be apparent by now that this is not an essay in 'deep ecology.' Fundamentalists would argue that the term 'green markets' is oxymoronic, and that most if not all production and consumption uses energy and produces waste. The focus of this essay is self-consciously pragmatic; it addresses some commercial activity that may produce positive benefits for the environment, and other activity that might be regarded as minimizing environmental harm. The terms 'environmentally appropriate' or 'less harmful' will be used throughout as alternatives to the oft-abused and loosely used 'environmentally friendly.'
2. The book was praised by Governor Clinton of Arkansas prior to his election as President of the United States and subsequently served as a model for Vice President Gore's report on reform of the federal public sector.
3. The collection of essays by Shearing and Stenning (1987) and, in particular, the contribution by Marx (1987) is richly illustrative. See also Johnston (1992) and Grabosky (1992).
4. The institutionalized participation of business and labor in public policy is the essence of European corporatism. Australian models of tripartism include regimes for the regulation of occupational health and safety and environmental protection. Here, governments may provide director grants to interest groups to facilitate their contributions to policy. On regulatory tripartism generally, see Ayres and Braithwaite (1992).
5. Commercial activity is subject to a variety of coordinating influences, most of which are nongovernmental (see Thompson, Frances et al. 1991).
6. The few scholars who have focused upon regulatory systems as systems, and upon the interaction of their components and instruments include Harter and Eads (1985) and Bressers and Klok (1988).
7. The term 'greenwash' has been used to refer to unjustified claims of environmental friendliness (see Greenpeace 1992).
8. It has been suggested that Americans' awareness of, and preference for, motor vehicle safety design was enhanced significantly by commercial advertising. For a discussion of 'the Volvo effect' and its wider implications, see *Harvard Law Review* (1994).
9. The salesperson's motives may not have been purely altruistic. Misuse or improper disposal of a product may result in significant harm to the public or to the environment; this in turn may produce legal action, adverse publicity and ultimately, financial loss for the manufacturer. But here again, we see the potential for market forces contributing to environmental improvement.
10. For discussions of various aspects of consumer boycotts, see Smith (1990), Friedman (1991), Fahey (1991), Joyner (1984), and Harper (1984).

11. For a review of recent developments in renewable energy products, see *Choice* (1993).
12. For a less optimistic perspective on the effects of ethical investing, see Dowie (1993).
13. For another illustration of the likely impetus of liability for commercial environmentalism, see note 9 above and accompanying text.
14. One prospective lender requires a comprehensive assessment of all risks associated with a proposed loan; a seventeen page environmental compliance checklist comprises part of the loan application (Schmidheiny 1992, 258). Canadian banks have begun to require detailed information from prospective commercial borrowers regarding all aspects of the latter's environmental exposure (Deloitte Touche Tohmatsu International 1993, 40).
15. While subsidies may be appropriate to assist the development of some products, they are generally regarded as inferior instruments which in time will induce a dependent orientation and will operate to suppress innovation (Porter 1990, 640).
16. See, for example, any issue of the UNEP periodical *UNEP Industry and Environment.*
17. It should be noted that eco-labeling, like other forms of certification and accreditation, need not be exclusive to the public sector. Private sector and hybrid public/private programs exist in a number of settings (see Cheit 1990; Grodsky 1993).
18. Assessing the full environmental implications and the relative merits of competing products is not always a simple task. For some of the difficulties surrounding eco-labeling programs, see Grodsky (1993), Israel (1993), and Howett (1992).
19. Cynics will observe that there is a limit to which a commercial enterprise can advocate reduced consumption of its product. The commercial viability of such demand reduction strategies depends upon the extent to which efficiencies may be realized upstream.
20. Another example: the Californians Against Waste Foundation encourages fast-food restaurants and their suppliers to create markets for environmentally friendly products by exercising their purchasing power (Reuters News Service 1993).

References

Australia Department of Administrative Services (1992) *Better Buying, Better World Strategy: Environmental Purchasing Policy.* Canberra: Australian Government Publishing Service.

Australian Bureau Of Statistics (1992) *Australia's Environment: Issues and Facts.* Canberra: Australian Government Publishing Service.

Ayres, Ian and John Braithwaite (1992) *Responsive Regulation: Transcending the Deregulation Debate.* New York: Oxford Univ. Press.

Beaucame, Andreas, and Thomas Girgensohn (1992) 'Environmental Based Consumption,' *Business Council Bulletin* (Jan–Feb): 22–27.

Beder, Sharon (1989) *Toxic Fish and Sewer Surfing: How Deceit and Collusion are Destroying our Great Beaches*. Sydney: Allen and Unwin.

Berle, Gustav (1991) *The Green Entrepreneur: Business Opportunities that Can Save the Earth and Make You Money.* Blue Summit Ridge, Pa.: Liberty Hall Press.

Boyer, Barry, and Errol Meidinger (1985) 'Privatizing Regulatory Enforcement: A Preliminary Assessment of Citizen Suits Under Federal Environmental Laws,' *Buffalo Law Review* 34: 833–964.

Braithwaite, John (1993) 'Responsive Regulation for Australia.' In *Business Regulation and Australia's Future*, edited by P. Grabosky and J. Braithwaite. Canberra: Australian Institute of Criminology.

Bressers, Hans, and Pieter-Jan Klok (1988) 'Fundamentals for a Theory of Policy Instruments,' *International Journal of Social Economics* 15 (3/4): 22–41.

Bruno, Kerry (1992) *Greenpeace Book of Greenwash*. London: Greenpeace.

Burch, D., R. Rickson, and H. R. Annels (1992) 'Agribusiness in Australia: Rural Restructuring, Social Change and Environmental Impacts.' In *Australian Environmental Policy,* edited by K. J. Walker. Sydney: New South Wales Univ. Press.

Burchell, Graham (1991) 'Peculiar Interests: Civil Society and Governing "The System of Natural Liberty."' In *The Foucault Effect: Studies in Governmentality,* edited by G. Burchell, C. Gordon, and P. Miller. London: Harvester-Wheatsheaf.

Cascio, Joe (1994) 'International Environmental Management Standards,' *ATSM Standardization News* (April): 44–49.

Chayes, Abram, and Antonia Chayes (1991) 'Compliance Without Enforcement: State Behavior under Regulatory Treaties,' *Negotiation Journal* 7: 311–30.

Cheit, Ross E. (1990) *Setting Safety Standards: Regulation in the Private and Public Sectors*. Berkeley: Univ. of California Press.

Choice (1993) 'Renewable Energy—How Close Are We?' *Choice* 34(9): 6–10.

Commoner, Barry (1990) 'Can Capitalists be Environmentalists?' *Business and Society Review* 75: 31–35.

Cramer, J., J. Schot, F. van Den Akker, and G. Maas Geesteranus (1990) 'Stimulating Cleaner Technology Through Economic Instruments: Possibilities and Constraints,' *UNEP Industry and Environment* 13 (April-May-June): 46–53.

Crook, Stephen, Jan Pakulski, and Malcolm Waters (1992) *Postmodernization: Change in Advanced Society.* London: Sage Publications.

Deloitte Touche Tohmatsu International (1993) *Coming Clean: Corporate Environmental Reporting*. London: Deloitte Touche Tohmatsu International.

Dowie, Mark (1993) 'Feel-Good Investing: Clean, Green and Guilt-Free Funds,' *Nation* April 26: 550–56.

Ehrlich, Eugen (1936) *Fundamental Principles of the Sociology of Law.* Trans. by Walter L. Moll. Cambridge: Harvard Univ. Press.

Elkington, John, Peter Knight, and Julia Hailes (1992) *The Green Business Guide*. London: Victor Gollancz.

Fahey, Patrick M. (1992) 'Advocacy Group Boycotting of Network Television Advertisers, and its Effect on Programming Content,' *University of Pennsylvania Law Review* 140: 647–709.

Fitzpatrick, Peter (1984) 'Law and Strikes,' *Osgoode Hall Law Journal* 22: 115–38.

Foucault, Michel (1991) 'Governmentality.' In *The Foucault Effect: Studies in Governmentality*, edited by G. Burchell, C. Gordon, and P. Miller. London: Harvester-Wheatsheaf.

Friedman, Monroe (1991) 'Consumer Boycotts: A Conceptual Framework and Research Agenda,' *Journal of Social Issues* 47(1): 149–68.

Gilboy, Janet (1992) *Government Use of Private Resources in Law Enforcement*. ABF Working Paper no. 9203. Chicago: American Bar Foundation.

Grabosky, Peter (1992) 'Law Enforcement and the Citizen: Non- Governmental Participation in Crime Prevention and Control,' *Policing and Society* 2: 249–71.

—— (1993) *Rewards and Incentives as Regulatory Instruments*. Administration, Compliance and Governability Program, Working Paper no. 13. Canberra: Research School of Social Sciences, Australian National University.

Gunningham, Neil (1993) 'Thinking About Regulatory Mix: Regulating Occupational Health and Safety, Futures Markets and Environmental Law.' In *Business Regulation and Australia's Future*, edited by P. Grabosky and J. Braithwaite. Canberra: Australian Institute of Criminology.

Greenpeace (1993) 'Body Shop Places Albright and Wilson on Environmental Probation,' *Greenpeace Business*, no. 6, 6 March.

Grodsky, Jamie A. (1993) 'Certified Green: The Law and Future of Environmental Labeling', *Yale Journal on Regulation* 10: 147–227.

Haggett, Scott (1992) 'Earth Friendly Canadian Pacific Hotels Rolls Out the Green Carpet,' *Reuters News Service*, 26 October.

Hahn, Robert W. (1993) 'Toward a New Environmental Paradigm,' *Yale Law Journal* 102: 1719–61.

Harper, Michael C. (1984) 'The Consumer's Emerging Right to Boycott: *NAACP v Claiborne Hardware* and its Implications for American Labor Law,' *Yale Law Journal* 93: 409–54.

Harter, Phillip J., and George C. Eads (1985) 'Policy Instruments, Institutions, and Objectives: An Analytical Framework for Assessing "Alternatives" to Regulation,' *Administrative Law Review* 37: 221–58.

Harvard Law Review (1994) 'Note: Harnessing Madison Avenue: Advertising and Products Liability Theory,' *Harvard Law Review* 107: 895–912.

Hayek, Frederick von (1991) 'Spontaneous ("grown") Order and Organized ("made") Order.' In Thompson et al., 1991.

Hornstein, Donald T. (1993) 'Lessons from Federal Pesticide Regulation and Paradigms and Politics of Environmental Law Reform,' *Yale Journal on Regulation* 10: 369–446.

Howett, Ciannat M. (1992) 'The "Green Labeling" Phenomenon: Problems and Trends in the Regulation of Environmental Product Claims,' *Virginia Environmental Law Journal* 11: 401–61.

Huppes, Gjalt, and Robert Kagan (1989) 'Market-Oriented Regulation of Environmental Problems in the Netherlands,' *Law & Policy* 11: 215–39.

Israel, Glenn (1993) 'Taming the Green Marketing Monster: National Standards for Environmental Marketing Claims,' *Boston College Environmental Affairs Law Review* 20: 303–33.

Johnston, Les (1992) *The Rebirth of Private Policing*. London: Routledge.

Joyner, Christopher C. (1984) 'The Transnational Boycott as Economic Coercion in International Law: Policy, Place and Practice,' *Vanderbilt Journal of Transnational Law* 17: 205–86.

Kamlet, Kenneth S. (1992) 'Environmental Management: The Ten Commandments,' *Internal Auditor* 49 (October): 36–44.

Levačić, R. (1991) 'Markets and Government: An Overview.' In Thompson, Frances et al., 1991.

Lury, Karen, and Stefano Hatfield (1992) 'Recycling Computer Products—More Enlightened Attitude from both Suppliers and Customers Needed for Success,' *Reuters News Service*, 24 September.

Marx, Gary T. (1987) 'The Interweaving of Public and Private Police in Undercover Work.' In Shearing & Stenning, 1987.

Mechlin, Stuart (1993) 'Comment—Savvy Bankers Remember Mother Nature,' *Reuters News Service*, 12 February.

Monks, Alan J. (1990) *Protecting the Environment Using Market Mechanisms*. Tasman Institute Occasional Paper no. B5. Melbourne: Tasman Institute.

Monks, Robert, and Nell Minow (1991) *Power and Accountability*. New York: Harper Business.

Morris, Gregory (1991) 'Responsible Care: Amoco,' *Chemical Week* 17 July: 74.

Organization for Economic Co-operation and Development (OECD) (1991) *Environmental Labelling in OECD Countries*. Paris: OECD.

——(1992) *The OECD Environment Industry: Situation, Prospects and Government Policies*. Paris: OECD.

Osborne, David, and Ted Gaebler (1992) *Reinventing Government: How the Entrepreneurial Spirit is Transforming the Public Sector*. Boston: Addison Wesley.

Platt, Nicholas (1992) 'The Rise of the Eco-Consumer Has Big Business Seeing Green,' *Reuters News Service*, 25 May.

Porter, Michael E. (1990) *The Competitive Advantage of Nations*. New York: Macmillan.

Reuters (1992a) 'It's Green for Go in Boots the Chemist,' *Reuters News Service*, 13 June.

——(1992b) 'N.Y. City Fund Wants Green Stance from 4 Companies,' *Reuters News Service*, 10 December.

——(1992c) 'Department of the Environment—Giant Global Market is the Prize for Business,' *Reuters News Service*, 19 November.

Reuters (1993) 'Fast Food Environmental Summit Lays Groundwork for Increased Communication and Cooperation,' *Reuters News Service*, 15 January.

Rose, N., and P. Miller (1992) 'Political Power Beyond the State: Problematics of Government,' *British Journal of Sociology* 43: 173–205.

Russell, Clifford S. (1988) 'Economic Incentives in the Management of Hazardous Wastes,' *Columbia Journal of Environmental Law* 13: 257–74.

Schmidheiny, Stephan (1992) *Changing Course: A Global Business Perspective on Development and the Environment*. Cambridge: MIT Press.

Schorsch, Jonathan (1990) 'Are Corporations Playing Clean with Green?' *Business and Society Review* 75: 6–9.

Schultze, Charles L. (1977) *The Public Use of Private Interest*. Washington, D. C.: Brookings Institution.

Sethi, S. Prakash (1990) 'Corporations and the Environment: Greening or Preening?' *Business and Society Review* 75: 4–5.

Shearing, Clifford D. (1993) 'A Constitutive Conception of Regulation.' In *Business Regulation and Australia's Future*, edited by P. Grabosky and J. Braithwaite. Canberra: Australian Institute of Criminology.

——, and Philip C. Stenning (eds.) (1987) *Private Policing*. Beverly Hills, Calif.: Sage Publications.

Simmons, Peter, and Brian Wynne (1993) 'State, Market . . . and Mutual Regulation? Socio-Economic Dimensions of the Environmental Regulation of Business.' Paper prepared for the Fifth Annual International Conference of the Society for the Advancement of Socio-Economics, 26–28 March, New York.

Smith, N. Craig (1990) *Morality and the Market: Consumer Pressure for Corporate Accountability*. London: Routledge.

Stewart, Richard B. (1992) 'Models for Environmental Regulation: Central Planning Versus Market-Based Approaches,' *Boston College Environmental Affairs Law Review* 19: 547–62.

——(1993) 'Environmental Regulation and International Competitiveness,' *Yale Law Journal* 102: 2039–2106.

Suart, Gregory (1992) 'Marketing Reports on Environmental Concerns in the Packaging Industry,' *Reuters News Service*, 20 August.

Teubner, Gunther (1983) 'Substantive and Reflexive Elements in Modern Law,' *Law & Society Review* 17: 239–86.

Thompson, Grahame, J. Frances, R. Levačić, and J. Mitchell (eds.) (1991) *Markets, Hierarchies and Networks: The Coordination of Social Life*. London: Sage Publications.

Van Goetham, Anne (1992) 'The European Eco-Label,' *European Environment* (December). Brussels: Europe Information Service.

Wheatley, Alan (1993) 'Firms Start to Warm to the Environment,' *Reuters News Service*, 7 March.

Designing Smart Regulation*

NEIL GUNNINGHAM AND DARREN SINCLAIR

Introduction

One of the crucial issues of our time is how to avoid serious, and perhaps cataclysmic, damage to the natural environment. The causes of such damage are both complex and controversial, and arise from a wide variety of social and economic pressures. The results, however, are more readily apparent. The evidence that pollution, land degradation, deforestation, ozone depletion, climate change, and the loss of biological diversity are inflicting serious and in some cases irreversible damage to the planet which sustains us, is increasingly compelling.[1] Indeed, it is arguable that the window of opportunity for averting major ecological disaster is a rapidly shrinking one, and that, in some cases, it may already be too late to prevent ongoing environmental degradation.

For policymakers, a variety of strategies are available that might, subject to political and economic constraints, enable serious environmental damage to be slowed down, halted, or ideally reversed. This article is about one of the most important of those strategies: environmental regulation. We use this term, deliberately, in the broadest sense, to include not just conventional forms of direct ('command and control') regulation but also to include much more flexible, imaginative and innovative forms of social control which seek to harness not just governments but also business and third parties. For example, we are concerned with self-regulation and co-regulation, with utilizing both commercial interests and Non-Government Organizations, and with finding surrogates for direct government regulation, as well as with improving the effectiveness and efficiency of more conventional forms of direct government regulation.

Regulation—even broadly defined—is not the only means of addressing environmental problems but will, in the very large majority of cases, undoubtedly be a crucial one. However, most existing approaches to regulation, are seriously sub-optimal. By this we mean that they are not effective in delivering their purported policy goals, or efficient, in doing so at least cost, nor do they perform well in terms of other criteria such as equity or political acceptability.

The major task of this article is to demonstrate how environmental regulation could be designed so that it would perform successfully in terms of those criteria (or at least come a lot closer to it). The central argument will be that, in the majority of circumstances, the use of multiple rather than single policy instruments, and a broader range of regulatory actors, will produce better regulation. Further, that this will allow the implementation of complementary combinations of instruments and participants tailored to meet the imperatives of specific environmental issues. By implication, this means a far more imaginative, flexible, and pluralistic approach to environmental regulation than has so far been adopted in most jurisdictions.

Towards Principle-based Regulatory Design

Because threats to the environment take many forms, the appropriate strategies to address environmental degradation are likely to be context-specific.[2] What sorts of policies work will be highly dependent upon the characteristics of the environmental issue under consideration. The strategies most effective in addressing point-source pollution from manufacturing are likely to be very different from those most suited to remedying land degradation or overfishing, as are the likely array of available instruments and institutional actors, and the political and economic contexts in which policy mixes must be designed. As a result, it would be futile to attempt to construct a single optimal regulatory solution that would be applicable to a wide variety of circumstances.

Does this mean that nothing of value can be said at a general and abstract level and that the most we can ever do is focus on solutions to particular types of problems (point-source pollution, land-clearing, soil degradation, etc.) with little hope of learning any wider lessons or of extrapolating from one policy area to another? We believe that such a conclusion is too bleak, and that, notwithstanding the context-specific nature of most environmental problems, it is possible to build a *principle based framework* for designing environmental regulation in any given circumstances. By this we mean an approach which, while falling short of providing determinative regulatory solutions, leads policymakers to assess their decisions against a set of design criteria which form the basis of reaching preferred policy outcomes.

In the remainder of this article, we address two elements we believe are crucial to successful regulatory design. First, and comprising the bulk of the article, we identify a series of *regulatory design principles*. We argue that adherence to these principles is at the very heart of successful policy design. Not least, we argue that policymakers should take advantage of a number of largely unrecognised opportunities, strategies and techniques for achieving efficient and effective environmental policy. These include:

- the desirability of preferring complementary instrument mixes over single instrument approaches while avoiding the dangers of smorgasbordism (i.e. wrongly assuming that all instruments should be used rather than the minimum number necessary to achieve the desired result);
- the virtues of parsimony: why less interventionist measures should be preferred and how to achieve such outcomes;
- the benefits of an escalating response up an instrument pyramid (utilising not only government but also business and third parties) so as to build in regulatory responsiveness, to increase dependability of outcomes through instrument sequencing, and to provide early warning of instrument failure through the use of triggers;
- empowering third parties (both commercial and non-commercial) to act as surrogate regulators, thereby achieving not only better environmental outcomes at less cost but also freeing up scarce regulatory resources which can be redeployed in circumstances where no alternatives to direct government intervention are available; and
- maximizing opportunities for win-win outcomes, by expanding the boundaries within which such opportunities are available and encouraging business to go 'beyond compliance' with existing legal requirements.

Second, we stress the importance of *instrument combinations* and discuss how such combinations might be inherently complementary, inherently counterproductive, or essentially context specific in nature. In recent years, policymakers begun to explore a much wider range of environmental policy instruments. However, there has been little systematic enquiry into how conceptually different instruments might interact with each other. Overall, there remains a tendency to treat the various policy instruments as alternatives to one another rather than as potentially complementary mechanisms.[3] As a result, policy analysts have tended to embrace one or other of these regulatory approaches without regard to the virtue of others.

It is important to earmark the issues we do not address in this article. First, we are not directly concerned with the debate on compliance. The extent to which different instruments are capable of being, or under a particular enforcement approach likely to be, effectively enforced, is obviously an important consideration in relation to their effectiveness and efficiency.[4] However, it is not necessary to enter into this debate in order to address our central concerns identified above. Second, we do not find it necessary to enter the debate concerning the prevailing regulatory culture of different jurisdictions and their relative effectiveness although this too, is likely to influence regulatory outcomes.[5] As we will see, our design principles can be applied successfully against the backdrop of a variety of enforcement practices and across a range of cultures.

Regulatory Design Principles

In this section we identify the core principles which should underpin regulatory design. Although these do not purport to prescribe specific solutions to specific environmental threats, our principles provide the guidelines and roadmaps which will enable policymakers to arrive at those solutions. The five principles described below are intended to be addressed sequentially.

Principle 1. Prefer policy mixes incorporating instrument and institutional combinations

There are very few circumstances where a single regulatory instrument is likely to be the most efficient or effective means of addressing a particular environmental problem. Certainly such circumstances exist. For example, a ban on the manufacture of certain highly toxic substances may be a highly effective way of preventing their use, without the need to invoke additional instruments. In the majority of circumstances, however, individual instruments have both strengths and weaknesses and none are sufficiently flexible and resilient to be able to successfully address all environmental problems in all contexts.

Command and control regulation has the virtues of high dependability and predicability (if adequately enforced), but commonly proves to be inflexible and inefficient. In contrast, economic instruments tend to be efficient but, in most cases, not dependable. Information-based strategies, voluntarism and self-regulation have the virtues of being non-coercive, unintrusive and (in most cases) cost-effective, but also have low reliability when used in isolation. Their success also depends heavily on the extent of the gap between the public and private interest.

Our general conclusion is that the best means of overcoming the deficiencies of individual instruments, while taking advantage of their strengths, is through the design of combinations of instruments. Similar arguments for regulatory pluralism apply with regard to regulatory participants. In most jurisdictions, the regulatory process been artificially restricted to government and industry. This reinforces outmoded notions of government as an omnipotent source of regulatory authority. A greater range of actors, including commercial third parties, such as banks, insurers, consumers, suppliers and environmental consultants, and non-commercial third parties, can assist in taking the weight off government intervention. Thus government can redirect is limited resources to those companies which are genuinely recalcitrant, and increasingly assume the mantle of facilitator and broker of third party participation in the regulatory process. An additional benefit is that a multiplicity of regulatory signals have the potential to be mutually reinforcing.

If one accepts this general approach of using combinations of instruments and participants, then there may be a temptation to succumb to a 'kitchen sink' approach to policy design,[6] throwing in every conceivable policy combination on the assumption that the severity of the environmental problems we confront, and their likely consequences for humankind, are such as to justify almost any level of resource input. However, this approach is likely to be seriously sub-optimal for a variety of reasons. First, there are practical limits to the capacity of industry to comply with a large range of regulatory and quasi-regulatory requirements—regulatory overload is now a well recognised phenomenon.[7] Second, the imposition on the public purse and the demand on public resources would also be excessive. Third and finally, not all combinations of instruments or institutions are likely to be complementary. On the contrary, a considerable number of combinations are either inherently, or in particular contexts, counterproductive, duplicative or sub-optimal (this issue is explored below).

Principle 2. Prefer less interventionist measures

Intervention has two principal components: *prescription* and *coercion*. Prescription refers to the extent to which external parties determine the level, type and method of environmental improvement. Coercion, on the other hand, refers to the extent to which external parties or instruments place negative pressure on a firm to improve its performance. By way of example, it may argued that industry self-regulation is higher in terms of its prescriptiveness than its coercion. That is, firms may be required to address specific issues and adopt certain behaviours, but there is little by way of external enforcement to ensure that their obligations are met.

In contrast, some economic instruments such as taxes and charges are high on coercion and low on prescription. That is, coercion is exercised through a price signal, which firms by and large cannot avoid. How they respond to that price signal, however, is independent of outside influence—they may choose to pay the higher tax or change their behaviour so as to limit its impact. If they choose the latter, then they also have total control over the type of remediation implemented. Ranking instrument categories according to the level of intervention therefore requires a balancing or assessment of the respective contributions of the two constituent components, prescription and coercion.

There are a variety of reasons why less interventionist approaches should be preferred to more interventionist ones. In terms of *efficiency*, highly coercive instruments usually require substantial administrative resources for monitoring and policing, without which they are likely to be ineffective. Highly prescriptive instruments lack flexibility and do not facilitate least cost solutions. They may also result in the unnecessary deployment of resources to policing those who would be quite willing to comply voluntarily under less interventionist options. Good performers may be inhibited from going beyond compliance with such regulation.

High intervention is unlikely to be as *effective* as alternative approaches essentially because conscripts generally respond less favourably than volunteers. Highly coercive measures may cause resentment and resistance from those who regard them as an unjustifiable and intrusive intervention in their affairs, rather than the constructive resolution of environmental problems. Unsurprisingly, high intervention also tends to score very badly in terms of *political acceptability*. This is particularly the case in sectors with a history and culture of independence from, and a strong resentment of, government regulatory intervention.

In contrast to the problems of high interventionism described above, low interventionist options, to the extent that they are viable, have the considerable advantages of providing greater flexibility to enterprises in their response, greater ownership of solutions which they are directly involved in creating, less resistance, greater legitimacy, greater speed of decision making, sensitivity to market circumstances and lower costs.[8] From a regulator's perspective, a focus on less interventionist approaches also has the attraction of freeing up scarce regulatory resources which may be redeployed against those who are unwilling or unable to respond to such measures and against whom there is no viable alternative to the deployment of highly intrusive instruments.

Implicit in this principle of 'starting with the least interventionist policy measure' is the assumption that the measure *actually works*. That is, the instrument must be capable of delivering the identified environmental outcomes. In some cases, this will mean that 'what works' requires a relatively high level of intervention, but even in such cases it should still be possible to apply to principle.

In applying the principle of least intervention, policymakers should bear in mind the capacity to raise the level of intervention, if and when required, with various instruments and/or instrument combinations. That is, it is not necessarily a matter of choosing one instrument in preference to another in a static sense, but rather that of invoking a temporal sequence of instruments, as described in the next principle below. Alternatively, firms may be segregated into different streams of regulatory intervention, for example, one might introduce a 'green track' of low intervention regulation for leading edge environmental performers, while retaining a more interventionist track for those firms which are merely complying with minimum standards or are recalcitrant.

Principle 3. Escalate up an instrument pyramid to the extent necessary to achieve policy goals

We asserted in the previous principle that preference should be given to the least interventionist measure(s) that will work. However, it is not always apparent to policy designers whether a particular measure they contemplate using will work or not, principally for two reasons. First, a given instrument may be effective in influencing the behaviour of some, but not of others (suggesting the need for regulation to be responsive to the different behaviour of different regulatees). Second, a particular instrument which, prior to its introduction, seemed likely to be viable in its entirety, may in the light of practical experience, prove not to be so (suggesting the need for instrument sequencing to increase dependability).

A window into solving the first problem is provided by John Braithwaite, whose 'enforcement pyramid' conceives of responsive regulation essentially in terms of dialogic regulatory culture in which regulators signal to industry their commitment to escalate their enforcement response whenever lower levels of intervention fail.[9] Under this model, regulators begin by assuming virtue (to which they respond with cooperative measures) but when their expectations are disappointed, they respond with progressively punitive/coercive strategies until the regulatee conforms.

Central to Braithwaite's model is the capacity for gradual escalation from low to high intervention, culminating in a regulatory peak which, if activated, will be sufficiently powerful to deter even the most egregious offender. It is possible to reconceptualize and extend this enforcement pyramid in two important ways. First, beyond the state and business, it is possible for third parties to act as quasi-regulators. Similarly, second parties in the for of business may themselves perform a (self-) regulatory role. In our expanded model, escalation would be possible up any face of the pyramid, including the second face (through self-regulation), or the third face (through a variety of actions by commercial or non-commercial third parties or both), in addition to government action.

To give a concrete example of escalation up the third face, the developing Forest Stewardship Council (FSC) is a global environmental standards setting system for forest products. The FSC will both establish standards that can be used to certify forestry products as sustainably managed and will 'certify the certifiers'. Once operational, it will rely for its 'clout' on changing consumer demand and upon creating strong 'buyers groups' and other mechanisms for institutionalizing green consumer demand. That is, its success will depend very largely on influencing consumer demand. While government involvement, for example through formal endorsement or though government procurement policies which supported the FSC, would be valuable, the scheme is essentially a free-standing one: from base to peak (consumer sanctions and boycotts) the scheme is entirely third party based. In this way, a 'new institutional system for global environmental standard setting' will come about, entirely independent of government.[10]

Second, Braithwaite's pyramid utilizes a single instrument category, specifically, state regulation, rather than a range of instruments *and parties*. In contrast, our pyramid conceives of the possibility of regulation using a number of different instruments implemented by across a number of parties. It also conceives of escalation to higher levels of coerciveness not only within an single instrument category but also across several different instruments and across different faces of the pyramid.

A graphic illustration of exactly how this can indeed occur, is provided by Joe Rees' analysis of the highly sophisticated self-regulatory program of the Institute of Nuclear Power Operators (INPO), which, post Three Mile

Island, is probably amongst the most impressive and effective such schemes worldwide.[11] However, even INPO is incapable of working effectively in isolation. There are, inevitably, industry laggards, who do not respond to education, persuasion, peer group pressure, gradual nagging from INPO, shaming, or other instruments at its disposal. INPO's ultimate response, after five years of frustration, was to turn to the government regulator, the Nuclear Regulatory Commission (NRC). That is, the effective functioning of the lower levels of the pyramid may depend upon invoking the peak, which in this case, only government could do. As Rees puts it: 'INPO's climb to power has been accomplished on the shoulders of the NRC'.

This case also shows the importance of integration between the different levels of the pyramid. The NRC did not just happen to stumble across, or threaten action against recalcitrants, rather there was considerable communication between INPO and the NRC which facilitated what was, in effect, a tiered response of education and information, escalating through peer group pressure and a series of increasingly threatening letters, ultimately to the threat of criminal penalties and incapacitation, the latter being penalties government alone could impose, but the former being approaches which in these circumstances at least, INPO itself was in the best position to pursue. Thus, even in the case of one of the most successful schemes of self regulation ever documented, it was the presence of the regulatory gorilla in the closet, that secured its ultimate success.

We do not wish to give the impression, however, that a coordinated escalation up one or more sides of our instrument pyramid is practicable in all cases. On the contrary, controlled escalation is only possible where the instruments in question lend themselves to a graduated, responsive and interactive enforcement strategy. The two instruments which are most amenable to such a strategy (because they are readily manipulated) are command and control and self-regulation. Thus it is no coincidence that our first example of how to shift from one face of the pyramid to another as one escalates and of how to invoke the dynamic peak, was taken from precisely this instrument combination. However, there are other instruments which are at least partially amenable to such a response, the most obvious being insurance and banking.

A combination of government mandated information (a modestly interventionist strategy) in conjunction with third party pressure (at the higher levels of the pyramid) might also be a viable option. For example, government might require business to disclose various information about its levels of emissions under a Toxic Release Inventory,[12] leaving it to financial markets and insurers (commercial third parties) and environmental groups (non-commercial third parties) to use that information in a variety of ways to bring pressure on poor environmental performers.[13]

In contrast, in the case of certain other instruments, the capacity for responsive regulation is lacking, either because an individual instrument is not designed to facilitate responsive regulation (ie its implementation is static rather than dynamic and cannot be tailored to escalate or de-escalate depending on the behaviour of specific firms) or because there is no potential for coordinated interaction between instruments. For example economic instruments have both these characteristics. In essence, either an economic instrument is in place and must be responded to, or it is not. An environmental tax (or the level of tax) for example, cannot be imposed depending upon whether or not an enterprise has responded positively to less intrusive instruments, but rather, is intended as a uniform price signal which will apply to all members of the target group equally, irrespective of their past behaviour. By the same token, there are significant limits to the extent to which broad based economic instruments, such as pollution taxes and tradeable emission permits, can be designed to interact in a coordinated and complementary fashion with other instruments, except by means of temporal sequencing as described below.

Another limitation for those aspiring to a coordinated and gradual escalation of instruments and coerciveness, is the possibility that in some circumstances, escalation may only be possible to the middle levels of the pyramid, with no alternative instrument or party having the capacity to deliver higher levels of coerciveness. Or a particular instrument or instrument combination may facilitate action at the bottom of the pyramid and at the top, but not in the middle levels, with the result that there is no capacity for gradual escalation. For example, lender liability gives banks and other financial institutions a considerable incentive to scrutinise the environmental credentials of their clients very closely before lending them money, and at this stage they may counsel a client towards improved environmental performance. However, subsequent to providing the loan, the only available sanction may be to foreclose, without credible intermediate options. In any of these circumstances, our proposed dynamic instrument pyramid still has some value but it will operate in a less than complete fashion.

In the substantial range of circumstances when coordinated escalation is not readily achievable, a critical role of government will be, so far as possible, to fill the gaps between the different levels of the pyramid, seeking to compensate for either the absence of suitable second or third party instruments, or for their static or limited nature, either through direct intervention or, preferably, by facilitating action or acting as a catalyst for effective second or third party action, as described in design principle five. In effect, a major role for government is thus to facilitate second and third parties climbing the pyramid.

Finally, there are two general circumstances where it is inappropriate to adopt an escalating response up the instrument or enforcement pyramid, irrespective of whether it is possible to achieve such a response. First, in situations which involve a serious risk of irreversible loss or catastrophic damage, then a graduated response is inappropriate because the risks are too high: the endangered species may have become extinct, or the nuclear plant may have exploded, before the regulator has determined how high up the pyramid it is necessary to escalate in order to change the behaviour of the target group. In these circumstances a horizontal rather than a vertical approach may be preferable: imposing a range of instruments, including the underpinning of a regulatory safety net, simultaneously rather than sequentially.[14] Second, a graduated response is only appropriate where the parties have continuing interactions—it is these which makes it credible to begin with a low interventionist response and to escalate (in a tit for tat response) if this proves insufficient. In contrast, where there is only one chance to influence the behaviour in question (for example because small employers can only very rarely be inspected), then a more interventionist first response may be justified, particularly if the risk involved is a high one.

Instrument sequencing to increase dependability

In the event that an instrument (or instrument combination) that seems viable in its entirety turns out not to be so, our proposed solution is to introduce instrument sequencing: enabling escalation from the preferred least interventionist option, if it fails, to increasingly more interventionist alternatives. For example, a particular industry sector may be allowed to conduct a voluntary self-regulation scheme *on the proviso* that if it fails to meet the agreed objectives, mandatory sanctions will be introduced. Such a solution is not only consistent with design principle 3 above, it also avoids a slide into smorgasbordism: rather than using all instruments and participants simultaneously, it is only when the least interventionist (viable) instrument(s) have demonstrably failed that one escalates up the pyramid and invokes a broader range of instruments and parties, and even then, only to the extent necessary to achieve the desired goal.

The precise nature of sequencing arrangements will be determined by the level of discretion that is associated with their implementation. That is, some sequencing arrangements will entail the automatic application of more interventionist measures if and when earlier measures fail, thus reducing the level of discretion, while others will require some further action by first, second, or third parties prior to their implementation, thus increasing the level of discretion. Minimizing the amount of discretion, once certain defined parameters have been breached, sends a powerful message to industry to deliver on less interventionist forms of regulation. Of course this does not preclude lobbying by business, but this is less likely to succeed if government has already publicly committed itself to a specified course of action. The following scenarios illustrate how the level of, for example, government discretion can be varied to address different environmental problems:

(i) The United States Climate Action plan aims to reduce the level of greenhouse gas emissions. The plan is based on a series of low intervention voluntary agreements with industry. Implict in the plan is a commitment to legislated targets if industry does not deliver on its promises. This redundancy provision contains a high level of discretion because the threat is: (a) implicit not explicit; (b) undefined; and (c) linked to a particular administration.

(ii) The New Zealand government has made similar voluntary arrangements with industry to reduce greenhouse gas emissions. It has, however, implemented a sequencing provision with far less discretion. If industry fails to achieve pre-specified reduction targets, a carbon tax will be introduced. This provision contains far less discretion because (a) it is explicit; and (b) it is defined. It is, however, still linked to a particular administration.

(iii) The Australian response to phasing out the use the of ozone depleting hydrochlorofluorocarbons (HCFCs) is similarly based on an industry wide voluntary self-regulation scheme. The sequencing provision in this case is in the form of a legislated tradeable quota scheme. If industry fails to meet pre-specified HCFC reduction targets, the tradeable quota scheme automatically comes into effect. This provision contains even less discretion than either of the previous two examples because (a) it is explicit; (b) it is defined; and (c) it is included in legislation, thus reducing opportunities for further political discretion. It would still be possible for a subsequent government to amend the relevant legislation. However, this is likely to require the expenditure of considerable political capital.

Triggers and buffer zones

Our proposed methods of sequencing are dependent on *triggers* to warn the authorities when less interventionist measures have failed. For example, under a scheme of self-regulation, the industry itself may invite government intervention. Alternatively, government and industry may agree to defined performance benchmarks. A failure to comply with these benchmarks would automatically trigger tougher regulations. Or it may be that public interest groups are able to identify serious breaches which would warrant intervention from governments or other third parties, possibly insurers.

In order to increase the dependability of sequencing provisions, several possible triggers would be preferable, though precisely which ones are most appropriate will depend upon the particular context. In broad terms, appropriate triggers might include: random government inspections; independent auditors; mechanisms for industry association reporting; in-house whistle blowers; community oversight; and compulsory firm reporting.

In relying on triggers to invoke sequencing, it is important that the triggers pre-empt unacceptable levels of environmental harm. That is, there needs to be a *buffer zone* between the point at which a trigger is set off and the level of environmental harm that is being monitored. For example, with Australia's self-regulatory scheme to phase out the use of HCFCs, the level at which mandatory quotas kick-in is well below that which is required to meet our international commitments under the Montreal Protocol—creating an effective buffer zone. The greater the degree of effectiveness that is required for a particular environmental issue, the greater the size of the buffer zones. This is similar to the concept of 'precautionary regulation', where tougher regulation acts as a safety net if and when other policies fail. The regulation is enacted, but the expectation is that it won't be used.

Circuit breakers

Another strategy, related to that of sequencing, is the use of *circuit breakers*. A circuit breaker is an instrument which is introduced as a short term measure (and ultimately withdrawn), the purpose of which is to pre-empt the anticipated failure of another instrument. Circuit breakers tend to be low intervention instruments introduced in anticipation that certain high intervention instruments, introduced in isolation, have a high chance of failure. For example, a ban on land clearing in South Australia was regarded as essential to halt widespread environmental degradation, but was also politically unacceptable and largely unenforceable in the absence of some complementary positive inducement. Compensation was introduced for those who were refused a permit to clear, in order to overcome both these problems and to facilitate the cultural change that was needed in the long term (i.e. from a belief that all landowners had an unencumbered right to clear, to a sustainable land use). Once this had been achieved (or at least that opposition to clearing bans had been largely overcome), the right to compensation was withdrawn.[15]

Circuit breakers are similar to sequencing in that there is an ordering of policy responses, beginning with less interventionist and then moving up to more intrusive regulations. The difference is that with sequencing, escalation up the enforcement pyramid occurs only when lower policies fail, whereas with circuit breakers, there is an expectation that they are only a short term measure, eventually to be replaced by other more conventional policy responses. It is important to recognise that the use of circuit breakers is a direct violation of the polluter pays and/or user pays principles (it may, nevertheless, be consistent with the precautionary principle). In some circumstances, however, this pragmatic approach may be necessary to achieve real progress in areas where regulatory resistance is high and external monitoring is difficult.

Principle 4. Empower participants which are in the best position to act as surrogate regulators

We argued earlier that there are a range of second and third parties, both commercial and non-commercial, which may play valuable roles in the regulatory process, acting as quasi-regulators. These range from industry associations (administering self-regulatory programs) through financial institutions to environmental and other pressure groups. All too often, however, policymakers have avoided or ignored the potential contributions of such parties, treating government as the sole regulatory provider. Yet by expanding the regulatory 'tool box' to encompass additional players, many of the most serious shortcomings of traditional regulatory approaches may be overcome.

There are several reasons why the recruitment of third parties into the regulatory process may provide for improved outcomes. First, in some instances third party quasi-regulation may be far more potent than government intervention. For example, the threat of a bank to foreclose a loan to a firm with low levels of liquidity is likely to have a far greater impact than any existing government instrument. Second, it may be perceived as more legitimate. For example, farmers are far more accepting of commercial imperatives to reduce chemical use than they are of any government mandated requirements. Similarly, participation by non-commercial third parties, in particular, may well be crucial in terms of political acceptability. Third, government resources are necessarily limited, particularly in an era of fiscal constraint. Accordingly, it makes sense for government to reserve its resources for situations where there is no viable alternative but direct regulation. The potential for Responsible Care to supplement government regulation of the chemical industry is a case in point.[16] Finally, even if resources were more readily available, governments are not omnipotent. There are many areas of commercial activity which impact on the environmental performance of industry where direct government influence is impractical. For example, where there are a myriad of small players, such that it is impossible even for government to identify, let alone regulate all of them.

Applying the principle of empowerment

The participation of second and third parties, particularly commercial third parties, in the regulatory process is unlikely to arise spontaneously, except in a very limited range of circumstances where public and private interests substantially coincide.[17] Such parties may have little existing interest in environmental performance, lack the necessary information even if they did, or indeed may have a commercial interest in maintaining or accelerating environmental degradation. For example, banks are unlikely to promote the conservation of remnant vegetation on farms where they perceive the clearing of land to provide increased earnings, nor are they likely to oppose the running of extra stock where this increases the ability to repay loans. There remains, therefore, a significant role for government in facilitating, catalysing and commandeering the participation of second and third parties to the cause of environmental improvement.

One powerful illustration of this principle can be drawn from Mitchell's work on pollution by oil tankers at sea.[18] Mitchell demonstrates how the imposition by the state of penalties for intentional oil spills (pursuant to an international treaty) was almost wholly ineffective, due in no small part to difficulties of monitoring, and, in some cases, to a lack of either enforcement resources or political will. Nor, in the absence of government intervention, did third parties have incentives to contribute significantly to the reduction of oil spills. However, all this changed when a new regime was introduced, requiring tankers to be equipped with segregated ballast tanks. Despite the increased cost of the new equipment, this regime has been extremely successful, a fact owed substantially to the role played by a range of powerful third parties. First, the new regime facilitated coerced compliance by three powerful third parties, namely non-state classification societies, ship insurers, and ship builders. As Mitchell demonstrates, none of these parties had any interest in avoiding the new regime yet ship-owners were critically dependent upon each of them.[19] Together, and in conjunction with state action, they achieved far more than state action alone was ever likely to.

There are a variety of mechanisms through which government may seek to engage second and third parties more fully in the regulatory process. Most of these will require government to seek out lateral means of extending its reach through innovative market orderings. An obvious starting point is the provision of adequate information. Without reliable data on the performance of industrial firms, those third parties which may be in a position to exert influence, for example in the commercial sphere (e.g. investors and banks), will be unable to make objective judgements about preferred company profiles. For example, it was only when government mandated collation and disclosure of toxic releases that financial markets were able to factor this information into share prices, thereby rewarding good environmental performers and disadvantaging the worst performers.[20]

Some strategies for empowering third parties will be specific to particular target groups. For example, Government may facilitate the activities of non-commercial third parties such as NGOs through the provision of funding support, the enactment of community right to know legislation and the provision of legal standing. In seeking to target banks, government might increase lender liability for a range of environmentally destructive behaviours. Insurers as regulators may be invoked by making insurance a condition of license, or a condition of authorization to engage in activities which have a high environmental risk.

Governments could also harness the very considerable power of supply chain pressure. For example, governments may make it a condition of regulatory flexibility that firms over a certain size not only adopt environmental management systems (a form of process based regulation) but also ensure that their major suppliers also conform to a simplified version of the system. Alternatively, such a condition could be included in an industry wide self-regulation program, as is already the case under the Product Stewardship code of practice of the chemical industry's Responsible Care initiative.[21] Thus the use of supply chain pressure by large firms to improve the environmental performance of smaller firms may be enhanced by a complementary combination with process-based regulation or self-regulation.

Consistent with our design principles, the preferred role for government is to create the necessary preconditions for second or third parties to assume a greater share of the regulatory burden rather than engaging in direct intervention. This will also reduce the drain on scarce regulatory resources and provide greater ownership of environmental issues by industry and the wider community. In this way, government acts principally as a catalyst or facilitator. In particular, it can play a crucial role in enabling a coordinated and gradual escalation up an instrument pyramid (described in principle 3), filling any gaps that may exist in that pyramid and facilitating links between its different layers.

This role can be illustrated by example. Insurance has the potential to be a useful instrument in the middle layers of the pyramid. Insurers have the capacity to conduct site visits, engage independent auditors, vary the size of premiums, and if necessary, withdraw their services altogether. Insurers are, however, dependent on the availability of reliable information on which to make their initial and subsequent assessments of firm performance, but commonly have great difficulty obtaining relevant information over and beyond that required to be disclosed by their clients.[22] As a consequence, there is a necessary role for government (at the bottom layers of the pyramid) to ensure that this information is accessible, for example, through the provision of compulsory pollutant inventory reporting by industry. It may also be that that insurers lack the necessary muscle at the top of the pyramid to deal with unrepentant recalcitrants. In such circumstances, insurers may advise government regulators of a firm's transgression and invite the full force of the law to be applied (whether they choose instead simply to cancel the insurance policy may depend substantially on the competitiveness of the market). Thus we have a combination of third party and government regulation coordinated between the different layers of the pyramid to provide the opportunity for coordinated enforcement escalation.

Principle 5. Maximize opportunities for win/win outcomes

A major criticism of conventional regulation are the lack of incentives for firms to continuously improve their environmental performance (for example an emission standard of 100 ppm gives no rewards for companies to substantially exceed this level) and the failure to encourage firms to adopt pollution prevention measures over end-of-pipe solutions (the same standard can be met by putting scrubbers on the chimney rather than developing cleaner technology).

The opportunities for both continuous improvement and pollution prevention will be considerably enhanced to the extent that firms can achieve higher levels of environmental performance at the same time as increasing productivity and/or profits: the classic win/win scenario. A key challenge for policymakers, therefore, is to ensure that regulatory solutions optimise the opportunity for win/win outcomes and facilitate and reward enterprises for going 'beyond compliance', while also maintaining a statutory baseline and a ratcheting up of standards.

Will firms voluntarily go beyond compliance?

It is increasingly argued that it is in business's own self-interest to move *beyond compliance* with existing legislative requirements and adopt a 'pro-active' stance on the environment, voluntarily exceeding mandated minimum performance standards. According to its proponents, firms going down this path may (in addition to improving profitability) enhance their corporate image, position themselves to realize new environment-related market opportunities, generally improve efficiency and quality, foster a greater consumer acceptance of their company and products, and reduce potential legal liability. Moving beyond compliance also gives firms the incentive to develop new environmental technologies to which can be sold into the rapidly growing and lucrative global market for environmental goods and services.[23]

And yet, despite the apparent benefits which may flow from improved environmental performance, the large majority of enterprises in the large majority of jurisdictions have taken very few steps to take advantage of them or to position themselves as environmental leaders. Assuming that considerable win/win opportunities do indeed exist (that is, even if proponents of this position may overstate the benefits, their basic position is sound), why have the majority of enterprises adopted a position which is, on the face of it, irrational? The most plausible answers are an emphasis on short-term profits, and bounded rationality.

The former is probably the single largest impediment to improved environmental performance.[24] Crucially, most environmental investments will only pay-off in the medium to long term, while the upfront investment is primarily short term. Because corporations are judged by markets, investors and others principally focussing on short-term performance, if they cannot demonstrate tangible economic success in the here and now, there may be no long term to look forward to.

Bounded rationality may also explain business's failure to adopt pro-active environmental policies even when it is in their economic interests to do so. Bounded rationality assumes not that people are irrational (although they sometimes are) but rather that they have neither the knowledge nor the powers of calculation to allow them 'to achieve the high level of optimal adaptation of means to ends that is posited by economics'.[25] For example, it is widely accepted that there are substantial energy efficiency improvements which industry could profitably adopt. And yet, most firms fail to take advantage of them. Only where energy is a large component of business input costs, have substantial investments in energy efficiency been made. In the least energy efficient industries where energy costs are only a minor component of overall business costs, energy efficiencies have been almost entirely ignored. This is bounded rationality at work: management focuses on core business functions and ignores lesser costs, even though these costs could be reduced through environmentally beneficial behaviour.

The role of government

Based on this analysis, the market, unaided, cannot be relied upon to deliver win/win outcomes. That is, a number of opportunities which would yield such outcomes are not, under present conditions, being taken up. Arguably, there is a role for government intervention to increase the uptake within firms of existing economically rational environmental improvements: in effect, seeking to compensate for both the inadequacy of markets (unaided) and of business rationality in order to maximise both the public (environmental) and private (economic) benefits.

But what form should this intervention take? Of course, government could simply mandate improved levels of business environmental performance. However, because there is a coincidence between self-interest and environmental improvement, other less interventionist measures should have a high chance of success, rendering prescriptive forms of intervention unnecessary or even counterproductive (see principle 2 above). Accordingly, the most appropriate role for governmental regulation lies in nudging firms at the margin towards cleaner production, heightening their awareness of environmental issues, and encouraging the re-ordering of corporate priorities in order to reap the benefits of improved environmental performance.

One way of increasing the chances of win/win outcomes is through the provision of information (e.g., cleaner production demonstration projects, technical support, databases and clearinghouses). A related strategy would be to encourage full cost accounting, on the assumption (for which there is much support) that unless business knows the costs and benefits, in environmental terms, of its current practices, it is unlikely to change them. Such strategies may be particularly important in addressing the problem of bounded rationality. Not only can government provide information to industry, but other non-government sources of information can also be harnessed and, in some cases, may be more effective.

Sometimes, because of institutional inertia, even when firms are made aware of potential cost savings they still will not exploit win/win opportunities. In such cases information alone is not enough, but is a necessary prerequisite. Here, information strategies can be supplemented by other voluntary promotional schemes which attempt to elicit and formalise a commitment from management to cost-effective environmental improvement. Examples include government sponsored schemes such as Golden Carrots and Green Lights in the United States and the PRISMA project in the Netherlands.

Governments might also consider some form of financial inducements to 'nudge' firms in the right direction, so overcoming narrow short-termism and bounded rationality. For smaller firms which may not have the internal resources and expertise to identify and implement win/win outcomes, government may subsidise the cost of external consultants preparing an environmental audit and management plan which seeks to exploit profitable environmental improvements. Again, once firms become aware of how to achieve win/win outcomes, and can easily access the consulting expertise and internal systems necessary to achieve them, they are far more likely to take action. Smaller firms may also require some assistance to cover up front costs and to more easily access capital.

However, it makes sense to target any financial inducements at those firms which are genuinely achieving beyond compliance rather than those firms that merely intend to comply with minimum standards. One way of achieving this is via a two-track, parallel regulatory system that provides incentives to those firms committed to higher levels of environmental performance which go substantially beyond compliance—increased flexibility, autonomy and public relations benefits less demanding administrative requirements, reduced license fees, preferential purchasing, etc. The intention is to attract as many firms as possible to the 'green track', but to maintain the conventional track as a fall back mechanism. Under this scenario it is not necessary for government to know the level of win/win opportunities available to each firm. Ultimately, it is up to each firm to determine whether financial benefits of minimal compliance are out-weighed by the benefits of being a 'green track' firm with higher levels of environmental performance. Firms should be able to move between tracks, but if they are placed on green track first, then deliberately fail to meet expectations, they should be regulated more harshly than if they had started off on the conventional track.

Moving the goals posts: turning win/lose into win/win

It is inevitable that even the most progressive companies will eventually reach a point at which win/win is no longer a viable option, and where any further spending on environmental protection will directly threaten corporate profits. Specifically, there are many circumstances under which the economic benefits of investing in environmental protection are tenuous or non-existent, and where the costs to business of implementing environmental protection measures will not be offset by any resulting savings from improved economic performance.[26]

At this point, two strategies are available to government. The first is to recognise the tension between environment protection and corporate profit, and to design policy instruments and enforcement responses accordingly. Here we simply restate the importance of a pyramidal enforcement response such as we advocated at principle three above. Regulators start at the bottom of the pyramid assuming that business is willing to comply voluntarily. However, they also make provision for circumstances where this assumption will be disappointed, by being prepared to escalate up the enforcement pyramid to increasingly deterrence-orientated strategies. Critically, at the peak of the pyramid will be a deterrence-orientated approach that makes it no longer economically rational for firms to avoid their environmental responsibilities.

A second strategy is for government to push back the point at which win/win becomes win/lose.[27] Michael Porter suggests that countries that have the most rigorous environmental requirements often lead in exports of affected products.[28] While such markets may evolve in the absence of government intervention, their scope and success can be influenced by such action. For example, Germany has had perhaps the world's tightest regulations in stationary air pollution control, and German companies appear to hold a wide lead in patenting—and exporting—air pollution and other environmental technologies. Conversely, those who weaken their regulations will fall behind in environmental exports. Thus as the United Kingdom's environmental standards have lagged, so to has its 'ratio of exports to imports in environmental technology fallen from 8:1 to 1:1 over the past decade'.[29]

However, Porter is at pains to emphasize that not all standards will lead to desirable trade outcomes, and that we need regulations that aim at outcomes rather than methods (that is, performance based rather than technology based standards), that are flexible and cost effective and which encourage companies to advance beyond their existing control technology. It must also be acknowledged that Porter's views have been strongly challenged from a variety of sources[30] and that empirical support for his position is somewhat tenuous.[31]

We agree with Porter that there is much that governments can and should do to encourage firms to develop environmental technologies and to harness environmental services markets. However, we disagree that more stringent regulation is necessarily the only or indeed the best means of achieving this outcome. Rather, there are a variety of other, less intrusive policy options than regulation, utilising not just government, but also second and third parties, which could also serve to drive environmental technological innovation and serve to create or expand global opportunities and markets for environmental services. As we argued earlier, such less-interventionist solutions have considerable attractions in terms of costs, effectiveness and legitimacy. Accordingly, in our view, the Porter solution (since it comes at the peak of an instrumental pyramid) should be regarded as a last rather than a first resort.

Take for example, the issue of pollution from the chemical industry. While it would certainly be viable, following Porter, to mandate tough standards, it would also be possible to adopt a self-regulatory scheme, as is the case with Responsible Care (with a proviso that if the scheme was not demonstrably achieving certain performance outcomes within a given period, government would intervene more directly). Such a scheme might be coupled with external audit, and government might itself require disclosure of results, enabling commercial third parties and to a lesser extent consumers and public interest groups to bring pressure on those who were achieving poorest results. Besides being less interventionist than the Porter solution, co-regulation has additional advantages of providing greater flexibility, giving industry ownership of the solution, and of avoiding much of the culture of resistance that may accompany government regulation.

Instrument combinations

In this article we have highlighted the importance of utilising combinations of instruments and parties to compensate for the weakness of stand-alone environmental policies. It cannot be assumed, however, that all instrument combinations will automatically be complementary. Some instrument mixes may indeed be counterproductive, while the outcome of others may be largely determined by the specific contexts in which they are applied. Unfortunately, the practical task of identifying which particular combinations are complementary, which counterproductive, and which context specific, is an especially daunting one. Not only is there an extremely large number of potential instrument combinations, but the answers to the question 'which ones are complementary or otherwise, and why?' are themselves both complex and qualified. To engage in the encyclopaedic task of exploring the full implications of all instrument combinations would not only be impractical but would not, we suspect, make for riveting reading. Instead, we have chosen to provide a brief overview of potential instrument interactions with some selective examples in order to sensitise policymakers to the importance of selecting judicious policy mixes.†

Inherently complementary combinations

Certain combinations of instruments are inherently complementary. That is, their effectiveness and efficiency will be significantly enhanced by using them in combination, irrespective of the circumstances of the relevant environmental issue being addressed. As such, policy makers can be confident in choosing these combinations over others. An illustrative example can be drawn from the combination of voluntarism (in which individual firms without industry-wide coordination voluntarily seek to improve environmental performance) and command and control regulation.

Voluntarism will complement most forms of command and control regulation, particularly where levels of environmental performance 'beyond compliance' are desired. In the case of performance based command and control regulation, a minimum performance benchmark is established, with voluntary based measures encouraging firms to achieve additional improvements. The United States EPA's 33/50 program is a good example of this approach.[32] Under the 33/50 program firms are encouraged to reduce the levels of their toxic chemicals releases, often at substantial cost, on a purely voluntary basis. Existing command and control regulations that apply to toxic chemical releases remain in force, with the 33/50 program delivering additional benefits.

The combination of the two instruments means that participating firms go beyond the command and control baseline, but that non-participating firms must still comply with this baseline. If voluntarism were introduced alone, then there would be no guarantee that non-participating firms would not increase their levels of toxic chemical releases, thus free-riding on those committed to higher standards. The combination of voluntarism and performance based command and control (which defines environmental outcomes, but does prescribe particular solutions) in this instance has produced environmental improvements additional to that which could have been achieved if either were employed in isolation. It is important to note that, in contrast to beyond compliance activities, if voluntarism and performance based standards were targeting the *same* level of behaviour then at best they would be a duplicative combination, and at worst, counterproductive.

Voluntarism may also work well with process based command and control regulation (where firms are required to adopt internal decision making processes designed to enhance environmental performance, but not guarantee it), for example, where the adoption of environmental management systems such as ISO 14001 have been mandated.[33] Because process-based prescriptions tend to be qualitative in nature, and therefore more difficult to measure quantitatively than performance or technology based standards, their full potential is difficult to enforce externally unless the regulated firm is committed to the concept. Voluntary based measures which seek to change the attitude of managers and the corporate culture may serve to reinforce a commitment to process based standards.

In contrast, technology based command and control regulation (which prescribes particular technological solutions) is unlikely to produce complementary outcomes when used in combination with voluntary measures. This is because technology based standards are highly prescriptive—firms can either comply or not, resulting in little room for beyond compliance achievements. In effect, technology based standards restrict the way in which firms respond to an environmental imperative, in terms of the method of environmental improvement, whereas voluntary measures are in principle designed to provide additional regulatory flexibility.

Inherently counterproductive instrument combinations

Certain combinations of instruments are either inherently counterproductive or, at the very least, sub-optimal. That is, their efficiency and effectiveness is significantly diminished when they are employed in combination. The example of command and control regulation and economic instruments is illustrative. Most command and control instruments, specifically performance-based standards (performance standards define a firm's duty in terms of the problems it must solve or the goals it must achieve) and technology-based standards, seek to impose predetermined environmental outcomes on industry. That is, even if the standards are not uniform (in that different requirements apply to different sectors or indeed different firms) individuals firms are not free to make independent judgements as to their preferred method of environmental improvement (in the case of technology based standards) or their overall level of environmental performance (in the case of performance standards). Economic instruments, in contrast, seek to maximize the flexibility of firms in making such decisions—government influences the overall level of environmental performance by providing a price signal relative to the level of pollution or resource consumption, or by creating a purchasable right to pollute or consume resources.[34]

If a command and control instrument were to be superimposed on an economic instrument that targets the same behaviour, or vice versa, then to the extent that the command and control instrument limits the choice of firms in making individual decisions, the economic instrument would be compromised. That is, there will be a sub-optimal regulatory outcome. This is because economic instruments are designed to exploit differences in the marginal cost of abatement between firms. It makes economic sense for those firms which can reduce their levels of pollution most cheaply to carry a greater share of the abatement burden, and for those were it is most expensive, to carry a lesser share of the same burden. The result is that the net cost of reducing the overall level of pollution (or resource consumption) will be lessened, or, for a given level of expenditure, a greater level of pollution reduction will be achieved. By simultaneously applying a prescriptive command and control instrument, for example a performance standard which mandates levels of energy efficiency for firms in tandem with a broad based carbon tax, free market choices would be artificially restricted thus undermining the basic rationale of the economic instrument.

There is, however, an extenuating circumstance which may justify the sub-optimal outcome in regulatory efficiency resulting from the combination of broad based economic instruments with prescriptive command and control. Where pollutants have highly localised impacts, through for example differences in assimilative capacities or proximity to local communities, effectiveness and equity issues may override the efficiency considerations. Localised impacts can be contrasted with global pollutants such as ozone depleting substances, greenhouse gas emissions, and to a lesser extent, sulphur dioxide emissions. In the case of highly localized pollutants, such as the run-off of agricultural chemicals into local river systems, it may be necessary to impose minimum levels of performance on firms/individuals in highly sensitive regions, or indeed a variety of different levels tailored to local conditions, even if there was a more general economic instrument in place. Although this would reduce the overall efficiency of the economic instrument, through the restriction of free market choice, this loss of efficiency may be justified on the grounds of effectiveness or equity.

One way of avoiding potentially dysfunctional results that can arise when applying incompatible instruments simultaneously (and of expanding the operational possibilities of compatible combinations) is to sequence their introduction. That is, certain instruments would be held in reserve, only to be applied if and when other instruments demonstrably fail to meet predetermined performance benchmarks. One type of sequencing is when an entirely new instrument category is introduced where previous categories have failed. Another version is when only the enforcement component of a pre-existing instrument is invoked to supplement the shortcomings of another. Logically, and consistent with design principle 2, such sequencing would follow a progression of increasing levels of intervention. The benefit of this approach is that considerable utility can be derived from otherwise counterproductive instrument combinations, and in the process, the overall dependability of the policy mix can be improved.

Combinations where the outcome will be context-specific

In addition to inherently compatible and inherently incompatible combinations, there will be other instrument combinations where it is not possible to state in the abstract whether the outcome will be positive or negative. Rather, much will depend on the particular context in which the two instruments are combined. For example, this is the case with combinations of voluntarism and self-regulation. These two instrument categories overlap to a substantial extent, and indeed, the borderline between them is significantly blurred—the main distinction for our purposes being that self-regulation entails social control by an industry association, whereas voluntarism is based on the individual firm undertaking to do the right thing unilaterally, without any basis in coercion. There is no inherent reason why these two instrument categories should be used in combination with each other, but equally no compelling reason why they should not.

In light of this, it is important for policymakers to distinguish between different instruments combinations that are inherently antagonistic, and those instruments combinations which are dysfunctional essentially as a result of the contextual features surrounding their application. In many cases, the *latter* will arise because of the existence of competing policy goals (rather than any inherent incompatibility of the instrument combinations themselves). For example, in the case of biodiversity conservation in Australia, the introduction of policies to preserve biodiversity have historically been undermined by incentives for clearing native vegetation on private land. Also in Australia, the introduction of a voluntary agreements with industry to reduce greenhouse gas emissions are compromised by the existence of generous tax subsidies for the use of diesel fuel. Where such conflicts exist, a priority for policymakers will be the removal of such perverse incentives.

Multi-instrument combinations

So far we have confined our discussion to bipartite mixes. There is, of course, no reason why mixes should not be multipartite, and they commonly are. The benefit of our examination of bipartite mixes has been to identify complementary and counterproductive mixes, with the result that we know, in the case of multipartite mixes, what combinations to avoid, and which complementary combinations we might build upon. The possible permutations of multipartite mixes are very large indeed, and it is not practicable to examine such combinations here.

Conclusion

Our general conclusion is that not only is it desirable to use a broader range of policy instruments, but also to the match those instruments: with particular environmental problems; with the party or parties best capable of implementing them; and with other compatible instruments. That is, it is in using complementary *combinations* of instruments and actors that policymakers can build on the strengths of individual mechanisms, while compensating for their weaknesses. And it is with government actively facilitating second and third party involvement that their potential as quasi-regulators is most likely to be realized. Thus the crucial policy questions became: how, in what circumstances and in what combinations, can the main classes of policy instruments and actors be used to achieve optimal policy mixes?

We have argued that successful regulatory design depends crucially upon adhering to a number of *regulatory design principles* which have hitherto not featured prominently on the policy agenda. In particular, we counselled policymakers not only to prefer combinations of instruments to 'stand alone' instrument strategies, but stressed the importance of preferring the least interventionist measures *that will work*. We also introduced the heuristic device of a three dimensional pyramid, as a means of escalating regulatory responses, and consistent with the pursuit of pluralistic regulatory policy, argued the importance of harnessing resources *outside* the public sector. We further addressed the extent to which it is possible to design environmental policy in such a way as to encourage and facilitate industry in going 'beyond compliance' with existing regulatory requirements.

Finally, we argued that, as not all regulatory instrument combinations are equal, it is incumbent upon policymakers, in seeking to introduce a broader range of regulatory solutions, to carefully select the most productive instrument combinations. We recognize that not all will necessarily agree with the precise conclusions we have arrived at, either in terms of design principles, nor preferred instrument mixes. Nevertheless, our intention is, in the first instance, to move the debate forward, and in the longer term, assist policymakers to introduce various forms of 'smart regulation'.

Notes

* This article is an abridged version of the concluding chapter in *Smart Regulation: Designing Environmental Policy* (N. Gunningham & P. Grabosky, Oxford University Press, Oxford, UK, 1998).

† A much more detailed exposition of instrument combinations is provided in 'Regulatory Pluralism: Designing Policy Mixes for Environmental Protection' (N. Gunningham & D. Sinclair *Law & Policy*, forthcoming 1998).

1. OECD, *Environmental Data 1995: Compendium*, November 1995, OECD, Paris; World Resources Institute, *World Resources 1994–95: A Guide to the Global Environment* (1994), Oxford University Press, New York; and OECD, *The State of the Environment* (1991), OECD, Paris.
2. J. B. Opschoor and R. K. Turner (eds.), *Economic Incentives and Environmental Policies: Principles and Practice* (1994), Kluwer Academic Publishers, Dordrecht.
3. T. Swanson, 'Book Reviews: J. B. Opschoor & R. K. Turner (eds.) *Economic Incentives and Environmental Policies: Principles and Practice* (1994)' (1995) 4(1) *Review of European Community and Environmental Law (RECIEL)* 85.
4. M. K. Sparrow *Imposing Duties: Government's Changing Approach to Compliance* (1994) Praeger, Westport.

5. D. Vogel *National Styles of Regulation: Environmental Policy in Great Britain and the United States* (1986) Cornell University Press, New York.
6. R. Hahn, 'Towards a New Environmental Paradigm (1993) 102 *Yale Law Journal* 1719.
7. D. Osborne and E. Gaebler, *Reinventing Government* (1992), Addison Wesley, Reading.
8. J. A. Sigler and J. E .Murphy, *Interactive Corporate Compliance: An alternative to regulatory compulsion* (1989), Quorom Books, New York.
9. I Ayres and J Braithwaite, *Responsive Regulation* (1992) Oxford University Press, UK.
10. E. Meidinger, 'Look Who's Making the Rules': The roles of the Forest Stewardship Council and International Standards Organisation in Environmental Policy Making' (1996), a paper presented to Colloquium on Emerging Environmental Policy: Winners and Losers, Oregon State University, Corvellis, Oregon, September 23.
11. J .V. Rees, *Hostages of Each Other: The transformation of nuclear safety since Three Mile Island* (1994), University of Chicago Press, Chicago, US.
12. N. Gunningham and A. Cornwall, 'Legislating the Right to Know' (1994) 11 *Environmental and Planning Law Journal* 274–288.
13. J. T. Hamilton 'Pollution as News: Media and stockmarket reactions to the Capital Toxic Release Inventory Data' (1995) *Journal of Environmental Economics and Management* 98–103.
14. N. Gunningham and M. D. Young, 'Towards Optimal Environmental Policy: The Case of Biodiversity Conservation' (1997) 24 *Ecology Law Quarterly* 243–298.
15. N. Gunningham and M. D. Young, 'Towards Optimal Environmental Policy: The Case of Biodiversity Conservation' (1997) 24 *Ecology Law Quarterly* 243–298.
16. N. Gunningham, 'Environment, Self-Regulation, and the Chemical Industry: Assessing Responsible Care' (1995) 17(1) *Law and Policy* 58–109).
17. N. Gunningham and J. Rees, 'Industry Self-regulation' (1997) 4 (19) *Law and Policy.*
18. R. Mitchell, *International Oil Pollution at Sea: Environmental Policy and Treaty Compliance* (1994) MIT Press, Massachusetts.
19. Ibid., ch. 8.
20. J. T. Hamilton, 'Pollution as News: Media and stockmarket reactions to the Capital Toxic Release Inventory Data' (1995) *Journal of Environmental Economics and Management* 98–103.
21. N. Gunningham, 'Environment, Self-Regulation, and the Chemical Industry: Assessing Responsible Care' (1995) 17(1) *Law and Policy* 58–109.
22. P. Freeman and H. Kunreather, 'The Roles of Insurance and Well Specified Standards in Dealing With Environmental Risk' (1996) 17 *Risk Management and Decision Economics* 513–530.

23. N. A. Gunningham, Beyond Compliance: management of environmental risk in Boer, Fowler & Gunningham (eds.) *Environmental Outlook: law and policy*, ACEL, Federation Press, 1994 and references cited therein.
24. A. Rappaport and M. Flaherty, 'Multinational Corporation and the Environment' (1991), Centre for Environmental Management, Tufts University.
25. H. Simon, *Economics, Bounded Rationality and the Cognitive Revolution* (1992), Edward Elgar, UK, p. 3.
26. N. Walley and B. Whitehead, 'It's Not Easy Being Green' (May-June 1994) *Harvard Business Review* 46–52.
27. M. Jacobs, *The Green Economy* (1991), Pluto Press, London, UK, p 157.
28. M. Porter, 'America's Green Strategy' (1991) April, *Scientific American*, p. 168.
29. M. Porter, 'America's Green Strategy' (1991) April, *Scientific American*, p. 168.
30. N. Walley and B. Whitehouse, 'Its Not Easy Being Green' (May-June 1994) *Harvard Business Review* 46.
31. J. C. Robinson, 'The Impact of Environmental and Occupational Health Regulation on Productivity Growth in US Manufacturing' (1995) 12(2), *Yale Journal or Regulation* 388.
32. S. Aora and T. N. Cason, 'An Experiment in Voluntary Regulation: Participation in EPA's 33/50 Program' (1995) 28 (3) *Journal of Environmental Economics and Management* 271.
33. W. L. Thomas, 'Using ISO 14001 to comply with the Management System Requirements of US EPA's RMP Rule and the EU's Seveso II Directive' (1988), *European Environmental Law Review* 335.
34. T. Schelling, *The Strategy of Conflict*, Harvard University Press, Cambridge.

PART V
International Environmental Law

Sleeping with an Elephant: The American Influence on Canadian Environmental Regulation*

GEORGE HOBERG†

Abstract

This article analyzes the American influence on Canadian environmental regulation in order to show the international sources of domestic public policy, especially the manner in which Canadian policy development is influenced by the United States, and the specific dynamics of Canadian regulatory policy. The United States influences Canadian domestic public policy by the export of costs and the export of knowledge. An analysis of major developments in the areas of air pollution, water pollution, pesticides, toxic substance regulation, and environmental impact assessment demonstrates that American influence over Canadian environmental regulation is pervasive. The most frequent pattern is emulation, where value convergence combined with U.S. leadership leads to Canadian borrowing of U.S. policy innovations. This process can be either elite-driven or activist-driven, the latter being characterized by an enlarged scope of conflict, media exposure, and pressure campaigns on policymakers.

Policy studies have shown increasing interest in the external influences on domestic public policy, but one special kind of external dependence has been largely neglected: small states dependent on one far larger neighbouring state. This class of relationships includes Ireland with the United Kingdom; Austria, the Netherlands, Belgium, with West Germany; and the subject of this chapter, Canada with the United States.[1] The difficulties faced by these small states was perhaps best expressed by Pierre Trudeau (1969) during his first trip to Washington, as Prime Minister of Canada:

> Let me say that it should not be surprising if these policies in many instances either reflect or take into account the proximity of the United States. Living next to you is

like sleeping with an elephant. No matter how friendly and even-tempered the beast, one is affected by every twitch and grunt.

In fact, Canada has always been preoccupied with how it is affected by its giant neighbour to the south, from the push for Confederation in 1867 to the free trade debate of 1988. In the environmental sphere, Canadian perceptions of American influence have been dominated by the acid rain issue, a case in which the United States exports its pollution to Canada, breeding resentment among the Canadian public and tensions in bilateral relations. The focus on acid rain has tended to obscure a much broader pattern of American influence on Canadian environmental regulation that is frequently much more positive.

This chapter outlines that pattern of influence. In so doing, it hopes to contribute to our understanding of the international sources of domestic public policy (Gourevitch, 1978; Katzenstein, 1985), the particular manner in which Canadian policy development is influenced by the United States,[2] and the specific dynamics of Canadian regulatory policy (Ilgen, 1985; Schreker, 1984). The first section of the paper outlines a number of ways in which the United States influences Canadian domestic public policy. In the second section, several areas of environmental regulation are reviewed—air pollution, water pollution, pesticides, toxic substance regulation, and environmental impact assessment—to analyze the magnitude of U.S. influence on Canada. The conclusion addresses under what conditions different forms of U.S. influence operate, and by so doing, places these international influences in the context of the domestic determinants of Canadian regulatory policy.

Patterns of Influence

The number of ways that the U.S. influences Canadian domestic public policy can be grouped into two broad categories: the export of costs and the export of knowledge. Perhaps the most evident category is when U.S. policies or actions impose *externalities* on Canada, by threatening some aspect of Canadian welfare. In this case, American actions more or less directly create policy problems for Canada. Perhaps the most extreme examples of this come in the environment area. In the cases of acid rain and Great Lakes water quality, the U.S. literally exports its pollution to Canada, causing widespread environmental damage.[3] This phenomenon has been characterized as 'environmental dependence', in that Canada depends on U.S. actions to improve its environmental quality (Munton, 1980–1).

There are many examples of externalities outside the environmental area as well. A classic example is economic policy. The international nature of financial markets means that Canadian monetary policy is highly constrained by American monetary policy. When the U.S. deregulated various transportation sectors, economic pressures mounted for Canada to do the same (Stanbury, 1988).

Second, Canada is also profoundly affected by the *economic dominance* of the United States. In this case, the U.S. is not imposing costs by explicit policy actions or transboundary physical phenomena, but through dependencies created by the sheer magnitude of the American market. Depending on the situation, economies of scale, factor mobility, and price differentials can render Canada highly vulnerable to forces emanating from the south. Historically, much of Canadian economic policy has been focused on resisting the natural north-south pull of economic activity in North America (Aitken, 1967; Williams, 1986). The overwhelming American presence was also the rationale behind the creation of prominent state enterprises such as the Canadian Broadcasting Corporation, Air Canada, and the Canadian National Railways.

The economic influence of the U.S. goes beyond its market dominance, to include a significant degree of American ownership of Canadian business (Levitt, 1970). Moreover, the problems of economic dominance may be magnified by the Canada-U.S. Free Trade Agreement (FTA) of 1988.[4] Many Canadians, including environmentalists, were concerned that the FTA would jeopardize cherished Canadian programs (Dover, 1988; Shrybman, 1988). In the environmental area, we will see how American economic dominance has profound implications for Canadian regulation.

Aside from exporting costs, the other major channels of U.S. influence lie in the exportation of knowledge. The dominant pattern in this case is *emulation*, in which Canada uses U.S. policies as a model. In this case, Canada is not forced to act by harm created by American actions, but instead borrows U.S. policy innovations in areas where Canada thinks they may be appropriate. In other words, American influence is not through dominance but leadership by example. For instance, the system of oil market regulation used in the Canadian west was borrowed from the Texas Railroad Commission (Richards and Pratt, 1979, 54 ff.). This type of 'lesson-drawing' (Rose, forthcoming) can be negative as well, where Canada deliberately avoids particular policies because of the undesirable consequences it sees resulting from U.S. policy. Frequently, Canadian policymakers modify American-inspired programs to make then suitable for the Canadian context. A prominent example of this phenomenon is the Canadian decision to entrench a charter of rights in its constitution, but then allow it to be overriden by legislatures through the so-called 'notwithstanding clause'.[5]

Emulation usually occurs through one of two primary modes. The first is elite-driven, when officials or policy specialists evaluating policy alternatives are attracted to the American experience. The second is activist-driven, when political activists use the existence of an American program or standard to support their argument for policy change in Canada. In this case, activists try to 'shame' the government into acting, with the logic that 'if it is good enough for them, it is good enough for us'. Examples of both these types can be found throughout the environmental field.

The transmission of this knowledge can follow a number of routes. First, it can occur through American *media* dominance. Canadians are routinely exposed to U.S. media. When an issue of importance emerges in the U.S. it is often picked up by Canadian policy activists or the media itself, forcing the government to respond. As the discussion below will demonstrate, this is a pervasive phenomenon in the area of toxic substances regulation.

Another channel of knowledge diffusion is through *scientific* dominance, resulting from the Canadian dependence on the scientific research performed in the United States. In the area of regulatory science, for instance, the U.S. is the world leader in toxicology research, and when studies there reveal concerns about a particular chemical, Canadian policymakers may be forced to respond as well. While Canada's more limited scientific resources make it dependent on others for the production of this vital information, it also has the advantage of being something of a free-rider. Science dependence frequently combines with media spill-over, as policy entrepreneurs pick up news of the discovery of new hazards and press policymakers for action.

A final channel for knowledge diffusion is through *transnational policy communities* linking the two countries. In many cases, formal meetings are scheduled between government officials in the two countries to share information and discuss common concerns. There are strong bilateral organizational links among some regulatory advocates, such as environmental groups and unions. Policy analysts in think tanks may share ideas (Stanbury, 1988). Industry officials in two countries frequently interact, either because Canadian firms are subsidiaries of American parent companies or through participation in related trade organizations.

These two major categories of influence vary significantly according to the degree of Canadian dependence on the United States. In the case of externalities and economic dominance, for instance, Canada is highly vulnerable to forces emanating from the United States. In the case of emulation, however, the mechanism of influence is more subtle. The mouse is not forced to react because of what the elephant is doing, but chooses to do so because it likes what the elephant is doing.

Of course, the U.S. is not the only international actor to influence Canadian domestic policy. Trade with other nations, multilateral trade arrangements, other international agreements, and broader international policy communities can all affect Canadian domestic regulation. Moreover, Canada can emulate policies of other nations than the U.S. However, the dominance of the United States in Canada's international environment gives it a unique influence over Canadian domestic public policy.

Air Pollution

Acid Rain

Acid rain is a classic case of the U.S. exporting costs to Canada. While pollutants flow across the border in both directions, prevailing winds and the greater amount of U.S. emissions ensure that Canada is far more affected by American-generated acid rain than the vice versa. Estimates are that 50 per cent of the acid rain falling in Canada comes from American sources, whereas a much smaller fraction, between 10 and 15 per cent, of U.S. acid rain originates in Canada (Canadian House of Commons, 1984, p. 41). Thus, Canada's ability to address its own acid rain problem is severely constrained by the United States (Munton, 1980–1).

As a result of environmental dependence, Canada aggressively pursued a bilateral treaty with the United States. In 1982, the Canadian government proposed an agreement whereby both nations would reduce sulfur dioxide by 50 per cent. However, the Reagan administration, which at this time refused formally to admit that acid rain was a human-made phenomenon, adamantly rejected the proposal. For some time, Canadian officials continued to place priority on achieving a bilateral agreement.

Over time, Canada shifted its strategy to emphasizing unilateral reductions. This shift was partly a result of the failure of international negotiations, but it also reflected a learning process about the relative stringency of Canadian air pollution regulations. The two foremost proponents of this shift were the Parliamentary Subcommittee on Acid Rain and the Canadian Coalition on Acid Rain. While the Parliamentary Subcommittee had been pushing for unilateral Canadian cuts as early as 1981, subsequent events significantly increased the force of its argument. In its 1984 report, *Time Lost*, it made the following argument:

The first principle to be adhered to, in the Sub-Committee's opinion, is that of arguing one's case from a position of strength. One cannot go to the United States and demand that closely pollution controls be implemented when Canada's record is obviously deficient in a number of important areas (Canadian House of Commons, 1984, p. 41).

The subcommittee noted that the U.S. powerplants had installed over 100 scrubbers—an advanced method of sulfur dioxide control—whereas no scrubbers existed in Canada.

The subcommittee efforts were supported by the most prominent Canadian environmental group on the issue, the Canadian Coalition on Acid Rain. Created in 1981, the group spent much of its resources in Washington, pushing Congress for action on acid rain. In 1983, when it realized it was adding little to the substantial lobbying efforts of the National Clean Air Coalition, the American lobby group, it returned to Canada to press its own government for unilateral action. The Coalition was a forceful advocate of using unilateral cuts to increase the pressure on the U.S. to cut its own emissions. In testimony before the subcommittee, it claimed: 'It is a peculiar logic in Canada to say to the United States that if they do not stop sending their pollution to us, we are just going to darn well continue to pollute ourselves' (Quoted in ibid., p. 43).

The changing perception of the desirability of unilateral action was greatly affected by American actions as well. In attempts to deflect pressures for action, American opponents of acid rain controls took some pleasure in pointing out the weakness of some of Canada's standards. Indeed, Adele Hurley of the Canadian Coalition on Acid Rain claims that 'the person most responsible for cleaning up Canada was John Dingell', the powerful Chair of the House Energy and Commerce Committee, a representative from Detroit, and persistent opponent of acid rain legislation. While this statement no doubt is somewhat hyperbolic, Dingell did play an important role in escalating the pressure on Canada to put its own house in order. In 1983, the somewhat naïve Ontario Environment Minister Keith Norton chose to pick a fight with Dingell about acid rain. Dingell had his army of aggressive staff members dig up information on the Canadian air pollution program, and shot back with an embarrassing list of questions exposing shortcomings in Canada's efforts to control its own sulfur dioxide emissions (Norton, 1983; Dingell, 1983).[6] These attacks were effective, they put Canadian policymakers on the defensive, and increased domestic pressure for unilateral cuts in Canada (Hurley and Perley, 1983).

In March, 1985, Prime Minister Brian Mulroney and a number of provincial premiers announced that Canada would reduce its emissions of sulfur dioxide by 50 per cent by 1994. While blaming the U.S. for blocking progress towards a bilateral accord, Mulroney also stated:

> [W]e did not go to any bargaining table on acid rain with clean hands. In point of fact we are behind the Americans in emission control in many significant areas. I believe you clean up your own act first before you can expect major concessions from someone with whom you are bargaining. The Government of Canada will be assuming its own responsibilities so that we can go to the table with clean hands (Keating, 1985).

Thus, the environmental dependence created by the U.S. export of acid rain forced Canadians to push Americans for policy reform. Through the resulting negotiations, Canada learned that some of its air pollution standards were in fact weaker than their American counterparts, jeopardizing its moral high ground in the negotiations. As a result, Canada was forced to tighten them in their continuing efforts to convince Americans to reduce their transborder emissions. While it had far more to do with domestic American politics, the U.S. Congress finally amended the Clean Air Act in Fall, 1990 to reduce annual sulfur dioxide emissions by approximately 10 million tons.

Automobile Emissions

In the case of emissions from automobiles, Canada has consistently followed American regulatory developments, with a lag in many cases of between five and 10 years. The U.S. has led the world in the regulation of automobile emissions, the first major policy enacted with the 1970 Clean Air Act, which required that cars reduce emissions by 90 per cent by 1975 (Jones, 1975; Krier and Ursin, 1977).[7] In 1973, Canada made an explicit decision not to follow the U.S. lead in reducing emissions by that amount, arguing that the less severe air pollution problems in Canadian urban areas did not warrant the additional expense (Duncan, 1973).

This divergence is somewhat surprising because of the nature of the automobile market in North America. With the 1965 Auto Pact between the two countries, the North American automobile market is highly integrated, with the U.S. the dominant player because of its market size (Beigie, 1972). The U.S. accounts for about 90 per cent of the market for cars produced in North America. Approximately 80 per cent of the cars manufactured in Canada are exported to the United States, while 75 per cent of the vehicles sold in Canada are manufactured in the United States (Canadian House of Commons, 1984, p. 16).

While the integrated market would seem to force convergence upon Canada, the particular nature of emission control technology allowed Canada the option to depart from U.S. standards. Rather than being integrated into the design of the engine, emissions were controlled through the simple addition of a catalytic converter, which could be added or left off with little cost or disruption of the production process. Ironically, cars were being made in Canada for sale in the U.S. that met the more rigorous U.S. standards, while cars made in the U.S. for sale in Canada were made to meet the more lax standards there.

Over time, however, pressure increased on Canada to adopt American standards. In 1985, the government finally adopted U.S. standards, to be implemented with the 1988 model year, seven years after the U.S. had implemented their standards (*Canada Gazette*, Part I, August 3, 1985, 4745–4754). This policy change was for the most part determined by American influences as well, as part of the larger acid rain story. Nitrogen oxides (NO_x) are one of the principle precursors to acid rain, and automobiles are the major source of nitrogen oxides. The fact that Canada's tailpipe standard for NO_x was three times less stringent than the American became, in the words of the Parliamentary Subcommittee on Acid Rain, an 'acute political embarrassment' and 'political liability' for Canadian officials (Canadian House of Commons, 1984, pp. 12, 42). This policy change was announced at the same time that Mulroney announced Canada's 50 per cent unilateral cut in sulfur dioxide emissions (Sallot, 1985).

A second major phase on Canadian regulation of automobile emissions is now in progress. Canada appears to be emulating the U.S. rather than reacting to a negative externality. The 1990 U.S. Clean Air Act Amendments require the adoption of a new stage of stringent air quality standards. While its air quality problems are still not as severe, Canada's new emphasis on adopting the 'best available control technology economically achievable' (BACTEA) has pushed it towards this new stage of U.S. standards.[8]

A federal 'plan' announced in 1989 adopted the California standards as proposed objectives (Transport Canada and Environment Canada, 1989). In the same year, the intergovernmental body responsible for environmental affairs, the Canadian Council of Ministers of the Environment (CCME), proposed to adopt California standards for the 1994 model year.[9] This move was strongly influenced by the Ontario Minister of the

Environment, Jim Bradley, who was inspired by a visit with officials from the coalition of northeastern states (Northeast States for Coordinated Air Use Management, or NESCAUM), who were preparing to implement more stringent standards even if the Clean Air Act Amendments had failed. Bradley apparently announced that Ontario was prepared to adopt the standards on its own, and was able to extract commitments from other provinces and the federal government (personal interviews).

This latest round of revisions reflects a process of elite-driven emulation. American leadership in automobile emission regulation, combined with Canada's new emphasis on choosing the best available technology, has produced convergence in this area.

U.S. economic dominance is usually considered a significant threat to Canadian interests, but the case of auto emissions is an interesting exception. The large U.S. market and integrated North American automobile market has produced a positive environmental externality for Canada. Until 1985, the flexibility of emission control technology permitted Canada to resist adopting American standards. But when Canada was prepared to move ahead in reducing emissions, American market dominance allowed easy adoption of the new standards that had already proven viable in the U.S. market.

These air pollution cases show several patterns of influence in operation. In the case of recent automobile emission standards, elite emulation seems to be the principal dynamic at work. In the 1985 decisions to reduce sulfur dioxide by 50 per cent and move to U.S. automobile standards, environmental dependence created powerful constraints on Canadian environmental officials. In the process of seeking a solution to that problem, Canadians learned that their own standards were lax in some areas, and dramatic action was taken so that Canada could pursue bilateral talks with 'clean hands'. In the case of auto emission standards, 'clean hands' meant emulating U.S. standards, and U.S. market dominance facilitated rather than deterred Canadian environmental initiatives.

Water Pollution

The case of water pollution is similar to air pollution in that there is a significant amount of environmental dependence as well as emulation. Pollution of the Great Lakes is an instance of the U.S. producing physical externalities that affect the Canadian environment, and thus constrain the ability of Canada to protect its own environment. As with acid rain, by virtue of its larger population and industrial production, the U.S.

contributes far more pollution to the shared ecosystem than Canada. Unlike the acid rain case, however, after a frustrating period of American reluctance, the two countries agreed in 1972 to a novel bilateral agreement to control Great Lakes pollution under the auspices of the International Joint Commission (Munton, 1980; 1980–1). Canada surrendered some of its policy sovereignty to an international body, in exchange for anticipated policy benefits as well as the commitment of the U.S. to do the same.

The Great Lakes Water Quality Agreement remains a monument to international collaboration on the environment. Bilateral collaboration among regulators and scientists has been substantial over several decades. Most recently, two major reports were issued resulting from extensive collaboration between national scientific bodies and even prominent 'think tanks' (U.S. National Research Council, 1985; Conservation Foundation and Institute for Research on Public Policy, 1990). While substantial environmental problems persist, the clean-up efforts have been successful in reducing many pollutants.

While Great Lakes pollution is a case of environmental dependence leading to successful bilateral cooperation, Ontario's recent reforms in its water pollution control policies are a classic case of elite-driven emulation. As one of several fundamental environmental initiatives by Ontario's recent Liberal government, Ontario issued a 1986 white paper proposing a new regulatory framework for the control of toxic water pollution labelled the 'Municipal-Industrial Strategy for Abatement', or MISA. The program is based on a strategy of requiring 'each direct discharger to meet standards attainable by the best available pollution abatement technology' (Ontario Ministry of the Environment, 1986, p. i). The report explicitly states that the new program was modelled on the U.S. approach:

> This approach was first spelled out in the United States as part of the Federal Water Pollution Control Act Amendments of 1972 and the Clean Water Act of 1977. Ontario will be basing its approach on the work of the United States Environmental Protection Agency (EPA), which has carried out extensive technical development of effluent limits based on technology (ibid., p. 31).

In other words, not only is the new regulatory approach modelled after the U.S., but Ontario is also intending to rely extensively on the technology-based standards in place in the United States. After receiving some criticism from industry for relying too much on an approach strongly opposed by U.S. industry, the government committed itself to carefully considering whether the adoption of U.S. standards would be 'most effective and practical for Ontario's unique conditions' (Ontario Ministry of the Environment, 1987, p. 7).

The inspiration for the adoption of the American model came from an Ontario Ministry official who was charged with developing a proposed strategy. The official, frustrated with Ontario's approach at that time, had visited the nearby EPA Region V office in Chicago, and was impressed with the comprehensiveness and stringency of the American approach and decided to propose it for Ontario (personal interview). Thus, MISA is a strong case of elite-driven emulation.

Pesticides

Pesticides are another case where Canadian regulation is strongly influenced by the United States. In this case, extensive scientific and media dominance produces a large degree of emulation, reinforced by economic dominance. Pesticide regulation requires a great deal of expensive scientific information, much of the which is generated in the United States. When new evidence of health risks from pesticides reaches the American media the news almost inevitably spills over into Canada, forcing regulators there to respond as well (Ilgen, 1985, p. 581). The much larger American markets, both for pesticides and agricultural products, also have important ramifications for Canadian regulation.

Canadian regulators are forced to rely on American regulators because of their relatively limited administrative capacities. Both countries are responsible for regulating a similar number of pesticide chemicals: there are 515 active ingredients in Canada, and approximately 600 in the U.S. But Canada's regulatory staff consists of about 70 people, whereas the U.S. staff is closer to 722. As one measure of resource levels, these figures mean that Canada has 0.1 regulators per active ingredient, while the U.S. has 1.2.

Partly because of its large size, but also because of its relatively rigorous regulatory requirements, the U.S. has taken a world leadership role in producing toxicology data (Brickman, Jasanoff, Ilgen, 1985, ch. 6). The smaller Canadian scientific community simply cannot match this, and is thus forced to rely on U.S. manufacturers, private laboratories, and government agencies for much essential information. Canadian reliance on American data has its costs and benefits. Canada realized how vulnerable it was to the U.S. when, in the late 1970s, the largest U.S. toxicology lab, Industrial Bio-test Laboratories (IBT), was discovered to have been routinely falsifying its reports. This scandal rendered much of the knowledge base of pesticide regulatory decisions in both countries invalid

(Castrilli and Vigod, 1987). On the plus side, Canada can essentially 'free ride' on U.S. data generation. In this way, Canada's more limited administrative capacity is less of a handicap than it would be otherwise.

Reevaluating Existing Chemicals

Pesticide regulation can be divided into three areas: reevaluating existing pesticides, licensing new pesticides, and establishing residue limits for pesticides in food. It is in the first of these that the American influence is probably felt the most strongly. One of the most challenging tasks of pesticide regulation is reevaluating pesticides that have been on the market for years, but were registered according to obsolete scientific methods and criteria. The greater analytical capacity of the U.S. means that in many cases Canada simply finds itself responding to American actions.

In most of the ten high-profile pesticide controversies since 1970, the two countries have taken similar actions. There is convergence on eight outcomes; the U.S. has gone further on one and Canada has gone further on one.[10] In terms of timing, the U.S. initiated action in seven cases, with Canada responding. In one case the timing was nearly identical (dinoseb), and in two cases Canada took action before the U.S. (captan and alachlor). But even in these two cases where Canada initiated action first, American influence was apparent. Both cases was so-called 'IBT chemicals', where previous studies were determined to be invalid because of the incompetence and corruption at the American laboratory. Replacement studies issued in the early 1980s raised concerns over the carcinogenicity of the substances. Canada responded quickly to the new information, but the studies emerged at the time when the Reagan administration's EPA was hostile to any new regulation (Hoberg, 1990a).

Perhaps the most extreme examples of the American influence on Canadian pesticide regulation were the cases of ethylene dibromide, better known by its acronym EDB, and daminozide, better known by its trade name Alar. In both cases, EDB in 1983–4 and Alar in 1989, environmental group pressure and media exposure led to a sense of national crisis in the U.S. In the EDB case, amidst headlines about 'killer muffin mixes', millions of dollars of grain-based merchandise were taken off the shelves and destroyed because they were found to contain trace quantities of EDB (Krimsky and Plough, 1988, ch. 2). In the Alar case, amidst a campaign by 'Mothers and Others for Pesticide Limits' organized by the Natural Resources Defense Council and led by actress Meryl Streep, dozens of school systems, including New York, Los Angeles, and Chicago, stopped distributing apple products in response to concerns about contamination by an Alar-related chemicals. After some reluctance, EDB was banned in the U.S. in several stages. In the case of Alar, market pressures and the threat of EPA action forced the manufacturer voluntarily to withdraw the product.

Both these media extravanganzas spilled over into Canada. The media reported the stories with a Canadian angle. Environmentalists, consumer activists, and opposition critics in Parliament demanded swift action from the government. In the case of EDB, they achieved a prompt response when the Canadian government banned the product four months after EPA initiated its ban. In the case of Alar, the Canadian government was more resistant. It disagreed with EPA's scientific assessment, and announced that it would wait for further results before deciding to ban the product (Health Protection Branch, 1989). Nonetheless, the Canadian subsidiary of the U.S. manufacturer announced that it was pulling the product off the market, one week after its parent company in the U.S. did so. At the request of the manufacturer, Canada cancelled its registration.

The EDB case was a clear instance of media dominance feeding activist-driven emulation. In the Alar case, the same forces were at work, but they were augmented by American market dominance. The Canadian supplier was responding both to pressures from Canadian apple growers preoccupied with the sensitivities of the American consumers who provided much of their market, despite the Canadian government's sympathies to its scientific argument. Here again, U.S. market dominance worked to the benefits of Canadian environmentalists.

The importance of American forces for convergence are also demonstrated by their absence in the two major cases of divergence. Canadian regulatory actions receive little media attention in the U.S., and American regulation is not affected by the same sorts of market pressures when Canada bans a product. In the case of alachlor, Canada banned the product, but the U.S. did not. The Canadian decision received only minor attention in the technical press in the U.S., and the American decision proceeded with little reference to the Canadian action. With the Canadian market accounting for only 3 per cent of alachlor use, the Canadian decision hardly affected the production logic of the manufacturer (Hoberg, 1990b).

In the case of dinoseb, the U.S. banned the product but Canada did not. Perhaps because of the different group at risk—that is, workers are the group most affected, residues on food are not an issue—dinoseb never became a major media issue in the U.S. There was thus no media spillover in Canada.[11] While the U.S. decision led to a reevaluation by Canada of dinoseb's regulatory status, that process was unaffected by public pressures as in the case of EDB and Alar. Thus, Canadian regulators had the freedom to choose a different balance of risks and benefits than their American counterparts (Pesticides Directorate, 1990).

Another measure of U.S. influence can be gleaned from the documents that Agriculture Canada issues to the public. In a survey of 27 documents issued between 1987 and August 1990, the actions of U.S. regulators were given prominent mention in 16.[12] In a number of cases, actions by the U.S. are given as the pretext for regulatory action in Canada. For instance, the opening of the announcement of one regulatory action reads as follows: 'The United States Environmental Protection Agency recently announced adoption of a regulatory position on tributyltins used as antifoulants for ship hulls'. After describing the U.S. action, the document then proceeded to describe the Canadian action:

> In view of the international movement of shipping traffic, Canada is also adopting an approach similar to that of the United States . . . Tributyltin based antifouling paints that meet the American criteria (see above) will be accepted for registration (Pesticides Directorate, 1989).

This case is an example of elite-driven emulation. The Canadian government does have its own list of priority chemicals for reevaluation, but their position in the queue is frequently altered by U.S. actions (personal interviews). These actions may be highly public, as in the cases of Alar and EDB, or much more quiet, as in the case of tributyltin.

During the 1980s, the U.S. developed a sophisticated process for the reevaluation of existing chemicals. The 1988 amendments to the Federal Insecticide, Fungicide, and Rodenticide Act accelerated this process and augmented its funding. The statute requires that all active ingredients be evaluated by 1998, and increased annual funding by $250 million (US).

A recent policy review of Canadian pesticide regulation explicitly recommends increasing the Canadian reliance on the U.S. process of reevaluation. The review team proposed the following process:

> The Bureau will develop a list of active ingredients that are registered in Canada but not in the U.S. The Bureau will then establish an appropriate reevaluation mechanism for those active ingredients, through appropriate consultation with stakeholders. The Bureau will attempt to benefit, as much as possible, from the current EPA reevaluation exercise for all active ingredients registered in both countries . . . The Bureau will review the U.S. decision on the regulatory status of the products, in light of the Canadian experience and within the context of Canadian circumstances (Pesticide Registration Review, 1990, pp. 28–9).

Thus, while Canada will not blindly adopt U.S. regulations, it will rely extensively on U.S. data generation and analysis. Therefore, even without the public exposure in cases like Alar and EDB, the Canadian regulatory agenda will be strongly influenced by the American regulatory agenda. In this case, the American influence occurs through a combination of scientific dominance and elite-driven emulation.

Licensing New Pesticides

In the case of approving new pesticides for use on the market, U.S. economic dominance is perhaps the most important channel of American influence. In fact, the Canadian agricultural sector is somewhat beholden to the activities of pesticide manufacturers and regulators in the United States. Because of its large market size, pesticide manufacturers seeking approval of a new product typically apply for registration in the United States first. If the product receives approval there, the large market allows relatively rapid recovery of the costs involved, including the often formidable costs of research, development, and regulatory review.

Only after getting approval in the U.S. do manufacturers then seek approval in smaller countries such as Canada. As a result, Canada is almost always 'following' the U.S. in the registration of new pesticides. Canada does not, however, simply adopt U.S. decisions. While much of the test data required is the same in both countries, Canada at least requires additional tests of the product's behaviour under Canadian field conditions (Peat Marwick Stevenson & Kellog, 1990). This situation places several important constraints on Canadian regulators. First, the more 'independent' they choose to be from the U.S. the more they drive up the costs of registering the product in Canada, which can discourage some manufacturers from applying. Second, growers place pressure on regulators to approve products in use in the U.S. so they do not suffer a competitive disadvantage (e.g., Pesticides Directorate, 1987).

The environmental consequences of this lag in new pesticide registrations depends on the environmental risks of the pesticides in question. If it is a question of a new, hazardous pesticide being used where none was before, then the Canadian environment might actually gain from this lag, despite the loss in income to farmers. However, if the new pesticide is in fact replacing a more dangerous alternative, then this lag may have significant negative environmental consequences. Canadian regulators have stated that the lack of effective alternatives—registered for use in the U.S., but not in Canada—frequently restricts their ability to phase out the use of more hazardous chemicals.[13] In this case, American market dominance has negative environmental consequences for Canada.

Residue Limits in Foods

Despite the various types of American pressures on Canadian pesticide regulation, Canada still has substantial discretion in some areas. This fact is perhaps best illustrated by comparing tolerances in the two countries, the limits that each country imposes on pesticide residues in food. If one compares the cases in which both countries have tolerances for a particular chemical in a particular food, for example Alar on apples, there is some convergence, but Canadian regulations are more stringent than U.S. regulations in a substantial number of cases. Of the 775 comparable cases, Canadian and U.S. tolerances are equivalent in 465, or 60 per cent of the cases. Canadian tolerances are more stringent in 298, or 38.5 per cent of the cases, while American tolerances are more stringent in only 12, or 1.5 per cent of the cases.

This divergence is somewhat surprising, given the large amount of trade in agricultural products between the two countries, and the relative strength of international organizations in the area of food safety (Salter, 1988; Frawley, 1987). The divergence results from methodological differences in the way the two countries establish tolerances. How can this divergence persist with such strong pressures for harmonization? There is no evidence that these disparities in tolerance cause any trade problems between the two countries, because the overwhelming majority of residues fall well below the limits in both countries. Thus, Canadian farmers do not suffer any real economic disadvantage from the more stringent tolerances, and thus don't pressure their government for relaxation to the U.S. level.[14]

This review of pesticide regulation demonstrates that Canadian pesticide regulation is strongly influenced by the United States. The much larger scientific and administrative capacity in the U.S. makes reliance on regulatory activities there inevitable. Canada's scientific dependence on the U.S, as well as elite emulation, have led to a significant amount of convergence. In several notable cases, media dominance has also led to activist-driven emulation. In what is no doubt the most extreme example, Meryl Streep not only set the U.S. regulatory agenda, but Canada's as well.

U.S. market dominance—in terms of demand for both agricultural products and pesticides—also plays a prominent role in pesticide regulation. Occasionally this has worked to the advantage of environmentalists, when bans in the U.S. lead to the withdrawal of products from the

Canadian market without Canadian regulators lifting a finger. In cases where the smaller Canadian market cannot support the production of more environmentally benign pesticides, U.S. market dominance may harm environmental interests. Canadian regulators still retain substantial discretion, as the cases of divergence on product regulation and food tolerances suggest. Nonetheless, in the case of pesticide regulation, American influence is indeed extensive.

Toxic Substances Regulation

The area of toxic substances regulation is replete with examples of American influence on Canadian regulation, both in terms of activities involving particular chemicals and the overall framework for toxic chemical regulation. As in the case of pesticides, much of the influence is channelled through scientific and media dominance, producing either elite- or activist-driven emulation.

Asbestos is a case with an interesting twist. Canada is the world's second largest producer of asbestos (behind the Soviet Union), and the United States is a world leader in asbestos regulation. Occupational standards for asbestos are more stringent in the U.S. than in Canada, and the EPA banned asbestos products in 1988. In this case, stringent American environmental regulation imposed severe economic costs on Canada. Canadian industry, the Province of Quebec, and the federal government have all denounced the EPA decision as unwarranted scientifically and politically motivated, and have joined in a lawsuit to overturn the EPA decision. In this case, Canada has failed to emulate the U.S. because of its economic interest in continued asbestos use (Hein, 1990).

In the case of formaldehyde-based foam insulation, Canada acted quickly to ban the material in late 1980 after an American study linked the substance to cancer in laboratory animals (Tataryn, 1983). In this case, Canada acted before the U.S. The U.S. Consumer Product Safety Commission also banned the product, but was overturned in federal court in a highly controversial decision (Weiner, 1986). While the timing of the two bans means the Canadian decision was not emulation, it was clearly based on scientific knowledge generated in the U.S.

The case of radon in homes is an example of aggressive Canadian resistance to pressures for emulation of American actions. Based on the results of an extensive national survey, the U.S. announced a 'national health advisory' in 1988, recommending that all homeowners test their homes for radon. The U.S. announcement was covered in the Canadian press, and it was revealed that American guidelines for homeowners taking action were five times more stringent than Canadian ones. Questions were raised in Parliament, and the responsible minister responded that he would take the issue under advisement. Canadian health officials strongly disputed American assessments of the radon hazard, and sought to deflect the issue. Activists failed to take up the issue, and it withered away without any policy change in Canada. This case shows that without activists pushing for emulation, reluctant officials can resist policy change with relative ease (Harrison and Hoberg, 1991).

Beyond these examples of specific chemical controversies, the Canadian regulatory framework for controlling toxic substances has also been strongly influenced by the United States. The only major federal statutory initiative during the 1980s in Canada was the Canadian Environmental Protection Act (CEPA), passed in 1988. As in the case of Ontario's MISA, the design of CEPA was strongly influenced by the American model, in this case the Toxic Substances Control Act and Clean Water Act. The cornerstone of CEPA is the Priority Substances List, a list of existing chemicals that are given priority for review and possible regulation. Background documents suggest this approach was strongly influenced by the U.S. Priority Pollutants list established in 1976 as a result of a settlement agreement between environmentalists and EPA (Canadian Environmental Advisory Council, 1987, pp. 70–1; 1988, p. 3).

An even more prominent example of borrowing from the EPA is CEPA's 'domestic substances list', a list of all chemicals used in the country in significant quantity. The consultative report that proposed CEPA recommended that this list be based initially on the pre-existing inventory developed by EPA under TSCA:

> A practical approach to the creation of the inventory is to adopt, as a starting point, an existing list of substances (the inventory developed under the U.S. Toxic Substances Control Act) and to allow a write-in system for the addition of substances found in Canadian commerce and not covered in the initial list (Environment Canada and Health and Welfare Canada, 1986, p. 9).

As in the case of pesticides, the much greater scientific and administrative capacity of the United States provides a resource for Canadian regulators.

Environmental Impact Assessment

Environmental impact assessment (EIA) is a classic case of partial emulation by Canada. The U.S. National Environmental Policy Act, enacted in

1970, is renowned throughout the developed world for its rigorous requirements for environmental impact statements and the intense legalism which has accompanied its implementation. In explaining the origins of its own EIA policy, Environment Canada cites NEPA as its inspiration:

> A critical breakthrough for EIA occurred when American President Richard Nixon signed in to law the National Environmental Policy Act (1970)—or as it is commonly called NEPA. With NEPA began experimentation, controversy, and increasing acceptance of EIA as a decision-making tool. In Canada, a small but growing number of officials, individuals in the business community, and citizens' groups began to see its potential (Couch, 1988, p. 5).

In late 1973, the federal cabinet established the Environmental Assessment and Review Process (EARP), and in 1975 Ontario enacted the first EIA statute in Canada, the Environmental Assessment Act.

Although attracted to the NEPA model of environmental impact assessment, Canadian governments have consistently rejected the accompanying legalism. The federal government, for instance, has historically opposed placing EIA requirements into a statute, because they thought it would undermine the process's flexibility (Fenge and Smith, 1986, p. 601). This coveted flexibility led to hostility to judical review so characteristic of the U.S. process. 'Ottawa simply recoiled from the spectre of additional bureaucratic paralysis through litigation' (Rees, 1980, p. 366).

As a result of a combination of recent events, federal officials may be losing this cherished autonomy. While Canadian policymakers remain hostile to American legalism, environmental groups in Canada are much more attracted to it (Gertler, Muldoon, Valiente, 1990). In two recent cases, at the request of environmental groups Canadian courts have intervened to block the construction of dams because the federal government did not follow its own cabinet guidelines on environmental impact assessment. These cases are significant because they presage an increased judicialization of the Canadian regulatory process (Lucas, 1989). As a result of the uncertainty generated by these cases, and strong public pressures for more rigorous environmental assessments, the federal government tabled legislation in June 1990 to incorporate EIA into a statute.

Environmental impact assessment is thus an example of partial emulation. Canada wanted to borrow U.S. policy without the process, which was viewed as inconsistent with parliamentary tradition. While there are signs of a creeping legalism in Canadian environmental policy, it is premature to predict its fate.

Conclusion

These case studies demonstrate that American influence over Canadian environmental, health and safety regulation is pervasive. While this influence has been negative in the case of acid rain and Great Lakes pollution, what is striking is the number of positive examples. Even American economic dominance, which Canadians have been struggling to cope with for over a century, occasionally has positive environmental benefits as the air pollution and pesticides case have shown.

The cases provide illustrations for each of the pathways of influence outlined in the first section. The U.S. has exported costs, making Canada dependent on the United States. Aside from the special case of physical externalities, dependencies arise when policy involves regulating commodities in international trade, be they automobiles, chemicals, or food. Canada is highly vulnerable to U.S. policies and action when markets are integrated and economies of scale exist. For instance, in the case of automobile emissions, the highly integrated market for cars and scale economies in the production process significantly reduced the cost to Canada of following the U.S. lead on tailpipe controls. In the case of pesticides and toxic substances, economies of scale in both the generation and interpretation of data, in combination with integrated markets in chemicals and food, make Canada highly vulnerable to the decisions of both U.S. manufacturers and regulators.

American influence on Canadian environmental regulation goes beyond situations of dependence. Perhaps the most pervasive dynamic behind U.S. influence is emulation. In this case, Canada's sovereignty is not as much at stake; instead, Canada is attracted to the American experience and chooses to emulate it in whole or in part. Emulation results from the transmission of knowledge, not the imposition of costs.

Canadian regulators do not adopt the American regulatory system lock, stock, and barrel. Despite the wealth of examples of policy convergence provided here, there is still a considerable amount of divergence on environmental policy between the two nations. The relevant question is then under what conditions Canada chooses to emulate the United States. Rose (forthcoming) describes 'contingencies of lesson-drawing'. In particular, he emphasizes the importance of institutional and value compatibility. The institutional differences between Canada and the U.S. have constrained emulation in some environmental impact assessment cases. Because of different institutional traditions, Canada wanted impact assessment without the institutional 'pathologies' of the U.S. NEPA. In fact, this desire to avoid 'Americanizing' Canadian regulatory processes is pervasive in Canada. At least until recently, Canada seemed relatively successful at adopting the U.S. policy without the institutional processes.

Perhaps the single most important force behind Canadian emulation is value consensus between the two nations. According to Rose, the greater the value consensus among nations, the greater the likelihood of emulation. Both nations place a high priority on environmental protection. Especially in the current climate of the second wave of environmentalism, the trajectory of policy in both countries is toward more rather than less regulation. In part because the environmental movement took greater hold earlier in the U.S., and in part because its greater population and industrial activity have created more severe environmental threats, the U.S. had tended to be ahead of Canada in programs for environmental protection. As Canada attempts to improve its environmental record, there is a natural tendency to look to U.S. standards and programs as a benchmark.

This value convergence combined with U.S. leadership also accounts for why there is so much emulation in Canadian environmental policy. One would expect that in other areas where there is less value convergence and the U.S. lags behind, such as health policy, emulation would not be evident.[15] U.S. environmental leadership also underlies the occasional instances where its market dominance has yielded environmental benefits for Canada. Clearly, if the U.S. had lagged behind Canada in regulating automobile emissions or pesticides, its market dominance would have been a powerful check on Canadian environmental policy.

While Rose's propositions take us a long way to understanding emulation, they do not encompass some of the dynamics of the process. For instance, this article has emphasized the distinction between elite-driven and activist-driven emulation. Rose does an effective job describing the elite process, where emulation is likely when policymakers (1) are dissatisfied with current policy, (2) share values with their foreign counterparts, and (3) have knowledge of foreign policies.[16]

But the dynamics of the elite-driven process are fundamentally different from the activist-driven one. Elite-driven emulation occurs when the scope of conflict is relatively narrow. In contrast, activist-driven emulation occurs in the context of an expanded scope of conflict, typically characterized by both media exposure and pressure campaigns on policymakers. When regulators agree with the activists, change is likely. But even if regulators disagree or are reluctant to act, sometimes their opposition can be overcome, as happened in the cases of high-profile pesticide controversies and automobile emissions in Canada. The presence or absence of activists is thus an extremely important determinant of whether emulation is likely to occur. In the case of radon and the pesticide dinoseb, for instance, Canadian regulators had knowledge of the more aggressive American program, but no activists chose to make an issue of it, leaving regulators the freedom to ignore American developments. Similarly, Canadian government opposition to more stringent asbestos standards has gone essentially unchallenged by activist groups.

This emulation is virtually but not completely unidirectional. The case of saccharin provides a glimpse into the atypical dynamics of U.S. emulation of Canada. While the U.S. had been studying the effects of saccharin on laboratory animals for many years, and was seriously contemplating removing the product from the market, regulatory action in both countries was triggered by the publication of results from a carefully controlled Canadian scientific study that linked saccharin to cancer in rats more convincingly than previously. This is one of the more dramatic examples of Canadian regulatory autonomy in the record. The U.S. Food and Drug Administration, under criticism for some time for delaying action, was forced to respond to the Canadian decision with its own ban.[17] The saccharin case is interesting for its rarity. As Margaret Atwood has said, the Canadian-American border is more than the longest undefended border in the world—it is the world's longest one-way mirror (quoted in McDonald, 1989, 27).

The two major categories of American influence—the export of knowledge and the export of costs—are quite different in what they imply for Canadian sovereignty. In the case of externalities and economic dominance, Canada is threatened by the elephant next door. In contrast, the emulation process is largely a response to the diffusion of knowledge from the U.S. to Canada, and thus is based on a more subtle type of influence. Canadian sovereignty is not threatened in the same way.

This distinction is extremely important, but it is probably very difficult for Canadian policymakers to discern. Regulating the environment is an extraordinarily complex task for policymakers. In the U.S., regulators struggle to perform their tasks in the face of resource and knowledge constraints and a political system that gives outsiders a great deal of power to structure the agency's agenda. In Canada, regulators face similar problems, although they are more insulated from their political environment than their American counterparts. However, they face additional constraints that Americans do not: international market constraints, dependence on U.S. science, and the influence of American activist groups channelled through the pervasive American mass media. Either because they are forced by international pressures or impressed by foreign experience, in small countries like Canada regulators are often not so much policy-makers as they are policy-takers.

Notes

* Research for this chapter was funded by the Social Sciences and Humanities Research Council of Canada. An earlier version was presented at the Annual Meeting of the American Political Science Association, San Francisco, August 30-September 2, 1990. I am grateful to Gregory Hein, Michael J. Hartley, Lee Lau, and Jeffrey Waatainen for research assistance, and Kathryn Harrison, Richard Rose, Richard Johnston, Toby Vigod, Mark Zacher, Peter Nemetz, Alan Cairns, and Ted Schrecker for helpful comments on an earlier draft.

† Political Science, University of British Columbia.

1. One article to address this small state/big state phenomenon is Rose and Garvin (1983). Measured by trade with the largest trading partner as a percentage of GDP, these pairs are ranked as follows (1983 figures): Ireland/UK (22 per cent), Canada/US (18 per cent), Belgium/Germany (16 per cent), Netherlands/Germany (15 per cent), and Austria/Germany (14 per cent). Canada's trade dependence on its large neighbour is far higher (75 per cent) than in the other countries, but its economy is not so open. Figures are derived from O'Connor (1989, p. 139).
2. See, for instance, Preston (1972). There is a robust tradition among nationalist Canadian scholars of emphasizing the U.S. influence on Canada (e.g., Lumsden, 1970), but more mainstream policy scholars have done little to incorporate the American influence into their explanatory frameworks. An admirable exception is Brooks (1989, esp. 96–103), but he has done little to conceptualize or analyze the various mechanisms of influence.
3. A special category of externalities is when U.S. exports hazardous wastes to Canada, which have in part resulted from the more lax regulatory standards north of the border (Handley, 1990). This issue will not be addressed here.
4. While the FTA increased economic interdependence, it also was intended to reduce the costs of American policy externalities in the form of trade actions affecting Canada.
5. In another example of emulation, the Canadian Supreme Court has relied extensively on American rights jurisprudence in its early interpretation of the Canadian Charter of Rights (Manfredi, 1990).
6. Dingell renewed this effort several years later during a Congressional hearing, which to this day remains one of the most valuable sources of data on the Canadian air pollution control program (U.S. Congress, 1987).
7. Actions by the U.S. Environmental Protection Agency and the U.S. Congress extended the deadlines for hydrocarbons and carbon monoxide by two and

three years, respectively, and relaxed the nitrogen oxides standards from a 90 per cent reduction to a 67 per cent reduction.

8. This emphasis on best available technologies apparently originated from Canada's international commitments in the United Nations Economic Commission for Europe (ECE) No_x Emission Control Protocol, signed in 1987. The U.S. is also a signatory to this agreement.
9. The ministers also proposed to adopt U.S.-style inspection and maintenance programs in areas with ozone problems (Canadian Council of Ministers of the Environment, 1989).
10. The cases are alachlor, aldrin/dieldrin, captan, daminozide, DBCP, DDT, dinoseb, EDB, heptachlor/chlordane, and 2, 4, 5-T. Canada has banned alachlor and the U.S. has not; the U.S. has banned dinoseb and Canada has not. In the remaining cases the outcomes are highly similar.
11. There has been some regional media attention in Canada to dinoseb contamination of well water, but it never became a national or high profile issue.
12. It should be noted that because only those cases where explicit reference to the U.S. was made were counted, this figure of 16 probably underestimates the extent of U.S. influence. In a number of other cases, it is likely that U.S. influence was important but just not mentioned by the authors of the documents.
13. One example of this constraint is the wood preservative pentachlorophenol.
14. Despite the apparent lack of trade distortion, the U.S.–Canada Free Trade Agreement explicitly required negotiations between the two countries to 'work towards equivalence' in pesticide regulation (*Canada–U.S. Free Trade Agreement*, Chapter 7, Schedule 7). In this case, if Canada is forced to adopt the American levels, or even if the two countries go half way, Canadian pesticide regulation will be weakened. Thus far, however, negotiations have focused exclusively on improving data exchanges between the two countries.
15. In fact, health policy is perhaps the most prominent example outside the environmental field where the U.S. is looking to Canada for lessons.
16. Physical proximity, transnational communities, and American media dominance make it particularly likely that Canadian policymakers will be aware of U.S. developments.
17. The FDA ban was overturned by Congress after an agressive industry lobbying campaign (Cummings, 1986).

References

Aitken, H. G. J. (1967). 'Defensive Expansionism: The State and Economic Growth in Canada', in Easterbrook, W. T. and Watkins, M. H. (eds.), *Approaches to Canadian Economic History.* Toronto: McCelland and Stewart.

Beigie, Carl E. (1972). 'The Automotive Agreement of 1965: A Case Study in Canadian-American Economic Affairs', in Richard Preston (ed.) (1972). *The*

Influence of the United States on Canadian Development. Durham, NC: Duke University Press.

Brickman, Ronald, Sheila Jasanoff and Thomas Ilgen (1985). *Controlling Chemicals*. Ithaca, NY: Cornell University Press.

Brooks, Stephen (1989). *Public Policy in Canada*. Toronto: McCelland and Stewart.

Canadian Council of Ministers of the Environment (1989). Information Release, 830–335/022, Charlottetown, Prince Edward Island, October 19.

Canadian Environmental Advisory Council (1987). *Review of Proposed Environmental Protection Act*. Ottawa (March).

—— (1989) *Listing Toxics Under CEPA–Is the Chemistry Right*? Ottawa (May).

Canadian House of Commons (1984). Sucommittee on Acid Rain, *Time Lost: A Demand for Action on Acid Rain*. Ottawa.

Castrilli, J. F. and Vigod, Toby (1987). *Pesticides in Canada: An Examination of Federal Law and Policy*. Ottawa: Law Reform Commission of Canada.

Conservation Foundation and Institute for Research on Public Policy (1990). *Great Lakes, Great Legacy*? Washington, DC and Ottawa, Ontario: The Conservation Foundation and Institute for Research on Public Policy.

Couch, William (ed.) (1988). *Environmental Assessment in Canada: 1988 Summary of Current Practice*. Ottawa: Federal Environmental Assessment Review Office (December).

Cummings, Linda C. (1986). 'The Political Reality of Artificial Sweeteners', in Sapolsky, Harvey (ed.) *Consuming Fears: The Politics of Product Risk*. New York: Basic Books.

Dingell, John (1983). Chairman. House Committee on Energy and Commerce, Letter to the Honourable Keith Norton, Ontario Minister of the Environment, July 25, 1983.

Dover, Glenn (ed.) (1988). *Free Trade and Social Policy*. Ottawa: Canadian Council on Social Development.

Duncan, Stephen (1973). 'Canada Won't Follow US on Auto Emissions', *Financial Post*, (June 13), p. 1.

Environment Canada and Health and Welfare Canada (1986). *Final Report of the Environmental Contaminants Act Amendments Consultative Committee*. Ottawa (October).

Fenge, Terry and Smith, L. Graham (1986). 'Reforming the Federal Environmental Assessment Review Process', *Canadian Public Policy*, 12, 596–605.

Frawley, John P. (1987). 'Codex Alimentarius—Food Safety—Pesticides', *Food Drug Cosmetic Law Journal*, 42, 168–173.

Gertler, Franklin, Muldoon, Paul and Valiente, Marcia (1990). 'Public Access to Environmental Justice', in Canadian Bar Association, *Sustainable Development in Canada: Options for Law Reform*. Canadian Bar Association: Ottawa.

Gourevitch, Peter (1978). 'The Second Image Reversed: The International Sources of Domestic Politics', *International Organization*, 32, 881–911.

Handley, F. James (1990). 'Exports of Waste from the United States to Canada', *Environmental Law Reporter: News and Analysis*, 20 ELR (February) 10061–6.

Harrison, Kathryn and Hoberg, George (1991). 'Setting the Environmental Agenda in Canada and the United States: The Cases of Dioxin and Radon', *Canadian Journal of Political Science*, 24, (March), 3–27.

Health Protection Branch, Health and Welfare Canada (1989). *Issues: Alar (Daminozide)*, (March 7).

Heclo, Hugh (1974) *Modern Social Policies in Britain and Sweden*. New Haven: Yale University Press.

Hein, Gregory (1990). *Regulating a Miracle Substance: The Politics of Asbestos in Canada and the United States*. University of British Columbia M.A. Thesis, Vancouver, BC (August).

Hoberg, George (1990a). 'Reaganism, Pluralism, and the Politics of Pesticide Regulation', *Policy Sciences*, 23, 257–289.

—— (1990b). 'Risk, Science, and Politics: Alachlor Regulation in Canada and the United States', *Canadian Journal of Political Science*, 23 (June) 257–278.

Hurley, Adele and Perley, Michael (1983). Canadian Coalition on Acid Rain, Testimony, Minutes of Proceedings and Evidence of Subcommittee on Acid Rain of the Standing Committee on Fisheries and Forestry (June 23), 4: 5–31.

Ilgen, Thomas (1985). 'Between Europe and America, Ottawa and the Provinces: Regulating Toxic Substances in Canada', *Canadian Public Policy*, 11, 578–90.

Jones, Charles O. (1975). *Clean Air*. Pittsburgh: Pittsburgh University Press.

Katzenstein, Peter (1985). *Small States in World Markets*. Ithaca, NY: Cornell University Press.

Keating, Michael (1985). 'Provinces to assist in cutting acid rain', *Globe and Mail*, (February 2), p. I.

Krier, James and Ursin, Edmund (1977) *Pollution and Policy*. Berkeley: University of California Press.

Krimsky, Sheldon and Plough, Alonzo (1988). *Environmental Hazards*. Dover, MA: Auburn House.

Levitt, Kari (1970). *Silent Surrender: The Multinational Corporation in Canada*. Toronto: Macmillan.

Lucas, Alistair (1989). 'The New Environmental Law', in Watts, R. and Brown, D. (eds.), *Canada: State of the Federation, 1989*. Kingston: Institute of Intergovernmental Relations.

Lumsden, Ian (ed.) (1970). *Close the 49th Parallel etc.: The Americanization of Canada*. Toronto: University of Toronto Press.

Manfredi, Christopher (1990). 'The Use of United States Decisions by the Supreme Court of Canada Under the Charters of Rights and Freedoms', *Canadian Journal of Political Science*, 23, 499–518.

McDonald, Marci (1989). 'Fields of Force', *Maclean's*, Special Report: Portrait of Two Nations, (July 3), p. 27.

Munton, Don (1980). 'Great Lakes Water Quality: A Study in Environmental Politics and Diplomacy', in Dwivedi, O. P. (ed.), *Resources and the Environment*. Toronto: McClelland and Stewart.

Munton, Don (1980–1). 'Dependence and Interdependence in Transboundary Environmental Relations', *International Journal*, 36, 139–184.

Norton, Keith (1983). Ontario Minister of the Environment, Letter to Congressman John Dingell, April 23.

O'Connor, Julia (1989). 'Welfare Expenditure and Policy Orientation in Canada in Comparative Perspective', *Canadian Review of Sociology and Anthropology* 26, 127–150.

Ontario Ministry of the Environment (1986). *Municipal-Industrial Abatement Strategy (MISA)—A Policy and Program Statement of the Government of Ontario on Controlling Municipal and Industrial Dischargers into Surface Waters*. Toronto (June).

Ontario Ministry of the Environment (1987). *Municipal-Industrial Abatement Strategy (MISA)—The Public Review of the MISA White Paper and the Ministry of the Environment's Response to It*. Toronto (January).

Peat Marwick Stevenson & Kellog (1990). *Review and Evaluation of the Pesticide Registration Gap Between Canada and the United States*, prepared for Pesticide Registration Review, Edmonton (June 25).

Pesticides Directorate, Food Production and Inspection Branch, Agriculture Canada (1989). *CAPCO Note 89–02*, Ottawa (February 28).

—— (1990). 'Dinoseb—Regulatory Position', *CAPCO Note 90–01*, Ottawa (February 14).

—— 'Oxyflourfen', (1987). *Discussion Document 87–01*, Ottawa (June 24).

Pesticides Registration Review (1990) *A Proposal for a Revised Federal Pest Management Regulatory System*. Preliminary Report of the Pesticide Registration Review Team, Ottawa (July).

Preston, Richard (ed.) (1972). *The Influence of the United States on Canadian Development*. Durham, NC: Duke University Press.

Rees, William (1980). 'EARP at the Crossroads', *Environmental Impact Assessment Review*, 1, 355–77.

Richards, John and Pratt, Larry (1979). *Prairie Capitalism*. Toronto: McClelland and Stewart.

Rose, Richard (forthcoming). *Lesson Drawing Across Time and Space*. Tuscaloosa: University of Alabama Press.

Rose, Richard and Garvin, Tom (1983). 'The Public Policy Effects of Independence: Ireland as a Test Case', *European Journal of Political Research*, 11, 377–397.

Sallot, Jeff (1985). '$150 million slated for smelter cleanup', *Globe and Mail*, (March 7).

Salter, Liora (1988). *Mandated Science*. Dordrecht: Kluwer Academic Publishers.

Schrecker, Ted (1984). *The Political Economy of Environmental Hazards*. Ottawa: Law Reform Commission of Canada.

Shrybman, Steven (1988). *Selling Canada's Environment Short: The Environmental Case Against the Trade Deal*. Toronto: Canadian Environmental Law Association.

Stanbury, William T. (1988). 'Reforming Direct Regulation in Canada', in Button, K. J. and Swann, D. (eds.) *The Age of Regulatory Reform*. Oxford: Oxford University Press.

Tataryn, Lloyd (1983). *Formaldehyde on Trial*. Toronto: James Lorimer & Co.

Transport Canada and Environment Canada (1989) *A Plan to Identify and Assess Emission Reduction Opportunities from Transportation, Industrial Engines and Motor Fuels*. Ottawa (May).

Trudeau, Pierre E. (1969). Address to the National Press Club, Washington DC, March 25.

US Congress, House Committee on Energy and Commerce, Subcommittee on Oversight and Investigations (1987). *U.S. Canadian Air Quality Effort*. Hearings, 100th Cong., 1st sess., (October 2).

US National Research Council and the Royal Society of Canada (1985). *The Great Lakes Water Quality Agreement: An Evolving Systems of Ecosystem Management*. Washington, DC: National Academy Press.

Weiner, Sanford (1986). 'Banning Formaldehyde Insulation: Risk Assessment and Symbolic Politics', in Sapolsky, Harvey (ed.) *Consuming Fears: The Politics of Product Risks*. New York: Basic Books.

Williams, Glen (1986). *Not for Export*. updated edition, Toronto: McClelland and Stewart.

Toward a New Conception of the Environment–Competitiveness Relationship*

MICHAEL E. PORTER AND CLAAS VAN DER LINDE†

The relationship between environmental goals and industrial competitiveness has normally been thought of as involving a tradeoff between social benefits and private costs. The issue was how to balance society's desire for environmental protection with the economic burden on industry. Framed this way, environmental improvement becomes a kind of arm-wrestling match. One side pushes for tougher standards; the other side tries to beat the standards back.

Our central message is that the environment-competitiveness debate has been framed incorrectly. The notion of an inevitable struggle between ecology and the economy grows out of a static view of environmental regulation, in which technology, products, processes and customer needs are all fixed. In this static world, where firms have already made their cost-minimizing choices, environmental regulation inevitably raises costs and will tend to reduce the market share of domestic companies on global markets.

However, the paradigm defining competitiveness has been shifting, particularly in the last 20 to 30 years, away from this static model. The new paradigm of international competitiveness is a dynamic one, based on innovation. A body of research first published in *The Competitive Advantage of Nations* has begun to address these changes (Porter, 1990). Competitiveness at the industry level arises from superior productivity, either in terms of lower costs than rivals or the ability to offer products with superior value that justify a premium price.[1] Detailed case studies of hundreds of industries, based in dozens of countries, reveal that internationally competitive companies are not those with the cheapest inputs or the largest scale, but those with the capacity to improve and innovate continually. (We use the term innovation broadly, to include a product's or service's design, the segments it serves, how it is produced, how it is marketed and how it is supported.) Competitive advantage, then, rests not on static efficiency nor on optimizing within fixed constraints, but on the capacity for innovation and improvement that shift the constraints.

This paradigm of dynamic competitiveness raises an intriguing possibility: in this paper, we will argue that properly designed environmental standards can trigger innovation that may partially or more than fully offset the costs of complying with them. Such 'innovation offsets,' as we call them, can not only lower the net cost of meeting environmental regulations, but can even lead to absolute advantages over firms in foreign countries not subject to similar regulations. Innovation offsets will be common because reducing pollution is often coincident with improving the productivity with which resources are used. In short, firms can actually benefit from properly crafted environmental regulations that are more stringent (or are imposed earlier) than those faced by their competitors in other countries. By stimulating innovation, strict environmental regulations can actually enhance competitiveness.

There is a legitimate and continuing controversy over the social benefits of specific environmental standards, and there is a huge benefit-cost literature. Some believe that the risks of pollution have been overstated; others fear the reverse. Our focus here is not on the social benefits of environmental regulation, but on the private costs. Our argument is that whatever the level of social benefits, these costs are far higher than they need to be. The policy focus should, then, be on relaxing the tradeoff between competitiveness and the environment rather than accepting it as a given.

The Link from Regulation to Promoting Innovation

It is sometimes argued that companies must, by the very notion of profit seeking, be pursuing all profitable innovations. In the metaphor economists often cite, $10 bills will never be found on the ground because someone would have already picked them up. In this view, if complying with environmental regulation can be profitable, in the sense that a company can more than offset the cost of compliance, then why is such regulation necessary?

The possibility that regulation might act as a spur to innovation arises because the world does not fit the Panglossian belief that firms always make optimal choices. This will hold true only in a static optimization framework where information is perfect and profitable opportunities for innovation have already been discovered, so that profit-seeking firms need only choose their approach. Of course, this does not describe reality. Instead, the actual process of dynamic competition is characterized by changing technological opportunities coupled with highly incomplete information, organizational inertia and control problems reflecting the difficulty of aligning individual, group and corporate incentives. Companies have numerous avenues for technological improvement, and limited attention.

Actual experience with energy-saving investments illustrates that in the real world, $10 bills are waiting to be picked up. As one example, consider the 'Green Lights' program of the Environmental Protection Agency. Firms volunteering to participate in this program pledge to scrutinize every avenue of electrical energy consumption. In return, they receive advice on efficient lighting, heating and cooling operations. When the EPA collected data on energy-saving lighting upgrades reported by companies as part of the Green Lights program, it showed that nearly 80 per cent of the projects had paybacks of two years or less (DeCanio, 1993). Yet only after companies became part of the program, and benefitted from information and cajoling from the EPA, were these highly profitable projects carried out. This paper will present numerous other examples of where environmental innovation produces net benefits for private companies.[2]

We are currently in a transitional phase of industrial history where companies are still inexperienced in dealing creatively with environmental issues. The environment has not been a principal area of corporate or technological emphasis, and knowledge about environmental impacts is still rudimentary in many firms and industries, elevating uncertainty about innovation benefits. Customers are also unaware of the costs of resource in efficiency in the packaging they discard, the scrap value they forego and the disposal costs they bear. Rather than attempting to innovate in every direction at once, firms in fact make choices based on how they perceive their competitive situation and the world around them. In such a world, regulation can be an important influence on the direction of innovation, either for better or for worse. Properly crafted environmental regulation can serve at least six purposes.

First, regulation signals companies about likely resource in efficiencies and potential technological improvements. Companies are still inexperienced in measuring their discharges, understanding the full costs of incomplete utilization of resources and toxicity, and conceiving new approaches to minimize discharges or eliminate hazardous substances. Regulation rivets attention on this area of potential innovation.[3]

Second, regulation focused on information gathering can achieve major benefits by raising corporate awareness. For example, Toxics Release

Inventories, which are published annually as part of the 1986 Superfund reauthorization, require more than 20,000 manufacturing plants to report their releases of some 320 toxic chemicals. Such information gathering often leads to environmental improvement without mandating pollution reductions, sometimes even at lower costs.

Third, regulation reduces the uncertainty that investments to address the environment will be valuable. Greater certainty encourages investment in any area.

Fourth, regulation creates pressure that motivates innovation and progress. Our broader research on competitiveness highlights the important role of outside pressure in the innovation process, to overcome organizational inertia, foster creative thinking and mitigate agency problems. Economists are used to the argument that pressure for innovation can come from strong competitors, demanding customers or rising prices of raw materials; we are arguing that properly crafted regulation can also provide such pressure.

Fifth, regulation levels the transitional playing field. During the transition period to innovation-based solutions, regulation ensures that one company cannot opportunistically gain position by avoiding environmental investments. Regulations provide a buffer until new technologies become proven and learning effects reduce their costs.

Sixth, regulation is needed in the case of incomplete offsets. We readily admit that innovation cannot always completely offset the cost of compliance, especially in the short term before learning can reduce the cost of innovation-based solutions. In such cases, regulation will be necessary to improve environmental quality.

Stringent regulation can actually produce greater innovation and innovation offsets than lax regulation. Relatively lax regulation can be dealt with incrementally and without innovation, and often with 'end-of-pipe' or secondary treatment solutions. More stringent regulation, however, focuses greater company attention on discharges and emissions, and compliance requires more fundamental solutions, like reconfiguring products and processes. While the cost of compliance may rise with stringency, then, the potential for innovation offsets may rise even faster. Thus the *net* cost of compliance can fall with stringency and may even turn into a net benefit.

How Innovation Offsets Occur

Innovation in response to environmental regulation can take two broad forms. The first is that companies simply get smarter about how to deal with pollution once it occurs, including the processing of toxic materials and emissions, how to reduce the amount of toxic or harmful material generated (or convert it into salable forms) and how to improve secondary treatment. Molten Metal Technology, of Waltham, Massachusetts, for example, has developed a catalytic extraction process to process many types of hazardous waste efficiently and effectively. This sort of innovation reduces the cost of compliance with pollution control, but changes nothing else.

The second form of innovation addresses environmental impacts while simultaneously improving the affected product itself and/or related processes. In some cases, these 'innovation offsets' can exceed the costs of compliance. This second sort of innovation is central to our claim that environmental regulation can actually increase industrial competitiveness.

Innovation offsets can be broadly divided into product offsets and process offsets. Product offsets occur when environmental regulation produces not just less pollution, but also creates better-performing or higher-quality products, safer products, lower product costs (perhaps from material substitution or less packaging), products with higher resale or scrap value (because of ease in recycling or disassembly) or lower costs of product disposal for users. Process offsets occur when environmental regulation not only leads to reduced pollution, but also results in higher resource productivity such as higher process yields, less downtime through more careful monitoring and maintenance, materials savings (due to substitution, reuse or recycling of production inputs), better utilization of by-products, lower energy consumption during the production process, reduced material storage and handling costs, conversion of waste into valuable forms, reduced waste disposal costs or safer workplace conditions. These offsets are frequently related, so that achieving one can lead to the realization of several others.

As yet, no broad tabulation exists of innovation offsets. Most of the work done in this area involves case studies, because case studies are the only vehicle currently available to measure compliance costs and both direct and indirect innovation benefits. This journal is not the place for a comprehensive listing of available case studies. However, offering some examples should help the reader to understand how common and plausible such effects are.

Innovation to comply with environmental regulation often improves product performance or quality. In 1990, for instance, Raytheon found itself required (by the Montreal Protocol and the U.S. Clean Air Act) to eliminate ozone-depleting chlorofluorocarbons (CFCs) used for cleaning printed electronic circuit boards after the soldering process. Scientists at Raytheon initially thought that complete elimination of CFCs would be impossible. However, they eventually adopted a new semiaqueous, terpene-based cleaning agent that could be reused. The new method proved to result in an increase in average product quality, which had occasionally been compromised by the old CFC-based cleaning agent, as well as lower operating costs (Raytheon, 1991, 1993). It would not have been adopted in the absence of environmental regulation mandating the phase-out of CFCs. Another example is the move by the Robbins Company (a jewelry company based in Attleboro, Massachusetts) to a closed-loop, zero-discharge system for handling the water used in plating (Berube, Nash, Maxwell and Ehrenfeld, 1992). Robbins was facing closure due to violation of its existing discharge permits. The water produced by purification through filtering and ion exchange in the new closed-loop system was 40 times cleaner than city water and led to higher-quality plating and fewer rejects. The result was enhanced competitiveness.

Environmental regulations may also reduce product costs by showing how to eliminate costly materials, reduce unnecessary packaging or simplify designs. Hitachi responded to a 1991 Japanese recycling law by redesigning products to reduce disassembly time. In the process, the number of parts in a washing machine fell by 16 per cent, and the number of parts on a vacuum cleaner fell by 30 per cent. In this way, moves to redesign products for better recyclability can lead to fewer components and thus easier assembly.

Environmental standards can also lead to innovation that reduces disposal costs (or boost scrap or resale value) for the user. For instance, regulation that requires recyclability of products can lead to designs that allow valuable materials to be recovered more easily after disposal of the product. Either the customer or the manufacturer who takes back used products reaps greater value.

These have all been examples of product offsets, but process offsets are common as well. Process changes to reduce emissions frequently result in increases in product yields. At Ciba-Geigy's dyestuff plant in New Jersey, the need to meet new environmental standards caused the firm to re-examine its wastewater streams. Two changes in its production process—replacing iron with a different chemical conversion agent that did not result in the formation of solid iron sludge and process changes that eliminated the release of potentially toxic product into the wastewater stream—not only boosted yield by 40 per cent but also eliminated wastes, resulting in annual cost savings of $740,000 (Dorfman, Muir and Miller, 1992).[4]

Similarly, 3M discovered that in producing adhesives in batches that were transferred to storage tanks, one bad batch could spoil the entire contents of a tank. The result was wasted raw materials and high costs of hazardous waste disposal. 3M developed a new technique to run quality tests more rapidly on new batches. The new technique allowed 3M to reduce hazardous wastes by 10 tons per year at almost no cost, yielding an annual savings of more than $200,000 (Sheridan, 1992).

Solving environmental problems can also yield benefits in terms of reduced downtime. Many chemical production processes at DuPont, for example, require start-up time to stabilize and bring output within specifications, resulting in an initial period during which only scrap and waste is produced. Installing higher-quality monitoring equipment has allowed DuPont to reduce production interruptions and the associated wasteful production start-ups, thus reducing waste generation as well as downtime (Parkinson, 1990).

Regulation can trigger innovation offsets through substitution of less costly materials or better utilization of materials in the process. For example, 3M faced new regulations that will force many solvent users in paper, plastic and metal coatings to reduce its solvent emissions 90 per cent by 1995 (Boroughs and Carpenter, 1991). The company responded by avoiding the use of solvents altogether and developing coating products with safer, water-based solutions. At another 3M plant, a change from a solvent-based to a water-based carrier, used for coating tablets, eliminated 24 tons per year of air emissions. The $60,000 investment saved $180,000 in unneeded pollution control equipment and created annual savings of $15,000 in solvent purchases (Parkinson, 1990). Similarly, when federal and state regulations required that Dow Chemical close certain evaporation ponds used for storing and evaporating wastewater resulting from scrubbing hydrochloric gas with caustic soda, Dow redesigned its production process. By first scrubbing the hydrochloric acid with water and then caustic soda, Dow was able to eliminate the need for evaporation ponds, reduce its use of caustic soda, and capture a portion of the waste stream for reuse as a raw material in other parts of the plant. This process change cost $250,000 to implement. It reduced caustic waste by 6,000 tons per year and hydrochloric acid waste by 80 tons per year, for a savings of $2.4 million per year (Dorfman, Muir and Miller, 1992).

The Robbins Company's jewelry-plating system illustrates similar benefits. In moving to the closed-loop system that purified and recycled water, Robbins saved over $115,000 per year in water, chemicals, disposal costs, and lab fees and reduced water usage from 500,000 gallons per week to 500 gallons per week. The capital cost of the new system, which completely eliminated the waste, was $220,000, compared to about $500,000 for a wastewater treatment facility that would have brought Robbins' discharge into compliance only with current regulations.

At the Tobyhanna Army Depot, for instance, improvements in sand-blasting, cleaning, plating and painting operations reduced hazardous waste generation by 82 percent between 1985 and 1992. That reduction saved the depot over $550,000 in disposal costs, and $400,000 in material purchasing and handling costs (PR Newswire, 1993).

Innovation offsets can also be derived by converting waste into more valuable forms. The Robbins Company recovered valuable precious metals in its zero discharge plating system. At Rhone-Poulenc's nylon plant in Chalampe, France, diacids (by-products that had been produced by an adipic acid process) used to be separated and incinerated. Rhone-Poulenc invested Fr 76 million and installed new equipment to recover and sell them as dye and tanning additives or coagulation agents, resulting in annual revenues of about Fr 20.1 million. In the United States, similar by-products from a Monsanto Chemical Company plant in Pensacola, Florida, are sold to utility companies who use them to accelerate sulfur dioxide removal during flue gas desulfurization (Basta and Vagi, 1988).

A few studies of innovation offsets do go beyond individual cases and offer some broader-based data. One of the most extensive studies is by INFORM, an environmental research organization. INFORM investigated activities to prevent waste generation—so-called source reduction activities—at 29 chemical plants in California, Ohio and New Jersey (Dorfman, Muir and Miller, 1992). Of the 181 source-reduction activities identified in this study, only one was found to have resulted in a net cost increase. Of the 70 activities for which the study was able to document changes in product yield, 68 reported yield increases; the average yield increase for the 20 initiatives with specific available data was 7 per cent. These innovation offsets were achieved with surprisingly low investments and very short payback periods. One-quarter of the 48 initiatives with detailed capital cost information required no capital investment at all; of the 38 initiatives with payback period data, nearly two-thirds were shown to have recouped their initial investments in six months or less. The annual savings per dollar spent on source reduction averaged $3.49 for the 27 activities for which this information could be calculated. The study also investigated the motivating factors behind the plant's source-reduction activities. Significantly, it found that waste disposal costs were the most often cited, followed by environmental regulation.

To build a broader base of studies on innovation offsets to environmental regulation, we have been collaborating with the Management Institute for Environment and Business on a series of international case studies, sponsored by the EPA, of industries and entire sectors significantly affected by environmental regulation. Sectors studied include pulp and paper, paint and coatings, electronics manufacturing, refrigerators, dry cell batteries and printing inks (Bonifant and Ratcliffe, 1994; Bonifant 1994a,b; van der Linde, 1995a,b,c). Some examples from that effort have already been described here.

A solid body of case study evidence, then, demonstrates that innovation offsets to environmental regulation are common.[5] Even with a generally hostile regulatory climate, which is not designed to encourage such innovation, these offsets can sometimes exceed the cost of compliance. We expect that such examples will proliferate as companies and regulators become more sophisticated and shed old mindsets.

Early-Mover Advantage in International Markets

World demand is moving rapidly in the direction of valuing low-pollution and energy-efficient products, not to mention more resource-efficient products with higher resale or scrap value. Many companies are using innovation to command price premiums for 'green' products and open up new market segments. For example, Germany enacted recycling standards earlier than in most other countries, which gave German firms an early-mover advantage in developing less packaging-intensive products, which have been warmly received in the market-place. Scandinavian pulp and paper producers have been leaders in introducing new environmentally friendly production processes, and thus Scandinavian pulp and paper equipment suppliers such as Kamyr and Sunds have made major gains internationally in selling innovative bleaching equipment. In the United States, a parallel example is the development by Cummins Engine of low-emissions diesel engines for trucks, buses and other applications in response to U.S. environmental regulations. Its new competence is allowing the firm to gain international market share.

Clearly, this argument only works to the extent that national environmental standards anticipate and are consistent with international trends in environmental protection, rather than break with them. Creating expertise in cleaning up abandoned hazardous waste sites, as the U.S. Superfund law has done, does little to benefit U.S. suppliers if no other country adopts comparable toxic waste cleanup requirements. But when a competitive edge is attained, especially because a company's home market is sophisticated and demanding in a way that pressures the company to further innovation, the economic gains can be lasting.

Answering Defenders of the Traditional Model

Our argument that strict environmental regulation can be fully consistent with competitiveness was originally put forward in a short *Scientific American* essay (Porter, 1991; see also van der Linde, 1993). This essay received far more scrutiny than we expected. It has been warmly received by many, especially in the business community. But it has also had its share of critics, especially among economists (Jaffe, Peterson, Portney and Stavins, 1993, 1994; Oates, Palmer and Portney, 1993; Palmer and Simpson, 1993; Simpson, 1993; Schmalensee, 1993).

One criticism is that while innovation offsets are theoretically possible, they are likely to be rare or small in practice. We disagree. Pollution is the emission or discharge of a (harmful) substance or energy form into the environment. Fundamentally, it is a manifestation of economic waste and involves unnecessary, inefficient or incomplete utilization of resources, or resources not used to generate their highest value. In many cases, emissions are a sign of inefficiency and force a firm to perform non-value-creating activities such as handling, storage and disposal. Within the company itself, the costs of poor resource utilization are most obvious in incomplete material utilization, but are also manifested in poor process control, which generates unnecessary stored material, waste and defects. There are many other hidden costs of resource inefficiencies later in the life cycle of the product. Packaging discarded by distributors or customers, for example, wastes resources and adds costs. Customers bear additional costs when they use polluting products or products that waste energy. Resources are also wasted when customers discard products embodying unused materials or when they bear the costs of product disposal.[6]

As the many examples discussed earlier suggest, the opportunity to reduce cost by diminishing pollution should thus be the rule, not the exception. Highly toxic materials such as heavy metals or solvents are often expensive and hard to handle, and reducing their use makes sense from several points of view. More broadly, efforts to reduce pollution and maximize profits share the same basic principles, including the efficient use of inputs, substitution of less expensive materials and the minimization of unneeded activities.[7]

A corollary to this observation is that scrap or waste or emissions can carry important information about flaws in product design or the production process. A recent study of process changes in 10 printed circuit board manufacturers, for example, found that 13 of 33 major changes were initiated by pollution control personnel. Of these, 12 resulted in cost reduction, eight in quality improvements and five in extension of production capabilities (King, 1994).

Environmental improvement efforts have traditionally overlooked the systems cost of resource inefficiency. Improvement efforts have focused on *pollution control* through better identification, processing and disposal of discharges or waste, an inherently costly approach. In recent years, more advanced companies and regulators have embraced the concept of *pollution prevention*, sometimes called source reduction, which uses material substitution, closed-loop processes and the like to limit pollution before it occurs.

But although pollution prevention is an important step in the right direction, ultimately companies and regulators must learn to frame environmental improvement in terms of *resource productivity*, or the efficiency and effectiveness with which companies and their customers use resources.[8] Improving resource productivity within companies goes beyond eliminating pollution (and the cost of dealing with it) to lowering true economic cost and raising the true economic value of products. At the level of resource productivity, environmental improvement and competitiveness come together. The imperative for resource productivity rests on the private costs that companies bear because of pollution, not on mitigating pollution's social costs. In addressing these private costs, it highlights the opportunity costs of pollution—wasted resources, wasted efforts and diminished product value to the customer—not its actual costs.

This view of pollution as unproductive resource utilization suggests a helpful analogy between environmental protection and product quality measured by defects. Companies used to promote quality by conducting careful inspections during the production process, and then by creating a service organization to correct the quality problems that turned up in the field. This approach has proven misguided. Instead, the most cost-effective way to improve quality is to build it into the entire process, which includes design, purchased components, process technology, shipping and handling techniques and so forth. This method dramatically reduces inspection, rework and the need for a large service organization. (It also leads to the oft-quoted phrase, 'quality is free.') Similarly, there is reason to believe that companies can enjoy substantial innovation offsets by improving resource productivity throughout the value chain instead of through dealing with the manifestations of inefficiency like emissions and discharges.

Indeed, corporate total quality management programs have strong potential also to reduce pollution and lead to innovation offsets.[9] Dow Chemical, for example, has explicitly identified the link between quality improvement and environmental performance, by using statistical process control to reduce the variance in processes and lower waste (Sheridan, 1992).

A second criticism of our hypothesis is to point to the studies finding high costs of compliance with environmental regulation, as evidence that there is a fixed tradeoff between regulation and competitiveness. But these studies are far from definitive.

Estimates of regulatory compliance costs prior to enactment of a new rule typically exceed the actual costs. In part, this is because such estimates are often self-reported by industries who oppose the rule, which creates a tendency to inflation. A prime example of this type of thinking was a statement by Lee Iacocca, then vice president at the Ford Motor Company, during the debate on the 1970 Clean Air Act. Iacocca warned that compliance with the new regulations would require huge price increases for automobiles, force U.S. automobile production to a halt after January 1, 1975, and 'do irreparable damage to the U.S. economy' (Smith, 1992). The 1970 Clean Air Act was subsequently enacted, and Iacocca's predictions turned out to be wrong. Similar dire predictions were made during the 1990 Clean Air Act debate; industry analysts predicted that burdens on the U.S. industry would exceed $100 billion. Of course, the reality has proven to be far less dramatic. In one study in the pulp and paper sector, actual costs of compliance were $4.00 to $5.50 per ton compared to original industry estimates of $16.40 (Bonson, McCubbin and Sprague, 1988).

Early estimates of compliance cost also tend to be exaggerated because they assume no innovation. Early cost estimates for dealing with regulations concerning emission of volatile compounds released during paint application held everything else constant, assuming only the addition of a hood to capture the fumes from paint lines. Innovation that improved the paint's transfer efficiency subsequently allowed not only the reduction of fumes but also paint usage. Further innovation in water-borne paint formulations without any VOC-releasing solvents made it possible to eliminate the need for capturing and treating the fumes altogether (Bonifant, 1994b). Similarly, early estimates of the costs of complying with a 1991 federal clean air regulation calling for a 98 percent reduction in atmospheric emissions of benzene from tar-storage tanks used by coal tar distillers initially assumed that tar-storage tanks would have to be covered by costly gas blankets. While many distillers opposed the regulations, Pittsburgh-based Aristech Chemical, a major distiller of coal tar, subsequently developed an innovative way to remove benzene from tar in the first processing step, thereby eliminating the need for the gas blanket and resulting in a saving of $3.3 million instead of a cost increase (PR Newswire, 1993).

Prices in the new market for trading allowances to emit SO_2 provide another vivid example. At the time the law was passed, analysts projected that the marginal costs of SO_2 controls (and, therefore, the price of an emission allowance) would be on the order of $300 to $600 (or more) per ton in Phase I and up to $1000 or more in Phase II. Actual Phase I allowance prices have turned out to be in the $170 to $250 range, and recent trades are heading lower, with Phase II estimates only slightly higher (after adjusting for the time value of money). In case after case, the differences between initial predictions and actual outcomes—especially after industry has had time to learn and innovate—are striking.

Econometric studies showing that environmental regulation raises costs and harms competitiveness are subject to bias, because net compliance costs are overestimated by assuming away innovation benefits. Jorgenson and Wilcoxen (1990), for example, explicitly state that they did not attempt to assess public or private benefits. Other often-cited studies that solely focus on costs, leaving out benefits, are Hazilla and Kopp (1990) and Gray (1987). By largely assuming away innovation effects, how could economic studies reach any other conclusion than they do?

Internationally competitive industries seem to be much better able to innovate in response to environmental regulation than industries that were uncompetitive to begin with, but no study measuring the effects of environmental regulation on industry competitiveness has taken initial competitiveness into account. In a study by Kalt (1988), for instance, the sectors where high environmental costs were associated with negative trade performance were ones such as ferrous metal mining, nonferrous mining, chemical and fertilizer manufacturing, primary iron and steel and primary nonferrous metals, industries where the United States suffers from dwindling raw material deposits, very high relative electricity costs, heavily subsidized foreign competitors and other disadvantages that have rendered them uncompetitive quite apart from environmental costs.[10] Other sectors identified by Kalt as having incurred very high environmental costs can actually be interpreted as supporting our hypothesis. Chemicals, plastics and synthetics, fabric, yarn and thread, miscellaneous textiles, leather tanning, paints and allied products, and paperboard containers all had high environmental costs but displayed positive trade performance.

A number of studies have failed to find that stringent environmental regulation hurts industrial competitiveness. Meyer (1992, 1993) tested and refuted the hypothesis that U.S. states with stringent environmental policies experience weak economic growth. Leonard (1988) was unable to demonstrate statistically significant offshore movements by U.S. firms in pollution-intensive industries. Wheeler and Mody (1992) failed to find that environmental regulation affected the foreign investment decisions of U.S. firms. Repetto (1995) found that industries heavily affected by environmental regulations experienced slighter reductions in their share of world exports than did the entire American industry from 1970 to 1990. Using U.S. Bureau of Census Data of more than 200,000 large manufacturing establishments, the study also found that plants with poor environmental records are generally not more profitable than cleaner ones in the same industry, even controlling for their age, size and technology. Jaffe, Peterson, Portney and Stavins (1993) recently surveyed more than 100 studies and concluded there is little evidence to support the view that U.S. environmental regulation had a large adverse effect on competitiveness.

Of course, these studies offer no proof for our hypothesis, either. But it is striking that so many studies find that even the poorly designed environmental laws presently in effect have little adverse effect on competitiveness. After all, traditional approaches to regulation have surely worked to stifle potential innovation offsets and imposed unnecessarily high costs of compliance on industry (as we will discuss in greater detail in the next section). Thus, studies using actual compliance costs to regulation are heavily biased toward finding that such regulation has a substantial cost.[11] In no way do such studies measure the potential of well-crafted environmental regulations to stimulate competitiveness.

A third criticism of our thesis is that even if regulation fosters innovation, it will harm competitiveness by crowding out other potentially more productive investments or avenues for innovation. Given incomplete information, the limited attention many companies have devoted to environmental innovations and the inherent linkage between pollution and resource productivity described earlier, it certainly is not obvious that this line of innovation has been so thoroughly explored that the marginal benefits of further investment would be low. The high returns evident in the studies we have cited support this view. Moreover, environmental investments represent only a small percentage of overall investment in all but a very few industries.[12]

A final counterargument, more caricature than criticism, is that we are asserting that any strict environmental regulation will inevitably lead to innovation and competitiveness. Of course, this is not our position. Instead, we believe that if regulations are properly crafted and companies are attuned to the possibilities, then innovation to minimize and even offset the cost of compliance is likely in many circumstances.

Designing Environmental Regulation to Encourage Innovation

If environmental standards are to foster the innovation offsets that arise from new technologies and approaches to production, they should adhere to three principles. First, they must create the maximum opportunity for innovation, leaving the approach to innovation to industry and not the standard-setting agency. Second, regulations should foster continuous improvement, rather than locking in any particular technology. Third, the regulatory process should leave as little room as possible for uncertainty at every stage. Evaluated by these principles, it is clear that U.S. environmental regulations have often been crafted in a way that deters innovative solutions, or even renders them impossible. Environmental laws and regulations need to take three substantial steps: phrasing environmental rules as goals that can be met in flexible ways; encouraging innovation to reach and exceed those goals; and administering the system in a coordinated way.

Clear Goals, Flexible Approaches

Environmental regulation should focus on outcomes, not technologies.[13] Past regulations have often prescribed particular remediation technologies—like catalysts or scrubbers to address air pollution—rather than encouraging innovative approaches. American environmental law emphasized phrases like 'best available technology,' or 'best available control technology.' But legislating as if one particular technology is always the 'best' almost guarantees that innovation will not occur.

Regulations should encourage product and process changes to better utilize resources and avoid pollution early, rather than mandating end-of-pipe or secondary treatment, which is almost always more costly. For regulators, this poses a question of where to impose regulations in the chain of production from raw materials, equipment, the producer of the end product, to the consumer (Porter, 1985). Regulators must consider the technological capabilities and resources available at each stage, because it affects the likelihood that innovation will occur. With that in mind, the governing principle should be to regulate as late in the production chain as practical, which will normally allow more flexibility for innovation there and in upstream stages.

The EPA should move beyond the single medium (air, water and so on) as the principal way of thinking about the environment, toward total discharges or total impact.[14] It should reorganize around affected industry clusters (including suppliers and related industries) to better understand a cluster's products, technologies and total set of environmental problems. This will foster fundamental rather than piecemeal solutions.[15]

Seeding and Spreading Environmental Innovations

Where possible, regulations should include the use of market incentives, including pollution taxes, deposit-refund schemes and tradable permits.[16] Such approaches often allow considerable flexibility, reinforce resource productivity, and also create incentives for ongoing innovation. Mandating outcomes by setting emission levels, while preferable to choosing a particular technology, still fails to provide incentives for continued and ongoing innovation and will tend to freeze a status quo until new regulations appear. In contrast, market incentives can encourage the introduction of technologies that exceed current standards.

The EPA should also promote an increased use of preemptive standards by industry, which appear to be an effective way of dealing with environmental regulation. Preemptive standards, agreed to with EPA oversight to avoid collusion, can be set and met by industry to avoid government standards that might go further or be more restrictive on innovation. They are not only less costly, but allow faster change and leave the initiative for innovation with industry.

The EPA should play a major role in collecting and disseminating information on innovation offsets and their consequences, both here and in other countries. Limited knowledge about opportunities for innovation is a major constraint on company behavior. A good start can be the 'clearinghouse' of information on source-reduction approaches that EPA was directed to establish by the Pollution Prevention Act (PPA) of 1990. The Green Lights and Toxics Release Inventories described at the start of this paper are other programs that involve collecting and spreading information. Yet another important initiative is the EPA program to compare emissions rates at different companies, creating methodologies to measure the full internal costs of pollution and ways of exchanging best practices and learning on innovative technologies.

Regulatory approaches can also function by helping create demand pressure for environmental innovation. One example is the prestigious German 'Blue Angel' eco-label, introduced by the German government in 1977, which can be displayed only by products meeting very strict environmental criteria. One of the label's biggest success stories has been in oil and gas heating appliances: the energy efficiency of these appliances improved significantly when the label was introduced, and emissions of sulfur dioxide, carbon monoxide and nitrogen oxides were reduced by more than 30 percent.

Another point of leverage on the demand side is to harness the role of government as a demanding buyer of environmental solutions and environmentally friendly products. While there are benefits of government procurement of products such as recycled paper and retreaded tires, the far more leveraged role is in buying specialized environmental equipment and services.[17] One useful change would be to alter the current practice of requiring bidders in competitive bid processes for government projects to only bid with 'proven' technologies, a practice sure to hinder innovation.

The EPA can employ demonstration projects to stimulate and seed innovative new technologies, working through universities and industry associations. A good example is the project to develop and demonstrate technologies for super-efficient refrigerators, which was conducted by the EPA and researchers in government, academia and the private sector (United States Environmental Protection Agency, 1992). An estimated \$1.7 billion was spent in 1992 by the federal government on environmental technology R&D, but only \$70 million was directed toward research on pollution prevention (U.S. Congress, Office of Technology Assessment, 1994).

Incentives for innovation must also be built into the regulatory process itself. The current permitting system under Title V of the Clean Air Act Amendments, to choose a negative example, requires firms seeking to change or expand their production process in a way that might impact air quality to revise their permit extensively, *no matter how little the potential effect on air quality may be*. This not only deters innovation, but drains the resources of regulators away from timely action on significant matters. On the positive side, the state of Massachusetts has initiated a program to waive permits in some circumstances, or promise an immediate permit, if a company takes a zero-discharge approach.

A final priority is new forums for settling regulatory issues that minimize litigation. Potential litigation creates enormous uncertainty; actual litigation burns resources. Mandatory arbitration, or rigid arbitration steps before litigation is allowed, would benefit innovation. There is also a need to rethink certain liability issues. While adequate safeguards must be provided against companies that recklessly harm citizens, there is a pressing need for liability standards that more clearly recognize the countervailing health and safety benefits of innovations that lower or eliminate the discharge of harmful pollutants.

Regulatory Coordination

Coordination of environmental regulation can be improved in at least three ways: between industry and regulators, between regulators at different levels and places in government, and between U.S. regulators and their international counterparts.

In setting environmental standards and regulatory processes to encourage innovation, substantive industry participation in setting standards is needed right from the beginning, as is common in many European countries. An appropriate regulatory process is one in which regulations themselves are clear, who must meet them is clear, and industry accepts the regulations and begins innovating to address them, rather than spending years attempting to delay or relax them. In our current system, by the time standards are finally settled and clarified, it is often too late to address them fundamentally, making secondary treatment the only alternative. We need to evolve toward a regulatory regime in which the EPA and other regulators make a commitment that standards will be in place for, say, five years, so that industry is motivated to innovate rather than adopt incremental solutions.

Different parts and levels of government must coordinate and organize themselves so that companies are not forced to deal with multiple parties with inconsistent desires and approaches. As a matter of regulatory structure, the EPA's proposed new Innovative Technology Council, being set up to advocate the development of new technology in every field of environmental policy, is a step in the right direction. Another unit in the EPA should be responsible for continued reengineering of the process of regulation to reduce uncertainty and minimize costs. Also, an explicit strategy is needed to coordinate and harmonize federal and state activities.[18]

A final issue of coordination involves the relationship between U.S. environmental regulations and those in other countries. U.S. regulations should be in sync with regulations in other countries and, ideally, be slightly ahead of them. This will minimize possible competitive disadvantages relative to foreign competitors who are not yet subject to the standard, while at the same time maximizing export potential in the pollution control sector. Standards that lead world developments provide domestic firms with opportunities to create valuable early-mover advantages. However, standards should not be too far ahead of, or too different in character from, those that are likely to apply to foreign competitors, for this would lead industry to innovate in the wrong directions.

Critics may note, with some basis, that U.S. regulators may not be able to project better than firms what type of regulations, and resultant demands for environmental products and services, will develop in other nations. However, regulators would seem to possess greater resources and information than firms for understanding the path of regulation in other countries. Moreover, U.S. regulations influence the type and stringency of regulations in other nations, and as such help define demand in other world markets.

Imperatives for Companies

Of course, the regulatory reforms described here also seek to change how companies view environmental issues.[19] Companies must start to recognize the environment as a competitive opportunity—not as an annoying cost or a postponable threat. Yet many companies are ill-prepared to carry out a strategy of environmental innovation that produces sizable compensating offsets.

For starters, companies must improve their measurement and assessment methods to detect environmental costs and benefits.[20] Too often, relevant information is simply lacking. Typical is the case of a large producer of organic chemicals that retained a consulting firm to explore opportunities for reducing waste. The client thought it had 40 waste streams, but a careful audit revealed that 497 different waste streams were actually present (Parkinson, 1990). Few companies analyze the true cost of toxicity, waste, discharges and the second-order impacts of waste and discharges on other activities. Fewer still look beyond the out-of-pocket costs of dealing with pollution to investigate the opportunity costs of the wasted resources or foregone productivity. How much money is going up the smokestack? What percentage of inputs are wasted? Many companies do not even track environmental spending carefully, or subject it to evaluation techniques typical for 'normal' investments.

Once environmental costs are measured and understood, the next step is to create a presumption for innovation-based solutions. Discharges, scrap and emissions should be analyzed for insights about beneficial product design or process changes. Approaches based on treatment or handling of discharges should be accepted only after being sent back several times for reconsideration. The responsibility for environmental issues should not be delegated to lawyers or outside consultants except in the adversarial regulatory process, or even to internal specialists removed from the line organization, residing in legal, government or environmental affairs departments. Instead, environmental strategies must become a general management issue if the sorts of process and product redesigns needed for true innovation are to even be considered, much less be proposed and implemented.

Conclusion

We have found that economists as a group are resistant to the notion that even well-designed environmental regulations might lead to improved competitiveness. This hesitancy strikes us as somewhat peculiar, given that in other contexts, economists are extremely willing to argue that technological change has overcome predictions of severe, broadly defined environmental costs. A static model (among other flaws) has been behind many dire predictions of economic disaster and human catastrophe: from the predictions of Thomas Malthus that population would inevitably outstrip food supply; to the *Limits of Growth* (Meadows and Meadows, 1972), which predicted the depletion of the world's natural resources; to *The Population Bomb* (Ehrlich, 1968), which predicted that a quarter of the world's population would starve to death between 1973 and 1983. As economists are often eager to point out, these models failed because they did not appreciate the power of innovations in technology to change old assumptions about resource availability and utilization.

Moreover, the static mindset that environmentalism is inevitably costly has created a self-fulfilling gridlock, where both regulators and industry battle over every inch of territory. The process has spawned an industry of litigators and consultants, driving up costs and draining resources away from real solutions. It has been reported that four out of five EPA decisions are currently challenged in court (Clay, 1993, cited in U.S. Congress, Office of Technology Assessment, 1994). A study by the Rand Institute for Civil Justice found that 88 per cent of the money paid out between 1986 and 1989 by insurers on Superfund claims went to pay for legal and administrative costs, while only 12 per cent were used for actual site cleanups (Acton and Dixon, 1992).

The United States and other countries need an entirely new way of thinking about the relationship between environment and industrial competitiveness—one closer to the reality of modern competition. The focus should be on relaxing the environment-competitiveness tradeoff rather than accepting and, worse yet, steepening it. The orientation should shift from pollution control to resource productivity. We believe that no lasting success can come from policies that promise that environmentalism will triumph over industry, nor from policies that promise that industry will triumph over environmentalism. Instead, success must involve innovation-based solutions that promote both environmentalism and industrial competitiveness.

Notes

* The authors are grateful to Alan Auerbach, Ben Bonifant, Daniel C. Esty, Ridgway M. Hall, Jr., Donald B. Marron, Jan Rivkin, Nicolaj Siggelkow, R. David Simpson and Timothy Taylor for extensive valuable editorial suggestions. We are also grateful to Reed Hundt for ongoing discussions that have greatly benefitted our thinking.

† Michael E. Porter is the C. Roland Christensen Professor of Business Administration, Harvard Business School, Boston, Massachusetts. Class van der Linde is on the faculty of the International Management Research Institute of St. Gallen University, St. Gallen, Switzerland.

1. At the industry level, the meaning of competitiveness is clear. At the level of a state or nation, however, the notion of competitiveness is less clear because no nation or state is, or can be, competitive in everything. The proper definition of competitiveness at the aggregate level is the average *productivity* of industry or the value created per unit of labor and per dollar of capital invested. Productivity depends on both the quality and features of products (which determine their value) and the efficiency with which they are produced.
2. Of course, there are many nonenvironmental examples of where industry has been extremely slow to pick up available $10 bills by choosing new approaches. For example, total quality management programs only came to the United States and Europe decades after they had been widely diffused in Japan, and only after Japanese firms had devastated U.S. and European competitors in the marketplace. The analogy between searching for product quality and for environmental protection is explored later in this paper.
3. Regulation also raises the likelihood that product and process in general will incorporate environmental improvements.
4. We should note that this plant was ultimately closed. However, the example described here does illustrate the role of regulatory pressure in process innovation.

5. Of course, a list of case examples, however long, does not prove that companies can always innovate or substitute for careful empirical testing in a large cross-section of industries. Given our current ability to capture the true costs and often multifaceted benefits of regulatory-induced innovation, reliance on the weight of case study evidence is necessary. As we discuss elsewhere, there is no countervailing set of case studies that shows that innovation offsets are unlikely or impossible.
6. At its core, then, pollution is a result of an intermediate state of technology or management methods. Apparent exceptions to the resource productivity thesis often prove the rule by highlighting the role of technology. Paper made with recycled fiber was once greatly inferior, but new de-inking and other technologies have made its quality better and better. Apparent tradeoffs between energy efficiency and emissions rest on incomplete combustion.
7. Schmalensee (1993) counters that NO_x emissions often result from thermodynamically efficient combustion. But surely this is an anomaly, not the rule, and may represent an intermediate level of efficiency.
8. One of the pioneering efforts to see environmental improvement this way is Joel Makower's (1993) book, *The E-Factor: The Bottom-Line Approach to Environmentally Responsible Business*.
9. A case study of pollution prevention in a large multinational firm showed those units with strong total quality management programs in place usually undertake more effective pollution prevention efforts than units with less commitment to total quality management. See Rappaport (1992), cited in U.S. Congress, Office of Technology Assessment (1994).
10. It should be observed that a strong correlation between environmental costs and industry competitiveness does not necessarily indicate causality. Omitting environmental benefits from regulation, and reporting obvious (end-of-pipe) costs but not more difficult to identify or quantify innovation benefits can actually obscure a reverse causal relationship: industries that were uncompetitive in the first place may well be less able to innovate in response to environmental pressures, and thus be prone to end-of-pipe solutions whose costs are easily measured. In contrast, competitive industries capable of addressing environmental problems in innovative ways may report a lower compliance cost.
11. Gray and Shadbegian (1993), another often-mentioned study, suffers from several of the problems discussed here. The article uses industry-reported compliance costs and does not control for plant technology vintage or the extent of other productivity-enhancing investments at the plant. High compliance costs may well have been borne in old, inefficient plants where firms opted for secondary treatment rather than innovation. Moreover, U.S. producers may well have been disadvantaged in innovating given the nature of the U.S. regulatory process—this seems clearly to have been the case in pulp and

paper, one of the industries studied by the Management Institute for Environment and Business (MEB).

12. In paints and coatings, for example, environmental investments were 3.3 per cent of total capital investment in 1989. According to Department of Commerce (1991) data (self-reported by industry), capital spending for pollution control and abatement outside of the chemical, pulp and paper, petroleum and coal, and primary metal sectors made up just 3.15 per cent of total capital spending in 1991.
13. There will always be instances of extremely hazardous pollution requiring immediate action, where imposing a specific technology by command and control may be the best or only viable solution. However, such methods should be seen as a last resort.
14. A first step in this direction is the EPA's recent adjustment of the timing of its air rule for the pulp and paper industry so that it will coincide with the rule for water, allowing industry to see the dual impact of the rules and innovate accordingly.
15. The EPA's regulatory cluster team concept, under which a team from relevant EPA offices approaches particular problems for a broader viewpoint, is a first step in this direction. Note, however, that of the 17 cluster groups formed, only four were organized around specific industries (petroleum refining, oil and gas production, pulp and paper, printing), while the remaining 13 focused on specific chemicals or types of pollution (U.S. Congress, Office of Technology Assessment, 1994).
16. Pollution taxes can be implemented as effluent charges on the quantity of pollution discharges, as user charges for public treatment facilities, or as product charges based on the potential pollution of a product. In a deposit-refund system, such product charges may be rebated if a product user disposes of it properly (for example, by returning a lead battery for recycling rather than sending it to a landfill). Under a tradable permit system, like that included in the recent Clean Air Act Amendments, a maximum amount of pollution is set, and rights equal to that cap are distributed to firms. Firms must hold enough rights to cover their emissions; firms with excess rights can sell them to firms who are short.
17. See Marron (1994) for a demonstration of the modest productivity gains likely from government procurement of standard items, although in a static model.
18. The cluster-based approach to regulation discussed earlier should also help eliminate the practice of sending multiple EPA inspectors to the same plant who do not talk to one another, make conflicting demands and waste time and resources. The potential savings from cluster- and multimedia-oriented permitting and inspection programs appear to be substantial. During a pilot multimedia testing program called the Blackstone Project, the Massachusetts Department of Environmental Protection found that multimedia inspections required 50 per cent less time than conventional inspections—which at that

time accounted for nearly one-fourth of the department's operating budget (Roy and Dillard, 1990).

19. For a more detailed perspective on changing company mindsets about competitiveness and environmentalism, see Porter and van der Linde (1995) in the *Harvard Business Review.*
20. Accounting methods that are currently being discussed in this context include 'full cost accounting,' which attempts to assign all costs to specific products or processes, and 'total cost accounting,' which goes a step further and attempts both to allocate costs more specifically and to include cost items beyond traditional concerns, such as indirect or hidden costs (like compliance costs, insurance, on-site waste management, operation of pollution control and future liability) and less tangible benefits (like revenue from enhanced company image). See White, Becker and Goldstein (1991), cited in U.S. Congress, Office of Technology Assessment (1994).

References

Acton, Jan Paul, and Lloyd S. Dixon, *Superfund and Transaction Costs: The Experiences of Insurers and Very Large Industrial Firms*. Santa Monica: Rand Institute for Civil Justice, 1992.

Amoco Corporation and United States Environmental Protection Agency, 'Amoco-U.S. EPA Pollution Prevention Project: Yorktown, Virginia, Project Summary,' Chicago and Washington, D.C., 1992.

Basta, Nicholas, and David Vagi, 'A Casebook of Successful Waste Reduction Projects,' *Chemical Engineering*, August 15, 1988, *95*: 11, 37.

Berube, M., J. Nash, J. Maxwell, and J. Ehrenfeld, 'From Pollution Control to Zero Discharge: How the Robbins Company Overcame the Obstacles,' *Pollution Prevention Review*, Spring 1992, 2:2, 189–207.

Bonifant, B., 'Competitive Implications of Environmental Regulation in the Electronics Manufacturing Industry,' Management Institute for Environment and Business, Washington, D.C., 1994a.

—— 'Competitive Implications of Environmental Regulation in the Paint and Coatings Industry,' Management Institute for Environment and Business, Washington, D.C., 1994b.

—— and I. Ratcliffe, 'Competitive Implications of Environmental Regulation in the Pulp and Paper Industry,' Management Institute for Environment and Business, Washington, D.C., 1994.

Bonson, N. C., Neil McCubbin, and John B. Sprague, 'Kraft Mill Effluents in Ontario.' Report prepared for the Technical Advisory Committee, Pulp and Paper Sector of MISA, Ontario Ministry of the Environment, Toronto, Ontario, Canada, March 29, 1988, Section 6, p. 166.

Boroughs, D. L., and B. Carpenter, 'Helping the Planet and the Economy,' *U.S. News & World Report*, March 25, 1991, *110*: 11, 46.

Clay, Don, 'New Environmentalist: A Cooperative Strategy,' *Forum for Applied Research and Public Policy*, Spring 1993, 8, 125–28.

DeCanio, Stephen J., 'Why Do Profitable Energy-Saving Investment Projects Languish?' Paper presented at the Second International Research Conference of the Greening of Industry Network, Cambridge, Mass., 1993.

Department of Commerce, 'Pollution Abatement Costs and Expenditures,' Washington, D.C., 1991.

Dorfman, Mark H., Warren R. Muir, and Catherine G. Miller, *Environmental Dividents: Cutting More Chemical Wastes*. New York: INFORM, 1992.

Ehrlich, Paul, *The Population Bomb*, New York: Ballantine Books, 1968.

Freeman, A. Myrick, III, 'Methods for Assessing the Benefits of Environmental Programs.' In Kneese, A. V., and J. L. Sweeney, eds., *Handbook of Natural Resource and Energy Economics*. Vol. 1. Amsterdam: North-Holland, 1985, pp. 223–70.

Gray, Wayne B., 'The Cost of Regulation: OSHA, EPA, and the Productivity Slowdown,' *American Economic Review*, 1987, *77*: 5, 998–1006.

—— and Ronald J. Shadbegian, 'Environmental Regulation and Productivity at the Plant Level,' discussion paper, U.S. Department of Commerce, Center for Economic Studies, Washington, D.C., 1993.

Hartwell, R. V., and L. Bergkamp, 'Eco-Labelling in Europe: New Market-Related Environmental Risks?,' *BNA International Environment Daily*, Special Report, Oct. 20, 1992.

Hazilla, Michael, and Raymond J. Kopp, 'Social Cost of Environmental Quality Regulations: A General Equilibrium Analysis,' *Journal of Political Economy*, 1990, *98*: 4, 853–73.

Jaffe, Adam B., S. Peterson, Paul Portney, and Robert N. Stavins, 'Environmental Regulations and the Competitiveness of U.S. Industry,' Economics Resource Group, Cambridge, Mass., 1993.

—— —— —— —— 'Environmental Regulation and International Competitiveness: What Does the Evidence Tell Us,' draft, January 13, 1994.

Jorgenson, Dale W., and Peter J. Wilcoxen, 'Environmental Regulation and U.S. Economic Growth,' *Rand Journal of Economics*, Summer 1990, *21*: 2, 314–40.

Kalt, Joseph P., 'The Impact of Domestic Environmental Regulatory Policies on U.S. International Competitiveness.' In Spence, A. M., and H. Hazard, eds., *International Competitiveness*, Cambridge, Mass: Harper and Row, Ballinger, 1988, pp. 221–62.

King, A., 'Improved Manufacturing Resulting from Learning-From-Waste: Causes, Importance, and Enabling Conditions,' working paper, Stern School of Business, New York University, 1994.

Leonard, H. Jeffrey, *Pollution and the Struggle for World Product*. Cambridge, U.K.: Cambridge University Press, 1988.

Makower, Joel, *The E-Factor: The Bottom-Line Approach to Environmentally Responsible Business*. New York: Times Books, 1993.

Marron, Donald B., 'Buying Green: Government Procurement as an Instrument of Environmental Policy,' mimeo, Massachusetts Institute of Technology, 1994.

Massachusetts Department of Environmental Protection, Daniel S. Greenbaum, Commissioner, interview, Boston, August 8, 1993.

Meadows, Donella H., and Dennis L. Meadows, *The Limits of Growth*. New York: New American Library 1972.

Meyer, Stephen M., *Environmentalism and Economic Prosperity: Testing the Environmental Impact Hypothesis*. Cambridge, Mass.: Massachusetts Institute of Technology, 1992.

—— *Environmentalism and Economic Prosperity: An Update*. Cambridge, Mass.: Massachusetts Institute of Technology, 1992.

National Paint and Coatings Association, *Improving the Superfund: Correcting a National Public Policy Disaster*. Washington, D.C., 1992.

Palmer, Karen L., and Ralph David Simpson, 'Environmental Policy as Industrial Policy,' *Resources*, Summer 1993, *112*, 17–21.

Parkinson, Gerald, 'Reducing Wastes Can Be Cost-Effective,' *Chemical Engineering*, July 1990, *97*: 7, 30.

Porter, Michael E., *Competitive Advantage: Creating and Sustaining Superior Performance*. New York: Free Press, 1985.

—— *The Competitive Advantage of Nations*. New York: Free Press, 1990.

—— 'America's Green Strategy,' *Scientific American*, April 1991, *264*, 168.

——, and Claas van der Linde, 'Green *and* Competitive: Breaking the Stalemate,' *Harvard Business Review*, September-October 1995.

PR Newswire, 'Winners Announced for Governor's Waste Minimization Awards,' January 21, 1993, State and Regional News Section.

Oates, Wallace, Karen L. Palmer, and Paul Portney, 'Environmental Regulation and International Competitiveness: Thinking About the Porter Hypothesis.' Resources for the Future Working Paper 94–02, 1993.

Rappaport, Ann, 'Development and Transfer of Pollution Prevention Technology Within a Multinational Corporation,' dissertation, Department of Civil Engineering, Tufts University, May 1992.

Raytheon Inc., 'Alternate Cleaning Technology.' Technical Report Phase II. January-October 1991.

——J. R. Pasquariello, Vice President Environmental Quality; Kenneth J. Tierney, Director Environmental and Energy Conservation; Frank A. Marino, Senior Corporate Environmental Specialist; interview, Lexington, Mass., April 4, 1993.

Repetto, Robert, 'Jobs, Competitiveness, and Environmental Regulation: What are the Real Issues?,' Washington, D.C.: World Resources Institute, 1995.

Roy, M., and L. A. Dillard, 'Toxics Use in Massachusetts: The Blackstone Project,' *Journal of Air and Waste Management Association*, October 1990, *40*: 10, 1368–71.

Schmalensee, Richard, 'The Costs of Environmental Regulation.' Massachusetts Institute of Technology, Center for Energy and Environmental Policy Research Working Paper 93–015, 1993.

Sheridan, J. H., 'Attacking Wastes and Saving Money... Some of the Time,' *Industry Week*, February 17, 1992, *241*: 4, 43.

Simpson, Ralph David, 'Taxing Variable Cost: Environmental Regulation as Industrial Policy.' Resources for the Future Working Paper ENR93–12, 1993.

Smith, Zachary A, *The Environmental Policy Paradox*. Englewood Cliffs, N. J.: Prentice-Hall, 1992.

United States Environmental Protection Agency, 'Multiple Pathways to Super Efficient Refrigerators,' Washington, D.C., 1992.

U.S. Congress, Office of Technology Assessment, 'Industry, Technology, and the Environment: Competitive Challenges and Business Opportunities,' OTA-ITE-586, Washington, D.C., 1994.

van der Linde, Claas, 'The Micro-Economic Implications of Environmental Regulation: A Preliminary Framework.' In *Environmental Policies and Industrial Competitiveness*. Paris: Organization of Economic Co-Operation and Development, 1993, pp. 69–77.

——'Competitive Implications of Environmental Regulation in the Cell Battery Industry,' Hochschule St. Gallen, St. Gallen, forthcoming 1995a.

——'Competitive Implications of Environmental Regulation in the Printing Ink Industry,' Hochschule St. Gallen, St. Gallen, forthcoming 1995b.

——'Competitive Implications of Environmental Regulation in the Refrigerator Industry,' Hochschule St. Gallen, St. Gallen, forthcoming 1995c.

Wheeler, David, and Ashoka Mody, 'International Investment Location Decisions: The Case of U.S. Firms,' *Journal of International Economics*, August 1992, *33*, 57–76.

White, A. L., M. Becker, and J. Goldstein, 'Alternative Approaches to the Financial Evaluation of Industrial Pollution Prevention Investments,' prepared for the New Jersey Department of Environmental Protection, Division of Science and Research, November 1991.

Index